The Path to Attainment

CLIMB THE HIGHEST MOUNTAIN® SERIES

The Path of the Higher Self
The Path of Self-Transformation
The Masters and the Spiritual Path
The Path of Brotherhood
The Path of the Universal Christ
Paths of Light and Darkness
The Path to Immortality
The Path of Christ or Antichrist
The Path to Attainment

The Masters and Their Retreats
*Predict Your Future:
Understand the Cycles of the Cosmic Clock*

CLIMB THE HIGHEST MOUNTAIN SERIES

The Path to Attainment

Mark L. Prophet · Elizabeth Clare Prophet

The Everlasting Gospel

SUMMIT UNIVERSITY PRESS
Gardiner, Montana

THE PATH TO ATTAINMENT
by Mark L. Prophet and Elizabeth Clare Prophet
Copyright © 2008 by Summit Publications, Inc.
All rights reserved

No part of this book may be reproduced, translated, or electronically stored, posted or transmitted, or used in any format or medium whatsoever without prior written permission, except by a reviewer who may quote brief passages in a review. For information, please contact Summit University Press, 63 Summit Way, Gardiner, MT 59030-9314, USA.
Tel: 1-800-245-5445 or 406-848-9500.
Web site: www.SummitUniversityPress.com
E-mail: info@SummitUniversityPress.com

Library of Congress Control Number: 2008927299
ISBN: 978-1-932890-14-3

SUMMIT UNIVERSITY ❦ PRESS®
The Summit Lighthouse, *Pearls of Wisdom*, Science of the Spoken Word, Teachings of the Ascended Masters and Keepers of the Flame are trademarks registered in the U.S. Patent and Trademark Office and in other countries. All rights to their use are reserved.
Printed in the United States of America

Image of Ikhnaton and Nefertiti © Agyptisches Museum Staatliche Museen Preussischer Kulturbesitz
Cover: *Tibet. Himalayas* (1933), a painting by Nicholas Roerich

Note: Our understanding of life and the universe is that all things are in polarity: plus/minus, Alpha/Omega, yang/yin, masculine/feminine. The worlds of Spirit and Matter are in polarity as two manifestations of God's universal Presence. In this relationship, Spirit assumes the positive-yang-masculine polarity, and Matter assumes the negative-yin-feminine polarity. Thus, while we acknowledge God as both Father and Mother, we have generally used masculine pronouns to refer to God and feminine pronouns to refer to the soul, the part of ourselves that is evolving in the planes of Matter. Also, in order to avoid the sometimes cumbersome or confusing expressions of gender-neutral language, we have occasionally used masculine pronouns to refer to the individual. These usages are not intended to exclude women.

12 11 10 09 08   5 4 3 2 1

And I saw another angel fly in the midst of heaven, having the everlasting gospel to preach unto them that dwell on the earth, and to every nation, and kindred, and tongue, and people,

Saying with a loud voice, Fear God, and give glory to him; for the hour of his judgment is come: and worship him that made heaven, and earth, and the sea, and the fountains of waters.

REVELATION

Contents

Preface xv

Introduction xix

1 Twin Rays 1

SECTION ONE
The Search for Wholeness 3
  The Creation of Twin Rays 5
  Descent into Form 8
  Separation of Twin Flames 9
  The Sacrament of Marriage 13
  Soul Mates 15
  Celibacy and Marriage 18
  Marriage as an Initiation on the Path 23
  Divorce 25
  Karmic Relationships 26
  The Search for the Twin Flame 28
  Oneness on Inner and Outer Planes 31
SECTION TWO
The Sacred Fire 36
  The Caduceus 37
  Spirit and Matter 39
  Misuse of the Sacred Fire 42
  The Transfiguration 44

SECTION THREE
Raising the Light   46
   Misuses of the Divine Polarity   47
   Family Planning   50
   The Disciplines of the Sacred Fire   51
   The Desire for Wholeness   53
   The Seventh Commandment   55
   The Flow of Alpha and Omega   57
   Raising the Light   61
   Reverence toward Life   65
   The Ritual of the Archangels   67

SECTION FOUR
The Alchemical Marriage   76
   The Victory of Love   78
   Meditation on the Oneness of Twin Flames   80

2 Integrity   83

SECTION ONE
Integration with the Source   85
   The Seamless Garment of the Christ   86
   The Return to God   88
   The Need for Brotherhood   89
   The Will to Integration   90
   Man Finds Freedom When Negative Karma Is Redeemed   91
   More than Forgiveness Is Needed for True Freedom   92
   Putting God First   93
   Finding Your Path   95
   Determination Is Needed   97
   Service to the World   98
   The Honor of God   99

Contents

    The Chart of Your Divine Self   102

SECTION TWO
The Science of Wholeness and the Tree of Life   106
    The Electronic Belt and the Tree of Life   107
    The Macrocosm and the Microcosm   111
    The Lines of the Clock   114
    Positive and Negative Manifestations on the Power Lines of the Cosmic Clock   117
    The Love Lines of the Clock   122
    The Wisdom Lines of the Clock   125
    Solar Hierarchies and the Mastery of the Elements through the Threefold Flame   129
    The Trines   139
    The Three Decans within Each Line   140
    Internalizing the Flames of the Hierarchies   143
    The Opportunity of One's Birth Sign   145
    Personal Cycles through the Hierarchies   146
    The Second Twelve-Year Cycle   149
    The Third Twelve-Year Cycle   155
    The Cycle of the Months   157
    The Conception of a Child   159
    Mastering Your Cycles   163
    Round the Clock Protection   165

SECTION THREE
The Dance of the Hours   170
    The Cycles of the Day   174

SECTION FOUR
The Teachings of Jesus on the Twelve Lines of the Clock   175
    The Power of the Spoken Word Reinforced by the Beatitudes   177
    The Crucifixion   190

The Antidote for Human Suffering
Is the Violet Flame   196
The Initiation of the Crucifixion
Must Come to Every Man   197
The Crucifixion of the Divine Feminine   199
The End of Banalities   202

SECTION FIVE
The Divine Inheritance   209
The Ritual of Adornment   210
The Search for the Tree of Life   212
Immortality   213

3 The One Path above the Many   215

SECTION ONE
The Search for Truth   217
The Path That Leads to God-Realization   218
An Open Mind Is Needed   220
Oneness with the Father Is Attainable by All   221
Incomplete Concepts of Salvation Are Ineffective   222

SECTION TWO
The Way of the Mystics   224
Each Age Brings New Revelations of God   225
Eight Pathways to God   229
Transforming the Soul   229
Origins of Mysticism   230
The Path of Mysticism   231
The Divine Spark   232
The Indwelling Presence of God   234
Mystical Contemplation and Prayer   236
The Threefold Path of Purgation,
Illumination and Union   238

The Dark Night   239
The Illuminative Stage   242
The Unitive Stage   243
The Spiritual Marriage   246
Becoming God   248
The Universal Path   250

SECTION THREE
The Eightfold Path   253
  The Four Noble Truths   254
  The Middle Way   255
  Eight Points of the Law   256
  Paths of East and West   261

SECTION FOUR
The Seeker and the Sought   265
  Seek Until Ye Find   266
  God Gave the Gift of the Future to Us All   267

4 The Great White Brotherhood   269

Renewed Opportunity   272
A Thirst for Brotherhood   273
The Great White Brotherhood's Reason for Being   274
The Formation of the Great White Brotherhood   276
Agents of the Brotherhood on Earth   276
Cosmic Service   278
The Mandala of a Root Race   278
The Representatives of God Come to Earth   280
The Ritual of Descent   282
The Manifestation of the Hierarchical Design   285
The Crystal Becoming the Mist   286
The First Three Root Races Ascend   288
The Interruption of the Cosmic Plan   289

The Creation of the Karmic Board   291
The Rescue Mission   292
The Establishment of God-Government   295
The Divine Right of Kings   296
Government Is Meant to Facilitate God's Plan   297
Foundations of God-Government   299
Blocks to the Brotherhood's Service   300
Branches of the Great White Brotherhood   301
Membership and Initiation   302
Religion   304
Progressive Revelation Denied   305
The "Push-Pull" System of Seeking God   307
The Highest Law Is Expressed in Many Ways   308
The Brotherhood Encourages
   Practical Spirituality   309
False Promises of the False Hierarchy   310
World Service   310
Spiritual Education in the Retreats   311
The Universities of the Spirit   313
Special Training   315
Protecting the Brotherhood's Focuses   316
The Brotherhood's Retreats
   Are Strategically Located   317
You Are Welcome to Study
   at the Brotherhood's Retreats   319
Impostors of the Ascended Masters   324
The Correct Use of the Ascended Masters' Names   326
The Functions of the Brotherhood   329

5   Attainment   335

    Dharma   337
    The True Teachers   338
    Measuring Attainment   339
    The Need for Hierarchy   340
    God Desiring to Be God   342
    The Guru-Chela Relationship   345
    The Need to Go Within   346
    Energy Is God   348
    The Purpose of Initiation   349
    The Law of Harmony   350
    Cycles of Initiation   352
    Withdraw from All Self-Indulgence   353
    Assessing Our Motives   356
    Nonattachment   357
    Affirmations for Attainment of the Christ Consciousness   360
    The Science of Mantra   364
    Attainment Is Rooted in the Dharma of God's Law   366
    The Solar Gift of Our Reality   367
    Attainment through Grace   368
    Muse Only upon Your Rate of Progress   369
    The Seed of Attainment Is within You Now   370

Afterword   373

Note from the Editor   378

Notes   381

Glossary   406

Charts and Illustrations

The T'ai Chi and Twin Flames   4
The Creation of Twin Flames   6
The Caduceus   37
The Seven Chakras   38
The Figure-Eight Flow of Energy
    through the Chakras   57
The Chart of Your Divine Self   105
The Electronic Belt   108
Categories of Negatively Qualified Energy
    in the Electronic Belt   109
The Tree of Life   110
The Purified Electronic Belt   112
The Four Quadrants   115
The Threefold Flame in Each Quadrant   116
The Twelve God-Qualities and Their Perversions   128
The T'ai Chi   129
The Twelve Solar Hierarchies   130
Representatives of the Twelve Solar Hierarchies
    to Earth and Her Evolutions   131
The Tests in the Etheric Body   135
The Tests of the Mental Body   135
The Trines of the Clock   136
The Tests of the Emotional Body   137
The Tests of the Physical Body   138
The Decans of the Twelve Lines of the Clock   142
Chart of Months   158
The Attainment of the Christ Consciousness
    through the Mastery of the Hours   172
Ikhnaton and Nefertiti with the Sun Disk   226

The Four Noble Truths
    on the Karmic Clock—Spirit   262

The Four Noble Truths
    on the Karmic Clock—Matter   263

The Middle Way—Eightfold Clock   264

The Mandala of the Manus
    and Their Twin Flames   281

Circle with 144 Points   283

The Seven Rays and the Five Secret Rays   284

Retreats of the Ascended Masters That Are Known
    to Be Open to Unascended Chelas   321

The Seven Rays and the Seven Chakras
    and the Beings Who Ensoul Them   332

Prayers and Decrees

Prayer for the Oneness of Twin Flames   33

Decree for the Resurrection Flame   62

Hail Mary   64

Heart, Head and Hand Decrees   70

Decree to Beloved Mighty Astrea   74

Meditation on the Oneness of Twin Flames   80

Round the Clock Protection   166

The End of Banalities   208

Radiant Spiral Violet Flame   252

Transfiguring Affirmations   361

Preface

THE PATH TO ATTAINMENT IS the ninth book in the Climb the Highest Mountain series. This book contains the final five chapters of the thirty-three that El Morya outlined in the conception of the work.

The thirty-three chapters of this series correspond to the thirty-three major initiations on the spiritual path—thirty-three spirals of self-mastery that have been the requirement of initiates of the Masters since time immemorial. The first chapter in the first book is "Your Synthetic Image." The final chapter of this book is "Attainment."

The Messenger has given some keys as to how we may assimilate the teaching and reach the goal of attainment: "These nine books all comprise the ascension spiral, out-pictured in physical form as the worded expression of that very flame. When you think of it in this way, you must understand that each chapter provides you with the opportunity for mastery.

"You must first master the concepts. As you are mastering these concepts mentally, the patterns of these concepts are interpenetrating and interweaving in your Light body, in your etheric body and in your soul. As you read the chapter again and you feel the flow of gratitude for the work and you feel the flow of the Spirit through it, your feeling body is exposed and is brought into alignment with the pattern. As you study some more, you find that physically you can actually eat of the Word. You may find that it is sweet in the mouth and bitter in the belly,[1] but you can eat of this book and this Word, and you can become it.

"As you read the work, you find that the tests will come swiftly on the heels of your study. Almost as soon as you turn around and lift your hand from the book, you will find a knock at the door and the stranger waiting to give to you the test. It may be the cleaning woman, it may be the milkman, it may be the neighbor, but you will find that your tests will come—through people you know or people you don't know, people on the street, people at work, people around you.

"We cannot be tested in a vacuum, even in the retreats of the Brotherhood. When you are admitted to these retreats between embodiments and at night, you are put right with the very people with whom you have difficulty on earth. And these are the tests of the century—to be able to make peace with God and peace with man, the very man that you find most obnoxious and most troublesome. So don't ever think that there is a surcease of strife until there is a surcease of strife within you.

"So it all starts in the flame in the heart, in the core of being, the white-fire core. It is a very tiny little atom at this moment, and yet it is going to expand. You have the opportunity to expand your awareness of your cosmos, your identity as you were created in the beginning, and all that you can become."[2]

If this is your first exploration of the Climb the Highest Mountain series, we welcome you to your study of these Teachings from the Ascended Masters, which have been called the Everlasting Gospel,[3] the scripture for the age of Aquarius. For those who are taking up this book after reading previous volumes, we wish you God-speed in your continuing journey to climb the highest mountain.

THE EDITORS

Introduction

ONE OF THE MIGHTY ANGELS John the Revelator encountered gave him a little book. The angel commanded him to "take it, and eat it up; and it shall make thy belly bitter, but it shall be in thy mouth sweet as honey."[1] The volume you hold in your hand is such a book.

It is a discourse on cosmic law set down in words that will bring to you the sweetness of divine illumination as you "eat it up." For in your exposure to the Law is found a sense of great joy and great sweetness of God consciousness. But when you begin to digest the Law, a chemicalization begins wherein darkness becomes Light.

The Light's encounter with the darkness of past karma is like the contact of two incompatible chemicals that produces an explosion. Darkness cannot contain Light, and therefore it is transformed. It is like turning a light switch on or off in a closed room. There is either light or darkness, but they don't occupy the same space.

During the years that I [Elizabeth] worked with Mark on the volumes of the Climb the Highest Mountain series, I would sit in my meditation room at La Tourelle in Colorado Springs and Messengers of God would come to bring scrolls of concepts that showed how they wanted them outlined in various chapters. The revelations were given, and they were so high that sometimes I would groan because of the influx of the concept and the consciousness of the Masters upon my consciousness. On many occasions, I had to say to the Messenger of God, "This is all I can take for today. I can't take any more." And I experienced this bitterness in the belly, the chemicalization of Truth in my consciousness.

My state of attunement had to be very, very high to be able to stand in the presence of Cosmic Beings delivering their outlines for this series, which is intended to be scripture for the new age. It was like the experience of John on the Isle of Patmos, when the angel of Jesus came to him and he was transported to a very high state of consciousness. And yet even when John, in this high state of consciousness, took in the concentrated energies of the little book, they exploded. And that bitterness began to transform his whole being.

The purpose of this series is to bring you to the level of attunement at which these revelations were made to me and to Mark. It is not merely to pass on to you intellectual knowledge. You can go up the mountain and sit down and read these books as the Everlasting Gospel, and you'll have the knowledge they contain. But my goal is for your consciousness to be raised so that you will have the same experiences that we had when we received the revelation.

Emerson says to go beyond a book's form to the essence behind it when he asserts: "Talent alone can not make a writer. There must be a man behind the book; a personality ... pledged to the doctrines there set forth.... If there be [not]

God's word in the man,—what care we how adroit, how fluent, how brilliant he is?"[2] The man behind these books is the hidden man of the heart, the Universal Christ, who will not leave you as he finds you.

The receipt of this series into Mark's and my consciousness demanded total sacrifice, total selflessness, total surrender of our personal lives, a laying down of our lives for the Masters. And we are dedicated to continuing this service in your behalf. We want you to know that as you read the Climb the Highest Mountain series, you can call to God and our Higher Self for understanding, for the integration of the Light into your being. We will be with you at inner levels. We will use the authority of our office to assist you in your spiritual quest.

The wise reader will understand that the Path is both simple and complex. The simple truths of life ingrained in every heart and mind are keys to a vast compendium of knowledge that the LORD has hidden from the worldly-wise and made known to the pure in heart. Thus continual study and a guileless application to one's Higher Self (the Christ within) are prerequisites to assimilating life's sweetest and most sacred mysteries.

These are the mysteries of the Ancient of Days, who has promised to write his laws in our inward parts so that all might know him, from the least unto the greatest.[3] And this he has done. Even so, many find it difficult to clearly understand the Law of their being. Its subtleties are inscrutable, because the Law is written in a language that is inaccessible to those who will read only outer signs and symbols where an inner sense (a holy innocence) is required.

But what, then, of those who are caught between the dark and the daylight? What of those who would touch the hem of the Master's garment and enter into the kingdom, yet they cannot because they see not? These need signposts along the way to guide them until they can hear the sound of his voice and the rustle of his robes.

As Messengers of the Great White Brotherhood, Mark and I have dedicated ourselves to creating those signposts, and many are included in this series. These teachings are calculated to lead seekers into the Promised Land of their own God-free being. Through this knowledge and the assistance of the Ascended Masters that accompanies the worded expression, the reader is offered a grander vision and a lifeline of hope in an age of crisis.

The Truth we present in this series is given in the tradition of progressive revelation. As one by one, students go unto their Father (the Presence of God within), greater revelations will be added unto them. It is our great desire that the keys in these volumes lay the foundation for a Golden Age that will come because the students of Ascended Master Law incorporate these keys into their lives.

When mankind en masse learn the higher way of living, of praying, and of invoking Light—practicing the sacred science —they will resurrect the cultures of civilizations that existed 300,000 to 500,000 years ago and even longer. And they will discover the secrets of health, longevity, alchemical precipitation —the mastery of the physical universe. But most important, they will also have dominion in spiritual realms and learn the way of the immortals.

The Truth we set forth herein is the Truth of the ages, the laws whereby the universes were framed. This is the Truth that is locked in the memory of the atoms and cells that compose the earth's crust and the being of man. This is the Truth that every soul knows. But without proper training and education it has remained lost, lying dormant just beneath the surface of the mind until it is brought to the fore by contact with the Light and renewed by the Teachers, the Ascended Masters, who stand waiting in the wings, ready to disclose the missing pieces to the puzzle of life.

All that man requires to complete his evolution and fulfill his divine plan will be revealed to him through the indwelling Christ, the indwelling Buddha and the memory of the soul awakened, quickened and mobilized by the Heavenly Hosts. Nothing will be withheld from those who diligently pursue the knowledge of the Law of Life. Man's fulfillment lies in the desire to be more of God, more of his higher consciousness, more of Life.

As Naaman the Syrian was required to dip into the river Jordan seven times to be healed of his leprosy,[4] so we ask that those desiring a transformation of consciousness—a healing of body, mind and soul—immerse themselves in the Light of the Seven Spirits of God that permeates these pages that they might receive their momentum of God-awareness, the momentum of Elohim.

In so doing, realize that reading this book (like all experience in the planes of Matter) is a means to an end, not an end in itself. The goal is God consciousness, which is always in turn a means to another end: greater God consciousness. For God is always growing, and you are a catalyst that fosters that growth even while your God Presence fructifies unfolding grace on earth.

As you read, we would have you hear the whispers of the universe in heart and mind, brood with the Great Spirit over the rites of creation, cast yourself in the cosmic drama reenacting the ritual of a cosmos, a rose, a cell, an idea. Involve yourself in Reality and thereby secure the mastery of self, of destiny.

As Messengers for the spiritual Hierarchy, we have been commissioned to speak the unspeakable, to utter the unutterable, and to set forth in writing what no man has written.

Ours is to make plain in earthly tongue what heretofore has been penned in the tongues of angels, to make clear the precepts of love.

Your newfound freedom will come not only from the formed but from the unformed as well, not just from what is said but from what remains unsaid. For words are but cups into which the mind and heart must pour the substance of experience and devotion, the distillations of soul-knowing and the formulations that are idling just beneath the surface of awareness waiting to be energized by the Christ mind.

The spinning wheel of life conspires so marvelously to produce the flax, so gossamer and filmy, that will one day become a garment of solar radiance, a garment of attainment. This wedding garment you will then wear as living devotion and love's perfect shield against all delusion, confusion and misunderstanding.

May you open the door of your heart to a renewal of your life in the alchemical furnace of He who loves you most. And may the angels from the realms of glory sit on your shoulder as you pursue these words and ever guide you into the Truth you seek.

In service to God in you,

Mark L. Prophet

Elizabeth Clare Prophet

MARK AND ELIZABETH PROPHET
Messengers of the Masters

Chapter 1

Twin Rays

And the LORD *God formed man of the dust of the ground, and breathed into his nostrils the breath of life; and man became a living soul....*

And the LORD *God caused a deep sleep to fall upon Adam, and he slept: and he took one of his ribs, and closed up the flesh instead thereof; and the rib, which the* LORD *God had taken from man, made he a woman, and brought her unto the man.*

And Adam said, This is now bone of my bones, and flesh of my flesh: she shall be called Woman, because she was taken out of Man....

Male and female created he them; and blessed them, and called their name Adam, in the day when they were created.

GENESIS

Twin Rays

SECTION ONE

The Search for Wholeness

ONE OF THE MOST BEAUTIFUL AND comforting concepts of all of the realities of heaven is found in the correct understanding of what have been called twin rays, or twin flames.* Truly, it was God himself who said: "It is not good that man [the manifestation of Himself] should be alone; I will make an help meet for him."[1] And thus, out of the Spirit, or active principle of creation, out of the masculine nature of God, came forth the feminine counterpart designed to be the vehicle for the expression and the expansion of the Lord of Creation.

The promise of twin rays, then, is one of wholeness. The principle of twin rays is the circle. The law of twin rays is the fulfillment in form of the masculine and feminine counterparts of the Deity.

To be sure, everyone has a twin ray either upon earth or in heaven. The spiritual complement of each soul does exist:

---

* The terms *twin ray* and *twin flame* have the same meaning, and they are used interchangeably in this chapter.

for the "other half" of the androgynous being of man lives to confirm the ultimate Truth of the law of polarities.

God never made an incomplete identity; male and female are actually parts of the individed Whole. One in Spirit, they must of necessity become twain in order to gain the fullest expression of the Godhead in form. The Lord of the Universe created neither man nor woman to be alone, but all-One with Himself. And this Oneness is beautifully consummated through reunion with one's own God Presence and with the God Presence of one's divine complement.

The words of Jesus used as the nuptial benediction to confirm the marriage vows on earth, "What, therefore, God hath joined together, let no man put asunder,"[2] were actually spoken by God as a fiat of the original creation—a sealing of the endowment of each flaming spherical identity with the fullness of the attributes of the Father-Mother God. The union was blessed; and the Spirit-sparks were commanded to take dominion over the world of form, to be fruitful and to multiply, and to replenish the earth in the Spirit of the Christ—the product of this heavenly union.[3]

Figure 1 The T'ai Chi and Twin Flames

The T'ai Chi is the ancient symbol from the East showing the two halves of the Divine Whole—the masculine and feminine, the Alpha and Omega of divine Being. In the Beginning, twin flames came forth from the one ovoid for the expansion of God's awareness in many planes of consciousness.

The Creation of Twin Rays

The mystical union of twin rays, or twin flames, originated with the creation itself, when Being came forth from God in the great white-fire sphere. This monadic expression of the Deity was endowed with the fullness of God's own Life; a sun of the Central Sun, it contained qualitatively all that was native to the Father-Mother God. Its purpose was to expand quantitatively the unique pattern with which it was endowed. In order to expand the consciousness of God throughout the creation, the white-fire body was divided in twain, both halves being endowed with an individual identity (an in-divided part of the Whole), which manifested as two I AM Presences, each surrounded by an identical Causal Body.[4]

It is the pattern of their Causal Bodies, then, that makes each pair of twin flames unique. This pattern is sealed in the white-fire body of the original monad; and when the division is made, each half of the Divine Whole retains the imprint of its destiny within the white-fire core that becomes the central sun of the individualized I AM Presence and Causal Body.

Just as each snowflake has a different design, so every monadic sun that comes forth from the center of God's Being bears a special quality that is all its own. Twin rays are one, then, by reason of their divine origin. Not by election but by divine appointment was the God Presence of each part of the Whole drawn forth from this unique ovoid of Light. Bursting forth from the Cosmic Egg, twin flames were endowed with identical Causal Bodies and a divine destiny that only they together could fulfill.

Thus, each set of twin rays has a unique assignment. Having been blessed with individuality, they have been sent forth to adorn the universe with their talented graces. No other monadic expression can fulfill their destiny, because no

Figure 2 The Creation of Twin Flames

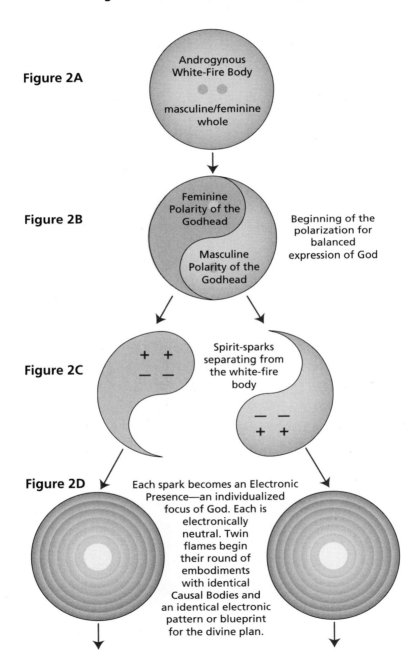

Figure 2E

The individual Christ Self is born out of the union of the Alpha and Omega spirals in the white-fire core.

Figure 2F

The soul in polarity with the I AM Presence goes forth to gain mastery in the world of form.

other has been given the same pattern to expand. This uniqueness in the pattern of their Causal Bodies also provides the basis for the union of twin flames. The law of attraction (like attracts like) governs their polarity; and no matter how far they may wander—though they be worlds apart—the love orbs that are their Causal Bodies are magnetized one to another like giant radar beacons.

Thus, the creation of the helpmeet for man was not an earthly creation—earth to earth, dust to dust, ashes to ashes—but a heavenly one. The true bride of man is his own feminine counterpart, the mother of his God-identity. And the bridegroom that cometh in the night of human desolation is the Christ, the masculine counterpart of the divine woman. This is the marriage that is "made in heaven" and sealed for eternity, whose vows can never be broken by a thousand earthly marriages.

Descent into Form

When the decree is issued for twin flames to embody, each God Presence responds by projecting extensions of itself into the world of time and space through the Christ Self and the crystal cord. The four lower bodies are then formed as chalices through which each individualized Christ Self may accomplish the mandates of destiny that the twin flames received as a scroll from Alpha and Omega.

No matter how far into the world of form twin flames may wander, destined as they are to outpicture the opposite polarities of their own divine pattern, their ultimate reunion is assured; for one day, after first rejoining their God Presence through the ritual of the ascension, they shall find reunion with one another. When this takes place, their individualized I AM Presences return to the focus of their white-fire body in the Great Central Sun, and they become forever a sun in the firmament of God's Being.[5]

Having graduated to cosmic heights, it is the destiny of twin flames to become Sun Gods and Goddesses. Representing the Father-Mother Principle, they are charged to nurture entire lifewaves and solar systems; for there is no end to the creative potential of the divine man and the divine woman created by God to expand the universe of His consciousness.

The universe is, in effect, their kingdom. They may go wheresoever they will and carry out those infinite degrees of expansion that the Godhead will deny to none who merit it. Thus, the man and woman go forth together into the eternal Garden of God, the Eden of God. Partaking of the fruit of the Tree of Life,[6] they live forever in such a union of bliss as is indescribable in mortal words or tongues.

This return to Oneness never destroys the individuality of either twin flame. Each retains the Edenic pattern of his or her identity, which can expand in infinite degree without sacrificing either the Allness of God or the uniqueness of his design for the Divine Whole. Such is the miracle of Life: the drop of water that slips into the sea can always be found as a molecule of love polarized to perfection.

Separation of Twin Flames

The parting of twin flames who go forth to do the will of God in the world of form is ordained by God in order that they might expand the talents he has given them and develop a greater individualization of their God flames in preparation for their eventual reunion in the octaves of Light.

In some cases, through their own freewill choice and with the approval of Hierarchy, one of the flames has held the focus of the will of God in the purity of higher octaves, while the other has descended into dense spheres on a holy mission of service, either to the earth or to one of the many other planetary homes upon which the evolutions of God are found.

Thus, some individuals on the planet have a twin ray who has never worn a physical garment, but who has continued to evolve in the higher reaches of Cosmos, benefiting from the experience gained on earth by the other half while adding his or her momentum of Light to the one who chose to brave the temptations of these dense spheres. Separation between the two has seemed very great; but the blessed tie that binds their union is a comfort of great magnitude, a promise of fulfillment that can never be gainsaid.

In other cases, both descended to participate in the world of experience and have moved through the octaves of mortal consciousness to the present hour. Sometimes this dual descent resulted in long periods of separation, as when one became caught on the astral plane while the other remained on the path of Light, seeking to hold the balance for the one who had temporarily lost his way. In some cases it has happened that both entered into negative spirals, and only by divine intervention were they able once again to climb the ladder of attainment.

It is sometimes the case that one twin flame is in embodiment while that one's counterpart may be in a state of transition between embodiments, either (1) studying in schools of Light, the temples of wisdom, or (2) caught in a net of astral delusion—the state known as purgatory. In the first instance, the one in embodiment may be the recipient of waves of heavenly joy and inspiration, which enable him, because of the added momentum of his twin ray, to perform mighty works of benevolence and creativity. In the second case, he may experience feelings of depression, anxiety and loneliness that seem wholly unnatural. The latter may be accounted for by the fact that his own twin flame is in need of help and is actually pulling on him for assistance to escape from the pits of astral darkness. Thus, he will be obliged to overcome not only the weight of his own karma, but also that of his other half, before he can move forward in the Light.

One of the greatest distresses that can ever arise in the universe is the suicide of any individual; for when men and women commit suicide, they often terminate the anchoring point of their twin ray in the world of form. Since this point of contact was intended to be an assistance to their counterpart, those who contemplate suicide should always consider their responsibility to their twin flame and ask themselves the question, "What effect will this act have upon my twin ray?" Suicide also interferes with the timetable set by Hierarchy for the coming together of twin flames. For instance, if a man is thirty and scheduled to meet his twin flame at the age of thirty-two, his suicide and subsequent reembodiment may result in his looking up at his twin flame from the cradle. Thus, neither will be able to fulfill their plan for that embodiment.[7]

The individual must realize, then, that his thoughts, his actions and his deeds are affecting not only himself but also his beloved one—even if that one is ascended! Yes, even the cosmic service of an Ascended Being may be held back by the unenlightened actions of his unascended counterpart. There is, indeed, a level of service in Hierarchy beyond which one cannot advance without one's twin flame. Many Ascended Beings are obliged to remain with the evolutions of earth long after their karma with unascended mankind has been balanced solely because their twin flames have not yet made the grade. Others may choose to remain in nirvana until the ascension of their twin flame. Those who have refused to come under the disciplines of the Law ought to consider the penalty that is being paid for their disobedience by loved ones in higher octaves.

Having an ascended twin flame is a great advantage to

one's service, especially in one's final embodiments upon earth. Likewise, a great deal can be accomplished for the planet when twin flames are united harmoniously in the service of the Light; for their union provides the anchoring point in the world of form for the completeness of the Father-Mother God.*

In many cases twin flames who are embodied upon the planet at the same time but who have not made contact with one another may be separated by divine decree because of the different stages of their spiritual advancement. For example, if one twin flame has gone the way of the world, he may be standing far off from his God Presence, and in an entire lifetime may not so much as come nigh the Presence either in thought or in contact.

When such is the case, it is often better that twin flames do not meet; for the heartbreak of being so near and yet so far from one's own self is often more than either can bear. Nevertheless, the one who is more advanced can do a great deal to invoke a momentum of victory for the day when his counterpart will accept the fullness of the Reality of God and of their divine destiny.

Then there are cases where twin flames meet and find that their paths are not compatible. This is always due to the fact that the accumulation of human creation within their electronic belts creates a clash in their personalities. Such clashes may arise because they have not been together for many embodiments and their involvements have taken them far from their original destiny. These differences can be overcome if both halves are willing to work together for the transmutation

---

* Saint Germain has said that he could not found a worldwide activity of Light without twin flames to guide its expansion, and thus he brought together our twin flames and ordained us as Messengers to spread abroad the Teachings of the Masters in this age.

of all density within their worlds. In all cases, love is the key to overcoming—with or without one's twin flame.

Every step Godward that is made by one half of the whole does directly and indirectly raise the other, and each backward step tends to retard the progress of both. Thus, once the individual is on the path of the ascension, he must never neglect his responsibility to guard the energies of his twin flame. Nevertheless, neither should give power to negation, whether from his own world or issuing from the world of the other.

The visualization of the violet fire encircling each half of the whole in a figure-eight pattern will assist in the transformation of all that is less than God's perfection and establish a point of transmutation between the two lifestreams. That point will be the Christ, who stands between the two poles of their individualization in form to keep the way of the Tree of Life. One may decree in the name of the Christ that the energies exchanged between oneself and one's twin flame pass over this fiery pattern and be purified ere they enter one another's worlds.

In giving their personal decrees, individuals may also insert in the preamble, after calling to their own God Presence and Holy Christ Self, the following phrase: "mighty I AM Presence and Holy Christ Self of my beloved twin flame." This practice will establish contact with the Higher Self of one's complement, whether he or she is ascended or unascended; for it is the Higher Self who counteracts all human influences and raises both halves of the Whole into their reunion in the Light.

The Sacrament of Marriage

Marriage was instituted by the Hierarchy for the purpose of preparing individuals for their ultimate reunion with the God Presence—the alchemical marriage—whereby permanent reunion with one's twin flame is achieved.* Personal sacrifices become necessary in the course of marriage in order to promote the greater good of the partnership and the offspring. Individual growth also occurs as the result of working side by side in loving grace with another soul for the welfare of family and community. All this is intended to develop the spiritual qualities and virtues that individuals require in order to realize the ultimate purpose of their divine destiny—including the unique service to be rendered with their twin flame.

Those who come together before the altar of God to be united in holy wedlock should do so in the understanding that their dedication is to the outpicturing of the attributes of the Father-Mother God. The family is the fundamental unit of service, the focus of the Holy Trinity and of the threefold flame. Marriage is, therefore, a holy union: first of two souls dedicated to the bringing forth of the Christ, and then of the family they establish under the aegis of Alpha and Omega.

The sacrament of marriage was originally sanctioned by Hierarchy for the evolution of twin flames upon this planet. However, because of the many ties that have been created through karma between souls who are not twin flames, it was decreed by the Lords of Karma that marriage should be a means whereby compatible souls can work out their individual and parallel destinies while serving side by side to expiate their personal karma.

Therefore, although man has only one divine counterpart, the purposes of his ultimate reunion with his God Presence and his twin flame may be served through his marriage to

---

* Jesus said, "When they rise from the dead, they neither marry nor are given in marriage" (Mark 12:25), showing that the marriage rite, while divinely ordained, is an earthly institution that does not endure beyond the grave. All should remember that the alchemical marriage, the marriage between the human and the Divine, is the most important union of all; for it implies a victory over outer conditions of life and the readiness of the ascension into the Light itself.

one who is not his twin flame. Furthermore, since earthly marriages are many times made between those who have already been joined together on high, marriage between those who are not twin flames may achieve the highest service and prove to be more harmonious than a marriage between twin flames who are not compatible in a specific embodiment. Such a relationship may be one of soul mates.

Soul Mates

Twin flames were created by God in the Beginning out of the same white-fire sphere of consciousness. Each half of the whole has the same electronic pattern, or blueprint, and that blueprint is not duplicated anywhere in cosmos. Twin flames are often alike, and yet they are often opposite in their manifestations, as they are intended to be the totality of the Father-Mother God in expression.

Soul mates are complementary souls who are working out a polarity of manifestation in one of the planes of consciousness. Their tie is for a particular mastery in time and space, whereas the ultimate union with one's twin flame is for eternity.

A soul mate is exactly what it says: It is a mate of the soul. The soul is something quite apart from the white-fire body, the white-fire core of your I AM Presence. So the term *soul mate* relates to a joint service and a mission on the Path that you might perform with someone other than your twin flame. The definition of the soul mate is someone with whom you are working on a project that is part of the fulfillment of the requirements of mastery on one of the seven chakras. Specifically, your soul mate would be one with whom you are working to focus the energies of Alpha and Omega in a specific chakra, and together you put forth your energies to make up the divine whole of that chakra.

One should not think of the primary quality of a soul mate relationship as being romantic in nature. Morya has called the pursuit of the will of God the sacred adventure. The path of discipleship itself, the finding and discovering of the divine lover of the soul—who is always Christ, one's own Christ Self—can be considered the true divine romance.

When people ask, "Can you have more than one soul mate?" they are often thinking strictly in terms of the romantic liaison. When I think of soul mates, I think specifically of project-orientation, when you work hand in glove to publish a book or to complete some project. Anything that involves team effort may involve soul mates. The definition of soul mate within that context would be two people holding the balance of an Alpha and Omega polarity for a project.

When people do not have a strong spiritual fortitude in their nature, any time they find themselves in that position of holding the balance of forces for worlds or for a project, it tends to also create a physical polarity. And those for whom the only excitement in life is romantic involvement can spend many embodiments going from affair to affair in rather rapid succession, because for them, the only meaning or feeling or depth to life is when there is a physical or a sexual overtone.

We find that this is particularly true of the fallen ones, because when they lose their point of Godhood, they lose the point of the threefold flame whereby their real joy in life is the figure-eight flow between themselves and their God Presence. The only way they have of feeling that they actually are alive and retaining their original vigor is to experience another and another and another such involvement. These relationships are always karma making, and they are karma making even when they are with soul mates or twin flames.

Partnerships, friendships and working together are necessary in every aspect of life. When you find one person with whom you fit together well for the accomplishment of a noble work, it is important to realize that even if the relationship is one of soul mates, this does not mean that it is an automatic fiat from life or from destiny that this is intended to be a romantic involvement. One may complete the project and be ready for the next initiation in the next chakra, which involves a whole new circle of people and perhaps another soul mate.

The connection between soul mates makes good brother/sister relationships, good family relationships and good marriages. These relationships have a quality of soul reflection; a certain element of completeness is found. In fact, you might be much more like your soul mate than your twin flame. Whereas you would be an opposite to your twin flame, you would be a parallel to your soul mate. This makes for happy, harmonious, fruitful relationships.

One of the greatest accomplishments of all time was made by a couple who were not twin flames but whose own twin flames were ascended and therefore able to assist them in their mission. Mary and Joseph, appointed by God to bring forth the Christ, were aided from on high by Archangel Raphael, the divine complement of Mary, and by beloved Portia, the Goddess of Justice, the complement of Saint Germain (who was embodied as Joseph).

Their lives are living proof of the fact that souls who come together dedicated in service to God and to the bringing forth of the Divine Manchild can succeed with the help of their twin flames. This help, when invoked, is always forthcoming from the God Presence of their twin flames, even though their twin flames may not yet be ascended.

Celibacy and Marriage

At this point let us make clear that among the spiritually elect of God upon earth, there are those who are masters and celibates, and there are those who are masters and family members. Down through the ages it has been necessary to bring avatars into existence upon the planet and to secure their transfer from higher octaves of Light into the world of form. Naturally it is more desirable to have them come through those who are themselves spiritually prepared to receive these incoming children.

Mary and Joseph were both specifically qualified as a part of the Essene community to receive the body and Being of that beautiful soul, Jesus, although they were not twin flames. Therefore, criticism or condemnation should never be leveled against any who bring forth children; for it is not man's prerogative to judge. Rather, it is the office of the Karmic Board and those Masters of Wisdom who can see the whole record of a lifestream to determine just what is and should be acting in the world of the parents.

Gautama Buddha explains that the paths of celibacy and of marriage both require a dedication to the Flame and to raising the Light: "Let all, then, arrest the spirals of unnecessary indulgence in the senses. Let all understand that there is a necessary balance that must be held by the devotees—the very precious balance of Light that is held in the chakras. We must, therefore, have a certain number of those who take the vow of celibacy who become the white Light of the crown of the Buddha and the Mother, that these might keep the balance for those who must tend the fires upon the altar of the family.

"Let those, then, who remain priest and priestess at the altar understand that it is not necessary to look to the right and to the left seeking that companionship of the husband or the wife.

But let those who are able know that this flame of the exaltation of purity must be held fervently, fervently with hope,... and that this high calling of the sons and daughters of God is reserved for those who see the requirement of the hour for constancy, for the release of the ruby ray, for energies that must be ready at the moment's notice for the defense of the Mother.*

"Let those, then, who keep the flame of family do so with consecration; and let not the flame of family be the opportunity or the excuse for the indulgence in lust, but let it be for the purity of the Virgin and for the attraction of the very highest souls. Let families, then, not be formed simply for the sake and in the name of giving birth to souls, but let families be formed for the higher consecration of love that will attract the avatars that are to be born....

"Let selfishness, then, be exposed. Let indulgence be exposed. And let those who are father and mother to the precious ones know that they are not excluded from the path of celibacy. They, too, may pursue the rituals and the initiations of the raising of the Light and the consecration of that Light. For after all, ye are not bound or in bondage but ye are free to be the Allness of God whenever you choose to be. And therefore, let the consecration of Light be your goal, and let the transmutation of all of the rituals of love in the marriage be the goal of this ritual—the raising, the exaltation, the consecration of new fires."[8]

Jesus affirmed the validity of the path of celibacy when he said, "For there are some eunuchs, which were so born from

---

* In the spiritual traditions of the East, these different callings may be a part of the natural cycles of life. The Hindu tradition describes four stages of life: (1) *brahmacharya*, the stage of strict chastity as a celibate religious student, (2) *garhasthya*, the stage of responsibilities to the world and to family as a married householder, (3) *vanaprastha*, the stage of retirement and meditation as a hermit or forest-dweller, (4) *sannyasa*, the stage of renunciation, when one is bound by neither work nor desire but can follow the path of a wanderer, freely pursuing knowledge of Brahman.

their mother's womb: and there are some eunuchs, which were made eunuchs of men: and there be eunuchs, which have made themselves eunuchs for the kingdom of heaven's sake. He that is able to receive it, let him receive it."[9] There is a need for spiritual orders after the priesthood of Melchizedek of men and women who take vows to be married to the Christ and to the Divine Mother. Unfortunately, this teaching has been misinterpreted by the Catholic Church and other churches that proclaim that the state of celibacy is holier and higher than that of marriage and therefore require priests to be celibate.

Jesus also affirmed the validity of human marriage. He performed his first public miracle at the marriage feast in Cana of Galilee, where he changed the water into wine.[10] By this he taught us that the water of the human consciousness is not adequate, that we must go through the alchemy of the Holy Spirit and that that wine of the Spirit must be a higher level of consciousness.

Jesus sanctified human marriage by his presence at this feast. To deny the holiness of the married state is to deny Jesus' sanctification of marriage and that of Saint Paul, who also proclaimed the holiness of the married state (while pointing out that celibacy was to be preferred if it could be kept).[11]

The Church's view that celibacy is holier than marriage denies the very heart of the sacrament of marriage celebrated by the Church itself. The imposition of a requirement of celibacy for priests has denied them the strength and protection that would be afforded in their service by their union in holy matrimony.

Mother Mary has explained that this requirement of celibacy is at the root of many of the problems of the Catholic Church. She said that when celibacy is forced on the clergy without an understanding of the true spiritual teaching behind it or how to maintain it, how to raise up the sacred fire on the altar of the spine of the temple of being, the results can be disastrous. She said:

"You find, then, that where the spiritual teaching as practiced in the Far East is not a part of the goal of celibacy, the end of that celibacy is far more heinous than the lawful marriage that is also ordained for those clergy outside of the Roman Church.... The misuse of the sacred fire, unlawfully according to the Laws of God, does place those priests outside of their vows, outside of a sense of personal dignity and truly outside of the holiness of the altar....

"Blessed hearts, it is good to place before oneself goals and self-discipline. Even the path of celibacy may be put on by married couples for a season of devotion, fasting and prayer, [voluntarily, by mutual consent]. These cycles, then, of conjugal love side by side with an acceleration of the marriage to the living Christ can therefore allow the individual to be balanced, to retain dignity, to know the beauty of family life yet not to be deprived of the priesthood of holy orders.

"Even so, the ancient prophets were married. Even so, some who later became saints and came apart from the world were married in the beginning, such as Siddhartha. And you know, beloved, that my own Son shared a beautiful love with his twin flame, Magda, who held the balance for him, even as I did, as he pursued a mission of immensity, holding the sacred fire of the Divine Mother in the full mastery of his chakras."[12]

The code of ethics sealed by the Lords of Karma for this epoch of earth's history requires that a man and a woman desiring to live and serve together present themselves at the church of their choice before a minister or priest of the Most High God. Under the laws of Hierarchy, the marriage contract is an agreement between husband and wife "for better or for worse" and "'til death do us part."* Although the pastor seals the earthly union using the words of the Lord's blessing already quoted, it should not be assumed that God automatically places his seal of approval upon the temporal union of husband and wife who are not twin flames; for they, by their own free will, enter into the marriage contract. If they have asked for guidance, they may feel confident that they have received it. Nevertheless, the free will that God has given to mankind also applies in matters of matrimony.

Unfortunately, many marriages are based on romance and physical appeal, the love of love, not on love between the souls. Because individuals see in their partners the alter ego of themselves, they fall in love with their self-created image. This drive toward union is a deep-seated spiritual need based upon their inner longing for their twin flames. When perverted by the ego, however, it manifests as selfishness. As the alter ego proves to be something less than the ideal, coolness of passion and appeal takes place, and the individual gradually withdraws his affection from his self-created image. The romance of the initial physical attraction dies away, and the marriage based upon selfishness fails. To be successful, marriage must be based on love between the souls, which in turn reflects as love between the persons.

One day spiritual marriage counselors will be able to assist those seeking advice through the study of their electronic belts. As we will explain in detail in the next chapter, every thought, word, emotion and deed that is less than God's perfection is

---

* The words "for better or for worse, for richer or for poorer, in sickness and in health" in the marriage vow mean that partners agree to bear the burden of one another's karma. Although each one continues to bear the responsibility of his own karma, the other stands by him while he goes through the trial. Each one may have karma with different lifestreams. Both share the burden. Each may be required to bring in one or more different souls. Both work together to provide a home, as representatives of the Father-Mother God, impartially meeting one another's needs and those of their offspring. The commitment embodied in the vow is to work out karma together and not desert one another because of karma.

deposited layer upon layer in the electronic belt. Individuals who have a momentum of misqualification in a certain area (for example, criticism, condemnation and judgment) will find that their momentum poles with, or is attracted to, an opposite misqualification (in this case, indecision, self-pity and self-justification).* Mistaking this attraction for genuine affection, such individuals often marry—to their later regret.

Lest any lose hope, however, let us quickly point out that this same substance, when transmuted into its divine qualities of God-power and God-harmony, can assist the couple to change a strictly human relationship into a truly spiritual one. Thus, all have the opportunity of advancing not only themselves but also their marriage partners toward the ultimate reunion with their twin flames.

Marriage as an Initiation on the Path

Let all relationships be consecrated in the Flame. Let us realize that marriage is an initiation on the Path, and the only real way it can succeed is if we make it an initiation and not seek from it that which it is not intended to give, which is the fulfillment of the endless desire for pleasure that is set before us as the goal by the world. We can never have that desire for pleasure satiated, because it is the desire of the carnal mind, and the carnal mind is the endless desire of the bottomless pit.

We must never compromise our alchemical marriage, our reunion with God—not for any human relationship. And that is the test on the Path: that no friendship, no family tie should stand between us and our God. Therefore, marriage is only

---

* Criticism, condemnation and judgment are plotted as the misqualifications on the 12 o'clock line of the electronic belt. Indecision, self-pity and self-justification are on the 6 o'clock line, the polar opposite. The corresponding positive qualities of the Causal Body are God-power on the 12 and God-harmony on the 6. For an explanation of the electronic belt and the misqualifications of energy that it contains, see chapter 2.

valid when the two partners can serve God better together than they can serve him alone.

The study of marriage as initiation is the study of the Path—the Path of the soul and her ultimate reunion with God. The Ascended Masters are really not concerned whether you are married in the human sense or not, and that decision and that relationship, which seems of such momentous import in the human scene, assumes a perspective to the Ascended Masters that is very clear, very disciplined and very to the point.

El Morya says that it doesn't matter if you are married or if you are not married—it matters that you pass your initiations on the Path. If these initiations can be passed and fulfilled in marriage, this is all well and good; and if they are to be passed as you maintain your union with God, all well and good. But it is the Path of initiation that counts.

When considering marriage, therefore, there are two questions to ask. First, "Have you considered whether your service will be enhanced, will be enriched and will be greater in the marriage union than it will be separately?" In other words, one plus one does not equal two in a marriage vow. One plus one always equals three, because it is you and your wife, or you and your husband, and the Holy Spirit between you. When that Holy Spirit ceases to be upon the altar of the marriage—whether in church or in the home or in the bedroom—then the marriage ceases to be valid in the Church or in the eyes of God. Every phase of marriage is intended to be sacred.

The second question is: "Are you deeply in love? Do you really have that deep fire burning in the heart, that fire that can commemorate your love for God?" Because if you don't have that love, your marriage will not withstand the onslaughts of the world. It will never be the whirling fire that is able to overcome every adversity.

Therefore, marriage has two requirements: the greater service to God, greater than you can render alone; and an intense fiery white-fire-core love.

Divorce

In the New Testament we find a statement of laws concerning marriage and divorce during that particular period of history. Jesus told his disciples, "Whosoever shall put away his wife, and marry another, committeth adultery against her. And if a woman shall put away her husband, and be married to another, she committeth adultery."[13]

The moral disciplines enforced from without at that time are intended to be imposed from within in periods of accelerated personal and planetary initiation such as the one through which we are now passing. At the end of this two-thousand-year cycle, when souls are being brought together for the redemption of karma, it is sometimes necessary for individuals to be married more than once in an embodiment in order to expiate the karma created by involvements in past lives.

Therefore, divorce has been sanctioned by the Lords of Karma—providing certain requirements of the Law are met. Only those earthly marriages that coincide with the heavenly union of twin flames created by God are sealed for eternity. But no contract should be broken except by mutual consent and for just cause under the laws of Hierarchy, many of which are reflected in the laws of the land regarding divorce.

The Golden Rule for marriage is to give all in service to the Christ in one's partner and not to surrender one's vows unless every step has been taken to preserve the harmony of the home. Where there is no harmony, no bringing forth of the fruits of Christ, there is not the proper representation of the Father-Mother God, and there is, therefore, karma in maintaining such a union. A discordant situation should either be healed in love or dissolved in love, both parties going their separate ways. But let each hear the solemn warning: unless he has given his all to preserve the union, he will be held accountable. The meeting of one's twin flame or a sudden shift of interests should not be construed as reason for deserting one who has been loyal and loving and has done his or her part to preserve the marriage contract.

Karmic Relationships

A note of caution should herein be sounded; for it is often a great temptation for those who have come to the knowledge of twin flames, who perhaps have been lonely or have experienced unfortunate problems in their marriages, to search for their twin flames and to imagine that they see their complement in those with whom they have nothing more than a karmic attraction. One must learn to distinguish between the inner confirmation that one is in the presence of one's divine complement and those attractions that spring from earthly desire and karmic involvements of the past.

Often lifestreams are brought together to balance past wrongs that they have committed against one another. The residue of their hatreds or quarrels from former embodiments creates a polarity of attraction that the Lords of Karma allow so that the individuals might balance, by the power of intense love, the cruelties that may have been practiced before. Hence, attractions between individuals may be for the balancing of karma, or they may indeed be a sign of the presence of one's twin flame.

Friendship maintained over a period of time, association without involvement or emotional attachment, will often reveal whether an attraction is based on the divine polarity or on the need for transmutation. Thus, it is always well to invoke a violet flame figure-eight pattern between oneself and such acquaintances in order that any magnetism based on human sympathy might be transmuted. If this is done conscientiously, it is often possible to avoid decisions and actions that will later be regretted. In either case, it will have to be ascertained by individual application to one's God Presence whether or not marriage vows provide the best opportunity for the balancing of karmic records and the fulfillment of the divine Law.

Sometimes the relationship of marriage provides the crucible and the intensity of love and service that is necessary to balance a certain karma, particularly when this requires the sponsoring of children. Such karmic marriages and other conditions of life may come and go, and they are for a purpose. So long as the karma remains (unless there be alternative means for working it out), they are binding. While we are in the midst of them, we can make of these marriages a celebration on earth of our inner union with our twin flame. This is lawful.

What is not lawful is to treat such a relationship halfheartedly or even resentfully and not give it the best and the most fervent love of one's heart because we say, "Well, this person is not my twin flame. And this is just a karmic situation, so I'll give it a token effort and bide my time until the real thing comes along." That is a very good way to prolong the resolution of karma and to make more karma.

We look at life with the understanding that whoever we are dealing with is God. The person is God—in manifestation. The divine flame is God. The potential is God. And we must love that person with our whole heart, with the purest and highest love that we would have for God and for our twin flame.

That love is liberating. It is a transmutative force. So it doesn't matter if you are married to your twin flame or if you have ever met your twin flame. What matters is that you realize the sacredness of marriage and the relationship of man and woman, and that this polarity is always representative of Alpha and Omega—the Masculine/Feminine co-creators of Life.

Beloved Chananda says: "We seek to direct the flames of the Holy Spirit and the Divine Mother in the earth. This we seek to do through companion souls, partners on the path of life. Truly it matters not whether (exactly) in the flesh you may be wed to your twin flame. What matters is that you maintain harmony, that you anchor the Light of that twin flame, and that you are happy, joyous, serving, free and full of the knowledge of the LORD with the one you have determined to share this journey with in earth. For, you see, in one respect every marriage is the marriage of twin flames. For every union is a celebration of that Light."[14]

The Search for the Twin Flame

Some individuals who, unfortunately, have not understood the balance and the divine assurance of the union of twin flames have spent entire lifetimes searching for their twin flames. Through the centuries, some of these blessed twin flames have made history in their search for one another; and this is understandable, although it is not recommended. The search for one's twin flame should definitely not become one's raison d'être. On the contrary, the meeting of one's twin flame should come about as a natural unfoldment of the divine plan.

As in all things, the sons and daughters of God should seek first to be joined unto their own I AM Presence in the assurance that, once they have found God, they can never lose their twin flame. The admonishment of Jesus "Seek ye first the kingdom of God, and his righteousness; and all these things shall be added unto you"[15] applies as much to twin flames and their search for one another as it does to every other facet of the path of victorious overcoming. The very fact that one's twin flame may be either ascended, between embodiments, in schools of Light, caught in the astral, or in the higher octaves from whence he has never descended into the world of form should make obvious the folly of searching without for that which is already within.

Chananda explains that the search for the twin flame should always be predicated on the desire for service and the spiritual path: "If the path of service is not your reason for being or seeking your twin flame, you have come to the wrong place! You who were born free to love, know this: This freedom carries with it the responsibility to set life free, to direct the Light garnered in the third-eye chakra into the denseness of selfish substance, exclusivity, hiding oneself, removing oneself from the universal community of the Great White Brotherhood, from the path of discipleship.

"Let not those who have failed as disciples of the Universal Light seek solace and sympathy in the embrace of one whom they call soul mate, counterpart or whatever term is chosen. If you are hurt, if you are bruised, if you are burdened by the encounter with God, with his emissary, with the living Christ abroad in the world, then I say, Take a deep breath, recite the mantra and run into the arms of your God. And let yourself be stripped and pummeled,* for thus you prepare to become the bride of Maitreya, of the Universal Light. Thus you are adorned. Thus you must prepare yourself also for the Beloved."[16]

It is important to bear in mind that physical union, even with one's own twin flame, cannot in any way produce a greater Oneness than that which the individual already enjoys by divine decree with his own divine complement. Man is

---

* "purified and made white, and tried" (Dan. 12:10)

already one with God. He cannot become more than God, but he can realize more of God through spiritual attainment as he transmutes the human creation in his electronic belt that separates his outer consciousness from his Creator.

Even as man is essentially one with God, so he is essentially one with his twin flame. In the world of time and space, the same human creation that separates him from God also separates him from his twin flame. In actuality, he cannot become "more one" with his twin flame than he already is, even as he cannot become "more one" with God. Whether or not he achieves this union is wholly dependent upon the spiritualization of his consciousness. This is the great tragedy of the misconception of twin flames. God has sealed them as one flesh in the original marriage vow—but the sealing is of the fire, and if the fire is not one, then the earth cannot be one. You could be married to your twin flame and not find your twin flame.

The physical reunion of twin flames must be left in the hands of the Father. Thus, it is not wise for individuals in embodiment to assume the role of matchmaker, although they may be acting in good faith on behalf of those whom they believe to be twin flames. In his good time, God will unite all who have earned the right to be together. Each son and daughter of God must rest in the certain knowledge that God, who has made all things and affinitized them correctly, will eventually unite the temporarily separated poles of the one true Being whom he has made.

Thus, after a process of soul refinement, molding of character and maturity in spiritual growth that always comes about as the result of the balancing of karma through service to Life and application to the sacred fire, individuals may find that they are reunited with their twin flames in spiritual service. This may take place early or late in an embodiment, or the Law may require that twin flames wait until another lifetime to be together physically. It is not uncommon for reunion to take place in temples of Light at the close of a particular period of initiation or an earthly sojourn.

Oneness on Inner and Outer Planes

Even before the physical reunion of twin flames may occur, their spiritual connection may be strengthened and anchored more fully in the earth. Chananda explains the importance of this: "Let us consider, then, why it is paramount to join forces with one's twin flame, especially in this hour, and why the Lords of Karma in recent years sent forth the dispensation for quickening, for acceleration of the uniting of twin flames[17]—discovering one another for a holy purpose and a physical one—and releasing the Light of the Causal Bodies of those who are of necessity separated in time and space but must serve, then, during the hours when the soul may take flight of the body and move at inner levels, or twenty-four hours a day; for the spiritual self is always one with the counterpart when and only when it is first one with God.

"Thus, the reason for the joint service of twin flames is this: The assignment from the beginning wherewith and whereto you were sent is something that must be fulfilled in the physical universe, in the physical Matter spheres, requiring the Divine Wholeness for the impetus of the movement of the T'ai Chi and the sphere of Light. Thus, when Causal Bodies of twin flames merge and they are one, 'as Above and so below,'* it is the manifestation of the fullness of the Godhead dwelling bodily in the twain. For the twain embody the Light

---

* on earth as in heaven, in outer manifestation as it is in the inner blueprint

[Christ consciousness] of Alpha and Omega, you see. No physical self has the capacity to be all in one. Thus the principle of helpmeet is balance, is helping each one meet the requirements of the Divine Wholeness for the mission.

"Now in this case, two halves do not equal one whole. Two halves equal two wholes. When the twin flame enters thy auric sphere, thou art whole. When you enter the auric sphere of the twin flame, he or she is whole. Thus, you see, in the completeness there are two manifestations of the fullness of the Causal Body—one therefore unlocking the Light of the other's. It is a divine interchange at the nexus of the Christ of both.

"Thus the union of the sacred fire in the mighty I AM Presence anchored here below enables each one to receive the release of Light from his or her own Causal Body. This is why some have said—as poets, as initiates, as devotees—that one is not complete without the twin flame.

"The twin flame, you see, in other words, is the only one in cosmos who holds the key to your Causal Body. These keys are held in the Holy Christ Self alone, for the LORD God would not allow even one's twin flame to violate the heights of one's Causal Body, just as you yourself are barred from access to that cosmic Light until you have become the initiate of the sacred fire.

"Nevertheless, the inner union can produce that release, as Above, so below. And in the meantime, the divine sharing below of the momentums garnered of mutual attainment works together for the fulfillment of the original assignment, the reason for being and for going forth."[18]

El Morya explains that karma is one factor that stands in the way of the reunion of twin flames: "I come to pierce the illusion that all problems are resolved by the meeting of twin flames or even soul mates. But I come with a statement of

Truth: that all problems *may* be solved by this union when it is founded upon the Rock of divine Reality.

"We come and we sponsor because your hearts have yearned, your souls have prayed, your minds have sought—sought to fulfill the reason for being in this life, sought to attain oneness with the perfect one. We will connect those for whom the connection results in a positive force for one another and for society. Where it would be detrimental in all ways or some, we recommend the accelerated path of the chela, humility before the Teaching of the Great White Brotherhood, which does give to you the knowledge of the violet flame and the call to Astrea (see page 74), which is the most powerful mantra to the Divine Mother that has been released in this octave....

"Understand that the highest and most perfect love begins with your individual expression of the heart, the expansion of that flame of love until all irritation is consumed and pride is not and you stand before your God truly worthy of whatever blessing can be given. Inasmuch as personal karma is the key factor separating twin flames and inasmuch as it is desirable that twin flames unite in service, the x factor that can make the difference is the entering in of one of the Ascended Masters or of Padma Sambhava or Gautama or Sanat Kumara to sponsor that union by pledging to take on the karma that does keep apart those souls. This sponsorship is like the sponsorship of the individual chela except it is the joint sponsorship of the twain.

"This, then, is a call you ought to include in your prayers. It is a call that says:

> O God, I desire to perform the best service and to fulfill my inner vow with my twin flame. If it be that karma does separate us and therefore our service, I pray,

let the LORD God set it aside for an hour and a year that we might show ourselves worthy, plow the straight furrow, enter into the service of our God and our country and of world freedom that together we may choose to balance that karma. And we do choose to do so, LORD God.

We pledge, then, no matter what may come, that if we be united, we will serve in harmony by the grace of God to first balance the karma taken on by an Ascended Master that that one need not carry for us the burden that is truly our own.

"Thus having so said, it is important to record on paper in your own writing this prayer and whatever you have added to it with the date carefully inscribed and with your signature. You may insert it in the book of the Everlasting Gospel.*

"You must remind yourself to call to Archangel Michael to defend the highest encounter and to bind all impostors of your twin flame. For as soon as the desire is set and the sail is raised on your ship, the false hierarchy will send in those of attraction, of glamour or of heavy karma or even the initiators that come out of the depths of darkness posing as the Krishna, the holy one of God that is thine own.

"To prepare for the perfect union, one must have the vision and the inner tie to God that tells one of the lurking danger. Thus keep the prayer and the call. And when all tests have been passed and the one sent is sent, remember that the purpose of that togetherness is truly first and foremost the balancing of that karma and the setting free of the Ascended Master who indeed has sponsored you and paid a price, the understanding of which will not be yours until one day you

---

* The Ascended Masters have spoken of the Climb the Highest Mountain series as the Everlasting Gospel prophesied in Rev. 14:6.

stand to offer yourself to pay the price for another."[19]

Whatever the outer circumstances of each one may be, the plan of God for twin flames is perfect and intact and it is cause for great rejoicing to the soul. It is a promise of fulfillment that will surely come if each one diligently strives to overcome, to improve his or her lot and to prepare, as a bride adorned for her husband, as the bridegroom who cometh to greet the bride, for the weaving of the wedding garment. This is the preparation for the alchemical marriage, and this is the marriage feast to which no man may come unless he wears the wedding garment.[20] The process whereby man weaves his wedding garment through the properly directed use of the sacred fire energies will be the subject of subsequent sections of this chapter.

SECTION TWO

The Sacred Fire

In the oneness of Life there is always polarity—never duality. The polarities of perfection consist of the masculine and feminine attributes of the Godhead. The perfect polarity between twin flames, created for one another out of the same white-fire body, enables each half of the whole to retain the divine magnetization. It is through this magnetization to perfection that man seeks the Divine; and thus, out of his incompleteness is born his reunion. The aloneness that man feels in the world of form before he has realized his reunion with his God Presence and his twin flame is, therefore, a blessing in disguise: for it propels man to his Source and to the ultimate goal for which he was created.

The Elohim Astrea pointed out that one of the methods used by man in seeking identification with Reality is that of sexual union: "As men or women seek one another, they are in reality seeking the other half of the Divine Whole; but they know it not. They think to achieve through physical union that wholeness that can be known only through the union of the soul with its Self—with the Higher Self and with one's own beloved twin flame. Such union brings both male and female into that wholesome state of the androgynous nature of God."[1]

In connection with their study of twin flames, it is essential that individuals on the Path understand the nature and function of sex, which means literally "sacred energy in action." Let them, then, approach the subject with reverence, remembering that Life is sacred and that Life is energy, that Life, or energy, belongs to God and is loaned to man in order that through its proper use he might multiply and expand the talents God has given him.

The Caduceus

The mastery of Life's sacred energies in action can only be accomplished through a proper understanding of the caduceus, the winged staff, which is the symbol of the medical profession. This symbol illustrates the entwining of the serpentine fire (the sacred fire) that rises upon the staff of Life (upon the spinal column) in the centripetal and centrifugal caduceus pattern. This fire is then anchored at the point of the third eye in the center of the forehead. Now let us see how the caduceus action is formed in man.

Figure 3 The Caduceus

As the sacred fire descends from the heart of the God Presence, flowing over the crystal cord, it travels along the spinal column to animate the temple of being through the seven major chakras and the other minor constellations of man's own physical-body universe.* The descending spiral

---

* Further information on the chakras and the caduceus is found in book 7 of this series, *The Path to Immortality*.

infuses the chakras with the masculine (positive) polarity, and the ascending spiral infuses them with the feminine (negative) polarity of the Godhead. Thus "The LORD shall preserve thy going out and thy coming in from this time forth, and even for evermore."[2] He shall preserve the going out of his sacred energies from the Holy of Holies into the body temple and their safe return to the I AM Presence via the caduceus pattern. Creation is being born each moment, each time an erg of energy completes the ritual of the descent and the ascent.

This mystery was revealed to Jacob in a dream. "And behold a ladder set upon the earth, [the spinal ladder] and the top of it reached to heaven [to the crown chakra—the pituitary center, which is man's focus of heaven on earth], and behold the angels of God ascending and descending on it."[3] Here the term "angels" symbolizes the electrons—particles of energy—that move in a continual flow up and down the spine, coming forth from the Presence and returning to it over the crystal cord.

The flowering of each of the seven chakras is thus attained by the victory of the caduceus action. Not only is the third eye opened as the result of the mastery of the sacred fire but also the purpose of the seven bodies of man is fulfilled as each of the seven chakras unfolds its destiny, each chakra being the focus of one of these seven bodies of man.

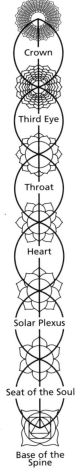

**Figure 4
The Seven Chakras**

The crown chakra, golden in color and depicted as the halo in the paintings of the saints, is the focus of the I AM Presence. The flame within the heart, vibrating with the love (pink) of God as it pulsates to the rhythm of the cosmos, is man's direct connection to his Christed Self; while the pure energies of the Causal Body, which holds the treasures of the ages and the immaculate concept of the divine plan, come through the third eye in the center of the forehead. The power of the spoken Word, which comes forth at the throat chakra, precipitates the etheric pattern in the physical form; while the chakra at the solar plexus is the anchoring point for the emotional body. The solar-plexus chakra is also destined to focus the energies of the Causal Body when the negative spiral known as the electronic belt is completely eliminated.

The seat-of-the-soul chakra, approximately two inches below the navel, is the focus of the (lower) mental body. When the passions of the carnal mind are overcome and the caduceus is raised, the creative intelligence of the Higher Mental Body (the Holy Christ Self) uses the sacred fire to bring forth the highest and noblest works of God. The chakra at the base of the spine is the focus of the physical body, which poles with the I AM Presence as its feminine counterpart in form. It is at this point that the energies of the caduceus return to the Presence, the positive becoming the negative for the return from the form to the formless.

Spirit and Matter

Life, as intelligent, self-luminous, creative energy, descends from the heart of the individualized I AM Presence over the crystal cord into the hands of the embodied soul. With the Christ Self acting as Mediator, this Life-force, as some call it, is intended to be expanded through the seven chakras in the body of man. Sex, then, or sacred energy in action, is nothing more than the release of the sacred fire—this energy that is first God's and then man's—through these chakras; but the term has come to reference its release through the base-of-the-spine and seat-of-the-soul chakras, which activate the genitals for the purposes of procreation.

The act of creation, whether of the Father-Mother God or of the sons and daughters appointed as co-creators in the world of form, necessitates the union of the divine polarity. Without the fullness in expression of the masculine and feminine aspects of the Deity, creation will not come forth, the soul will not pass through the portals of birth, the flowers will not bloom, the planets will not find their orbits, the stars will not shine, nor will any portion of the destiny of the universe be brought into manifestation.

The body of Nature, or the physical universe, is the womb of man (of the *man*ifestation of God). This passive aspect of the Deity is described in the Book of Genesis: "The earth was without form, and void; and darkness was upon the face of the deep." Then, "the Spirit of God moved upon the face of the waters. And God said, Let there be light; and there was light."[4] (Earth and water are the yin, or feminine, elements. Air and fire are the yang, or masculine, elements of creation.)

Thus, into the universal womb, the Holy Spirit of God did project the great energy stream of the Divine Logos. This stream carried the precious seed, the Word that in the Beginning was with God, without which there was nothing made that was made.[5] Matter (Mater) was impregnated with Life; and out of the union of Spirit and Matter came forth the divine archetype, the Christ, the only begotten Son of God, that the world through him might have eternal Life. The sons and daughters of God and the entire creation were formed after this Christic pattern.

In the union of Spirit and Matter, then, Matter transcends itself and becomes Spirit while Spirit takes on the vestiges of form and dimension. The finite is transformed when it becomes the bride of the Infinite. The energies that God has invested in the material universe, through the laws of transcendence and transmutation, become Spirit immortally vested. The product of their union is the Christ, who possesses the power to transcend both Spirit and Matter, time and space, the power to mediate between the Mother and the Father, between the God Presence and the human monad that is Matter in the state of becoming Spirit.

The grandeur and the purpose of creation, then, was for the bringing forth of the Son (Sun) through the union of the Father-Mother principle. When Jesus made the statement, "I and my Father are one,"[6] he was referring to the alchemical union that must take place between the embodied soul and the divine God-Presence before the individual can enter the fiery ovoid and therein find ultimate reunion with the twin flame.

In the alchemical marriage, God becomes man and man becomes God. God and man meet at the nexus of the figure eight, at the cross of the Christ from which the masculine energies—Spirit—descend and the feminine energies—Mater—ascend. In this divine union, the Spirit of the I AM Presence exchanges its masculine polarity with its feminine polarity focused in the world of form. Out of this perfect union there comes forth the Christ in every man, whose destiny it is to overcome all outer conditions, to demonstrate the alchemical principle of creation in the world of form, to heal the sick, to cast out sin and to overcome the last enemy, which is death.

The divine man and the divine woman (womb-man) need only look up and examine the ebb and flow of the universe to discover how they are destined to fulfill in the microcosm the glories of the Macrocosm. When husband and wife exchange the sacred energies in the marriage rite, they should do so in full awareness of the majesty of God's creation and their own momentum of wholeness, which is found in Christ. These sacred energies should always be dedicated to the reunion of the lower self with the Higher Self. This is accomplished as the marriage partners invoke the figure-eight pattern of the sacred fire around their four lower bodies when they come together.

The greatest secret of Life, the secret of creation, is sacred. The union of the divine man and the divine woman for the fulfillment of this highest and noblest purpose, the bringing of the children of God into the world of form, should always be consecrated by the vows of holy matrimony and the dedication of the bearers of the divine seed to the bringing forth of the Christ. It is this dedication to the Christ that spiritualizes the function of marriage and ennobles the offspring of the union.

Human marriage is sanctified by God as a circle of protection for sons and daughters of God. It is blessed by offspring and the offspring of the mind and the heart—mutual creations of the Spirit that bless all Life. The sanctification of the body, the heart, the mind and the soul in the wedding ceremony is not unlike the inner sanctification in the secret chamber of the heart. When protected by the great circle of God, sex is not sinful when it is revered as the sacred fire of the Divine Mother. The divine love that is shared at all levels of the chakras is the giving and receiving of the masculine and feminine elements, offering a foretaste to man and wife of that wholeness the soul shall realize when she is ultimately bonded to her Lord.

Misuse of the Sacred Fire

Unfortunately, the Achilles' heel of mankind has been their misuse of the sacred fire. This creative force, this Light, this power, this energy that descends hourly and momentarily from God to man, must be properly used and understood if man is to master his world. For it is the key to immortal Life. Throughout this series we have dealt with the Ascended Masters' instruction on the control and mastery of this energy; here we shall deal with the actual techniques of the mastery of the sacred fire as it pertains to the mystery of creation.

Just as mankind have learned to build canals and dams for the control of the earth's waters, so from past use man has built within himself channels into which he has directed the returning energies of the sacred fire. Some have a momentum of directing that energy to the crown chakra—these are devoted to learning and teaching. Some have directed it to the heart center—these have a great momentum of divine love, which becomes a magnet that holds the energies of the planet in balance. In others the flow of the sacred fire has been directed largely through the base-of-the-spine and seat-of-the-soul chakras. These individuals, without even consciously directing the flow of their energy, find that their genital areas are easily and almost continuously stimulated.

Such individuals may say they have a problem with sex, but in actuality this is not the case. What they are really saying is that the abundance of God's Life that flows to them hourly is being directed by them subconsciously to the lower chakras.

Men should not feel condemned by temptation or by frustration, nor should they feel a sense of being helpless sinners in their inability to cope with this misdirected flow of energy. They need only summon the determination and the will of God to raise these energies into the proper function throughout the four lower bodies.

When individuals realize the ultimate goal of the use of the sacred fire and the sacredness of its use in the procreative process, they will understand that the emphasis of life is not intended to be upon the fulfillment of man's lust, but in the use of this marvelous energy to attain limitless power, grace, self-mastery, health, longevity and blessings for all life.

The Transfiguration

The Ascended Master Lord Ling* has explained the action of the caduceus in connection with the transfiguration of beloved Jesus the Christ. He said that when the caduceus is operative in the proper manner around the spinal ladder, the flames of freedom and of the sacred fire rise up the spine and throughout the entire nervous system. When the initiate is in complete mastery of the sacred fire, as Jesus was, the spiritual power of the Light flows through his form, transforming the blood into golden liquid Light.

This is the true meaning of the transfiguration, and this is what occurred on the Mount of Transfiguration. Lord Ling says, "When I appeared on the Mount of Transfiguration, the fullness of that action was manifest in the body temple of Jesus, and it was but a short time thereafter that he demonstrated his mastery over death—the last enemy that is overcome after the mastery of the caduceus." Lord Ling revealed that the caduceus action was the secret of Jesus' power over life and death. He said that Saint Germain also knew this teaching before his ascension and it was through its proper use and demonstration that he lived for hundreds of years in one body.[7]

Before man's fall from grace and his misuse of the sacred fire, creation sprang forth by the power of the spoken Word through the throat chakra. Twin flames faced one another and uttered the fiat of the Light by which the power of the divine seed and the action of the caduceus produced a living form

---

* One of the many important embodiments of this Son of God was Moses, who led the children of Israel out of bondage in Egypt and who, in his ascended state, appeared with Jesus during his transfiguration (Mark 9:2–8; Matt. 17:1–8).

instantaneously, and thereby a Son of God stepped forth in radiant manifestation. The Light rays flowing between the masculine and feminine polarities of the father and mother were able to weave the garment of the flesh form in a short time. The child could, then, step forth as a smaller figure and almost in the twinkling of an eye, through an accelerated process, manifest in an adult form with the full waking consciousness of Being, resplendent with the memory of all past lives as an integrated Whole. This meant that there was no break in the continuity of the soul's evolution. The shedding of the body form was not regarded as a sorrowful event, but a joyous one, when the so-called outworn parts could be exchanged for a totally new physical form. In those days wills were made leaving the treasures gathered in one life unto the self to be redeemed upon one's return.

Lord Ling revealed that it was in this manner that Melchizedek was born without father and without mother,[8] without descent, without beginning of days and without ending. His God-parents were Masters of Light—a Son and Daughter of God; thus, he was without earthly mother and father but not without heavenly parents. This is the secret of the Order of Melchizedek.

In commemoration of the beauty of this spiritual creation, the Holy Spirit descended upon the apostles on the day of Pentecost in twin flames of Light; and with these flames came the benediction that was spoken to the children of Israel of old, "Behold, ye are gods."[9]

SECTION THREE

Raising the Light

THE LORD GOD WHO MADE heaven and earth is an androgynous Being. Therefore, when creating man, he said, "Let *us* make man in *our* image, after *our* likeness."[1] And thus it is recorded, "male and female created he them,"[2] because he himself was possessed of the divine polarity. Each individualized I AM Presence, being a replica of the Electronic Presence of the Father Supreme, is also androgynous. When the white-fire body was divided for the purposes of expansion, each point of Light (each half of the I AM THAT I AM) that was to serve as a focus of the Deity for the incoming soul was given an equal portion of God.

But to serve the purposes of divine magnetism in the world of form, the souls who went forth clothed with the veil of flesh were endowed with a 60–40 ratio of the divine attributes. The one who would embody the masculine aspects of the Deity was, therefore, polarized with 60 percent of the masculine attributes and 40 percent of the feminine, while the one who would embody the feminine aspects of the Deity was endowed with 60 percent of the feminine attributes and 40 percent of the masculine. It is this imbalance that creates the desire for oneness with one's counterpart; this is the blessing that keeps man on the path of the grand search for his divinity through the search for his twin flame.

In a masculine embodiment, the soul has a greater opportunity to master and expand the masculine virtues of the Christ, and in a feminine embodiment, the soul learns to develop the feminine attributes of the Deity, associated with the Holy Spirit. In order to maintain the balance in each individualized Causal Body and for purposes of balancing karma and gaining new experience, a change of roles and polarities is assumed by twin flames in successive embodiments.[3] All of this is for the purpose of the soul's expansion of her understanding of her relationship to the Deity; for God himself manifests to us in the souls of all of the actors who play in the drama of life with us as we evolve in earth's schoolroom.

Misuses of the Divine Polarity

Unfortunately, where the sacred energies have not been brought under control, some individuals find it difficult to adjust to the change in polarity that occurs when twin flames are obliged to assume opposite roles. At times there is a manifest rebellion against their sex, women desiring to assume the masculine role and men tending toward the feminine. When such tendencies to go against one's karma and dharma are allowed to go unchecked, they may take the form of homosexuality, if not in this embodiment then in the next.

With each incarnation, male or female, we are given a certain charge at the base-of-the-spine chakra. There are three energies that rise in the Kundalini, the *idā, pingalā* and *sushumnā*.[4] This energy comes out of the Mother flame, and it is the same energy that Jesus raised from the base of his pyramid of Life in the transfiguration, the resurrection and the ascension.

If a male chooses to engage in the practice of homosexuality, he will thereby pervert the masculine ray of these three, the alpha current. If it is misused continually, he will be depleted of that masculine ray, and this often produces an effeminate nature. If a female chooses to engage in the practice of lesbianism, she will thereby misuse the feminine aspect, or the Omega spiral, of self. This deprives the person of the fullness of the feminine potential. It may cause a shift over into a less intuitive and less exalted state, into a more crude and perverted masculine way of life.

The Masters teach us that homosexuality was introduced on Lemuria in the shrines of the Mother when the priests and priestesses misused the sacred fire of the Mother flame. We have been given free will, but when we choose this way, we are not choosing the balance of our forces. We cannot, therefore, look forward to the resurrection and the ascension until we have rebalanced our energies.

Where there are large numbers of individuals engaged in these practices and thus perverting the sacred fire and unbalancing their own forcefields, this imbalance may also be reflected in nature. The Bible records that the overwhelming misuse of the creative force by the people of Sodom and Gomorrah, including the ungodly misuse of sex by men and women together,[5] was the cause of the destruction of the twin cities of the plain.[6]

The purpose of man's descent into the world of form is to gain mastery over the sacred fire and thereby to bring about the perfect polarity of the Godhead in the four lower bodies.

Through experience in earthly schools, man is intended to become the Christ; and when he does, the masculine and feminine attributes of the Deity are in expression equally. He is then outpicturing half of the masculine aspects of the Deity and half of the feminine. This perfect balance marked the difference between Jesus the Christ and his disciples. The reunion of twin flames in the white-fire body after their ascension gives each half of the Divine Whole the full complement of the masculine and feminine expressions of the Deity, intended by God to be the crown of their achievement. Only then can they be called co-creators with God in the fullest sense of the word.

The practice of homosexuality does not further these goals; on the contrary, it results in the imbalance becoming greater the longer it is practiced. Once individuals allow themselves to be caught in this spiral, it becomes increasingly difficult to break the pattern with each successive embodiment in which it is indulged. This, of course, is true of every habit that is formed through man's misuse of the sacred fire.

Homosexuality is therefore not a way of life but an inverted attempt to find one's other half. Its continued practice can only lead the individual farther and farther away from one's God Presence and from ultimate reunion with one's twin flame. Those who truly seek to be free from this should realize that when they turn the problem over to God, he will supply the strength to overcome.

Energies that flow within us carve deep river beds. When we habitually express irritation or anger or a use of sexual energy, we are carving a deep pattern within us. Energy tends to flow in that channel we have created. If we are going to close off one channel and open up another, we have to be patient with ourselves. We have to be understanding. We must never condemn but attempt to move forward on that path of self-mastery. The generous use of the violet flame and a sublimation of one's energies in the service of the Christ in all assures man his freedom from every unprofitable practice.

The determination of one's sex is not an accident of biology, but a preordained opportunity for the soul to gain needed balance in the expression of Christly virtue. Therefore, attempts to alter one's sexual polarity through homosexuality or by medical operations are not in keeping with the will of God. Rebellion against one's sex can only be based on ignorance of the Law of one's own being and of the wide variety of godly attributes capable of being developed by both sexes.

Family Planning

While on this subject, we should point out that the attempt to predetermine sex by parents will not alter the sex of the incoming soul, but it may result in their having a soul other than the one intended for them by the Lords of Karma. Parents who deny birth to their assigned soul by using scientific methods to prearrange the sex of the child are not absolved of their responsibility to that soul. If they do not give birth to that child in this life, they may be called upon to do so in the next.

The Hierarchy does expect, however, that parents should plan intelligently for a family that is within their means. The Goddess of Liberty has stated the position of the Karmic Board on family planning: "You ought not to bring forth more children than you are able to care for and for whom you may adequately express your love."[7]

If parents are unable to exercise God-control for the required period, they may use contraceptives as long as these are not harmful to the health of the parents and do not become the means of dodging their responsibilities to incoming souls for whom they vowed to provide body temples.⁸ Those who deny the opportunity for reembodiment when they have the means, the health and the capacity to bear children should consider the time when they may be pleading before the Lords of Karma for another round in the world of form. Then, their own record will be their judge.

The Disciplines of the Sacred Fire

The movement toward "free love" does not have the sanction of Hierarchy, for it effectively does away with the disciplines of the sacred fire that are necessary for the soul to earn the ascension. Also, when individuals allow themselves to become sexually involved with one or many outside of the vows of marriage, they ignore the true function of sex, which is procreation; and in neglecting their responsibilities to bear children, they may incur grave karma. The pagan attitude captured in the phrase, "Make love, not babies,"⁹ defiles the purposes of creation and the intent of the Father-Mother God.

Let all understand that man's most precious gift of life is his seed, his ability to impart life. For in being the keys to procreation, the sperm and the ovum actually contain the archetypal pattern of each one's Christed Self.* Therefore, when man gives his seed to a woman, he is giving her the most precious part of himself; he is giving to her the key to his divinity.

Sons of God must always bear in mind that the potential of their seed may be either expanded or limited by the consciousness of the woman to whom they entrust it. Having gained custody of his identity pattern, the woman can control

---

* Each seed bearing after its kind follows the unique pattern that the Universal Christ has stamped upon it. Therefore, the seeds of plants also contain the powerful imprint of the Universal Christ Mind that provides the impetus of their reproduction.

the man for good or for ill depending on the state of her consciousness.¹⁰

Sometimes active and sometimes dormant, the memory patterns of all sexual involvements that have ever been experienced by the individual are recorded in the electronic belt. This reservoir of negative spiraling energies* raises its head as a potent force, even in the lives of those who have dedicated themselves in the service of the Light. The negative spirals, past momentums and records of sexual involvements all work together, then, as a sexual magnetism against the ascendant spiral of eternal Life that is the gift of God to every man.

Seeing that God has ordained husband and wife as representatives of Alpha and Omega to bring forth sons and daughters in the image of the Christ, the necessary respect between them must be upheld in order that they might fulfill that role. Premarital involvements detract from the sanctity of the purposes of marriage and tend to separate the responsibilities of procreation and the security of a deep and abiding love that must accompany it from the sex act, making it a biological function.† This attitude furthers man's image of himself as an animal rather than a representative of Hierarchy. The proper instruction on the use of the sacred fire will give to all the divine blueprint of life that each individual may follow at his own pace.

Whereas schoolchildren are being taught that sex is a necessary part of life, they are not being taught its proper use. Ironically, those who are called upon to teach sex education

---

* Those who associate sin with immorality may be interested to know that the word "sin" simply means "*s*acred *e*nergies in a *n*egative spiral."
† Another negative effect of such involvements is that when people indulge in premarital relationships, most sexual involvements are simply an exchange of energies at the electronic belt level. They take on some of the electronic belt patterns of their partner, and these remain with them. Within the circle of marriage and its sealing in the Trinity, on the other hand, there is the opportunity, through spiritual attunement and the raising up of energies through meditation, for there to be an exchange through all of the chakras of the Great Causal Body—the great spheres of cosmic consciousness.

are often ill-equipped for the job—through no fault of their own, having as they do an incomplete knowledge of their subject. It must be understood that the scientific use of the sacred fire is necessary for the proper functioning of the physical form. The daily charging of that form with the energies that descend from the God Presence, the blessing of the chakras with these waters of Life, the nourishing of the body by the flow of the sacred energies up and down the spinal column—this is what is necessary to the health, happiness and longevity of a lifestream.

However, as we have noted in book 7 of this series, *The Path to Immortality,* there are entities that goad mankind into every type of abuse of the sacred fire. These may hound people for months and years, frustrating them to the point where they feel they have no alternative but to engage in some illicit form of sex. Using the force of the individual's own past records, together with the race consciousness of sex, they project sex fantasy and intense desire at unsuspecting souls, who identify these projections as their own.

More than half of mankind's problems with sex are manufactured by the sinister force, whose sole intent is to engage people's energies in the misuse of sexual energy in order to steal Light that was given to them by God for the nourishment of the chakras and the four lower bodies. This is just one more method, and a very prevalent one indeed, that is used by the forces of darkness to deprive mankind of immortal Life and the joys of their God-given inheritance while they are on earth.

The Desire for Wholeness

The desire for union as the desire for wholeness is the desire of the presence of Alpha and Omega within our own temple to be One. Symbolically, then, the point of Omega is the base of the pyramid where the white fire of Life burns. The point of Alpha, the golden Light of victory, is the crown. When the two are one, wisdom has the power of purity to perform its perfect work, and the Mother has the wisdom to go forth through her sons and daughters and take dominion over the earth.

In Matter, Alpha without Omega is powerless. The powerful stream of the rising ascension flame makes wisdom become God in action through us. Omega without Alpha is simply the pure stream of the cosmic force without the direction of the Mind of God. There is a way to attain wholeness within the individual temple, and the path is the locking of these twin spirals of the balance of Alpha and Omega, the Father-Mother God, within the very heart that leaps as a threefold flame.

The violet flame is a most direct and efficient means of clearing the channel so that the flame may rise as a stream, clearing the pathway. At each stop along the way, like a subway station, there are accumulations, and therefore the Mother flame does not continue unobstructed. The soul must follow the stream, yet the stream cannot rise because of the karmic conditions that result from the misuse of the seven rays, beginning with the base of the spine, the white fire, then the seat of the soul as the violet flame, the solar plexus as the purple and gold, the heart as the mighty pink fire, the blue-flame chakra of the will of God in the throat, the third eye and the crown, the green and the gold.

In centuries of misqualification of these planes of being, we have wittingly or unwittingly erected obstructions, barriers, dams to the rising flow of Life. Therefore we have invented, after the way of the fallen ones, various ways and means of overcoming the stoppage of the flow. Some people invent tantrums, others gossip or hatred. They use the release of the throat chakra temporarily to relieve that pathway of Light of the effects of the obstructions of past karma.

Sexual indulgence that is rampant on earth today is a means of releasing that Light so as to avoid the pain of the pressing through of the green shoot of the stalk of the lily. This, of course, neutralizes any burden of pressure that might arise in any of the given chakras. However, it also reduces to a stubble the power of the individual to rise in his own dominion. The plant does not even begin to grow before it is cut down, and therefore the individual loses the will to be, to live, his own sense of integrity—which is integration with Alpha and Omega. He loses his sense of self-worth, because all self-worth is defined as individual wholeness. He cannot hold even his head erect because there is not enough flow of the ascension fire to support the head of the flower upon the stalk.

The soul's natural state is union through the Father-Mother God. This wholeness is maintained by the ascent of the Mother Light to the point of the Father. In the presence of this divine union, and only in its presence, do we know the bliss of the Divine One. God has ordained the celebration of this union on earth in this evolution in the ritual of marriage. This celebration of the union is given to us for the procreation of life, for life begetting Life. The union is the Alpha-Omega of Life, and therefore, in its sacred fire it produces the new manifestation of life.

The Seventh Commandment

The understanding of the original marriage of the soul to this Light of the Mother gives us the meaning of the Sun behind the sun of the seventh of the Ten Commandments, "Thou shalt not commit adultery."[11] In its higher understanding, this means, "Thou shalt not use the Life-force in any of the seven chakras for any activity whatsoever that would deprive the Divine Mother of her lawful Light from your soul."

Every form of discord or self-indulgence steals from the Divine Mother the Light that belongs to her. We see, then, that adultery in a broader sense is the entire ramification of the misuse of any of the seven chakras.

The Ten Commandments were given to an idolatrous generation. They were the reinforcement at the physical level of spiritual Laws that had application far beyond the simple understanding of the physical law. Adultery, in a literal sense, is the act by one who is married in a lawful marriage on earth of engaging in sexual intercourse with another who is either married or unmarried. This law is the fundamental principle, the physical law, upon which the spiritual Law does thrive.

We cannot disobey the physical law while maintaining the keeping of the spiritual Law. In other words, the spirit of the Law does not obviate the letter. We cannot say we are modern and we are beyond the requirement of the seventh commandment in the very narrow and basic interpretation of it. But if we keep the commandment and do not commit adultery, we must also realize that in order to win our eternal union with God, we must begin to celebrate that union on earth. Therefore we must also keep the spiritual Law. If we profess to be initiates on the path of the ascension, for us the literal interpretation of the seventh commandment is not enough. We must be disciplined in the maintenance of the Light of the T'ai Chi in each of the seven chakras.

The exercise of holding the attention and the sublime adoration of the Mother at the point of the third eye can be given each day, especially while giving the violet flame, the "Heart, Head, and Hand Decrees" (see page 70) or any other decrees or spiritual exercises. Archangel Michael is the defender of the Divine Woman, and therefore, to visualize the rising River of Life with a blue-fire sheath gives protection to that Light within you that it not be violated by any records that continue to exist in the other chakras until they are transmuted. Visualizing the violet flame in each of the seven chakras will assist in transmuting old momentums by which the pressure that comes about because of the blockages of old records and misqualified substance has been released in the past.

The Flow of Alpha and Omega

The problem of integration could sum up all other problems that people have on the spiritual path—the problem of not having the white sphere of identity won, the problem of not drawing the circle of the figure eight through the heart connecting the lower and the higher energies and continuing this figure-eight movement within the self so that the lower energies are constantly rising to nourish the upper chakras and the spiritual force of God is descending as a sacred fire to cleanse.

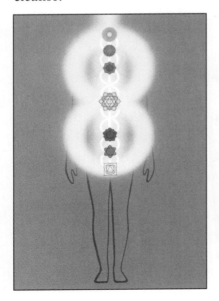

Figure 5 The Figure-Eight Flow of Energy through the Chakras

The heart is the anchor point in the four lower bodies of the energy that descends over the crystal cord from the I AM Presence and Christ Self. From here, the light is distributed to the seven major chakras. The chakras above the heart have a masculine / plus / Spirit polarity, and the chakras below the heart a feminine / minus / Matter polarity.

We know of the interaction of fire and water, Alpha and Omega. When you look at the chart of the figure-eight flow through the chakras, remember that the white fire as spiritual energies proceeding from the heart to the upper chakras is the focal point of Alpha; below the heart it is as the water energies of Omega. As the flow passes through the heart, the fire descending becomes water purified for the purification of the lower vehicles, the organs below the heart. It provides all that is required for the sustainment of life. As that energy returns to the heart, passing through the nexus, it becomes fire again, so that continually working in our members is the baptism of fire of beloved Alpha and the baptism of water of Omega.

The water baptism is for repentance and the cleansing of sin. The fiery baptism is for the anchoring of the I AM Presence in your form. We need this energy. If there is a leak anywhere because of old momentums, then we lose it—we are allowing a leak to occur in one of the chakras or one of the planes of being that drains us of the Life-force of Alpha and Omega. Then we find ourselves not able to fulfill our tasks or our divine plan, to charge forth in life with determination and energy to accomplish all that is before us in each twenty-four hours.

It becomes very important, then, to understand that the commandment to not commit adultery is absolutely essential to the survival of the soul and the soul's ascent to the Mount of Transfiguration. This is a daily and an ongoing process. If we would have the full faculties of our Christ Mind and our mighty I AM Presence, we must be fastidious in determining what are the leaks.

In the nineteenth century, Freud told us that all of these problems are sexual problems. You could look at it this way. And from this perspective, it might be said that if only you had a perfect sexual life, all of your problems would be over.

However, the fact of the matter is that even if one could conceive of and have the perfect sexual life—whatever that might mean to any individual—coming back to the question of wholeness, it would not solve the problem. This has been proven again and again. Therefore, what is the problem and what is its solution?

El Morya has said, "Tell them that the problem in the mastery of the Life-force is a problem not of sex, but of flow."

People are no better and often far worse in the sexual experience; therefore, we must come to grips with the higher law and the higher manifestation of the Light of the Mother within us. We must come to the realization that old patterns of centuries persist. Very human momentums are carried over from lifetime to lifetime. Even the shape of your bones, the size of your hands, the number of the hairs on your head, a disposition to thinness or to some other body condition—all of these characteristics may be seen repeating again and again in each embodiment. If this is true, then we can see that we are cast from the mold of the divine blueprint of the etheric plane as well as the blueprint that we create and superimpose upon it. Therefore, something so fundamental as the individual's sexual habits might very well be seen to carry over from one embodiment to the next.

We live in a civilization of promiscuity; therefore we do not have a natural inclination in our training from childhood to strive for the mastery of energy. Even the expression of negative emotions is not considered to be bad but a necessary release. We shouldn't bury our hatreds, we shouldn't suppress our anger; if we do this we will have psychological problems, we will have physical problems—so they tell us.

It is true: we must not suppress. But often this is used as a justification to have an outburst, to become angry, to express oneself emotionally to clear the channels of being so that things flow again. There is always the easy way out. "There is a way which seemeth right unto a man, but the end thereof are the ways of death."[12] At every hour of the day we may take the easy way—or we may have the divine habit of the discipline of the Life-force in all that we do.

It is essential, if we would walk the earth in the Electronic Presence of the World Mother, that we understand what is pleasing to the Mother and what is not. She carries the greatest power in all of Matter, and her demand is that we discipline our energy. There is only one way to discipline energy, and it is by the perfect love of the Mother. Without that perfect love, we do not summon the will to break through those old patterns of centuries, we do not summon the will to bind the demons that stand at the threshold, the very gates of the chakras, to prevent that Mother flame from entering and from rising.

Lightbearers must summon the Life-force within them to resolve the problem of the economics of the system of the four lower bodies. This world we live in, this temple we occupy must be governed according to the law of supply and demand. The supply of Light within you is the Mother Light and your threefold flame. The demand is that you need all of it and then some to make your ascension.

Because we have squandered this Light in previous lives, even the natural flow that we receive each day—using all of it for the glory of God in the service of one another—is not enough to make our ascension. That is why, when we give our dynamic decrees, we invoke the presence and the multiplication factor of the Christ consciousness of the saints, the Ascended Masters. We ask them to send their momentum of Light to multiply our own heart's Light, our own magnet, so that we may have more than simply our daily allotment. We need more for our own healing, for our own balancing of karma, and we need more to hold the balance for planet

Earth and those who are still squandering their Light. If we could go it alone on our own threefold flame and our own rising Mother Light, we would not need the Great White Brotherhood.

If we have squandered the Life-force, we must now invoke it again and raise it up. If by the use of drugs or chemicals in our bodies we have interfered with the natural flow of God's wisdom, the natural flow of the Mother Light to the crown and our soul's upward ascent, we must look for healing in life itself—life in every level, life as the path of our diet, our fasting, our prayer, our violet flame. We must seek the restoration by Light itself of those cells of the body, injured by marijuana or other forms of drugs.

We need every source of Light we can get. We need the Kundalini. We need the threefold flame. We need the violet flame. We need the decrees in all of the seven rays. We need the Light of every chakra. We need the Central Sun in the very heart of the earth, in the heart of Helios and Vesta. We need the heart-fire of every Ascended Master, and we need the Life-force preserved in the right food.

This is why the path of the ascension is a total path. If we violate any one of its laws, we find that we cannot carry out the discipline on the other side of that law. We all see this, we all know it; but it takes a twenty-four-hour vigil to take care of the body as the vessel of the Spirit.

Raising the Light

It is essential to understand, then, that everybody has the creative force and that everybody is using it—whether or not they are actually involved with sex. It is a force that is active from the cradle to the grave and beyond; and it must, therefore, be controlled here and now if we would have our freedom both here and hereafter. How we use this force, how we direct it, determines what we are going to be and to accomplish.

The rising of the flow of the waters of Life from the lower centers can be accomplished by the frequent use of the simple yet all-powerful decree:

> I AM the resurrection and the life of every erg of energy sent forth from my Presence for the nourishment of my body temple. I AM the resurrection and the life of the divine plan made manifest within the seven centers of Light. I AM the resurrection and the life of every cell and atom of my four lower bodies now made manifest.

The raising of these energies may also be accomplished through the giving of the "Transfiguring Affirmations" of beloved Jesus (page 361) and the decrees to the resurrection and ascension flames.

Those who are determined to raise the sacred fire to the third eye will find a most powerful means of accomplishing this goal in the decree to Astrea (page 74). The decree may be given thirty-three times, once for each of the thirty-three major initiations leading to the ascension. As it is given, the disciple visualizes the ascension spiral rising around the spinal column. Beginning at the base of the spine, he focuses an intense concentration of white fire around each of the thirty-three vertebrae, holding each focus as a flame for the duration of one decree. This exercise may also be given with the violet and purple flames as well as the healing green. Any decree from those sections of the decree book, given thirty-three times in this manner, will complement the action of the Astrea ritual. (These, however, should not be used as a substitute for the Astrea decree but in addition to it.)

The Hail Mary and the rosary are a meditation given to the West for the raising of the energies of the sacred fire through the chakras.[13] Djwal Kul explains: "When you give the salutation to the Mother ray in the recitation of the Hail Mary, you are giving praise to the energies of the Mother locked within the flame in the hidden chamber of the heart and sealed in the base-of-the-spine chakra. In this gentle yet powerful salutation, you are day by day drawing the energies of the white-fire core and the base of the spine—yes, even the serpentine fires of the Goddess Kundalini—up the spinal altar for the nourishment and the wholeness of Life in all of its centers.

"And so, you see, down through the centuries, the precious rosary given by the saints as an offering to the holy Mother has been the means whereby the Ascended Masters have introduced into Western culture an aspect of the science practiced by the yogis of the Himalayas in the raising of the Kundalini and the purification of consciousness thereby. The personification of the Mother in Mary in the West and the adoration of that Mother image by all who acknowledge her Son as the Christed One is the means, altogether safe, whereby the soul might experience the reunion with the Father-Mother God in the tabernacle of being.

"This ritual can be actualized in this very life here on earth without forcing the chakras and without disturbing the delicate balance of karmic cycles. On a parallel with this experience is the transmutation by the fires of the Holy Spirit of the energy layers of the electronic belt, which is comprised of the records, held in the subconscious strata of the mind, of individual causation and the memory of the soul's previous incarnations since the descent into Matter."[14]

Mother Mary has explained that the rosary may be used "as a universal adoration of the Mother flame by people of all faiths. For, you see, the salutation 'Hail, Mary' simply means 'Hail, Mother Ray' and is an affirmation of praise to the

Mother flame in every part of life. Each time it is spoken, it evokes the action of the Mother's Light in the hearts of all mankind.

"Thus the rosary is a sacred ritual whereby all of God's children can find their way back to their immaculate conception in the heart of the Cosmic Virgin. The New Age rosary is the instrument for mankind's deliverance from the sense of sin and from the erroneous doctrine of original sin. For every soul is immaculately conceived by Almighty God, and God the Father is the origin of all of the cycles of man's being. That which is conceived in sin is not of God and has neither the power nor the permanence of Reality. All that is real is of God; all that is unreal will pass away as mankind become one with the Mother flame. The daily giving of the rosary is a certain means to this oneness."[15]

Mary said that students of the Masters ought not to affirm their sinful nature, but rather their rightful inheritance as sons and daughters of God; nor should they dwell upon the hour of death, but rather upon the hour of victory. She promised to assist Keepers of the Flame, disciples of Christ and devotees of the Mother flame in winning their victory and the victory for all mankind if they would pray thus to her:

> Hail, Mary, full of grace.
> The Lord is with thee.
> Blessed art thou among women
>   And blessed is the fruit of thy womb, Jesus.
>
> Holy Mary, Mother of God,
>   pray for us, sons and daughters of God,
>   now and at the hour of our victory
>   over sin, disease and death.

Guilt, repression and frustration should not be allowed to enter the forcefield or consciousness of the seeker for Truth.

There must be an objective analysis of one's present position and potential, a realization that the goal of freedom can be accomplished through the Christ, through the proper use of the sacred fire, and the invocation of the Law that will set the captives free. Only by these means can the aspirant gain the proper perspective for his victory.

God does not require that this mastery be attained overnight. And as we have said, the Lords of Karma have sanctioned the institution of marriage for the working out of all human problems, including that of sex.

Reverence toward Life

Let the students of the Masters act with reverence toward Life and toward the God who made man and woman to be as one flesh, to be fruitful and multiply and replenish the earth.[16] Let them acknowledge the Father-Mother God as the source of all true love, and let them command the return of all energies used in love's fulfillment to the fount of everlasting Life. It is by thus sanctifying every activity of our lives that we transform the mundane into the spiritual, and through the transforming process, transcend the finite and become one with the Infinite.

We find that each initiation passed brings man more glorious experiences in the arms of Divine Love. Patiently, the lower self gives way to the Higher Self. Progressively, man experiences a higher union. A change from one to the other must never be sacrificial, nor should it ever be forced; for ascendancy in every area of life is a natural by-product of the spiritualization of man's consciousness.

Therefore, let not the problem of sex be a stumbling block to true religion; for it is the desire of the Most High God to extend comfort to man, no matter what his stage of development. When each partner to the marriage vows assumes the role of the Holy Comforter, whose responsibility it is to raise not only his own energies but also those of his mate, together they will weave the wedding garment, the action of the caduceus providing the pattern thereof. Commending the use of their sacred energies into the care of their Christ Selves, they likewise place their overcoming victory in the hands of God. As in all matters of mastery, surrender is the key. The pronouncement of the words of Jesus will never fail to evoke a response from the tender heart of God: "I of mine own self can do nothing. It is the Father in me who doeth this work."[17]

Let all gain in the knowledge of the LORD God of Hosts, whose continuing beauty is paraded before us, not only in the Pleiades and the bands of Orion, but in the whole conclave of heaven and in the microcosm here below. The infinite firewheels of Light embody the mysteries of the Sacred Cause, and in the body of man there is a counterpart—as Above, so below.

Hermes Trismegistus, that great initiate of old, has wisely spoken, saying, "O people of earth, men born and made of the elements, with the Spirit of the divine man within, rise from your sleep of ignorance—be sober and thoughtful, realize that your home is not in the earth, but in the Light."

God created man to become like Him, to be a co-creator and to procreate as He procreates. At all times let us revere the use of the sacred fire as a commemoration of the creation that went forth in the beginning in response to the divine decree—"Let there be light."[18] This decree has the power to raise the energies of man and to bring his four lower bodies into proper alignment. Through the mastery of the caduceus, man balances the threefold flame and prepares himself for his final initiations in the temple at Luxor—the transfiguration, the resurrection and the ascension.

Man need never feel that he is deprived of sex through

the study of religion, for as we have seen, God has given to man the sacred fire, and He will never deprive him of its proper use. It is man who deprives himself of the sacred fire through the improper use of sex. The guarding of these sacred energies brings man the reward of bliss through the immaculate conception, the reunion with his twin flame and the alchemical marriage—an ecstasy that can never be compared with physical union.

The Ritual of the Archangels

The Archeia Charity gives a ritual for the sealing of the sacred circle of marriage: "O my children, the demons of the night are jealous of your love. They would claw the very body of the Mother if they could. They come as vultures to devour the flesh and blood of the children of God before the hour of the consecration of the body and the blood by the Sacred Eucharist of our Lord. They are not the eagles who gather together at the place of the Corpus Christi.[19] They are not the sons and daughters of God who follow the flame of the Mother enshrined in the tower of the lighthouse—a beacon to guide the souls to victory—but they are the discarnates sent by the dragon to devour her child as soon as it is born.[20]

"Cradle the child of your love. Wrap the child in the swaddling garments of the Holy Spirit. Let honor and reverence for one another be the pivot of a cosmic love unfolding in Mater to the glory of the eternal Christos. Remember the story of Sleeping Beauty.[21] Each time the innocence of love is veiled in flesh, each time the Mother flame is born anew in Mater preparing to unite with the knight champion of the Holy Spirit, there appears on the scene, lurking in the shadows, the representative of the great whore[22] who comes to poison that rosy-cheeked innocence.

"O my children, let your love be the commemoration of the fusion of the cloven tongues of the Spirit. Now then, take the ritual that the Archangels practice at the rising and the setting of the sun when the torch of love is passed by angels of the dawn and angels of the dusk. Take the ritual of the Archangels and make it all your own, and prove thereby the victory of love on Terra. Prove that your love is the holy habitation of the LORD God of Hosts and that this love, by your will firmed in the fire of God-determination, will not be defiled by the hordes of the night.

"Stand together facing the chart of the I AM Presence and make your inner attunement with the star of your divinity. Meditate upon your heart and the flame therein and behold the arc ascend into the center of the Divine Monad. Now take your right hand and dip it into the fires of your heart and draw the circle of our oneness around yourselves as you stand in adoration of the One. Visualize this circle, twelve feet in diameter, as a line of sacred fire. It is your ring-pass-not. Within that circle of oneness is the forcefield of Alpha and Omega; and you focus the T'ai Chi, the plus and minus of cosmic energies, where you are.

"Let the flow of your love be not in imitation of the idolatrous generation. Let it not be the mechanization of sex as the Luciferians have popularized their sordid and sadistic ways. The flow of the Holy Spirit twixt father and mother is for the birth of the Divine Manchild, first within each heart and then in the Bethlehem babe. Seek not the thrills of sensuality or the titillation of mind or body, but seek the bliss of mutual reunion in the Presence.

"Let your love be the reenactment of the alchemical marriage. Let your love be consecrated for the soul's ultimate reunion with the I AM Presence. So is the marriage ritual intended to be the rehearsal for the great drama of your soul's assumption into the flame of love for the rolling-up of the scroll of identity into the Great Silence of your own I AM THAT I AM and for the fusion of those twin flames of the Godhead when the I AM Presence of each half of the Divine Whole merges in the hallowed circle of God.

"Seek the bliss of the raising of the Mother Light—of *sushumnā*, *idā* and *pingalā*—as these form the caduceus energies that reveal your real identity in Christ. Let your bliss transcend the earthly senses, and let your Light flow from all of the chakras to reinforce the divine polarity of the Father-Mother God in every level of consciousness to be outpictured in the seven major chakras and the five chakras of the secret rays.

"Your marriage is made in heaven and you are wed to God. Daughters of the flame: Behold, thy Maker is thine husband.[23] So be, with Mary, the handmaid of the Lord.[24] Sons of the flame: The golden band you wear is the halo of the Cosmic Virgin, the bride descending out of heaven[25] to consummate your love on earth.

"As Above, so below, the cosmic flow of Father-Mother God is intended to be shared in the sanctuary of the Holy Family. And it is intended to be sealed with the blessing of the true ministers of the Logos and to be guarded by purity in the Holy of Holies. The ark of the covenant is also a matrix of the protection of twin flames joined together in holy matrimony for a life of service to God and man. And the Covering Cherubim must be invoked daily, for they are the guardians of love in the planes of Mater.

"Understand, O wise ones pursuing the law of the Logos, that if the fallen ones can destroy love, they can destroy all. For love is the foundation and the fountain of life. Love is the essence of creation. Without love, life is desolate and the skies are dreary and elemental life is despondent."[26]

Heart, Head and Hand Decrees
by El Morya

Violet Fire

Heart

    Violet fire, thou love divine,
    Blaze within this heart of mine!
    Thou art mercy forever true,
    Keep me always in tune with you.

Head

    I AM Light, thou Christ in me,
    Set my mind forever free;
    Violet fire, forever shine
    Deep within this mind of mine.

    God who gives my daily bread,
    With violet fire fill my head
    Till thy radiance heavenlike
    Makes my mind a mind of Light.

Hand

    I AM the hand of God in action,
    Gaining victory every day;
    My pure soul's great satisfaction
    Is to walk the Middle Way.

Tube of Light

Beloved I AM Presence bright,
Round me seal your tube of light
From Ascended Master flame
Called forth now in God's own name.
Let it keep my temple free
From all discord sent to me.

I AM calling forth violet fire
To blaze and transmute all desire,
Keeping on in freedom's name
Till I AM one with the violet flame.

Forgiveness

I AM forgiveness acting here,
Casting out all doubt and fear,
Setting men forever free
With wings of cosmic victory.

I AM calling in full power
For forgiveness every hour;
To all life in every place
I flood forth forgiving grace.

Supply

I AM free from fear and doubt,
Casting want and misery out,
Knowing now all good supply
Ever comes from realms on high.

I AM the hand of God's own fortune
Flooding forth the treasures of Light,
Now receiving full abundance
To supply each need of life.

Perfection

I AM life of God-direction,
Blaze thy light of truth in me.
Focus here all God's perfection,
From all discord set me free.

Make and keep me anchored ever
In the justice of thy plan—
I AM the Presence of perfection
Living the life of God in man!

Transfiguration

I AM changing all my garments,
Old ones for the bright new day;
With the sun of understanding
I AM shining all the way.

I AM light within, without;
I AM light is all about.
Fill me, free me, glorify me!
Seal me, heal me, purify me!
Until transfigured they describe me:
I AM shining like the Son,
I AM shining like the Sun!

Resurrection

I AM the flame of resurrection
Blazing God's pure Light through me.
Now I AM raising every atom,
From every shadow I AM free.

I AM the light of God's full Presence,
I AM living ever free.
Now the flame of life eternal
Rises up to victory.

Ascension

I AM ascension Light,
Victory flowing free,
All of good won at last
For all eternity.

I AM Light, all weights are gone.
Into the air I raise;
To all I pour with full God-power
My wondrous song of praise.

All hail! I AM the living Christ,
The ever-loving One.
Ascended now with full God-power,
I AM a blazing Sun!

Decree to Beloved Mighty Astrea—
"The Starry Mother"

In the name of the beloved mighty victorious Presence of God, I AM in me, mighty I AM Presence and Holy Christ Selves of Keepers of the Flame, Lightbearers of the world and all who are to ascend in this life, by and through the magnetic power of the sacred fire vested in the threefold flame burning within my heart, I call to beloved mighty Astrea and Purity, Archangel Gabriel and Hope, beloved Serapis Bey and the Seraphim and Cherubim of God, beloved Lanello, the entire Spirit of the Great White Brotherhood and the World Mother, elemental life—fire, air, water and earth! to lock your cosmic circles and swords of blue flame in, through and around my four lower bodies, my electronic belt, my heart chakra and all of my chakras, my entire consciousness, being and world.

[You may include here prayers for specific circumstances or conditions for which you are requesting assistance.]

Cut me loose and set me free (3x) from all that is less than God's perfection and my own divine plan fulfilled.

        1. O beloved Astrea, may God Purity
           Manifest here for all to see,
           God's divine will shining through
           Circle and sword of brightest blue.

First chorus: Come now answer this my call
                 Lock thy circle round us all.
                 Circle and sword of brightest blue,
                 Blaze now, raise now, shine right through!

        2. Cutting life free from patterns unwise,
           Burdens fall off while souls arise
           Into thine arms of infinite love,
           Merciful shining from heaven above.

3. Circle and sword of Astrea now shine,
   Blazing blue-white my being refine,
   Stripping away all doubt and fear,
   Faith and goodwill patterns appear.

Second chorus: Come now answer this my call,
Lock thy circle round us all.
Circle and sword of brightest blue,
Raise our youth now, blaze right through!

Third chorus: Come now answer this my call,
Lock thy circle round us all.
Circle and sword of brightest blue,
Raise mankind now, shine right through!

And in full faith I consciously accept this manifest, manifest, manifest! (3x) right here and now with full power, eternally sustained, all-powerfully active, ever expanding and world enfolding until all are wholly ascended in the Light and free!

Beloved I AM! Beloved I AM! Beloved I AM!

[Give each verse, followed by the first chorus; repeat the verses, using the second chorus; then give the verses a third time, using the third chorus.]

SECTION FOUR

The Alchemical Marriage

THE TEACHINGS GIVEN BY SERAPIS Bey in the Ascension Temple include training in the governing of the sacred energies in action whereby they are withdrawn from the matrices of sex fantasy and used to weave the mystical robe referred to by Jesus as the "wedding garment." When an individual is found wearing the wedding garment, it signifies that he has correctly used his vital energies; when he is not, it signifies that his energies are still engaged in sustaining the matrices of error.

The parable of the wedding garment recorded in the twenty-second chapter of Matthew gives this teaching in code. When the king (the I AM Presence) sent forth his servants to call them that were bidden to the wedding of his son (the alchemical marriage), they would not come. This shows that mankind are not prepared for the union of the lower self to the Higher Self. They are not ready to surrender their sacred energies for the weaving of the wedding garment; instead they go the way of their sexual fantasies, "one to his farm, another to his merchandise." Thus, they made light of the marriage feast and even slew the servants of the king who bid them attend.

Then the king sent forth armies (the spiritual Hierarchy) and destroyed those murderers and burned up their cities (summoned them to the Last Judgment and the Trial by Fire), and they passed through the second death because they had not the wedding garment. Then the king said to his servants, "The wedding is ready, but they which were bidden were not worthy."

When the chosen ones had rejected the opportunity to become one with the Christ, the king extended the opportunity to all who might be found worthy, not by calling but by their own individual acceptance and demonstration of the Law. "So the servants went out into the highways, and gathered together all as many as they found, both bad and good: and the wedding was furnished with guests."

It is recorded that "when the king came in to see the guests, he saw there a man which had not on a wedding garment.... Then said the king to the servants, Bind him hand and foot, and take him away, and cast him into outer darkness; there shall be weeping and gnashing of teeth."

This most forceful teaching makes clear that those who do not have the wedding garment when they are summoned to the Last Judgment will not endure the Trial by Fire.[1] Nor will these be admitted into the halls of Luxor where the initiations for immortality are given; nor can they come in to the Holy of Holies, to their own I AM God Presence, there to receive the sacred ritual of the marriage ceremony.

Jesus concluded his parable with the oft-quoted words, "Many are called, but few are chosen." In reality, many are called to come Home, but few choose to surrender God's energies, which they have made their own, in order that the divine pattern (the Kingdom) might be manifest on earth.

The Victory of Love

The deathless solar body is the ultimate body of manifestation, which God wants to bestow upon everyone. In that body incorruptible, man and woman ascend into the perfection of their Presence and become as God intends every son and daughter to be, a King of kings and Lord of lords, complete within the unity of their twin flames. Even exchange is no robbery, and when a soul can claim reunion with God, the prodigal son has returned to the arms of the Father. And every son is acclaimed with the same clasp of joy that was bestowed upon the prodigal in the parable.[2]

The directing of the waters of the sacred fire into higher channels of purpose and service is not a question of can or can't. God has never made a Law that man cannot obey if he will invoke the strength to overcome and to do the will of God.

Has he, the LORD, not said, "Prove me now herewith, saith the LORD of hosts, if I will not open you the windows of heaven, and pour you out a blessing, that there shall not be room enough to receive it. And I will rebuke the devourer [the demons who consume man's sacred energies] for your sakes, and he shall not destroy the fruits of your ground [he shall not prevent the sacred fire from rising in the caduceus pattern]; neither shall your vine cast her fruit before the time in the field [neither shall these energies be prematurely lost through the misuse of the sacred fire], saith the LORD of hosts."[3]

You do not have to wait until your ascension or another life or until you get out from your current burdens or relationships to experience, first, the union with your I AM Presence, and second, the union with your twin flame. The union is here and now. And the forces of hatred, the hordes of darkness, always seek to make us believe that the perfect love that we are anticipating is somewhere in the beyond—somewhere, tomorrow, some time, some place.

This is the ultimate lie of the hordes who pervert the flame of love. To experience the beauty of love must never be postponed into the future, nor should we think about it as a past experience that we are forevermore deprived of because of the parting of death or separation or because in this life we didn't happen to meet the right person. When love is true, when love is real and when love is nourished and it is that whirling fire, nothing can overcome it—not even your own subconscious, not even your own electronic belt patterns. Nothing can overcome love, because love is the greatest power of the universe.

Meditation on the Oneness of Twin Flames

Souls of infinite fire, twin flames of Light arcing the love of light-years across the galaxies, I call thee forth in the name of God, I AM THAT I AM. By the Light of the Mother flame, come forth now. Stand before the altar of the Most High God. Bow before Alpha and Omega; embrace the eternal Christos. Twin flames of universal Light, come now into the center of the AUM.

Hail, celestial spirits of infinite fire. Seraphim and Cherubim, now gather round and pass the sacred fire through twin flames united in love for the cosmic service on earth as in heaven. Lords of Karma, I call to thee. Now establish by the Light of Alpha and Omega that burning love within our hearts and the arcing of the Light in the white-fire core of Being—twin flame unto twin flame.

Beloved Archangel Michael and Faith, beloved Jophiel and Christine, beloved Chamuel and Charity, beloved Gabriel and Hope, beloved Raphael and Mary, beloved Uriel and Aurora, beloved Zadkiel and Holy Amethyst, establish now the Light of twin flames for our God-mastery in the seven planes of being.

Come forth, O Light of God that never fails. Come forth, Mother Light. Restore our consciousness. Elohim, accelerate the contact now. Elohim, in the name of Jesus Christ and Saint Germain, seal the flow of infinite love. Seal the flow of sacred fire. Let fire, air, water and earth converge in the center of Being, I AM THAT I AM.

O my beloved God Self, O my beloved Christ Self, O my beloved twin flame in the heart of God, we are one. In the heart of Elohim we are one. In the heart of Archangels we are one. Blaze forth thy Light.

O God, fill the aura with sacred fire. Sweep now the

mighty violet flame through all centers of Light. Let the twin flames now appear as Covering Cherubim, as cloven tongues of fire. Let us be these cloven tongues within the great sphere of our wholeness, within the womb of cosmos. Let us merge and turn for the turning of the cycles of being. Blaze forth thy Light, Alpha and Omega. Cleansing Light, purifying Light, energizing Light, rejuvenating Light, come forth now!

We invoke the Great Blue Causal Body that we might fulfill our sacred labor in time and space. Let the great spheres of power, wisdom and love descend. Seal our hearts in threefold flame from the altar of the living God. Bathed in the sunlight of the Eternal Presence, standing in the celestial City Foursquare, we survey the vast panorama of being, Hierarchies of Light, our origin, our evolution, our souls spiraling through infinity capturing time and space for a season, entering once again infinity. With Elohim, our souls return, return to the plane of action where we must forge and win by our karma, by our dharma, in love—only love.

Hand in hand, twin flames become son and daughter, lover and the beloved, husband and wife, twins of sacred fire moving through earth, moving through air and sea and sky and land, moving with elemental life and angelic hosts. Twin flames, manifest the glory of the One, manifest the glory of the Great Central Sun.

On earth we vow to be the allness of thyself, O God. In heaven we vow to be the fullness of that Self-awareness.

I am born and being born. I am come and I am becoming the Whole and the One. Let life become Life. Let truth now manifest the higher Truth. O accelerate, sacred fire. O accelerate, sacred Being. Accelerate, sacred consciousness. Soul, now be sealed in sacred fire.

Souls of twin flames, be sealed now—now, and forever in the mystery of our Oneness—and go forth to meet thy God.

Chapter 2

Integrity

To him that overcometh will I give to eat of the tree of life, which is in the midst of the paradise of God....

And he showed me a pure river of water of life, clear as crystal, proceeding out of the throne of God and of the Lamb.

In the midst of the street of it, and on either side of the river, was there the tree of life, which bare twelve manner of fruits, and yielded her fruit every month: and the leaves of the tree were for the healing of the nations.

REVELATION

Integrity

SECTION ONE

Integration with the Source

THE WORD *INTEGRITY* MEANS having a sense of honor before people and before God. Integrity means honesty, fair play, justice and always the attitude of kindness. Integrity also relates to "integral" or "integration"—being integrated with life, with how other people feel, how you make them feel, being integrated with God and with your Holy Christ Self.

Integration with all of life is our goal. Quality life, then, begins with personal integrity and self-respect. Only when you have self-respect will you have respect for others. And there can be no personal integrity unless that respect is present. The ramifications of this one simple concept are far-reaching.

The first prophet and spiritual leader who ever came to the earth to show the way declared those eternal principles that, had they been obeyed and accepted by man, would have turned earth into a paradise here below. In fact, these principles did, in past Golden Ages, actually create an earthly paradise for humanity. These epochs are known to us as Lemuria (or Mu) and Atlantis.[1]

In every succeeding age the same eternal principles have been told and retold. Enoch, the seventh from Adam, was translated that he should not see death[2] because he accepted them. Unfortunately, they have been rejected by many and accepted by the few.

For this reason, in a very real sense, man, the monad, has become a wandering soul, to quote the words of Saint Peter, "to whom is reserved the mist of darkness forever."[3] In this case, "forever" is the set of man's sails determined by his eternal free will as it manifests finitely and acts in steering his course. As long, then, as men and women embrace a quality that is less than perfection, a quality that is more dark than it is light, so long shall they sail forever into that darkness that is an absence from the Light.

But let it be clearly understood that the mercy of God, which endureth forever,[4] has declared in his Laws that so long as man does not destroy the total battery of being by using up the substance of his soul and thus becoming a castaway from life's opportunities, there is still a chance for him to turn around. Through the long-suffering of God, there is the possibility for him to return to that integration with the wholeness of God that comes by sweet surrender and a willingness to accept the will of God.

The Seamless Garment of the Christ

The scriptures mysteriously declare, "For whosoever hath to him shall be given, and he shall have more abundance: but whosoever hath not, from him shall be taken away even that he hath."[5] This shows that momentums that men develop act as magnets to pull them either down or up.

God, having long ago surrendered himself to man as the gift of Life and the instinct of Life, has permitted man to digress from the pursuit of the cosmic plan and pursue a downward course. God has permitted man to languish in ignorance as a prodigal son simply because this was the misplaced desire of the will of man—a desire born of ignorance and sustained by it. There is only one way to reverse the currents of energy that have been directed to the downfall of man, and that is to seek integration with the cosmic wholeness of God. In a very real sense, this wholeness was manifest in the seamless garment of the living Christ.

Those who know the inner laws of Being and understand the long history of the Master Jesus will recognize, in the great drama of his soul, Abel, the son of Adam, and also Joseph, the son of Jacob, the idle dreamer who wore the coat of many colors. Jesus had other embodiments after this, which we will not now go into. These were significant and symbolical of the seven color rays, which became blended together in his final lifetime as one whole garment, the seamless garment.[6]

While this garment was of a so-called rude homespun, beautiful and white, its main virtue was its ability to retain the spiritual energies of the Lord Christ. For the true seamless garment that the Christ wears is a garment of Light, the auric field.

We see in Lloyd Douglas' story *The Robe* a beautiful example of how men and women can leave behind them, on the sands of Life, footprints that do indeed guide another's spiritual energy and elevate the soul.[7] The wisdom of Jesus was to teach mankind concerning their real need to integrate themselves with God, to become one with God.

The Return to God

While the idea that men have come forth from God is inherent within every soul—though latent in many as an idea having any practical value—there is something in man that seems to regard as a loss any attempt to retrace the steps back from individuality toward the wholeness of integration, or integrity.

But when man returns to God and is a part of God, he does not lose his identity. The only way he can lose his identity, be a castaway, is to go into the exterior world and lose his soul in exterior things, dissipate his substance, destroy himself. When he comes home to God in the ascension, he doesn't lose anything, he gains everything.

It should be understood that the purposes of creation are served by right experience calculated to develop the soul of man and ready him for a position in the kingdom of God. The Father has never intended that any life expression should actually fail to apprehend the integrity of God himself.

Conscience, morals, ethics and a sense of purity, the quality of forgiveness and of mercy, a sense of beauty and the desire for righteousness, a search for the Laws of God or spiritual illumination, a communion with the Holy Spirit and a sense of Oneness with the Eternal Father—all these are fragments of the integrity of God himself. The nameless qualities of God, the numberless facets of his Being are yet the birthright and inheritance of the elect. There is no false pride or humility in the sense of election, but only a joyous feeling of gratitude that God and his purposes can become identified with the integrating soul.

The Need for Brotherhood

As souls integrate with their Source, they cannot fail to draw nigh unto one another. For like does indeed attract like, and unlike repels. "Birds of a feather," as has been said, "flock together." In the world of human affairs this quality often makes for narrowness of concept. (For example, some attorneys and physicians are unable to hobnob with others save those of their own craft.) However, in the spiritual quest the universal man is being developed, and broader understanding and larger concerns make for the integrity that, by the power of example, gives rise to faith in other men.

The Great Divine Director speaks of the necessity for this integration in a world of scientific advancement: "As men have expressed a greater measure of scientific rapport and have exhibited a greater control over the forces of Nature, instead of becoming *more* spiritual, they have become *less* spiritual and have done despite to the spirit of grace that has released the secrets of Nature into their hand.

"And thus, with succeeding generations, unless perchance the spiritual laws of the universe and of brotherhood shall come forth to greater measure, they will, through the perverseness of their nature, enter into warlike covenants with themselves, desiring to express one facet of themselves and then another portion of life, another facet of themselves. And these two facets in extreme war will extinguish both facets, and both shall cease to be.

"And thus the world will be rent by war and mankind's bodies torn because of the jagged concepts they now hold. This will come to pass without question unless men exercise some spiritual control over their being, some control of virtue and integrity. For integrity is a sense of universal integration whereby each monad desires to become one with his own immortal Presence. When this occurs properly, there is never in outer manifestation a need for human discord, for all are in effect one with one another as they become one with God! This is law and it cannot be denied."[8]

The Will to Integration

The will of God is unquestionably the will of integration and of divine integrity. Yet it is true that there are men who question the purposes of the Divine. These have not known him, neither have they understood his compassion and the necessity for his Laws, functioning as they do upon the earth plane. There are those who, perceiving the manifestation of that which men call evil—of disease, destruction, pain or injury—say, "If God possesses omnipotent power, why does he not instantly terminate these awful conditions? Why does God permit man to suffer and to languish in ignorance?"

Why, indeed! Because man must master, by his conscious use of free will, the energies entrusted to him. For he is destined to become a co-creator with God, who made him in his image and likeness.[9] If man, then, is destined for this great glory, he must prove that he can fulfill his responsibilities upon earth.

If God were to step in and save man from the conditions he has created, he would never learn how to use the Law correctly. It is a tribute to the integrity of God that he upholds Universal Law in the face of man's disobedience and misappropriation of that Law. For without the justice of the Law, the infinite love and mercy of God might very well dictate the dissolving of those very conditions, unpleasant though they may be, that will ultimately lead man to his victory.

However, because men have lacked integrity, they have lacked the desire to seek the Law, to pursue it. They have felt in their own consciousness and intelligence that they were a law that was sufficient unto themselves.

Man Finds Freedom When Negative Karma Is Redeemed

Since the dawn of Christendom, the concept that "what men do not know does not hurt them" and "what I can get away with does not hurt me" has held a pernicious influence over the consciousness of men. We live in a time when many people feel that it is quite all right to do anything they get away with—it doesn't matter. However, karmically speaking, everything we do does matter. There is never any need for men and women to entertain this aborted sense of life, for it simply is not true.

We remember Jesus' prophecy, "That which is done in secret shall be shouted from the housetops."[10] We also know that the eternal Keeper of the Scrolls of each man's life is accurate in all that he records. There are no instruments of human creation that have such a perfected degree of accuracy as the system of Almighty God wielded by and in the hands of the Karmic Board. Two statements come to mind: "Therefore, for every thwarting of the Law there comes a day of reckoning," and "though the mills of the Gods grind slowly, they grind exceedingly small."[11]

Unfortunately, many see the Law of God as a law of disaffection and disavowal. They envision a God who has no use for us but is simply the Lawgiver who stands ready to strike mankind with a rod of punishment. But God does not deal our karma to us as punishment. Karma is a manifestation of an impersonal law as well as a personal one. The purpose of our bearing our karma is that karma is our teacher. We must learn the lessons of how and why we misused the energy of life.

Until that day comes when we recognize the Law of God as a Law of love, we will probably encounter difficulties. But if we will only hasten that day's coming into our own life, we will recognize that karma is actually grace and beauty and joy.

We should understand, then, that the Law that comes to us is the Law of love. When it becomes chastening, it is the chastening of love. When it becomes the fruit in our life of our own advancement, this is the fruit of that love.

More than Forgiveness Is Needed for True Freedom

Integrity is a garment that men should welcome, that they should wear gladly. For in reality, it is a garment of freedom. Unfortunately, this law has not been understood correctly, and in the very idea of forgiveness of sin, men have erred. They have thought that by the simple cry, "Forgive me," or "I am sorry," they have wiped out the entire record of their error. This is not true, for the Universal Law requires not only the asking of forgiveness, but also the righting of the wrongs that have been done, so that the error itself might be corrected and blight removed by the instigator thereof. Until this is accomplished, the karma remains.

However, men are not only instigators of evil. They are also benefactors of others. Thus the karmic record shows not only infamy but also beautiful service. All lives are mixed as sand and sugar, with a grain here and a grain there of mingled Truth and error.

Tumbling over the heap composed of human error and human victory, of good and bad momentums, men struggle toward the top, seeking to expand in the domain of self the Laws of God, so that those Laws may be established in their lives and recorded with their heartbeat upon the substance, the real substance, of Self.

Putting God First

None should flout the Laws of God or man, and all should remember the words of the Lord Jesus, who said, "Render to Caesar the things that are Caesar's, and to God the things that are God's."[12] We are prone to remember the former (in America, the Internal Revenue Service has seen to that) but to forget the latter. In fact, the kingdom of heaven must come first—the kingdom of God must be placed above all other conditions.

The Maha Chohan has said: "Honor and integrity are the virtues of which immortality is made. Integrity refers to your 'integral integration' in your I AM Presence. When you have honor and integrity, you weave strong ties to the Infinite, to the immortal realms of Life. When you have no honor and no integrity, beloved, you are like the shifting sands. You are double-minded and therefore unstable in all your ways,[13] and you can accomplish nothing.

"It is not simply honor and integrity toward one's fellow men of which I speak, but honor and integrity toward God himself. When you align yourself with the first commandment, 'Thou shalt have no other gods before me,' you place God first. After that there are descending hierarchies in your life to which you assign greater and lesser importance.

"When you make it your duty each morning to put God first, to honor his flame in your loved ones and to consecrate all your enterprises to him, then all goes well. The key is to put God first in the day and last in the day and to rehearse throughout the day the magnificence of the beauty of life he has given you."[14]

The needs of humanity and the needs of God to expand his Light must be taken into account by every person, and the kingdom of God must be put first. In this way, his kingdom will manifest upon earth with greater speed, and the days of travail will be shortened as the fullness of the majesty of the King of Truth is enthroned within the hearts of all men as the integrity of his uniting love.

Some men have a quantity of earthly needs and a cup that resembles a bottomless pit of desire. These are never satisfied with worldly goods or even with spiritual treasures. They remain perpetually hungry. Truly, when one commits himself to God, it is to commit his desires to God that He may satisfy them according to the divine plan that the Father holds for every lifestream.

The reason the prodigal son sought of the Father to have his portion and to go unto earth and spend that portion was that he wished to be on his own. Many men and women today resent any intrusion into their personal lives. They wish to be able to direct those lives in the course they choose. God has not interfered, nor will he interfere with such as these. He leaves them strictly alone, and many of these are involved in a whole series of misfortunes created by themselves, for themselves and through themselves in an ignorance of which they are unaware.

However, there is never a loss in invoking the will of God, in invoking the divine plan and in requesting integration with the Spirit of Truth. Such invocation is but an invitation to God to bring the gifts of his superiority into the relatively speaking inferior manifestation of individual life. God, the great giver, welcomes the opportunity to give, and man should welcome the opportunity to receive. This is a form of integration, a form of cosmic integrity.

In the schema of life, there are many below the level of

almost any given individual. While there may be a bottom to the heap, very few seekers are at the bottom. Therefore, although men may lament their lot, there are always those whose lives need and require such guidance as they can give. Man does not have to be perfect outwardly in order to be a teacher of good things. God has ordained that greater men—that is, those who have attained more of his intelligence and knowledge—shall serve lesser men and their needs, even as God serves the needs of greater men and serves all. No one, then, should fear both to receive and to give the grace of God, which should be multiplied upon earth.

Finding Your Path

One unfortunate condition in the world today is the spirit of competition between so-called spiritual individuals—this is truly spiritual wickedness in high places.[15] In many cases, these individuals have worked for centuries, embodiment after embodiment, in conflict with one another and in opposition at both political and spiritual levels. Certainly the time must come when the integrity of living souls causes them to desire spiritual harmony more than they desire autonomous glory.

When one considers the great soul-hunger of man for true religion, it must be recognized that it is a sin of monumental proportions for anyone deliberately or even ignorantly to break the confidences men place in them by reason of a supposed spiritual stature. Every religious teacher, priest and representative of God has a solemn responsibility to bear to the world a message of love and hope in the bonds of a cosmic integrity manifest upon earth.

Archangel Raphael speaks of the true purposes of religion and spirituality: "There are many churches, many schools, many paths of healing and religion. What is most important for your discernment in deciding your chosen way, and that which will be the acceleration of your life, is to determine what is the greatest need of your soul and your four lower bodies, what is the weakest link in the chain of being of your lifestream, then to find the teacher and the teaching, the path and the system, whether of prayer and fasting or any kind of remedies that may be from the highest source that would be the ones that would help you most to attain a greater integrity and a greater wholeness.

"Let the goal, then, of thy life be wholeness—knowing full well that the sphere of wholeness becomes the divine magnet for every good thing from God to the twin flame and all in between. Then, knowing that wholeness is the goal, observe through the eyes and heart of Mother Mary that portion of yourself requiring the greatest attention. Go after this. Bring the spirit of Light and the dynamic decree to it. Approach it from all of the four lower bodies and the chakras.

"Bring up, therefore, the lowest vibrating frequencies of your being. And if you do not know what these are, ask. Knock, and it shall be answered.[16] Call unto the Lord Christ. We are his servants and we will deliver to you that word of the magnificent God-free being who helps you now in this very hour, even the Ascended Master Jesus Christ.

"Blessed ones of the noble lineage of the house of David, you who are the seed of that ancient Light, come now and understand that not only individual wholeness but wholeness of the cells in the Body of God makes for a greater wholeness in the entire Mystical Body. Thus, we seek spheres of Light that may interconnect and form therefore a surface of Light, a body of Light, a magnet of healing.

"See what will contribute to the greatest good for your inner integrity, but do not stop there. Look what will contribute to the greatest good of the integrity of the community.

Then see how the community itself may help more and more on the Path who struggle, are burdened, are bowed down and still fall beneath the weight of the cross of personal karma."[17]

Determination Is Needed

In the word *integrity,* the word *grit* is embodied, and it may often require that individuals have what men call spunk, but which spiritual masters call God-determination, to let nothing deter them from pursuing their appointed course. Some men and women have lived many years beyond their allotted span simply because of an intensified will to live. The will to do is the catalyst of integrity, and those who would have integrity must first recognize their lack of it and then determine that they will pursue it boldly.

The Elohim Cyclopea speaks of the determination that is necessary on the path to reunion with God: "You must have a breakthrough, beloved hearts, by your own God-determination! You must throw over that infilling of your temples with drugs and with chemicals of all types, interfering with the logical mechanism of your own infinite and scientific body of God! You must realize that it will take a fervent love, a consuming fire and a God-determination to reach that point of your own Christ consciousness—not by animal evolution but by the divine solution, which is to enter the capsule and the sphere of your own Causal Body and live!

"You must demand it! You must command it! You must not take no for an answer! You must have the breakthrough for which you have been striving! And you must be the one who shatters the density that allows you to sleep when you ought to rise up and take dominion over this planet!"[18]

Service to the World

Integrity is a spiritual gift, and the purpose for acquiring it should be to assist in the God-realization of all men. So long as individuals are dedicated to the expansion of spirituality only within the domain of their personal selves, they make even the pursuit of divine grace a selfish act.

Yet God does not ask that men shall utterly spend themselves upon those of their fellow men who do not welcome their ministrations. Let the child of the Light who would be free understand that his first responsibility is to God; his second is unto himself—to make himself a noble worker in the kingdom; and the third is to the world and *all* in the world who will welcome his service—and they are many.

This is the golden Light of cosmic Truth that binds men and women of every race and creed into a mighty Body of God on earth, an army of Light upon the planet who will expand Truth to all areas of human endeavor, even as they expand gratitude into cosmic realms of limitless Light. When this is done, the angels, Cosmic Beings, Ascended Masters and hosts of Light may all rejoice in the gratitude of men of good will—those who bow their knees to the glory of God and his purposes by manifesting whenever possible the bonds of his integrity through the holy lives they lead.

Although there may be no higher religion than Truth, a truth that is believed must become a truth that is enshrined within all that man shall do. Unless this is done, men will only lack, they will never have the abundant Life; and the looseness of their morals—the qualities of the mercy they strain through the filters of human deceit and density—will continue to milk mankind of the kindness of God and the fire of his good will.

Rather, let them utilize his good will daily by the power of example, the power of Truth, the power of divine friendship between peoples the world around. In this way, expansion will occur in the human domain, broadening the power of men to help themselves—until the illumination that God has given through his Son, the Universal Christ, will be the forte of all men. Then the universities and the educational systems of the world will be slanted to the development in the young child of the "way in which he should go."[19]

The Honor of God

El Morya speaks of integrity as honor, a quality he exemplified in his embodiments on earth: "As the love of God's holy will is manifest in the integrity, in the honor of sons and daughters serving together to let Thy will be done as in heaven so on earth, I am here to tell you of the great worth of heaven's Sons and Daughters working together in the Great White Brotherhood for the precipitation upon earth, in the hearts of devotees, of the fires of the will of God, the armour of the will of God and a spiral of devotion such as the world has not known before.

"I AM a Chohan. The Lord of the First Ray you call me, and so I have been called of God. In my embodiments of old I perceived honor as the will of God, the integrity that does not allow one word, one erg of energy to pass from the lips, the heart, the mind that is not in reverence, in defense of Truth and the immaculate heart of the Cosmic Virgin.

"You have known me as Thomas More, chancellor and servant of King Henry VIII.[20] You will recall that in my devotion to that honor, I wore the hair shirt to deprive myself, to remind myself in humility of the high office of service in government to which God had called me—and I was and I remain his servant first and the king's second. And some of you have heard the words of another Thomas who served another Henry, Thomas Becket—another name, another flame of the Lord of the First Ray, when the hair shirt also worn reminded of the cosmic honor.[21]

"Never allow, precious hearts, a conflict of interest in your lives, for service to God must override all other considerations in life. There can be no consideration other than his plan, his will, his Light, his love, for in that fiery white honor is found the crystallization of the blue ray—as the intense white fire of purity, of devotion, becomes the steely blue of determination to be that purity in action in the world of form....

"Integrity begets love, love begets harmony, and all three equal the divine manifestation of thy kingdom come on earth, O God."[22]

What shall it profit a man if he shall gain the whole world and lose his own soul?[23] The course of human life is a steady flowing of sand through the glass of the hours, and the stream will spurt to an end one day, signifying the end of a cycle. Being is composed of many cycles leading to one sublime cycle of realization and attainment. This is the springboard of all Reality, the ascension in the Light.

Goddess of Purity speaks of Truth as a corollary of integrity and honor: "I come to renew your dedication to the cosmic honor flame and to infuse you with the power, Light and love of honor. Honor is the power that gives to all, to every ray, to every son and daughter of God serving every ray, the action of integrity. And integrity, when espoused, leads to the integration of the soul with the Spirit of God that is known as the alchemical union, the marriage of the Lamb. For the Lamb is the I AM Presence, and the Lamb's wife is the soul. Thus in allegory from the very foundation of twin flames' coming forth from the ovoid of God's Being, man knows and is aware of the desire for the return to Oneness, the return to union, and the un-i-tie that binds him to all that is real.

"With integrity, with honor, comes Truth. And with Truth, the flaming sword to keep the way of the Tree of Life,[24] to keep the way of the Edenic consciousness. And this two-edged sword is for the cleaving asunder of the Real from the unreal. Without honor man cannot remain in paradise. Without honor he cannot claim his friendship with God and with the Brotherhood.

"Therefore know the Truth and the Truth shall make you free.[25] Confess your sins before God. Write them one and all on paper and then commit them to the flame, to the Lords of Karma. Let there be nothing that is hidden, that is not revealed, within you. Come clean and present yourselves robed in white, prepared as the bride adorned for her husband.

"Precious hearts, the flame of purity is the flame whereby you are prepared to receive the initiations of the Holy Spirit and of the sacred fire. Let all, then, surrender to God all that is not of the Light that they might become the integrity and the integration of the allness of God and the allness of man in manifestation, as Above, so below."[26]

Let all rejoice in the potential of integrity in their lives. Yet all must choose for themselves. All must begin in this domain from whatever level they are on, until the illustrious Spirit of Universal Love has made of the consecrated offering of their thoughts and feelings, of their lives and their energies, a beauteous integrity with the soul of immortal God-loveliness.

The Chart of Your Divine Self

THE CHART OF YOUR DIVINE Self is a portrait of you and of the God within you. It is a diagram of you and your potential to become who you really are. It is an outline of your spiritual anatomy.

The upper figure is your "I AM Presence," the presence of God that is individualized in each one of us. It is your personalized "I AM THAT I AM." Your I AM Presence is surrounded by seven concentric spheres of spiritual energy that make up what is called your "Causal Body." The spheres of pulsating energy contain the record of the good works you have performed since your very first incarnation on earth. They are like your cosmic bank account.

The middle figure in the chart represents the "Holy Christ Self," who is also called the Higher Self. You can think of your Holy Christ Self as your chief guardian angel and dearest friend, your inner teacher and voice of conscience. Just as the

I AM Presence is the presence of God that is individualized for each of us, so the Holy Christ Self is the presence of the Universal Christ that is individualized for each of us. "The Christ" is actually a title given to those who have attained oneness with their Higher Self, or Christ Self. That is why Jesus was called "Jesus, the Christ."

What the Chart shows is that each of us has a Higher Self, or "Inner Christ," and that each of us is destined to become one with that Higher Self—whether we call it the Christ, the Buddha, the Tao or the Atman. This "Inner Christ" is what the Christian mystics sometimes refer to as the "inner man of the heart," and what the Upanishads mysteriously describe as a being the "size of a thumb" who "dwells deep within the heart."[1]

We all have moments when we feel that connection with our Higher Self—when we are creative, loving, joyful. But there are other moments when we feel out of sync with our Higher Self—moments when we become angry, depressed, lost. What the spiritual path is all about is learning to sustain the connection to the higher part of ourselves so that we can make our greatest contribution to humanity.

The shaft of white Light descending from the I AM Presence through the Holy Christ Self to the lower figure in the Chart is the crystal cord (sometimes called the silver cord). It is the "umbilical cord," the lifeline, that ties you to Spirit.

Your crystal cord also nourishes that special, radiant flame of God that is ensconced in the secret chamber of your heart. It is called the threefold flame, or divine spark, because it is literally a spark of sacred fire that God has transmitted from his heart to yours. This flame is called "threefold" because it engenders the primary attributes of Spirit—power, wisdom and love.

The mystics of the world's religions have contacted the

divine spark, describing it as the seed of divinity within. Buddhists, for instance, speak of the "germ of Buddhahood"[2] that exists in every living being. In the Hindu tradition, the Katha Upanishad speaks of the "light of the Spirit" that is concealed in the "secret high place of the heart" of all beings.[3] Likewise, the fourteenth-century Christian theologian and mystic Meister Eckhart teaches of the divine spark when he says, "God's seed is within us."[4]

When we decree, we meditate on the flame in the secret chamber of our heart. This secret chamber is your own private meditation room, your interior castle, as Teresa of Avila called it. In Hindu tradition, the devotee visualizes a jeweled island in his heart. There he sees himself before a beautiful altar, where he worships his teacher in deep meditation.

Jesus spoke of entering the secret chamber of the heart when he said: "When thou prayest, enter into thy closet, and when thou hast shut thy door, pray to thy Father which is in secret; and thy Father which seeth in secret shall reward thee openly."[5]

The lower figure in the Chart of Your Divine Self represents you on the spiritual path, surrounded by the violet flame and the protective white Light of God. The soul is the living potential of God—the part of you that is mortal but that can become immortal.

The purpose of your soul's evolution on earth is to grow in self-mastery, balance your karma and fulfill your mission on earth so that you can return to the spiritual dimensions that are your real home. When your soul at last takes flight and ascends back to God and the heaven-world, you will become an Ascended Master, free from the rounds of karma and rebirth. The high-frequency energy of the violet flame can help you reach that goal more quickly.

Figure 6 The Chart of Your Divine Self

SECTION TWO

The Science of Wholeness and the Tree of Life

THOSE WHO ARE FAMILIAR WITH the Great Law and understand its higher action know that Life is sacred; that Life is immortal and that Life is *God*. These know that the Tree of Life standing in the midst of the garden described in Genesis[1] is an allegorical representation of the individualized I AM Presence. In order to eat of the twelve manner of fruits thereof, man is required by Law to attain a consciousness of God-power, God-love, God-mastery, God-control, God-obedience, God-wisdom, God-harmony, God-gratitude, God-justice, God-reality, God-vision and God-victory together with a sense of ultimate purpose in the expression of the Laws of God through the fulfillment of his individual divine plan.

When God is experienced by man as he partakes of the fruit of the Tree of Life, man is able to gild each moment of his life with the crown of God-perfection. Each moment is thus immortalized, and moment by moment he himself is becoming immortal. Thus he is brought to a state of Eden once again, having the opportunity to make use of the treasures of his own Causal Body and those treasures that are stored in the Great Blue Causal Body—which contains all of the good that has ever been externalized by man.

The Garden of Eden is in allegory the Causal Body of man, and the Tree of Life in the midst thereof is the I AM Presence. Eden means *Energy-den*—the place where there is a concentration of God's energy, or the Causal Body. One of the meanings of den is "center of secret activity," which is also descriptive of the hub of the Causal Body.

The Electronic Belt and the Tree of Life

In Figure 7 you will see an illustration of the electronic belt. This belt extends from the waist to beneath the feet. It is shaped like a large kettledrum. It contains the aggregate records of man's negative thoughts, feelings, words and deeds, hence negative karma. Whereas the four lower bodies were God's provision for self-mastery in the world of form, the electronic belt is the spiral of negatively qualified energy (referred to as the "negative spiral") that developed coincidentally with man's descent into the consciousness of duality.

The entire contents of this electronic belt—the records and accumulations of man's own misqualified substance—is the karmic weight that holds him earthbound and prevents him from overcoming the pull of gravity and ascending into the Light. This is the weight that puts him in the category of mortality; this is the weight that ties him to the mass consciousness.[2] Figure 8 shows how the misuse of the four elements pollutes the four lower bodies of man and causes them to be out of alignment.

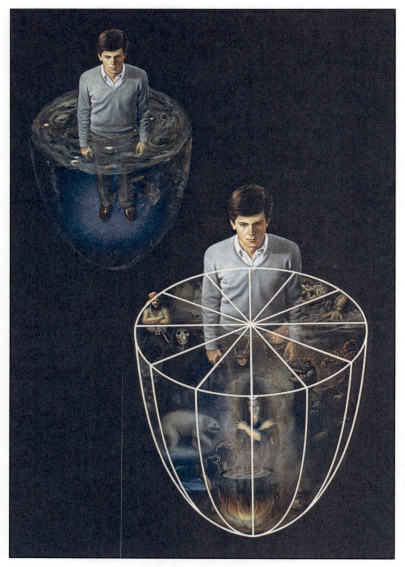

Figure 7 The Electronic Belt

The electronic belt is formed of the individual's misqualification of God's energy as it collects and intensifies in the subconscious to form a negative spiral shaped like a kettledrum surrounding the chakras below the heart. This forcefield contains compartments where different momentums of negativity are lodged. These momentums coalesce as thoughtforms in the electronic belt and in the subconscious of the individual.

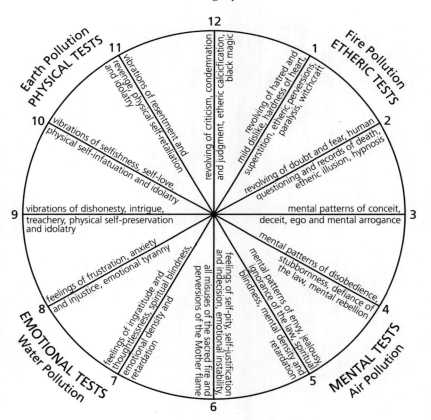

Figure 8 Categories of Negatively Qualified Energy in the Electronic Belt

The twelve categories of negatively qualified energy in the electronic belt may be plotted as the lines of a clock.

In Figure 9 you will see the chart of the Tree of Life showing the twelve manner of fruit and the leaves of the Tree that are for the healing of the nations.³ Here we see the archetype of the Causal Body of man. This chart shows how the four lower bodies are realigned through the balancing action of the threefold flame and the transmutation of all shadowed substance in the electronic belt by the power of the Holy Spirit.

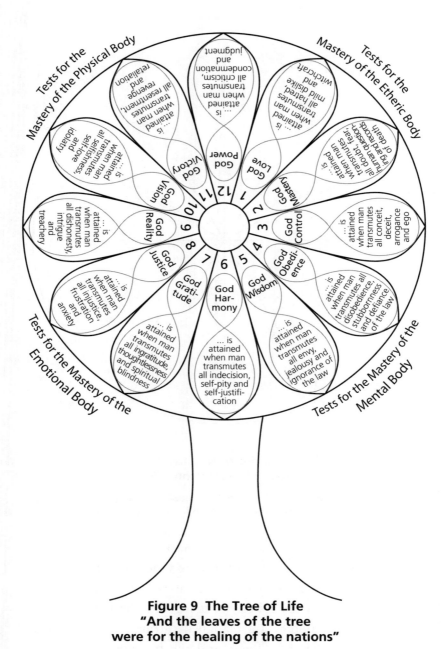

Figure 9 The Tree of Life
"And the leaves of the tree were for the healing of the nations"

The God-quality of each line is attained through the I AM Presence with the help of the Holy Christ Self when man transmutes the negative quality of that line of the electronic belt. The God-qualities are also plotted as the lines of a clock.

The Macrocosm and the Microcosm

We understand the Macrocosm to be the entire warp and woof of creation, known and unknown, visible and invisible. We understand the microcosm to be man himself—the epitome of the creation confined within a framework of individuality. Each microcosmic world is a cell in the Macrocosm, a crystal fragment of the Greater Crystal, reflecting a portion of His glory. The key to infinity is won through the mastery of the lesser self (the microcosm) by the power of the Greater Self (the Macrocosm). Through man's correct use of the sacred gifts of Life, including free will, his consciousness in the microcosm can identify with the fullness of God's consciousness in the Macrocosm. But first, it is essential that he learn how to make the contact, how to establish and maintain his relationship with the Superconscious Ego.

The figure-eight pattern is used to illustrate the principle of exchange between the Macrocosmic world Above and the microcosmic world below. At the nexus, the point where the lines in the figure eight cross, the virtues of the Greater Reality of oneself, of the Superconscious Ego, flow downward into the microcosm, and the aspirations of the lesser reality of oneself, of the ego, flow upward into the Macrocosm. This exchange is accomplished through the consciousness of the Christ, the Super Ego, who, positioned in the center of the cross, is the agent of the alchemical transformation that takes place between the energies of God and man.

In Figure 8 and Figure 9 we see diagrammed the Causal Body of man as his personal Macrocosm and the electronic belt as his personal microcosm. Whereas the microcosm is intended to reflect all that is contained in the Macrocosm—fulfilling the fiat, "As above, so below"—those who have departed from grace have filled their lower vehicles—the four lower bodies and the electronic belt—with the debris of their disobedience to the Laws of God. This debris, which we often refer to as "human creation," must be cleared out of these vehicles before the Light can penetrate from on high and man's consciousness can thereby become the repository of the Christ consciousness and all that was intended by God-Good.

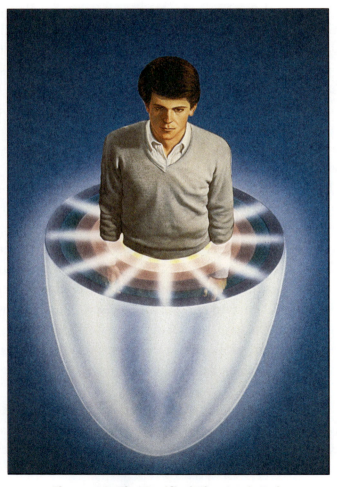

Figure 10 The Purified Electronic Belt

The electronic belt is intended to reflect all that
is contained in the Causal Body of man.

And so it came to pass that those who ate of the tree of the knowledge of good and evil caused the "fall," or lowering of the vibrations in the lower half of the figure eight, bringing about the gradual densification of the four lower bodies and the formation of the negative spiral that we call the electronic belt. Because the Tree of Life was protected by the flaming sword,[4] the upper half of the figure eight remained inviolate as the Holy of Holies—the God Presence and the Causal Body of man retained the image and the records of his true identity. Thus, at this stage of man's evolution, the Christ Self stands at the crossroads of his dual being to mediate between the divine perfection of the God Self and the imperfection of the human, as both seek to manifest in the forcefield of his consciousness.

It is the purpose of this study, then, to show how the disciple may indeed clear away the debris of the human consciousness by the use of the sacred fire and replace it with the Light of the twelve godly attributes, even as he prepares for his ultimate reunion with his Creator.

Examining the two charts, which we have diagrammed according to the design of a clock, we see that the divisions of man's consciousness follow the pattern of twelve, a pattern that prevails throughout the universe. On each line of the electronic belt in Figure 8 are listed the perversions of the divine attributes on that line in the Causal Body of Figure 9. The chart of the Tree of Life shows the twelve manner of fruit, the twelve attributes of the Godhead that are amplified through the Twelve Hierarchies of the Sun. These Hierarchies assist mankind in overcoming the categories of misqualified substance that accumulate on the lines of the clock in the electronic belt.

Each of the leaves of the Tree of Life is for the "healing of the nations," the nations being the twelve "tribes" or departments of human creation outlined in the chart of the electronic belt. As man replaces his human creation with the twelve principal godly attributes designated on the leaves of the Tree, the flowering of the corresponding virtues takes place on that line in the Causal Body. These virtues are also reflected in the electronic belt and in the four lower bodies—and man is seen in the image of his Maker.

These virtues come forth from the white-fire core of the corresponding godly attribute, first as a threefold flame, and then as the flowering of the twelve-thousand-petaled lotus expanding from the threefold aspect of his divinity into manifestation. Multiplied by the twelve attributes, these virtues comprise the 144,000 flames that are consecrated by God for the fulfillment of each cosmic pattern. (A further explanation of the 144,000 will be given later in this section.)

Thus, each of the twelve leaves shows the potential of the Godhead intended to become the forte of expression in man. The realization of that God-potential takes place as the flowering of the lotus of man's divinity in the world of form. Here again, we see that Spirit (the potential of the Godhead) gains identity throughout Matter (the realization of the Godhead in form).

The Lines of the Clock

Let us begin our examination of the electronic belt by pointing out that the 12, 6, 3, and 9 o'clock lines are the north, south, east and west of man's being. Each of these lines marks the beginning of a series of tests involving one of the four elements and its corresponding lower body. Thus, the 12 o'clock line introduces the tests of fire and the etheric body; the 3 o'clock line the tests of air and the mental body; the 6 o'clock line the tests of water and the emotional body; and the 9 o'clock line the tests of earth and the physical body. These four quadrants also correspond to the four aspects of God: Father, Son, Mother and Holy Spirit.

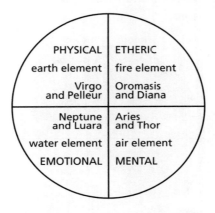

Figure 11 The Four Quadrants

Each of the four quadrants corresponds to one of the four planes of Matter and one of the four lower bodies.

Each of these tests is administered by the individual's own Holy Christ Self and the hierarchs of the element under examination. Thus, Oromasis and Diana assist the Christ in directing the tests involving the mastery and purification of the fire element and the etheric body, on lines 12, 1 and 2. Aries and Thor work closely with the Christ in administering tests of mastery and purification for the air element and the mental body on lines 3, 4 and 5. Tests of the water element and the emotional body on lines 6, 7 and 8 are under the direction of the Christ and Neptune and Luara. To complete the cycle of purification and mastery, the Christ and the hierarchs of the earth element, Virgo and Pelleur, administer the tests of earth and the physical body on lines 9, 10 and 11.

We also see the trinity of manifestation in each quadrant. The threefold flame of Life burns within each of the four lower bodies, in every side of the Pyramid of Life. In each aspect of God, the Trinity is fulfilled: the blue ray of the Father, the yellow of the Son, and the pink of the Holy Spirit—power, wisdom and love.

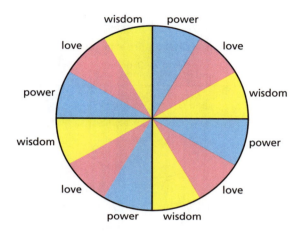

Figure 12 The Threefold Flame in Each Quadrant

The manifestation of the threefold flame in each quadrant divides the circle into twelve—the twelve lines of the Cosmic Clock. The plumes of the threefold flame are blue (power), yellow (wisdom) and pink (love).

The dot in the center of the clock is called the fulcrum of compensation. The term *compensation* has been defined as "a psychological mechanism by which an individual attempts to compensate for some real or imagined deficiency of personality by developing or stressing another aspect of his personality or by substituting a different form of behavior."[5] Now as we study the lines of the clock, let us look at the opposite poles of each of our numbers in order to see how mortals compensate for their own misqualified energies by misqualifying more of God's energy. Let us begin with the 12-6 and 3-9 axes, which come under the heading of the power plumes.

Positive and Negative Manifestations on the Power Lines of the Cosmic Clock

On the side of the north at the 12-6 axis, we have the lodging of misqualified substance accumulated from the revolving of criticism, condemnation and judgment.

Revolving is an activity of the memory body. It is the process whereby we go over and over again, as though we were on a treadmill, our memories of the past: our mistakes, our victories, the fortunate and unfortunate events in our lives. This is done in order to keep alive our memories of the past; for unless human beings revolve these records, they fade away into the subconscious recesses of the mind (the subterranean levels of the electronic belt), no longer to appear on the surface as conscious memory.

Nevertheless, the etheric body and the electronic belt do retain the records of the past until they are transmuted. This fact has been proven by experiments in hypnosis, whereby individuals recall, while in a trance state, experiences of childhood and even those of former embodiments, the detailed memories of which may be long forgotten to the conscious mind.

It should be noted, then, that the mere forgetting of past wrongs and injustices must not be construed as the overcoming of these conditions. Man overcomes only "by the blood of the Lamb"[6]—that is to say by the sacred fire—which he must invoke in the name of the Christ and by the power of the Lord's Spirit. When we put the memories of unpleasant happenings "out of mind" so that they will be "out of sight," we are only burying them in the etheric body and in the electronic belt. In order to remove permanently the energy patterns that have impressed upon our consciousness the records of past mistakes, we must transmute them by invoking the sacred fire, in service to life and in holy prayer.

God's energy misqualified through our criticism, condemnation and judgment of ourselves as well as other parts of life piles up in the etheric body and manifests as etheric calcification (an impaired memory). The activities of criticism, condemnation and judgment are compensated in the human personality by the opposite qualifications of self-pity, self-justification and indecision, which appear on the side of the south at the 6 o'clock line as shadowed substance. This compensation takes place in the emotional body and manifests there as emotional instability.

One does not need to be a psychoanalyst to see that it is a part of human nature to feel sorry for oneself while criticizing others as the cause of one's misfortunes. People justify their own wrongs while judging the sins of others. Thus, the return of 12 and 6 o'clock substance causes the individual to become emotionally indecisive and unstable because these misqualified energies result in the forfeiture of the memory of his divine plan originally recorded in the etheric body.

Now let us look at the sides of the east and the west, the 3-9 axis. At the 3 o'clock line we find in the mental body patterns of conceit, deceit and ego, which manifest as mental arrogance and the assertion "Je suis le droit" ("I am the law"). These are the traits that cause men to say, "I am not subject to the laws of God, but I make the laws to suit my own will." This is the line of human pride, the line on which Lucifer himself fell, and it takes in the entire gamut of intellectualism and the false premises and conclusions of the carnal mind.

Compensating for the assertion of the ego at the 3 o'clock line are vibrations of intrigue and treachery. These manifest on the 9 o'clock line as the need for physical self-preservation. Now we see that the arrogance of the ego that steps outside of the bonds of the Laws of God must cover up for itself through intrigue and treachery. Therefore, we observe all manner of crimes committed in defense of the dying ego—dying because it has cut itself off from the vine of the abundant Life. This Life flows freely to man when he is in the state of grace, but now that he has been put out of the Garden of Paradise, he must secure it by illegitimate means.

Although the 3 o'clock line is the line of the lie and the liar, both are to be seen on every line of the clock, for it is the entire gamut of human consciousness that supports and sustains the human ego. There is no other way to defend the negative 3 o'clock position than through dishonesty; for the human ego is dishonest from its original premise, "I am the law." Therefore, since it cannot employ the Laws of God to defend its position, it uses a perversion of those Laws: logic based on cause and effect in the world of human creation.

Human creation found at the 12-6 and 3-9 axes of the electronic belt is overcome through the invocation of the will of God—the blue ray. We note on the chart of the Tree of Life these leaves are God-power, God-control, God-harmony and God-reality. Each of these is the blue plume of the threefold flame in its quadrant. When all shadowed substance of those lines is transmuted, man beholds the Star of Bethlehem manifest in his world as the pinwheel of cosmic faith.

The four leaves of the Tree that manifest the will of God show how that will overcomes the human creation of those lines. On the side of the north, God-power, invoked through the qualities of faith, intelligence and goodwill, teaches man that the power of God is able to rebuke a wayward generation, that God himself is the avenger of all wrong, for did he not say, "Judge not, that ye be not judged," and "Vengeance is mine; I will repay"?[7]

Therefore, there is no need for individuals to criticize, to condemn or to judge one another, for through the flaming will of God manifest in our consciousness, God himself does correct the wrongs of the race. We have but to hold to the immaculate concept of each one's true identity, and we will thereby draw unto ourselves and our fellow men the power of God that will change all conditions in the being and world of man that are less than his perfection.[8]

At the 3 o'clock line, on the side of the east, the blue plume manifests the quality of God-control. We see that it is through our own desire for the perfection of God and our determination to rely utterly upon his Laws that we invoke the will of God, that we learn to control those human tendencies that continually thrust the ego into prominence. Those who defy the authority of the Divine Ego, the I AM Presence, and who thus fail to retain the power of their God-control, are obliged to use intellectual argument to defend their unlawful position.

On the side of the south at the 6 o'clock line, the blue plume manifests the universal harmony of the will of God. God-harmony keeps man in tune with every part of life because the will of God is the blueprint, the God-design within the white-fire core—the central sun magnet—of every atomic particle of life. Hence, when man lovingly submits himself to the will of God, he is harmonious with all that lives and moves according to the divine will.

Out of God-harmony proceeds the universal and individual manifestation of supply. Therefore, each time the individual allows the harmony of his communion with the Holy Spirit to be broken, he cuts the cable of his supply. The abundant Life can come to man only through the alchemical formula—the form of a perfect sphere—which is sustained through man's harmonious relationship with his God.

Discord manifesting in the world of the individual becomes, therefore, a sin against the abundant Life; hence, it is a sin against the Holy Spirit. Atonement for the sin of inharmony comes about as man replaces his justification for the inconsiderate acts of the human self (i.e., acts that do not take into consideration the will of God) with the adoration of the Divine Self. This adoration manifests through the emotional body when that body is purified, when it has relinquished personal desires and replaced them with God-desire.

Man's complete adoration of God makes him regard harmony as the highest law of his being, simply because harmony is the will of God that framed universal Being. There is no real existence outside of God-harmony. Harmony brings into focus the eternal mandate: Peace with honor. Harmony refutes self-pity and the vacillation of indecision, which are dishonorable states of consciousness; for there is only one decision to be made, and that is the decision to follow the way of harmonious overcoming through service to the will of God.

The law of harmony through the divine will enables man to overcome the problems of an ego-centered existence that manifest as misqualified substance on the 12-6 and 3-9 axes. Harmony is the key to God-power, God-control and God-reality. When God-harmony is the goal, we can with Christ say to any one of our four lower bodies that may be assailed with self-concern: "What is that to thee? Follow thou Me."[9]

When one has gained his mastery over the 6 o'clock substance, he can affirm the Master's words with confidence, "Behold the fowls of the air: for they sow not, neither do they reap, nor gather into barns; yet your heavenly Father feedeth them. Are ye not much better than they? Which of you by taking thought can add one cubit unto his stature? And why take ye thought for raiment? Consider the lilies of the field, how they grow; they toil not, neither do they spin: and yet I say unto you, That even Solomon in all his glory was not arrayed like one of these."[10]

On the side of the west at the 9 o'clock line, the will of

God manifests as God-reality. We know the Reality of God by following his will, and his Reality displaces all dishonesty. When we realize in the consciousness of God that "I AM Real," there is no need to idolize the synthetic image, or to seek to preserve the physical self. Those who seek to preserve their human creation through their offspring, through chemical formulae or historical record have missed the point of life entirely. Immortality can be conferred only upon that which is Real, that which is perfect, that which is God. All else is transitory.[11]

The Love Lines of the Clock

Let us now examine the love plumes, the 1-7 and 4-10 axes of the electronic belt; through these axes the love of Christ is intended to manifest in the lower vehicles. The 1 o'clock line is the second line of the etheric body, which comes under the tests of fire. These tests concern the revolving of feelings ranging from intense hatred to those of mild dislike. Beloved Saint Germain has taught us that mild dislike is just as destructive as hatred; it is simply a lesser form of the same evil (energy-veil). For the energy of mild dislike, after being thrust upon the ethers, amalgamates with islands and pockets of hatred floating in the mass consciousness, thereby contributing to the reservoir of misqualified energies used by the black magicians to wreak havoc against unsuspecting souls.

Patterns of human hatred, referenced by Jesus as "hardness of heart," lodge at the 1 o'clock line and are sustained in the etheric body through perversion of the fire element. Hatred, in order to be sustained, must first be revolved in the memory and then energized in the emotional body through feelings of ingratitude on the 7 o'clock line. Vendettas and feuds of long standing accumulate large quantities of misqualified substance at the 1 o'clock line of the electronic belt and ultimately manifest as etheric perversions and paralysis. These hatreds and the perversions they effect in the memory body carry over from one embodiment to the next and can be observed as instant dislike experienced between individuals upon their first encounter.

Just as the sharp knife of criticism, condemnation and judgment is the basis of all black magic, so hatred and mild dislike form the basis of all forms of witchcraft. The practice of the latter results in the manifestation of emotional density on the 7 o'clock line, along with feelings of ingratitude and thoughtlessness. Unless they are transmuted, these by-products of etheric perversions and paralyses will eventually be outpictured in the mental and physical bodies ere they come full cycle for redemption through the sacred fire.

The only way in which one can have mild dislike for another child of God is through an inability to appreciate his divine qualities. This inability we call ingratitude, and it manifests as emotional density—a clogging of the very pores of the senses of the soul. Human creation lodged at the 1-7 and 4-10 axes, being a perversion of divine love, can only be overcome through the flame of divine love, together with the assistance of one's God Presence and the Heavenly Hosts who have overcome the world and all things in it through the power of love.

To begin the transmutation of the 1-7, 4-10 axes, then, we magnetize the power of God's love at the 1 o'clock line through the pink plume. God-love overcomes perversions in the etheric body and God-gratitude overcomes all density in the emotional body. Gratitude is a flowing stream, a bubbling brook that cleanses and rejuvenates the dried-up riverbeds of the four lower bodies and the electronic belt with the purity of God's love—the love that is able to see the Christ in every man, that is able to accentuate his goodness and to be grateful for it.

When one is grateful for the Flame of Life manifesting in all of the many sons of God, one becomes keenly sensitive to the needs and abilities of others. In this awareness, one can have no hatred or mild dislike; nor is there any need to practice witchcraft in order to achieve one's ends, for one realizes that love is the fulfilling of the Law.

At the 4 o'clock line mental patterns of disobedience, stubbornness and defiance of the Law manifest as mental rebellion. This, too, is a perversion of divine love; for we see that in their rebellion, mankind show the little love they have for the Creator and his Laws—Laws that he enacts only that his children might receive his infinite blessings.

The reason for this rebellion is plainly seen as it manifests on the 10 o'clock line as selfishness and self-love. Mankind rebel against God's laws because they love themselves more than their Creator. Thus, the idolatrous habits that manifest in the physical body as self-indulgence, self-infatuation and the catering to the physical senses are compensations for man's disobedience to the Laws of God. Taken a step further, it can easily be seen that the mind furnishes the rationalization for the selfishness of the physical body, the desires of which are fed by feelings of ingratitude and memories of past hatred.

Alas, stubbornness is a product of selfishness, even as selfishness is a product of stubbornness. Both are overcome by the divine qualities of God-obedience at the 4 o'clock line and God-vision at the 10. Through supreme adoration of our Divine Source, the Giver of Life who ordained an individualized focus of himself for every monad made in his image, we become obedient to the Laws of God. Through God's love for us and our love for him, we see the vision of our divine plan, and this vision of our glorious opportunity as heirs of Christ gives us the courage to overcome the flesh. The byword of the overcomers of self-love is "He who seeks to save his life shall lose it,"[12] for he shows thereby that his real concern is not with the Father but with the lower self.

The Wisdom Lines of the Clock

Now let us examine the wisdom plumes, the 2–8, 5–11 axes, through which the Mind of Christ is intended to manifest in the electronic belt and four lower bodies of man.

The third test of fire in the etheric body is man's confrontation with the records of death he has accumulated during his entire involvement in mortality since his descent into the world of form. This includes his revolving of doubt and fear and his human questioning of the divine plan. All of these states of consciousness, including death, are illusions; therefore, this substance in the electronic belt tends to cloud Reality and to make the world of the finite appear to be real.

The power of the risen Christ and of his God-mastery over sin, sickness and death gives all who would follow in his footsteps the assurance, wrought by the resurrection flame, that man can overcome the effects of mortality. Descending into the plane of the emotional body, these records create feelings of anxiety, frustration and injustice, which come to the fore as emotional tyranny. Man feels caught within the confines of mortality, trapped by his own records. Frustration builds into anxiety and is reinforced by the concept that life is unjust.

Mortals compensate for this closed-in feeling with outbursts of emotional tyranny. Instead of ruling themselves and others through divine wisdom, they resort to a blind tyrannical misuse of power and authority, forcing their own and others' energies into subservience to the mortal will, thereby creating more illusion. God-justice is the key to the undoing of this buildup of records and emotions, together with the quality of God-patience, which submits all of one's human creation to the adjudication of one's Christ Self and the Lords of Karma.

The process of undoing the patterns of mortality may be painfully disquieting and even discouraging, but those who determine that they will follow the divine plan by exchanging their emotional imbalances and undisciplined energies for the crown of God-mastery and God-justice will find the rewards well worth the effort. For by submitting themselves to the wisdom of God's Laws, they are freeing themselves from the records of mortality, from the round of rebirth and from the emotional consequences of mankind's identification with the finite world.

On the 5-11 axis, we see the perversion of the illumination plume in the mental and physical bodies. On the 5 o'clock line, mental patterns of envy, jealousy and ignorance of the Law manifest as mental density and retardation. We can only retard our growth and the expansion of the Light of the Christ within us if we engage our energies in the coveting of that which other sons of God have brought forth from the Creator.

The persistent indulgence of one's energies in various aspects of jealousy, together with a willful ignoring of the Laws of God that are written in man's inward parts,[13] manifests as density and incompetence in the mental faculties. Eventually, the buildup of envy and jealousy manifests on the 11 o'clock line as a seething resentment and an explosion of revenge all the way from petty fights to global warfare.

Retaliation, whether against one's own self (masochism) or against other parts of life (sadism), is another mark of idolatry, for it is a placing of the image of the finite man in the place where the Christ ought to appear. Only God-wisdom and God-victory can rescue the mortal from his plight of spiritual blindness: his total inability to see the Christ in self or in others and to understand that in the precepts of the Law is the balanced outpicturing of the Law in all of its aspects in every part of life.

May we quote once again the words of the Goddess of Justice: "There is no injustice anywhere in the universe. But in the consciousness that has not become wholly Real, there is an attitude of injustice that impairs the universal plan. Therefore, long ago I espoused the virtue of God-justice and I determined to bring that quality of the wholeness of the motherhood of God on behalf of her children in that flame of justice, which would liberate all mankind, ultimately even from the karmic cycles of their own initiation.

"Man initiates the cycles of injustice. He must arrest those cycles and commence in their place spirals of freedom, spirals of justice and equality. The key to divine justice is in the realization that all life is one."[14]

Greatness, nobility and beauty are qualities of the soul, which, when earned, cannot be denied to those who have worked diligently in the Father's kingdom. Karmic penalties that manifest as deformity, accident, poverty, ignorance and the unfortunate circumstances of life—these have also been earned. To take revenge against another for one's own shortcoming is the mark of the unillumined soul.

Likewise, those who cannot see that what one man has done, another man can do—those who are jealous of the accomplishments of others—are often too lazy to apply the precepts of the Law that would afford them the same progress. (However, this same tendency may also manifest as fierce competition.)

"Study to show thyself approved unto God, a workman rightly dividing the word that needeth not be ashamed."[15] This is the admonishment that overcomes the 11 and 5 o'clock substance, for when we know the Law, we cannot be fooled by vibrations of envy, jealousy and ignorance, which precipitate the compulsions of resentment, revenge and retaliation.

Figure 13 The Twelve God-Qualities and Their Perversions

Line of the Clock	God-Quality in the Tree of Life	Misqualification in the Electronic Belt
12	God-power	Revolving of criticism, condemnation and judgment, etheric calcification, black magic
1	God-love	Revolving of hatred and mild dislike, hardness of heart, superstition, etheric perversions, paralysis, witchcraft
2	God-mastery	Revolving of doubt and fear, human questioning and records of death, etheric illusion, hypnosis
3	God-control	Mental patterns of conceit, deceit, ego and mental arrogance
4	God-obedience	Mental patterns of disobedience, stubbornness, defiance of the law, mental rebellion
5	God-wisdom	Mental patterns of envy, jealousy, ignorance of the law, spiritual blindness, mental density and retardation
6	God-harmony	Feelings of self-pity, self-justification and indecision, emotional instability, all misuses of the sacred fire and perversions of the Mother Flame
7	God-gratitude	Feelings of ingratitude and thoughtlessness, spiritual blindness, emotional density and retardation
8	God-justice	Feelings of frustration, anxiety and injustice, emotional tyranny
9	God-reality	Vibrations of dishonesty, intrigue and treachery, physical self-preservation and idolatry
10	God-vision	Vibrations of selfishness, self-love, physical self-infatuation and idolatry
11	God-victory	Vibrations of resentment and revenge, physical self-retaliation and idolatry

Solar Hierarchies and the Mastery of the Elements through the Threefold Flame

As we compare the chart showing the cross-section of the electronic belt (Figure 8) with that of the leaves of the Tree of Life (Figure 9), let us bear in mind that the Great Central Sun Magnet is focused at the core of every atom (Adam) of manifestation and that inherent in the creation is the pattern of the circle divided into twelve sections.

The Taoist symbol, on the other hand, provides us with the concept of the masculine and feminine polarity of the Deity, of Alpha and Omega.[16] All Life revolves around this Yin (feminine or passive) and Yang (masculine or active) principle. Within Oneness there is always polarity—never duality[17]—and out of that polarity comes forth the balanced manifestation of the Christ.

Figure 14 The T'ai Chi

Throughout all of nature, in Spirit and in Matter, the pattern of the T'ai Chi, of the Alpha-to-Omega and of the Spirit/Matter universes, is repeated again and again. This represents the first division of the circle of the One. As each half again divides into two, and as each resulting quadrant manifests the threefold flame, we see the division of the circle into twelve sections.

Thus, we will observe that the God-qualities on the 6 through the 11 o'clock lines focus the feminine aspect of God through the emotional and physical bodies of man, while the

God-qualities on the 12 through the 5 o'clock lines focus God's masculine attributes through the etheric and mental bodies. Therefore, the polarity of God-qualities on the 12-6, 1-7, 2-8, 3-9, 4-10 and 5-11 axes is in perfect balance and designed to bring into focus the flame of the Christ through the four lower bodies. We will now explain how this balance is simply a reflection of the Twelve Solar Lords and the sun qualities they magnify.

Raying out from the Great Central Sun Magnet and positioned around the Great Central Sun, according to the design of the clock, are the twelve suns of manifestation that are ensouled by the Twelve Solar Hierarchies. While the Central Sun is occupied by beloved Alpha and Omega, supreme representatives of the Father-Mother God, the twelve lesser suns are occupied by the Hierarchies bearing the names commonly assigned to the signs of the zodiac (Figure 15).

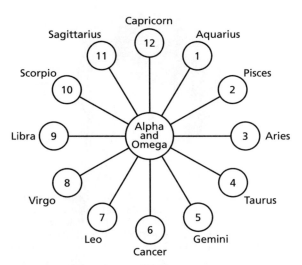

Figure 15 The Twelve Solar Hierarchies

The Twelve Solar Hierarchies are twelve suns of manifestation around the Great Central Sun. They are known by the names of the signs of the zodiac. The stars in these configurations are not the Hierarchy—the beings of the Hierarchy simply use these and many other stars to release their energy.

These twelve Hierarchies are represented at the Court of the Sacred Fire on Sirius by the Twenty-Four Elders. The Twenty-Four Elders are twelve sets of twin flames, each set having mastery and authority over one of the twelve lines of the Sun in manifestation.

The Twenty-Four Elders have appointed representatives to assist mankind in overcoming their human creation at the twelve points—which, as we have seen, are actually twelve opportunities for self-mastery—within the electronic belt. The Ascended Masters appointed by the Four and Twenty Elders as their representatives, along with the Heavenly Hosts who serve with these divine appointees, are shown in Figure 16.

Both the Masters and their Hosts work directly under the Four and Twenty Elders, who in turn dispense the blessings of

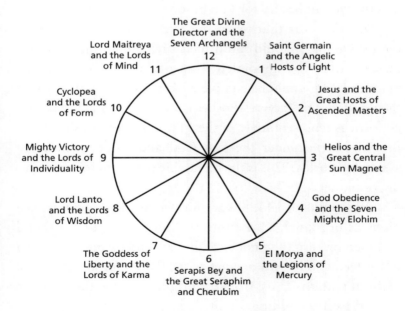

Figure 16 Representatives of the Twelve Solar Hierarchies to Earth and Her Evolutions

the Twelve Solar Hierarchies. It should be noted that each of these Hierarchies has 144,000 Cosmic Beings in their service and that each of these in turn has 144,000 angels at his command.

It is precisely because these twelve Ascended Masters and their twin flames (if they are ascended) have manifested their victory over the human creation on the particular line on which they serve that they have been appointed by the Twenty-Four Elders to assist each one evolving upon earth to attain self-mastery.

The Knights of the Round Table were also intended to hold the focus for the Twelve Hierarchies of the Sun and the twelve heavenly attributes that bring to fruition the consciousness of the Christ. Serving directly under the king, who held the office of the Christ, were twelve knights, each of whom had twelve candidates for knighthood serving under him.

The plan was that when the twelve knights on each of the twelve lines should fulfill their divine plan through self-mastery over the appointed lines of human creation, the matrix of 144 would be complete. Each of the knights would then initiate one thousand other candidates, and they would go forth as representatives of the 144,000 priests of the sacred fire who serve under the Sun God and Goddess of every system of worlds. This is the hierarchical pattern for each unit of cosmic service.

Other units of 144,000 are formed as the original twelve disciples or "knights" rise into the initiations of Christhood and thereby earn the right to gather around themselves nuclei of twelve, who in turn magnetize the flames for another hierarchical pattern. Thus, from the original twelve, there will be formed twelve additional units, and each of these will eventually magnetize twelve others. This spiraling expansion of Hierarchy explains the spiritual cause behind the phenomenon of the expanding universe. At the end of the cycles of expansion, the trend is reversed as the consciousness of the Creator recalls these servant Suns who were sent forth to expand the godly attributes.

The parable of the unprofitable servant, which begins appropriately "For the kingdom of heaven is as a man...,"[18] gives the description of this cosmic activity. Herein is revealed not only the pageant of the "Cosmic Homing," but also the ritual of the Last Judgment wherein those who have multiplied their talents are received with highest honors at Luxor and "the unprofitable servant [is cast] into outer darkness: [where] there shall be weeping and gnashing of teeth."[19] These events were reviewed in book 7 of this series, *The Path to Immortality*.

Now, as the earth revolves each year around the sun of this system, presided over by Helios and Vesta, it passes through and comes under the influence of the Twelve Hierarchies, also known as the Twelve Houses of the Sun. These Hierarchies, whose focuses are maintained in the Great Central Sun, extend their influence through the sun-focus of Helios and Vesta for the benefit of all who are evolving in this solar system. We shall explore the functions of these Hierarchies on the lines of the clock after briefly showing the relationship of the four elements to the four lower bodies of man and his planetary home.

As we have seen in previous volumes of this series, the earth itself has four lower bodies. While we live on the physical body of the earth, the planet also has an emotional body, which is known as the astral plane; a mental body, referred to as the mental belt; and an etheric, or memory, body, which is called the etheric plane. Therefore, we may conclude that the earth also has an electronic belt; for the electronic belt is actually the negative spiral that is formed of the substance that has been misqualified through the four lower bodies—whether of a man or of a planet.

Thus, the misqualified substance lodged in the electronic belt of the planet Earth is the accumulation of the mass karma and effluvia of all of the evolutions who have ever lived upon this planet.[20] We may conclude, then, that the electronic belt of the earth reflects the electronic belts of its inhabitants. Therefore, the evolutions of the earth must work out their collective karma according to the pattern of the electronic belt of the earth. Simultaneously, each lifestream must balance his own karma according to his individual pattern.

Each of the four lower bodies of man and of the earth relates to one of the four elements, and each body is tested through the mastery of the element to which it corresponds. The physical body corresponds to the earth element, the emotional body relates to the water element, the mental body to the air, and the etheric body to the fire element. These, in turn, correspond to the four seasons and should be studied in relation to the four quadrants of the clock.

The tests of fire in the etheric body occur on the 12, 1 and 2 o'clock lines during the months of January, February and March.* The Hierarchies of Capricorn, Aquarius and Pisces assist the planet in overcoming the accumulation of etheric effluvia (malicious animal magnetism) by radiating to the earth the qualities of God-power, God-love and God-mastery.

While these Hierarchies are in the etheric, or fire, quadrant, they also teach mastery over earth, air and water respectively (as they occupy positions on these trines—see Figure 19). Therefore, within the "fire body" the other elements are tested and balanced as the planet as a whole comes to grips with the effluvia resulting from mankind's misuse of the fire element.

At the spring equinox, which falls on the 3 o'clock line, we

---

* The change from one hierarchy to the next occurs on the change of the sun sign.

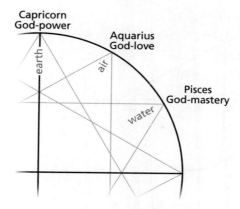

Figure 17 The Tests in the Etheric Body

have the beginning of the tests of the mental body through the air element. All human effluvia resulting from misqualification of this element through the mental body is dealt with by the planet as a whole during the cycle of spring.

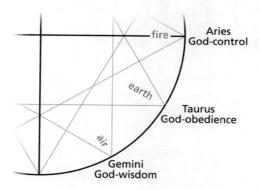

Figure 18 The Tests of the Mental Body

This is the time of year for the victory of the mental body and for the victory in man of the divine qualities of God-control, God-obedience and God-wisdom through his mastery

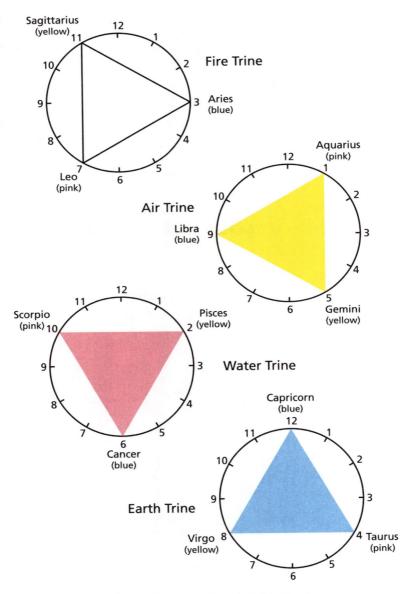

Figure 19 The Trines of the Clock

Comparing these diagrams with Figure 12 shows that the vertices of each trine themselves form a threefold flame. For example, Aries is the blue plume in the mental quadrant, Leo the pink plume in the emotional quadrant, and Sagittarius the yellow plume in the physical quadrant.

over fire, earth and air. These qualities are focused during the months of April, May and June by the Hierarchies of Aries, Taurus and Gemini, who assist mankind in demonstrating the principles of mastery over all ignorant animal magnetism in the electronic belt of the earth.

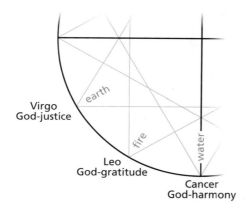

Figure 20 The Tests of the Emotional Body

With the coming of the summer solstice on the 6 o'clock line, the planet is faced with the tests of the water element and the emotional body. This effluvia is lodged at the 6, 7 and 8 o'clock lines and is sustained through mankind's momentum of sympathetic animal magnetism. The Hierarchies of Cancer, Leo and Virgo, manifesting the power of God-harmony, God-gratitude and God-justice through the mastery of the water, fire and earth elements respectively, assist mankind in passing these tests.

With the coming of the autumn equinox, the planet is faced with the tests of the physical body and the earth element. Human effluvia lodged at the 9, 10 and 11 o'clock lines is sustained through delicious animal magnetism—the indulgences of the senses—and it is overcome with the assistance of the Hierarchies of Libra, Scorpio and Sagittarius, who teach the mastery of air, water and fire during the months of October, November and December.

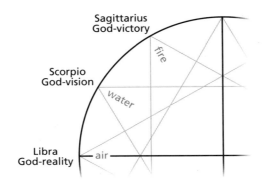

Figure 21 The Tests of the Physical Body

As we explained in the beginning of our study of the chart of the electronic belt, the four quadrants relate not only to the four lower bodies but also to the tests of fire, air, water and earth. These tests, coming under the etheric, mental, emotional and physical bodies follow the pattern of the threefold flame within each of the four lower vehicles.

For instance, the victory of the manifestation of the Christ in the etheric body comes about through the balanced action of the blue, pink and yellow plumes on the 12, 1 and 2 o'clock lines. When all human creation is overcome and transmuted on those lines, the threefold flame blazes forth in balanced action through the etheric body as God-power (blue), God-love (pink) and God-mastery (yellow). The victory of the Christ in each of the other three lower bodies is based on the same triune mastery of the blue, pink and yellow plumes. One should become familiar with the three phases of mastery that occur within the etheric, mental, emotional and physical bodies by studying them in sequence on the Charts.

The Trines

Now, let us take a larger look at the Tree of Life and see how the Twelve Hierarchies of the Sun test man's mastery over the four elements, not only through the body to which each of the elements relates, but also through each of the other lower bodies.

Referring to Figure 19, we see that the tests of the mastery of air come under the Hierarchies of Aquarius, Gemini and Libra. We notice immediately that these Hierarchies divide the electronic belt into three equal parts forming a threefold flame. Aquarius uses the pink plume (this sign is the pink plume of the threefold flame of the etheric quadrant) to teach the mastery of the air element through the power of divine love on the 1 o'clock line. Gemini uses the yellow plume to teach the mastery of the air element through the attribute of God-wisdom on the 5 o'clock line, and Libra establishes the authority of God-reality in the world of the aspirant by teaching him the mastery of the air element through the blue plume on the 9 o'clock line.

The perfect balance of this configuration of the threefold flame is a requirement for the proper alignment of the four lower bodies and the intermeshing of those bodies by the power of the Holy Christ Flame. The mastery of the three phases of each of the elements under the Hierarchies of the Sun creates four threefold flames on the circle. When this is accomplished, the threefold flame (which is a sphere) gains the power of the cosmic square through its manifestation in the four lower bodies—what is known as "the squaring of the circle."

Following this pattern, we see that the Hierarchy of Pisces

uses the yellow plume to teach the mastery of the water element through the power of God-mastery on the 2 o'clock line. The Hierarchy of Cancer teaches the mastery over this same element by the authority of God-harmony and supply, using the blue plume on the 6 o'clock line, while the Hierarchy of Scorpio uses the pink plume on the 10 o'clock line to teach the mastery of the water element through the power of God-vision.

Tracing the mastery of the fire element, we note that the Hierarchy of Aries teaches the mastery of fire through the blue plume on the 3 o'clock line. Here the key is the attribute of God-control, whereas the Hierarchy of Leo teaches this same mastery through the pink plume on the 7 o'clock line by the power of God-gratitude. Finally, the Hierarchy of Sagittarius uses the yellow plume to teach the mastery of the fire element on the 11 o'clock line through the attribute of God-victory.

Again, we see another triad forming in the mastery of the earth element. On the 4 o'clock line, the Hierarchy of Taurus teaches through the love plume the mastery of the earth element with God-obedience as the mark of attainment. The Hierarchy of Virgo teaches the mastery of the earth element on the 8 o'clock line through the illumination plume and the power of God-justice. To complete this cycle, the Hierarchy of Capricorn teaches the mastery of the earth element through the power ray on the 12 o'clock line. Here God-power enables man to achieve his mastery and to take dominion over the earth.

The Three Decans within Each Line

The period of the influence of each Hierarchy is divided into three equal parts. These thirds are referred to as *decans*, each one representing ten degrees on the circle. The power of the Christ that flowers on each of the leaves of the Tree of Life relates to the action of the threefold flame *within* each of the signs of the Solar Hierarchies. The threefold flame within the signs actually shows the relationship of the three phases of each element to one another. Let us explain:

Capricorn, Taurus and Virgo, as we have said, teach the mastery of the earth element through the threefold flame. But within the thirty-degree cycle of each of these sign is the complementary expression of the other two. The first decan (approximately ten days) of Capricorn is under the blue ray and the double influence of the Hierarchy of Capricorn itself. The second decan is influenced by the Hierarchy of Taurus (pink) under Capricorn; the third decan is ruled by Virgo (yellow) under Capricorn.

The first decan of Taurus, being under the Hierarchy of Taurus, would be ruled by the pink plume; the second decan would be ruled by Virgo (yellow) under Taurus; and the third decan would be ruled by Capricorn (blue) under Taurus.

The first decan of Virgo, in turn, is under the yellow plume of Virgo's Hierarchy; the second is influenced by Capricorn's blue under the yellow of Virgo; the third is guided by the pink of Taurus under the yellow of Virgo.

Thus, we can figure the decans of each of the Twelve Hierarchies by marking the first as that of the sign itself, the second as that of the next sign of that element as it appears in order on the clock, and the third decan as the influence of the remaining sign in the triad.

Each year the dates of the influence of these signs vary slightly; therefore, one should consult a current calendar in order to determine the exact dates of these divisions.

Figure 22 The Decans of the Twelve Lines of the Clock

Line of the Clock	God-Quality in the Tree of Life	Qualities of the Decans, Which Form a Threefold Flame on Each Line
12	God-power	God-faith God-intelligence Good will
1	God-love	God-diplomacy God-comfort God-grace
2	God-mastery	God-discipline God-purity God-patience
3	God-control	God-perfection God-desire God-reliance
4	God-obedience	God-unity God-understanding God-devotion
5	God-wisdom	God-forgiveness God-tolerance (largesse of heart) God-intuition
6	God-harmony	God-supply God-science God-wholeness
7	God-gratitude	God-honor God-awareness God-happiness
8	God-justice	God-mercy God-balance God-judgment
9	God-reality	God-truth God-dominion God-destiny
10	God-vision	God-freedom God-protection God-determination
11	God-victory	God-illumination God-peace God-brotherhood

Internalizing the Flames of the Hierarchies

The manifestation of the threefold flame within each of the elements shows the relationship within the sacred Trinity of Father (blue), of Son (yellow) and of Holy Spirit (pink)—or to express it in Hindu terms: of Brahma, the Creator (blue), of Vishnu, the Preserver (yellow), and of Siva, the Destroyer (pink). The progressive interaction of these aspects of the Deity throughout the solar year teaches us the phases of the sun and of our own inner being, if we will but be alert to these winds of God that blow with cyclic regularity, unfolding the Christ consciousness as a flame each hour, each day and each month of the year.

Poised in the center of his God-design at the fulcrum of the Christ, man sees that his life's opportunity is a flame. Bowing before the Hierarchy of Capricorn, he takes up the flame of God-power and "keeps" it during their approximately thirty-day reign. At the end of the cycle of Capricorn, he lays down the flame as a knight places his sword in the scabbard. Turning thirty degrees and facing the Hierarchy of Aquarius, he receives the flame of God-love, which he adores and expands as the just steward who multiplies his talents and then returns them to God.[21]

Passing through each of the Twelve Solar Hierarchies in this way, the expansion of the kingdom of God on earth comes about as man takes up each opportunity—each flaming aspect of the Sun—and makes it his own.

As he enters into and becomes a part of the consciousness of the flame, he leaves a portion of himself in the flame and receives in return a portion of the flame. The twain having been made one, neither is ever again the same. To this ritual of regeneration by the flames of God and the ever-new quality of the Light, there is no end. We commend you to the glorious discovery of the twelve thousand virtues that blossom from the trinity of Light on each branch of the Tree of Life. The prayer of Jesus for each one who pursues this divine calling assures us of its realization: "Father, make them one [with the flame] even as we are one."[22]

As we study and compare our two charts, let us realize that the pattern of the Great Central Sun and the twelve lesser suns revolving around it is also outpictured in the microcosm of man's being, in Nature and in our own solar system. The Son of God, the Eternal Christos, moves through the years as a great solar body wending its way through the stellar highways and sojourning in the houses of the sun.

The star of man's divinity—the I AM Presence—works closely with each of the Hierarchies of the Sun to assist him in overcoming the tests that unfold in each month of the year and in each twelve-year cycle. The son of God who goes forth to conquer the world and to take up the cross of his own victorious overcoming understands the opportunity afforded by each of the Hierarchies. He does not attribute earthly qualities to these Hierarchies as do other forms of astrology, but he realizes that the association of imperfect conditions with the signs of the zodiac has come about only through a confusion of the godly attributes with their human perversions.

It is these perversions that the great Hierarchs of the Sun assist man to eliminate. The closer he draws to his own divinity, the greater will be his attunement with all who have gone before him and who have earned the right to serve under the Sun Hierarchs who govern the energies that are released to the earth and to man each month.

The Opportunity of One's Birth Sign

Whatever sign an individual is born under, that is the sign through which he must conquer during that embodiment. If he is born during the period when the planet is under the influence of the Hierarchy of Pisces, then his assignment for that embodiment is to overcome individual and world karma involving the 2 o'clock creations of doubt, fear, human questioning and records of death. Born under the sign of Pisces, he must always remember that he has need of the assistance of these Hierarchs, else he would not be assigned to their school. He is given the responsibility of attaining mastery over the water element through the mastery of his etheric body and the axes of which his sign is a part. The godly attributes found on the 2-8 and 5-11 axes magnified by the power of illumination's flame will be prominent in his life, and through these, he will find the key and the balance to the tests on the other lines.

One's birth sign should be taken as one's opportunity to gain self-mastery over all conditions opposing the universal services of the Hierarchy in command. No matter what tests he is facing, the son of God always remembers to see each test in the perspective of the line of his birth, for therein he discovers the secrets of his destiny and the mysteries of his overcoming. Under the tutelage of these great Hierarchs, he learns to see the universe and all creation through the lens of their consciousness.

As each successive embodiment affords another view and another opportunity, he gradually magnetizes the perspective and the potential of the entire sphere of God's consciousness; and his innermost being pulsates with the grand design of the Creator that can be contained by none but must be outpictured by all.

Personal Cycles through the Hierarchies

In addition to the major personal initiation of an embodiment under one of the Hierarchies, you also have personal cycles through the Hierarchies yearly and monthly. Let us look first at the yearly cycle.

At the hour that you were born, you began your first initiation, the initiation of the Hierarchy of Capricorn, of God-power. (Cycles always begin at the 12 o'clock line.) The initial thrust of God-power was your first breath and your first cry, and the initiation you passed was to seize the flame of life and take it and claim it as your own.

All through the first year of your life, you were serving under the Great Divine Director and the Hierarchies of Capricorn, testing the power as that power manifested in the stretching of the limbs, in the flow of the energy of the heart, in the exact working of the physical body.

On your first birthday came the first yearly initiation in this life under the Hierarchy of Aquarius, and God-love infused your soul with a new wonder. Your identification with love and with loved ones increased.

On your second birthday come the initiations of Pisces in the water element. It is a testing in the etheric body of the flow of water—the emotions. It is the flame of God-mastery. In this year you master many things.

Then at three comes the awareness of the Christ Child. The child gains a tremendous sense of identity, of "I AM WHO I AM," the awareness of the name, and "I want to do it all by myself!" This is the development of the ego; it is the Divine Ego aborning in the child. The greatest mistake the parent can make is to do for that child what the child diligently desires to do for himself; and when the child cries that you have done something for him, quickly undo it and let him do it himself. It is very important that the flame of individuality develop in this third year under the Hierarchy of Aries. It is focusing the balance for a lifetime.

In the fourth year comes the test of the Hierarchy of Taurus. More and more we are precipitating into the physical, gaining mastery of the physical. There is now a certain stubbornness that is positive that carries through the flame of individuality. It is a will to be, to have a separate identity. Children are mastering the physical element, the earth plane of Taurus. The entire year is marked by this energy.

Taurus is a sign of love. It is by love that we precipitate determination, and it is actually a determination within the soul of the child to conform to the law of the inner being. The problem here is that not all children have the sense of the inner law, and they have laws imposed upon them from without that society and parents and schools deem more important than the inner law of the child. So the child is taking into himself, line upon line, whatever he contacts and composing the law of his life at subconscious and conscious levels.

On the fifth birthday, the child comes under the Hierarchy of Gemini, which tests the wisdom of the Christ Mind. It is a sign of air. The mental development increases. The child is precocious. The child wants to learn.

On the 6 o'clock line, the sixth birthday, the child learns under the Hierarchy of Cancer the flow of energies-in-motion, the flow of harmony. This is a time when parents must take care to see that the child is not allowed to have tantrums and to throw energy in order to control others. For the next three years the child will be testing the emotional body and the flow of energy: What can the child get away with? What can the child do with energy?

At age seven the child is dealing again with an action of love, this time under Leo and the mastery of God-gratitude

—learning manners, learning politeness, learning to say "Thank you," developing an awareness of social action and interaction.

On the 8 o'clock line, the Hierarchy of Virgo anchors into this earth sign the flame of God-justice, the equality of the flow of energy in the four lower bodies.

At the age of nine, the child comes again into a new increment of awareness—awareness of life as the Holy Spirit and the flame of God-reality. A greater measure of independence is coming at this time, and parents must take care to see that the child is taught what is real and what is not real.

The tenth birthday marks God-vision, dealing with the energies of Scorpio, the test of the ten, selflessness, a lesson of giving, a lesson also in the water element.

In the eleventh year the flame of God-victory—the fire of Sagittarius anchoring in the earth quadrant the sign of victory, the development of the physical body.

Each twelve years of life marks the turning of a cycle of the Cosmic Clock. On the twelfth birthday the child returns to the place of origin and now has a set of records to be dealt with from the first turn of the clock. The child faces the initiations of puberty on the 12 o'clock line in a new cycle of God-power surging through the four lower bodies, and he will also deal with all of the records of impressions of the first year of his life.

The age of twelve also marks the year when the first increment of karma from previous lifetimes descends. Unless the child is an advanced soul, an initiate, or has requested that the karma be given earlier, it is the plan of the Lords of Karma to allow children, parents and teachers twelve years before the descent of karma in which to instill in the child's consciousness the blueprint of life, the mastery of the mind, the standards of culture, the standards of religion—all the things that children should be taught as the legacy of the thousands of years of culture on this planet.

Unfortunately, parents are sometimes ignorant of this culture and of this teaching, and our educational institutions do not ensoul it. Therefore we find many times that in the first twelve years of the life of a child, more harm is done than good. Nevertheless, these twelve years are the supreme opportunity to pass on to children the torch of all of the values we hold dear, spiritual knowledge and an understanding of the cosmos.

The Second Twelve-Year Cycle

During the first twelve years of life, the pattern of what the child will bring forth is set. Ideally, the child will have developed a strong sense of cosmic law, which parents call right and wrong. But right and wrong, of course, move on the scale of relativity as the decades roll by, and so we prefer to speak of cosmic law itself as the measuring rod of right and wrong.

After the first twelve years, when the child has that grounding, he faces the tests of karma and the tests of puberty. If he has a firm foundation in the law, he is equipped to face that energy which is oncoming and which presents a great testing in the next twelve-year cycle, the years between twelve and twenty-four.

On the twelfth birthday, the child receives the impetus of God-power—a sphere of light that descends from the Causal Body. It is a blue sphere of energy. It is delivered to the Christ Self, to the Christ flame, just as cosmic Hierarchies deliver a sphere of Light at winter solstice for the turning of the planetary cycle of the year.

However, as the I AM Presence delivers the sphere of fire, of God-power, so the Lords of Karma, through the Christ Self, also deliver the package of karma that contains the misuses of God-power in previous lifetimes. The child can choose to increase his momentum of power by invocations to the blue flame and to the masters who serve on that ray, especially to the Great Divine Director, or he can choose to indulge that condemnation as it cycles back to him for transmutation. Instead of letting it go into the flame, he may become hypercritical of everything and everyone, including himself.

Where there is ignorance of what is taking place, people can go through an entire year, taking the momentum of karma that is returning and re-creating it. For an entire year they can be misqualifying the flame of God-power. And when the cycle turns and that flame and that torch which ought to have been carried is to be exchanged for the flame of God-love on the line of Aquarius, the flame that has not been carried cannot be exchanged for a new flame. We see that initiation is cumulative. What we earn on one line has to be carried to the next line, and it becomes the foundation for mastery in that line.

Therefore, on the thirteenth birthday, the child who has correctly used the flame of God-power lays it upon the altar, and the momentum of God-power gives him the mastery to claim the love of Aquarius and to anchor that love as purity, as divinity.

The age of thirteen is for the testing of love in many ways. It is a time when love must be garnered in the heart, when the wise parent will show the child how to raise the energies coursing through the body, how to release that energy in the heart, how to expand the heart chakra, to begin to understand life as a path of service, and to continually be giving in love in order to use these new energies which are arousing new feelings within his form. These energies can be used for the service of life, and the child can gain a great sense of mastery of that flow in this year.

However, with the release of that flame of love, the karma of hatred and mild dislike, which are the misuses of love, also comes up for transmutation. We find that young people at this age like to get together in groups and cliques and clubs, and there is the stratification into social levels. Some are left out and some are included, and intense likes and dislikes build up. All of this can be dissolved by the alchemy of divine love when parents and teachers are there to show the child how to use these energies.

At the fourteenth birthday on the 2 o'clock line, we find that there is mastery to be gained, especially over the increments of karma coming at this age. With that increment of God-mastery and the walk with Jesus, the Master of this line, there comes the increment of karma that is a momentum of fear and doubt, including all past records of the experience and the initiation of death. At fourteen there is a great deal of torment that the adolescent faces in coming to grips with past records of death. In this year we find young people across the world even considering suicide and the forms of violence that come from these records of death.

Coming to the fifteenth birthday on the 3 o'clock line, the child enters into his own sonship—his awareness of himself as the Christ. He truly comes into the awareness that "I AM a son of God." He is not simply affirming this, but he is realizing what it means to be a son of God. The Christ Self releases an increment, a momentum, of the Great Central Sun, and the Christ flame actually blazes forth through the child.

When children at age fifteen face that awareness and potential of the Christ, they also are faced with an increment of karma that is the ego, or the carnal mind. It is an age when young people become aware of themselves as personalities, and they often push the personality and the ego to the fore to the neglect of the soul and the development of the Christ flame.

At age sixteen, there is a supreme opportunity for building, for anchoring the talents of the child in the earth plane in the earth sign of Taurus. This year also falls in the mental quadrant. It is the year when application in school is very important: preparation and decisions for the sacred labor are being made. And the application of the flame of love, in study, will bring the reward of the foundation that is necessary for life.

Unfortunately, there are many distractions at this age. Besides the increment of the flame of love and God-obedience that is given on this birthday, there is also that package of karma—the record of all that the Lords of Karma require the sixteen-year-old to transmute of past records of rebellion, disobedience, stubbornness and defiance of the law—the inner law of being. The age of sixteen (and even younger) is the age when experimentation with all forms of abuses of the body takes place, including the taking of drugs. Unfortunately in the modern world, young people of this age, led by their peers, do not have the guidance needed to pass the tests on this line, and usually they make more karma than they balance.

With the seventeenth birthday on the 5 o'clock line comes an intensification of God-wisdom by the Hierarchy of Gemini. The age of seventeen is an age when a great deal of knowledge can be gleaned from the Causal Body. The increment of karma that comes up for transmutation in this year is the increment of envy, jealousy and ignorance of the law. When the individual is personality-oriented from age fifteen on, there are envies and jealousies and vying for relationships. Sometimes this all-consuming energy takes all of the young person's time in relationships with the opposite sex. If this energy can be transmuted and placed in its proper perspective, the mind of the seventeen-year-old, freed from these other concerns of personality, has the capacity for amazing input, study and accomplishment, especially accomplishment in the sacred labor.

At the age of eighteen, on the 6 o'clock line, comes the testing in the flame of God-harmony and the Divine Mother. Eighteen marks the beginning of a three-year cycle when the feeling body is at its prominence and there is the testing by the substance of karma that must be consumed if we would gain our mastery under the Hierarchies of Cancer, Leo and Virgo.

The karma that comes to the fore under Cancer is indecision, self-pity and self-justification—for example, feeling sorry for oneself for not being accepted in college, not going on to higher opportunity as others are doing, feeling sorry for oneself because of one's own failures. There is that idling of energy, the inability to make a decision. "What will I do with my life? I'm out of school. Now where will I go?"

The mastery of this flow is necessary to forge ahead into the higher learning of advanced educational institutions, which were intended by the Masters to be the focal point for the release of the culture of the Divine Mother. The high-school years are intended to be the release of the energies of the Christ Self, the Christ mind. Entering college, vocational school, business school or some training after high school is a time to glean from the hand of the Mother the knowledge of one's sacred labor and to complete this training in the four years that culminate on the line of the Holy Spirit, the 9 o'clock line.

When we come to the line of the Holy Spirit after that training, it is time to go forth into the world of form to make our mark, to get a job whereby we precipitate with our hands that which we are intended to manifest in this life. The years twenty-one, twenty-two and twenty-three are periods when we can take advanced training, mastering further phases of postgraduate work in the increments of the Holy Spirit, or we can go forth, our training completed, to take our place in the world community.

There are also misuses of these lines to watch for in those years. At nineteen, under the Hierarchy of Leo, there is ingratitude and disturbance in the emotional body and a certain anxiety and nervous tension. At twenty there is the mastery of Virgo—the sense of human injustice, the outrage about particular experiences or individuals you are interacting with who you feel have been unfair. It is a time to take up social causes. It is also a time to be careful that we don't squander this increment of the Light of God-justice by getting completely caught up in a sense of injustice, whereby we re-create and amplify injustices in our personal life and on a planetary level.

At twenty-one the testing of Libra, of God-reality, comes again. On this line we find the perversion of Libra as unreality. It is the deceit, the deception, the intrigue and the treachery that the ego uses to justify its position.

Twenty-two, the year of Scorpio, is the year of the testing of the sacred fire, the testing of the uses of sex energy. This testing comes all through adolescence, but the testing in this year comes as the release of the karma of many misuses of the sacred fire in the past. This is also a year when people often start families. It is a year for the mastery of the flow of the sacred fire and the using of that energy to bring forth children. It is the year of vision—of seeing the plan of life, carving out that vision, selecting one's life partner.

The momentum of selfishness from the past is very strong in this year. We must see to it that we do not base our lives, our plans or our marriages on selfishness or possessive love. Partnerships based on residual karma that is not transmuted will not be lasting. We must call forth the sacred fire from the Hierarchy of Scorpio and the Elohim Cyclopea for clear seeing and for the transmutation of these misuses of energy so that we can make our decisions based on that clear seeing.

Finally, completing this second twelve-year cycle with the twenty-third birthday, we have the Hierarchy of Sagittarius giving us an impetus for the victory of life. Opposing this victory is the entire dragon of the carnal mind—our own human creation symbolized in the form of the dragon in the Book of Revelation—and this energy comes with a momentum of resentment, revenge and retaliation. When we are eleven years old and playing, it is the year when we have the hostilities and the cruelties that children are noted for. This comes again at age twenty-three, and we must see to it that we do not allow resentment, even in a subtle form of silent seething, to take from us the crown of victory, which is a release of victorious, golden illumination.

The Third Twelve-Year Cycle

Coming back to the 12 o'clock line, we are at the twenty-fourth birthday. The next cycle of twelve years is for the mastery of the Christic Light and the Buddhic Light. In these twelve years we have the opportunity to become the Christ and the Buddha. At age thirty-three, Jesus manifested the victory of the Christ consciousness and earned his ascension. At age thirty-six, Siddhartha attained enlightenment. We have the opportunity to do likewise.

Now if all follows like clockwork and all we outpicture throughout our lives are the God-qualities of the twelve hierarchies, of course we ascend. That is the spiral of the ascension that you weave with the threefold flame in each of the four quadrants. The threefold flame becomes the fire in the center of the base of the pyramid that begins to turn as a spiral when you are nigh your ascension. It envelops your form, your four lower bodies, and you return to the heart of the Father-Mother God.

Jesus came into embodiment with 93 percent of his karma balanced. As he went through the cycles of his clock during the years from his birth to the age of twelve, he received from his Causal Body only increments of the twelve flames of God—of God-power, God-love, God-mastery, God-control, God-obedience, God-wisdom, God-harmony, God-gratitude, God-justice, God-reality, God-vision and God-victory. As the Avatar of the age, however, he was required to balance planetary karma even while increasing the sphere of the Christ consciousness during these first twelve years.

At the age of twelve, he was given the opportunity to balance personal as well as planetary karma and to begin the initiations for Christhood. His acceptance of this responsibility even when it conflicted with family obligations is evident in his statement to his parents when they found him discoursing with the doctors in the temple, "Wist ye not that I must be about my father's business?"[23]

During the next eighteen years—one and a half cycles round the clock—he prepared for his three-year mission, both in and out of the retreats of the Great White Brotherhood in the Near and Far East. Each line was a major initiation under Lord Maitreya, who was his guru and who put him in contact with the Cosmic Christ. With each increment he was fortifying himself with the God flames of the Solar Hierarchies for the three-year ministry that culminated in his crucifixion, his resurrection and the demonstration of the ascension.

If we come into embodiment with karma and yet qualify God's energy and the returning energy of our karma with the flames of God, we have the opportunity to consume that karma by invocation to the sacred fire and by the momentum of Light in our Causal Body, and to manifest considerable attainment in the Christ consciousness by our thirty-third birthday. This is the year that we enter our divine mission: we go forth with our ministry able to deliver the Teachings of the Ascended Masters to the world, to serve the souls involved in the karma of our mandala of life.

The next three-year mission then culminates in the fulfillment of the power of the three-times-twelve. Three times going forth in the cycles of the Cosmic Clock brings us to the age of thirty-six and the Buddhic initiation.

The Cycle of the Months

In addition to this yearly cycle, the clock also unfolds month by month. Your year begins on the day of your birth. New Year's Day might be the beginning of the year for the planet, but for you as your own microcosm, your year begins on your birthday. The one o'clock line is the same day of the next calendar month. Then simply continue around the clock in this way for all the remaining lines.

For instance, if your birthday is June 5, June 5 is on the 12 o'clock line, July 5 on the 1 o'clock line, August 5 on the 2 o'clock line, and so on (see Figure 23). This will tell you, month by month, how your personal initiations fall under the Twelve Hierarchies of the Sun.

The day of your birthday is the day when you start your initiations under the Hierarchy of Capricorn—the 12 o'clock line. Three months later to the day (e.g., September 5), on the 3 o'clock line, you will be initiated under the Hierarchy of Aries, and for one month you will have the initiations of God-control.

Six months after your birthday to the day (e.g., December 5), you will have the testing of the Hierarchy of Cancer, the testing of the Mother flame, the testing of your harmony; you will have the testing of the flow of water in the emotions. Nine months after your birthday to the day (e.g., March 5), on

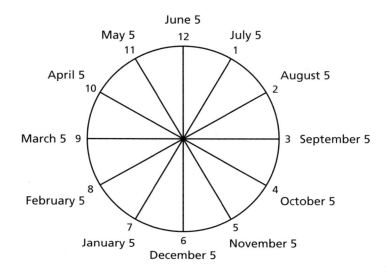

Figure 23 Chart of Months

This example shows the chart for someone born on June 5.

the 9 o'clock line, you will have the test of the hierarchy of Libra.

Therefore, for your yearly cycle, you are on the line of the Hierarchy for that year according to your age, and within that year you will walk through the Twelve Hierarchies month by month. For example, if you are twenty-six, you are on the 2 o'clock line of Pisces for your year; but on your birthday, you start the first month of that year under the Hierarchy of Capricorn. (Remember, all cycles begin in Capricorn.) It is like two dials on a meter that measures electricity—one dial is for the yearly cycle and one dial is for the monthly cycle.

When you are in your Capricorn month, you can anticipate that from your Causal Body will descend your attainment of God-power. You have God-power in that great sphere of Light, the Sun behind the sun. It is a momentum that you stored in previous initiations under that Hierarchy. You have momentums of God-love, God-mastery, God-control, and so on, and when the corresponding month comes, it's like the opening of the door of the Causal Body. The Light of your good karma comes down. At the same time, the negative karma on the same line rises out of the electronic belt. Therefore, every month of your life you can anticipate exactly what kind of energy of your personal karma will be up for transmutation.

The Conception of a Child

A key time to be aware of these cycles is in the conception and birth of a child. Let us consider now the plotting of the chart of a lifestream from the moment of conception.

The conception of the child, or the birth of the ego, occurs at the 3 o'clock line after the soul has been examined by the Lords of Karma and assigned to another round in the world of form. Since the etheric body is carried over from one embodiment to the next, it is intact at the moment of conception; thus we begin our chart at the 3 o'clock line rather than the 12. The mental, emotional and physical bodies being formed during the period of its confinement within the womb, the birth of the child occurs at the 12 o'clock line after nine months of gestation.

It is the solemn responsibility of the parents to cooperate with the Solar Lords in anchoring the divine pattern in the four lower bodies of the child. The following keys will assist in this work:

(1) During the first three months of gestation, the mental body is being formed (note the dominance of the head of the fetus). The vehicle for balance of the Christ Mind is developed through the blue, pink and yellow plumes and the qualities of God-control, God-obedience and God-wisdom with the

assistance of the Hierarchies assigned to the 3, 4 and 5 o'clock lines. This, the first phase of prenatal development, is under the Lords of Illumination (those God-free Beings who serve the Christ through the flame of wisdom).

(2) During the second three-month period, the accent is on the development of the emotional body. The balance of the heart flame is achieved through the blue, pink and yellow plumes as they appear on the 6, 7 and 8 o'clock lines as the qualities of God-harmony, God-gratitude and God-justice. During this cycle, the soul begins to identify with the form, and the auras of mother and child are as one luminous orb. This second phase of prenatal development is under the Lords of Adoration (those God-free Beings who serve the Christ through the flame of love).

(3) During the third three-month period, the physical form comes into greater prominence. The balance of the masculine and feminine polarities of the Godhead are anchored within the delicate frame as the Christ child prepares to emerge from the state of involution to begin his evolution in the world of form. The blue, pink and yellow plumes enfold his consciousness and body temple with the power of God-reality, God-vision and God-victory. This final phase of prenatal development is under the Lords of Action (those God-free Beings who serve the Christ through the flame of power).

(4) During the three months preceding conception (or whenever parents are hoping to conceive a child) and the three months after birth, special attention should be given to the restoration of the Edenic image within the etheric body of the child, which is designed to mirror the perfection of God.

The qualities of God-power, God-love and God-mastery, manifesting as the blue, pink and yellow plumes on the 12, 1 and 2 o'clock lines, focus the pure radiance of the Christ that resurrects the divine blueprint of life for the incoming child.

The three-month periods before conception and after birth are under the Hierarchies of Purification (those God-free Beings who serve the Christ through the flames of purity, freedom and Truth).

During the first three months of the life of the child, the memory of past lives is most vivid, for he is passing through his etheric tests. It is during these three months that the child must orient himself to his new surroundings. By the end of the third month, after he has passed through the memories of the past, he begins to identify with the line of his birth year or birthday. At that time he begins his mental development, and his memory of the past begins to recede.

Since babies do not talk, they cannot tell us of their memories of the past, but we personally have observed children who during the first three months of their post-natal development have looked for and been very much involved with individuals that they have known in the past. At this time their memories of the past are most vivid. Some bring back the memory of their experience in higher octaves and schools of Light; others who have reembodied very quickly may be more aware of their immediate past life than of higher octaves.

It is important for parents to give special attention to the purification of the etheric body during the formative period of the child, for the following reasons: (1) the etheric body contains the records of all past embodiments, which eventually will have to be worked out as karma through the mental, emotional and physical bodies; and (2) the amount of Light that can manifest in these three lower vehicles may be limited by the accumulation of human effluvia in the etheric body. This purification is best accomplished through the use of decrees to the white flame of purity, the violet flame of transmutation (including purple) and the green flame of healing.

Throughout the pregnancy, parents may also give decrees

to the blue, pink and yellow rays, adding the following inserts in the preamble: (1) After addressing their own God Presence, add "mighty I AM Presence and Holy Christ Self of the incoming child," and (2) at the close of the preamble, add "I decree for the incoming child, all incoming children, their parents and teachers." Throughout the decree, parents may substitute either the pronouns "him" and "his" or "them" and "theirs" for "us" and "our," so that the decree may apply to their child (when a more concentrated service is being given for his specific evolution) or to all incoming children collectively.

Bearing in mind that during each of the three cycles of the nine months of gestation the incoming child will be coming to grips with phases of his own misqualified energy indicated on the lines of the clock, parents may assist the child greatly by invoking the violet fire generously on his behalf. For example, during the first month (3 o'clock line), they may make the following invocation at the end of the preamble of each violet flame decree:

"I decree for the transmutation of all past momentums of conceit, deceit and ego manifest as mental arrogance, together with the cause, effect, record and memory of all misqualified substance lodged at the 3 o'clock line of the incoming child. In the name of the Christ, I claim that energy repolarized for the victory of the Light and the manifestation of his God-control!"

A similar invocation may be made each month with the appropriate inserts taken from the "Round the Clock Protection" decree (see page 166).

Parents who understand their role as representatives of Alpha and Omega, of the Father-Mother God, will see the nine-month period in which the soul's lower vehicles are being readied for the mission of an entire lifetime as the cosmic moment that will pave the way for him to take his God-dominion over the earth—including his personal karma. The Twelve Hierarchies of the Sun stand ready to give each soul the opportunity to attain self-mastery over every aspect of human creation. Therefore, each day the parents may assist in this process by invoking on behalf of the child the transmutation of the twelve categories of human creation by giving the "Round the Clock Protection" decree.

Mastering Your Cycles

By following the cycles of self-mastery as they evolve each year and month under the Solar Hierarchies, disciples can prepare themselves for each sacrifice of human creation that may be required for their victory. By studying the charts, they will be mindful of the categories of human effluvia that are "up" for transmutation both within themselves and on a planetary scale. This means that that section of the electronic belt or the subconscious is open—like an open door. Patterns will flow through the mind, perhaps not the total experience, but the tip of the iceberg of the experience.

For example, you may have been involved in condemning someone in a previous life. All of a sudden, in the first month of your birthday cycle, you will meet a person who will begin to condemn you. You may say to yourself, "What have I done? Why is this person condemning me? I haven't done anything wrong. I haven't done anything to this person. This is unjust!"

You may make this arc to Virgo, the earth sign, and get a sense of injustice about this terrible condemnation that is coming down upon you, and then arc over to Taurus, another earth sign, and become very rebellious against this person. You say, "I won't stand for this injustice," and you rebel against this condemnation. When you do this, you are getting involved in human qualities and reacting against an opportunity to balance life.

Karma is exact and it is exacting. When you have people condemning you, it is a perversion of the light of Capricorn and of God-power. Depersonalize it immediately. It doesn't matter if you did it or if they did it. You impersonalize the energy and you put it into the flame. Withdraw from the person. Bless this one who has been the carrier of the message of your own karma. Go home and take out your violet flame decree and invoke that flame.

You may say, "In the name of Jesus the Christ, I call to my own I AM God Presence, to Almighty God, to release the Light of the violet flame and the pure energies of Saint Germain to transmute this condemnation into God-power. I call for that energy to be freed in the name of the Father, the Mother, the Son, and the Holy Spirit." And then give fifteen minutes or a half hour of decrees for in the violet flame, consciously directing the flame to this person, calling on the law of forgiveness for this person and calling upon the law of forgiveness for yourself.

It really doesn't matter who started the action of this karma. The point is to stop it. You want to stop it, cut it off right now. We call this arresting the spiral.

Karma moves in spirals. You don't want to allow that energy to keep on cycling through your consciousness. You want to put an end to it. Whether it's yours or anybody else's, you don't want to live in that environment. You don't want to live in that consciousness. There is only one way to get rid of it permanently, and that is to put it into the flame of the Holy Spirit. Put it into the sacred fire. Pass the violet flame through it. Become detached.

This is the value of nonattachment. We get so attached to the fact that somebody is condemning us. The key is to separate the person from the condemnation. Put the flame through the condemnation, cut the individual free who has been victimized by this vibration, and behold, you may find a new individual, a Christed one standing before you. You may make a new friend out of an old enemy just by disengaging the perversion from the God-quality.

When we do this on each line of the clock, we can look forward with joyous anticipation to each opportunity for soul advancement that may be won through the ritual of adornment—the sweet surrender of the self to God as a lover to the Beloved, giving his all and receiving All in return.

Round the Clock Protection

Two of the requirements for the ascension—the alignment of the four lower bodies and the balanced expansion of the threefold flame—can be greatly enhanced through the use of decree patterns on the electronic belt. The "Round the Clock Protection" decree provides a systematic pattern for this purpose.

The decree may be given in any of the following four ways: (1) following the preamble, give sections A, B and C straight through, ending with the closing; (2) give the decree twelve times, using one insert each time from sections A, B and C, beginning with number 12; (3) give the trines on lines 12, 4, 8; 1, 5, 9; 2, 6, 10; 3, 7, 11, in sections A, B, and C; or (4) give the crosses on lines 12, 3, 6, 9; 1, 4, 7, 10; 2, 5, 8, 11, in sections A, B and C.

While giving these decree patterns, the visualization of the balanced threefold flame should be held in consciousness as the matrix for one's self-mastery over the elements and over their perversion in the four lower bodies: this can only be accomplished by the power of the Christ.

Round the Clock Protection

In the name of the beloved mighty victorious Presence of God, I AM in me, Holy Christ Selves of all mankind, all great powers and legions of Light:

In the name of my mighty I AM Presence, I lovingly surrender all substance on all lines of my clock and I demand and command in the name of the Christ that every single cycle of every single cell and atom within my form that is not outpicturing the perfect cycles of the Christ consciousness is now dissolved, is now arrested and turned back by the authority of my God Presence. This which I call forth for myself, I call forth for all mankind and the planetary body. And I call for the victory of the Light of the sun in _____ and the moon in _____.

A (12) Beloved Great Divine Director and the Seven Archangels,
  (1) Beloved Saint Germain and the angelic hosts of Light,
  (2) Beloved Jesus and the great hosts of Ascended Masters,
  (3) Beloved Helios and the Great Central Sun Magnet,
  (4) Beloved God Obedience and the Seven Mighty Elohim,
  (5) Beloved El Morya and the legions of Mercury,
  (6) Beloved Serapis Bey and the great Seraphim and Cherubim,
  (7) Beloved Goddess of Liberty and the Lords of Karma,
  (8) Beloved Lord Lanto and the Lords of Wisdom,
  (9) Beloved Mighty Victory and the Lords of Individuality,
 (10) Beloved Mighty Cyclopea and the Lords of Form,
 (11) Beloved Lord Maitreya and the Lords of Mind,

beloved Lanello, the entire Spirit of the Great White Brotherhood and the World Mother, elemental life—fire, air, water, and earth! I decree:

Seize, bind, and lock! Seize, bind, and lock! Seize, bind,

and lock!

B (12) all revolving of criticism, condemnation and judgment, etheric calcification, black magic and all moon substance*
- (1) all revolving of hatred and mild dislike, hardness of heart, superstition, etheric perversions, paralysis, witchcraft and all moon substance
- (2) all revolving of doubt and fear, human questioning and records of death, etheric illusion, hypnosis and all moon substance
- (3) all mental patterns of conceit, deceit, ego and mental arrogance, and all moon substance
- (4) all mental patterns of disobedience, stubbornness, defiance of the Law, mental rebellion and all moon substance
- (5) all mental patterns of envy, jealousy, ignorance of the Law, spiritual blindness, mental density and retardation, and all moon substance
- (6) all feelings of self-pity, self-justification and indecision, emotional instability, all misuses of the sacred fire and perversions of the Mother flame, and all moon substance
- (7) all feelings of ingratitude and thoughtlessness, spiritual blindness, emotional density and retardation, and all moon substance
- (8) all feelings of frustration, anxiety and injustice, emotional tyranny and all moon substance

---

* The moon governs the astral, or water, body. In the perfection of cosmic astrology, the satellites of the planets are intended to be reflectors of the pure feelings of the lifewaves of the planet. As soon as mankind began to misqualify their feelings, the moon began to amplify this energy. Therefore, the moon no longer reflects the pure Light of the sun; instead, the light of the moon is the reflection of man's misuses of solar energy. "Moon substance" is a term used to describe energy that has been misqualified under the influence of the moon.

(9) all vibrations of dishonesty, intrigue, treachery, physical self-preservation and idolatry, and all moon substance
(10) all vibrations of selfishness, self-love, physical self-infatuation and idolatry, and all moon substance
(11) all vibrations of resentment and revenge, physical self-retaliation and idolatry, and all moon substance

back to my first embodiment in Mater, and all that is not of the Light into Mighty Astrea's cosmic circle and sword of blue flame of a thousand suns, and lock your cosmic circles and swords of blue flame of thousands of suns from the Great Central Sun and blaze megatons of cosmic Light, blue-lightning rays and violet fire in, through, and around all that opposes or attempts to interfere with the fulfillment of

C(12) my God-power and my divine plan fulfilled in all cycles
  (1) my God-love and my divine plan fulfilled in all cycles
  (2) my God-mastery and my divine plan fulfilled in all cycles
  (3) my God-control and my divine plan fulfilled in all cycles
  (4) my God-obedience and my divine plan fulfilled in all cycles
  (5) my God-wisdom and my divine plan fulfilled in all cycles
  (6) my God-harmony and supply and my divine plan fulfilled in all cycles
  (7) my God-gratitude and my divine plan fulfilled in all cycles
  (8) my God-justice and my divine plan fulfilled in all cycles
  (9) my God-reality and my divine plan fulfilled in all

cycles
(10) my God-vision and my divine plan fulfilled in all cycles
(11) my God-victory and my divine plan fulfilled in all cycles

and my victory in the Light this day and forever!

And in full faith I consciously accept this manifest, manifest, manifest (3x) right here and now with full power, eternally sustained, all-powerfully active, ever expanding and world enfolding until all are wholly ascended in the Light and free! Beloved I AM, beloved I AM, beloved I AM!

The material in this section provides an introduction to the principles of the Cosmic Clock. This science of the law of cycles has many applications in life. It is one of the key teachings that the Ascended Masters have given to help us anticipate and pass the tests of life on the spiritual path. Additional information about the clock and its many applications may be found in Elizabeth Clare Prophet, *Predict Your Future: Understand the Cycles of the Cosmic Clock*.

SECTION THREE

The Dance of the Hours

How many cycles it will take before individual man is perfected can only be determined by his own application. Each day and each hour is a key to his salvation if he will only utilize the precious moments as flames of God that are for his self-realization, for his elevation to the place where conscious reunion with the Son of God takes place. Lord Maitreya, who is known as the Great Initiator, once made the statement:

"Progress individually and collectively shall move in man by the rhythmic dance of directed hours!... The idea that each man is directly connected with God and that a beautiful stream of pure energy is flowing into him hourly for his use, while not new, is always new to contemplate.

"Unfortunately, most individuals do not realize that they are the custodians of this great energy and that they are the receivers and directors of its flow. Nevertheless, this precious cosmic energy, which is incoming through their lifestreams every minute and hour, flows out from them as thought and feeling.

"It is true that there are times when nothing is actually being impressed upon the radiation of the God-power that pours through an individual. It is as though an interval of rest were being sent forth (comparable to the rest symbol in a measure of music). However, the important fact for men to remember is that they *are* qualifiers and that each hour of the day they are qualifying this holy stream of energy.

"The negative qualities, which far too frequently are permitted to express in life, take a tremendous toll upon the four lower bodies of the lifestream who initiates them. I refer here to the vibratory actions of hate and hate creations, of discord and ill feelings—feelings of frustration and fear concerning the individual and his relationship to the cosmos and feelings of insecurity. All of these take their toll.

"The hobgoblins of human mischief, released from the Pandora's box of men's thoughts and feelings, must be resisted, for although they abide in the atmosphere of earth they are not the pure creation of God but entirely human in origin. These must be transmuted, and transmutation must come about as much through right qualification as through the power of the God flame itself.

"Discrimination, then, rests within the duty and province of each individual to pause hourly to consider for himself just what qualities he wishes to send forth into the universe. He must choose either the qualities of his heavenly Father or the qualities of men with all of their imperfections. 'Choose you this day whom ye will serve.'"[1]

We have included with this chapter a chart showing the "rhythmic dance of directed hours." It is based on the twenty-four-hour cycle of the individual manifestation of the threefold flame (see Figure 24, page 172).[2]

If the disciple will consider the fact that each hour is a

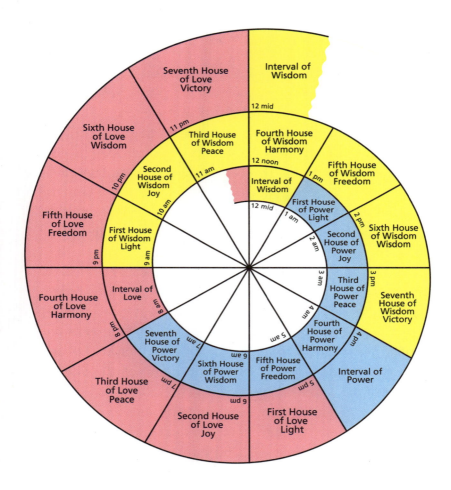

Figure 24 The Attainment of the Christ Consciousness through the Mastery of the Hours

flaming opportunity to don the Christ consciousness and to qualify God's energy with an aspect of his being, as Maitreya explained, he will "pick up" the flame of the hour and he will consciously qualify it with such attributes of God-dominion as are indicated on the chart.

At the end of the hour, he will lay down the flame as though it were the petal of a flower, and he will tenderly pick up each succeeding flame, drawing it to his heart and cherishing it as an immortelle from the garden of God's consciousness.

The "Dance of the Hours" from *La Gioconda* by Ponchielli and "Barcarolle" from *Tales of Hoffman* by J. Offenbach may be used as meditations for establishing the rhythmic flow of the flames of God throughout the twenty-four-hour cycle.

One can hear the rhythm of the flame in the sound of the flutes as the orchestra expands the motif of the "Dance of the Hours." And the 6/8 time of "Barcarolle" gives us the lilting feeling of the waltz of the threefold flame. The swelling of the music carries the momentum of Light that increases as we invoke the flames of God each hour.

The elementals join in the ballet and in the waltz, for they, too, are flames of God; and they know that when mankind is perfected, they, too, will receive the gift of immortality. Those who tune in to the "dance of the hours" should be prepared to entertain not only "angels unawares"[3] but also "elementals unawares."

All of the beings of nature sing and dance and work and play to the ritual of the threefold flame, and thus we can readily see that the "rhythmic dance of directed hours" is the key to the harmonious cooperation of the kingdoms of angels, elementals and men: the angels contribute the love ray, the elementals the power ray, and Christed man the wisdom ray.

The Cycles of the Day

The day begins with an "interval of rest," as Maitreya put it, charged with the illumination of the "midnight sun." From 1 AM to 8 AM the four lower bodies of man are recharged with the flame of the will of God. At 1 AM the Light of power is released; at 2 AM the joy of power; at 3 AM the peace of power; at 4 AM the harmony of power; at 5 AM the freedom of power; at 6 AM the wisdom of power; and at 7 AM the victory of power.

At 8 AM his consciousness "changes gears," so to speak, in an "interval of rest" qualified by the love ray as he prepares to go forth to manifest the Mind of God in his day's calling.

At 9 AM he receives the influx of the Light of illumination; at 10 AM the joy of illumination; at 11 AM the peace of illumination; at 12 noon the harmony of illumination; at 1 PM the freedom of illumination; at 2 PM the wisdom of illumination; and at 3 PM the victory of illumination.

At 4 PM another "interval of rest," this time of the power ray, enables him to recharge and to reorder his energies in preparation for the release of God's love at eventide.

At 5 PM the adoration of his heart flame swells with the incoming tide of the Light of love. At 6 PM he basks in the joy of love; at 7 PM in the peace of love; at 8 PM in the harmony of love; at 9 PM in the freedom of love; at 10 PM in the wisdom of love; at 11 PM in the victory of love.

At midnight, during the interval of illumination, his higher bodies go forth to take instruction in the temples of Light while the physical form rests secure in the faith that a new day will dawn with another opportunity to express God's hope and his charity. Thus is the soul bidden by God to go forth to balance the threefold flame in the rhythmic dance of the hours and to attain thereby the consciousness of the Christ.

SECTION FOUR

The Teachings of Jesus on the Twelve Lines of the Clock

IT IS THE POWER OF THE SPOKEN Word that is opposed by the defenses of the human ego that manifest on each of the twelve lines of the electronic belt. The power of the spoken Word comes forth from the mighty I AM Presence in the center of the Causal Body—the sphere being the symbol of the mouth of God—and it is made relevant to the human consciousness through the Mind of Christ. Just as there is a fulcrum of compensation at the level of the human ego, so there is a fulcrum of compensation at the level of the Christ, whose consciousness is the crossroads of the Divine in manifestation (in manifest action).

By examining the chart of the Tree of Life (page 110), we can see how the qualities of God work together in man to bring about the manifestation of the Christ through the four lower bodies. The Sons of God who have been sent to teach mankind the Way have always taught in terms of the twelve cycles of God-realization that unfold the opportunities for initiation that are open to the evolving consciousness of man. These opportunities, when fulfilled, bring out in the individual his complete God-identity.

It would be well for us to examine the simple Teachings of one of these Avatars. Having overcome the world and all things in it, he was and is qualified to teach the mystery of the sacred fire as it spirals through the four lower bodies of man, manifesting the threefold flame in perfect balanced action on the twelve lines of man's individualization.

Jesus of Galilee selected twelve disciples, each of whom had the assignment of attaining self-mastery over one of the twelve lines of human creation.* This mastery was intended to be an atonement for all mankind—not that the disciples' or any man's works should be the salvation of another, but that their actions might serve as a pledge to the Deity that if twelve should overcome and thereby set the example for the age, so many could do likewise after them.

To the Christ and to all who are anointed to that office, standing in the center of the clock at the fulcrum of compensation, is given the responsibility for drawing enough of the Divine Trinity to compensate for the entire accumulation of the world's karma. His Light must hold the balance for the collective manifestation of mankind's misqualified energies, until one by one they themselves are able to meet the challenge of the Word: "Take dominion over the earth."[1]

He who holds the office of the Christ on behalf of his brethren (until they themselves rise to that initiation) must face

---

* The twelve apostles are placed on the lines of the Twelve Hierarchies in the following order, starting with the 12 o'clock line: Andrew, Philip, Thomas, Peter, Bartholomew, Matthew, James the Greater, Jude, James the Less, John, Judas/Matthias and Simon. For more information about the apostles and their positioning on these lines, see the fourth book of this series, *The Path of Brotherhood*, pp. 151–74.

the multitudes and the energies of the carnal mind that are directed against the manifestation of the Light of the Divine Manchild on all of the lines of the clock. The requirement of his disciples is that they each hold the balance for only one of the twelve lines. It is, therefore, in his service of holding the balance for the evolutions of a planet that the Christ—whose office has been held by Jesus for the last two thousand years—is the Saviour and the hope of the world.

The Power of the Spoken Word Reinforced by the Beatitudes

Let us then review the account in the fifth chapter of Matthew of the Master Jesus' instruction on the twelve phases of human creation. The observations of the scribe are significant.

"And seeing the multitudes, he went up into a mountain and when he was set, his disciples came unto him: And he opened his mouth and taught them, saying,…"

"Seeing the multitudes," Jesus was completely aware of the categories of human creation, of the belief in an existence apart from God and of separation from Oneness. Those who had eaten of the fruit of the tree of the knowledge of good and evil, whose consciousness was dual, would not be able to understand his teaching. Therefore, he retreated to the mountain, to the summit of his Being, symbolizing the I AM Presence; and when he was set in the consciousness of his God-Self, in the center of the Sun, he called his disciples and appointed them representatives of the Twelve Hierarchies of the Sun.

To each one he gave the commission to overcome the world, and he explained in the Beatitudes how the sense of the beautiful, together with the attitude of be-ness—the attitude of being one with God—would enable him to refute the testimony of the material senses and to acknowledge the Christ in man each step of the way. This acknowledgment of the Christ would enable the disciples to heal and to perform the feats of alchemy that Jesus was to demonstrate before them at the conclusion of his Sermon on the Mount and throughout his ministry.

Being a Messenger of God, he opened his mouth and the Word of God came forth saying:

1. Blessed are the poor in spirit: for theirs is the kingdom of heaven.

This be-attitude challenges man's misqualified energy lodged at the 1 o'clock line. The poor in spirit are those who acknowledge their spiritual need. They are ready to surrender the self and to be disciplined by the love of the Christ, whose first precept makes clear that the sense of duality must go down before the understanding of the allness of God and the Oneness of Life.

It is freedom from personality and personal attachment, from the self juxtaposed against other selves, that gives man his freedom from hatred and mild dislike. In the allness of God, there can be no object for hatred or dislike, but only God aware of himself in manifestation in man—God loving himself in man, and man loving himself through God. This is the first step of discipleship. Having clothed himself with the spiritual armour of Oneness, man goes forth to conquer all of the other lies of duality.

2. Blessed are they that mourn: for they shall be comforted.

This is the be-attitude that overcomes the world of human creation that manifests at the 2 o'clock line. The records of death are the records of man's involvement in mortality, his belief that he is a mortal moving among other mortals. In this frame of mind, he questions, he doubts and he fears. Only the comfort of the risen Christ and his Reality, outlined as the image of immortal Life, can give him his freedom from the illusions of death.

Here the comforting Truth that makes man free is the realization that all human suffering, which is the direct result of man's identification with mortality, can be overcome through the understanding that man is now and always the beloved son of God, that he is alchemically wed to his God-Presence through the Christ and the crystal cord—the blessed tie that binds the soul to her Maker. The soul's atonement for all mortal sin, whereby the individual attains his at-one-ment with God, takes place as he pierces the illusion of duality with the sword of Truth, invokes the Flame of Life and rejoices in the resurrection of his true identity.

3. Blessed are the meek; for they shall inherit the earth.

The meek are those who have attained such an awareness of God and of the Divine Ego that they no longer have any need to defend the human ego or to resist those egos that still consider themselves to be outside of the consciousness of God. To the belligerent sense of the carnal mind, this meekness appears as cowardice, servility or weakness of character; but to those who are One in the Spirit of God, meekness is the gentleness that David experienced when he said, "Thy gentleness hath made me great."[2] Meekness is that spiritual quality that overcomes the intellectual arrogance that feels the need to affirm its own self-sufficiency by proclaiming, "I am the law." Meekness is the sublime humility of the Christ who kneels before the Almighty and inherits the earth by his submission to the will of God.

The earth that he inherits is the substance misqualified in

the electronic belt that he has willingly placed upon the altar of the sacred fire. There it is purified and then returned to him for his use in building the kingdom and in service to God and man. Thus having surrendered his all to God, God surrenders unto him His All; and the Christ declares, "All power is given unto me in heaven and in earth."[3]

Those who are truly humble are qualified to rule the earth as divine stewards of the full potential of the Godhead. Humility is the quiet assurance of Oneness that overcomes the pride of human personalities and their need to maintain an existence separate from the Body of God. True humility is the mark of the spiritual devotee who knows that the wholeness of the Christ can never be offended by the incompleteness of the human ego.

4. Blessed are they which do hunger and thirst after righteousness, for they shall be filled.

The deep desire to know and to be the Law of God in action counteracts the resistance of human egos to the Divine Ego that manifests at the 4 o'clock line as disobedience, stubbornness and defiance of the Law.

After the prodigal son has pursued the temptations of the world, after he has tasted the fruits of rebellion, he comes to the place where he is no longer satisfied with the husks of human consciousness.[4] He is hungry for the fruits of the Spirit, he is tired of the intellectual arguments that entertain the mortal consciousness for a time, and he yearns to hear the sweet words of righteousness—of the "right use" of the Laws of God—gentle Truths that are taught by the Mother of the World. He yearns for the succor of "Home," he longs to be filled. And so the desire for God creates a vacuum in man's consciousness that God is obliged to fill with the flame of love that begets obedience.

The Christ is victorious in the mind of man when that mind is willing to be tutored by the heart, and He shall be victorious in the world order when the nations respond to the Laws that God has written "in their inward parts."[5] These Laws are the foundation of God-government in heaven and on earth.

With Christ as the chief cornerstone, the law of order that prevails in the City of God (the City Foursquare) is destined to be lowered into manifestation in the cities of men.[6] Then the ruling of the nations by the rod of iron[7] will hail the victory of the Christ in every man, woman and child. No longer subject to the tyranny of unbridled egos, all shall be governed by the Light from within that will unite the nations—not by force but by love—to the will of the Great Architect and his blueprint for the Golden Age. Then, obedience to the Laws of God will be seen as the open door to the beauty of the Deity made manifest in the energy patterns invoked by the Sons and Daughters of the Flame. Because the beauty of their creations shall be wedded to the archetypal patterns of the Law, they shall not perish from the earth but shall have the seal of immortality.

5. Blessed are the merciful, for they shall obtain mercy.

This beatitude is a restatement of the Golden Rule, "Do unto others as you would have them do unto you."[8]

The Christ expresses the quality of mercy that is both compassionate and benevolent[9] toward a suffering humanity, i.e., toward those who suffer because they have not yet mastered the world of their own human creation. This he is able to do because his own innate sense of well-being—the result of his total identification with God—gives him an awareness of the Truth of his own Reality. And he knows that what is true about himself holds true for every other part of Life.

In this realization of every man's completeness in his I AM Presence, the Christ is illuminated to the point where he need not be envious or jealous of the attainment of another, of his talents and blessings received from God, or even of his human situation; neither will he take advantage of his brethren. For he knows that what one part of God has experienced or attained, all other parts of God may experience and attain. Indeed, God is universally available to his creation.

The penalties for one's ignorance of the Golden Rule are the same whether such ignorance stems from a lack of understanding or from a more willful ignoring of the Law. These penalties can only be atoned for through a higher understanding of the Mind that framed the universe and its unerring Laws. For this Mind imparts to the creation a sense of wellbeing, of having been created in the Image and Likeness of God; and this Image, which is radiantly manifest in the whitefire core of every atom, structures in man an intuitive merciful awareness of cosmic law. Mercy, expressed as the Golden Rule, is the open door to wisdom: He who has taken wise dominion over his energies by a proper application of the Laws of God is found holding compassionate reverence for Life in all of its manifestations. "Be ye therefore wise as serpents and harmless (merciful) as doves."[10]

6. Blessed are the pure in heart, for they shall see God.

Whereas the consciousness that is based on the knowledge of good and evil conceives of itself as separate from the Creator—hence outside of his frame of reference—purity of heart invokes that singleness of vision that restores man to his rightful place: the Image Most Holy focused within the All-Seeing Eye of God. It is the sense of separation from the Allness of God that forces the synthetic image to justify its position and to feel sorry for itself, while the pull of the yin and yang of human consciousness keeps individuals in a constant turmoil of indecision.

Through harmony with the Christ, man enters into a powerful alliance with his Presence, who is the conqueror of all misqualified substance in the electronic belt. Devotion to God-harmony and faith in the abundant Life will ultimately raise man's consciousness back to the original conception of his wholeness in the sight of God. By guarding the unity of man's consciousness, the flames of God-harmony and abundance clear the way for the descent of the Holy Spirit, who performs the alchemical marriage between the lower self and the Higher Self, making of twain "one new man."

It is the magnet of God-harmony that draws to man the supply of every good and perfect thing, but harmony is never complete without total surrender. Therefore, let us remember that surrender of the self, with its sense of duality, through the purification of the heart is essential if the individual would apprehend the purity of the will of God and bring it into practical manifestation.

7. Blessed are the peacemakers; for they shall be called the children of God.

Those who can express gratitude for the manifestation of the Christ in themselves and in every other part of God are known as the peacemakers because they have risen to that consciousness of oneness where they perceive themselves as neither the accuser nor the accused. They emulate the Divine Mother, who sees the Christ in all of God's children and is unmoved by any activity that may be contrary to His nature. Therefore, the peacemakers are supremely qualified to carry the flame of God-gratitude—gratitude that is realized through the power of love, undivided and all-inclusive.

The peace that flows from a grateful heart is established in man through the trinity of the Christ flame, which consumes the veil that separates the lower self from the Higher Self. Paul referred to this peace that cometh from reunion with God when he said, "He is our peace who hath made both one and hath broken down the middle wall of partition between us ... for to make in him of twain one new man, so making peace."[11]

Through the realization of the Christ, "I and my Father are one,"[12] man conquers the sea of emotional substance that rages in his electronic belt. Christ, the beholder of the perfect concept of our divinity, overcame the world through the singleness of his vision. He who keeps his eye focused upon the Christ is also able to demonstrate the laws of alchemy. By acknowledging the power of love, he calms the sea, walks upon the waters and finds the peace that passeth understanding, a peace that glows from the soul immersed in God-gratitude for all that is.

8. Blessed are they which are persecuted for righteousness' sake, for theirs is the kingdom of heaven.

Jesus blessed the consciousness that willingly sacrifices the ego, revealing thereby a mystical awareness of its own ultimate Reality and reward. Such a consciousness is not plagued with feelings of frustration, anxiety and injustice on the 8 o'clock line, for it knows with absolute certainty that God-justice is the supreme arbiter of man's destiny.

In order to feel a sense of injustice, individuals must admit to an external and opposing force that resists their God-identity. This admission reveals that the basis of their consciousness is that of duality. In order to be persecuted, individuals must still be retaining a sense of ego. Total immersion in the oneness of the Christ affords man the knowledge of the Law of God, which states that there is no injustice anywhere in the universe.[13] The Laws of God are exact and exacting, and the working out of man's karma determines that as he sows, so shall he reap.[14]

Justice is the universal awareness of God's Laws in action, and it precludes the need to dominate the lives of others through emotional tyranny or any other form of hypnotic control. The idea that one has been wronged or that one has wronged another shows one's ignorance of the fact that in all things God is the doer. The only actions that the Christ acknowledges are those that are done by him, through him, and in him. All else is subject to transmutation. Through the flame of freedom, God wipes out our sense of injustice, and we see in place of the defender and the defendant the pure Son of God in whose oneness is found the true balance of Life.

Those who have wrongly used the power of God are cast down by the sword of Truth, by the power of the spoken Word that shatters the matrices of injustice and reestablishes the blueprint of "Thy kingdom come." To the observer this appears as the battle of Armageddon, but to the Christ it is simply the canceling out of the imperfect pattern by the penetration of his Light.

9. Ye are the light of the world. A city that is set on an hill cannot be hid. Neither do men light a candle, and put it under a bushel, but on a candlestick; and it giveth light unto all that are in the house.

This teaching from the Sermon on the Mount is directed to the ego consciousness that opposes the manifestation of God-reality through the machinations of intrigue and treachery. These are among the defense mechanisms that the ego employs to preserve the physical self as an idol ("I"-dol—the doll of the id) in place of the Higher Self, who alone has the right to proclaim "I AM Real!"

In this be-attitude Jesus is telling the disciples that there is never any need to resort to treachery or intrigue to defend the ego and to further its aims, for the Real Identity of man is the Light of the world. This Christed Self, who lives in all, can never be hid; furthermore, the realization of "who I AM" gives man the victory over the perversions of the ego. Only when man truly knows who he is can he summon the courage to proclaim the Truth of his identity: "I AM that I AM!" Thus, having invoked the Light of the threefold flame, he places it on a candlestick and holds it high to give Light unto all who dwell in the temple of God's Being.

As long as man conceives of himself as a sinner, he feels the need to hide his sins. But when he realizes that he is destined to become the fullness of the manifestation of the Christ, the beloved Son of God, he accepts the responsibility of being the Light of the world, and he vows to hold out that Light until all mankind are drawn into the consciousness of God-reality to walk the earth as kings and priests unto God.

10. Let your light so shine before men, that they may see your good works, and glorify your Father which is in heaven.

God-vision, singleness of purpose won through loving obedience to the Law, enables man to overcome the densities of selfishness and self-love that manifest on the 10 o'clock line as infatuation, not only with his own physical self, but also with the physical selves of others. The records of man's self-indulgences are based on his idolatrous sense of mortals moving and mingling their misqualified energies outside of the framework of the Oneness of God.

Jesus explains to those who would "decrease that He might increase"[15] that if a man do good works by the power of the Light of the Christ and give the glory to God, then all who behold his works will glorify the Father, which is in heaven, instead of giving unto him the glory that is his only to reflect.

The challenge of the All-Seeing Eye of God is met as one raises the attention from the lower self to the Higher Self both in himself and in others. This is what is known as holding the *immaculate concept;* it simply means that man now beholds man as the Image of God, perfect in His sight. As the disciple keeps his eye upon his God Presence, the human self disappears, even as Jesus' did from Bethany's hill.[16] In this beatitude men will gaze upward to perceive the Son of God ascending into a cloud of glory—the upward spiral of the ascension current that accelerates the momentum of the Real Man until he is no longer visible in the time-space dimension.

11. Think not that I am come to destroy the law, or the prophets: I am not come to destroy, but to fulfill. For verily I say unto you, Till heaven and earth pass, one jot or one tittle shall in no wise pass from the law, till all be fulfilled.

This beatitude teaches that in the consciousness of the Christ is the fulfillment of the Law. Jesus declares that the Law is above all human personality—even that personality falsely attributed to him by the Pharisees—and functions with exactitude, their human arguments notwithstanding. Standing in the doorway between time and eternity, the Son of God as the Initiator of man's victory sees to it that not one jot or one tittle of his creation shall escape the judgment of the Almighty.

The power of God-victory secured in the Law enables the disciple to overcome his momentums of resentment and revenge on the 11 o'clock line and heals any desire he might have to retaliate against himself or another part of Life. Revenge is a form of idolatry, for in order to take revenge, one must first conceive of the oppressor and the oppressed. Both are idols that are first raised by the ego and then cast down in order that it might retain its sense of importance.

Man's illumined obedience to the commandment "Thou

shalt have no other gods before me"[17] gives him everlasting victory over the idols that men raise out of the marshes of duality. It is the victorious understanding of the Laws of God that causes man out of his own free will to worship the one God and to exclaim, "Hear, O Israel:" (Hear, all that is Real) "The LORD our God is one LORD"[18] (the LORD our God is the LORD of all that is Real).

12. Ye have heard that it was said by them of old time, Thou shalt not kill; and whosoever shall kill shall be in danger of the judgment: but I say unto you, That whosoever is angry with his brother without a cause shall be in danger of the judgment; and whosoever shall say to his brother, Raca, shall be in danger of the council: but whosoever shall say, Thou fool, shall be in danger of hell fire.*

This commandment of the Christ reveals the dangers of the abuses of God-power through the revolving of etheric misqualifications. Just as criticism, condemnation and judgment may bring on depression, a sudden drop of energy levels, illness and even the untimely death of those against whom it is leveled, so the return cycle will surely bring the same to those who persistently engage in such practices.

"With what measure ye mete, it shall be measured to you again."[19] Here Jesus further amplifies his warning, "Judge not lest ye be judged,"[20] and he reveals the possibility of psychic murder through the projection of anger and condemnation. Those who engage in such cursings are in danger of receiving the recompense of their abuse of the fire element. To those who have misused the sacred fire, the destruction of their

---

* "Raca" (Aramaic *reka*, vain, empty, worthless): a Jewish expression of scorn or contempt. Matthew Henry interprets this as implying a sense of pride or superiority in the speaker. The word "fool" (Greek *moros,* foolish, impious, godless) could also be understood as "rebel" (Young's Literal Translation) or "renegade" (Jerusalem Bible). Henry interprets this accusation as deriving from hatred.

human creation by its purifying power appears not as a blessing but as "hell fire." Therefore, those who do not challenge by the power of the Christ the vestiges of 12 o'clock substance in themselves and in others may be burned when the fire comes in contact with their human creation.

Jesus devoted the remainder of the Sermon on the Mount to the matter of black magic, witchcraft and hypnosis, appearing on the 12, 1 and 2 o'clock lines, all of which deal with the perversions of the fire element.

One may study the remainder of the fifth chapter of Matthew with this in mind, taking special note that Jesus summed up his final admonishments on the mastery of human creation under two headings:

I. But let your communication be, Yea, yea; Nay, nay: for whatsoever is more than these cometh of evil.

Here the Master gives the law of affirming the Real Self and the good in all life and denying the synthetic image and all that proceeds from the consciousness of duality. Taking the flaming sword of Truth in hand, the disciple goes forth to conquer by cleaving asunder the Real from the unreal. If he can at all times keep his consciousness at the razor's edge, he will never again be fooled by the illusions of the world, and he will live forever in the calm and certain knowing of what is Truth.

II. Be ye therefore perfect, even as your Father which is in heaven is perfect.

Here Jesus states the law of correspondences: As Above, so below—God is omnipotent, omniscient and omnipresent. Even as the I AM Presence, who dwells forever in the Causal Body of man, is perfect, so the disciple may become perfect as he overcomes the temptations of the twelve lines of the electronic belt and transmutes the humanly misqualified substance that has formed deposits there throughout his many embodiments. Once and for all time, Jesus declares the present possibility of the perfectionment of man.

The remainder of his Sermon on the Mount, which is given in chapters six and seven of the book of Matthew, is devoted to a further clarification of the overcoming of the world and its effluvia outside of themselves. Jesus explains how the disciples must become qualified to meet this creation both in themselves and in others.

After he completed the setting forth of the law of overcoming, Jesus came down from the mountain—down from his attunement at the summit of Being—summoned by God to go into the world and demonstrate the Laws and principles that he had taught. Immediately, he healed the leper and the centurion's servant. The fever left the mother of Peter's wife at the touch of his hand. He rebuked the winds and the sea, and he cast out the devils in the country of the Gadarenes.

Seemingly miraculous demonstrations such as these continued throughout Jesus' entire three-year ministry. However, his miracles were not really miracles, but the divine manifestation of the Christ standing poised in the center of Being. At the fulcrum of compensation, he drew forth the Light of his own God Presence and Causal Body, which not only compensated for human creation wherever it was found but also completely transmuted it, together with its cause, effect, record and memory.

The Crucifixion

The initiation of the crucifixion is one through which every son and daughter of God must pass before they are found worthy for the initiation of the resurrection. The following commentary on Mark 15:1–39 explains how the steps of Jesus' passing through this initiation relate to the lines of the Cosmic Clock.

Verse 1 begins **"And straightway in the morning** [indicating the 9 o'clock line] **the chief priests held a consultation with the elders and scribes and the whole council, and bound Jesus, and carried him away, and delivered him to Pilate."** This is the treachery and intrigue, the deceit of the world that attempts to capture the Christ by the arguments, the logic of the carnal mind. The carnal mind, of course, cannot bind the Christ, and therefore it binds the human form, Jesus, because it too is self-deluded and it thinks that the vessel is the Flame because it is in the idolatrous state.

Verse 2 is the questioning of Pilate, who says, **"Art thou the King of the Jews?"** Jesus refuses to declare himself the King of the Jews and says merely, **"Thou sayest it."** While Pilate is calling him the King of the Jews, Jesus is not affirming it, he is not calling himself the King of the Jews. **"The chief priests accused him of many things; but he answered nothing. And Pilate asked him again, saying, Answerest thou nothing? behold how many things they witness against thee. But Jesus yet answered nothing; so that Pilate marvelled."**

Verses 2 to 5 illustrate the test of the 10 o'clock line, where the ego is given one last opportunity to preserve its identity through selfishness, self-love, idolatry and a perversion of the momentum of self-preservation that is in the Flame of Life itself. Jesus was without any ego. He could not be prodded into making any defense of himself because he knew that his self was his God Self. The test is a threefold flame to see if the ego will attempt to preserve itself through a perversion of the blue, the yellow and the pink plumes.

Verse 6 explains that it was customary at the feast of the Passover **"to release unto them a prisoner, whomsoever they desired." Here we see the test of the 11 o'clock line. The resentment, revenge and retaliation of the mass mind is directed against the Christ and not against the figure Barabbas, who is the personification of the sins of the people. Barabbas was a murderer and an insurrectionist, which shows the misuse of the energies of the 10-4 axis. Insurrection is the rebellion against the law on the 4 o'clock line. Murder is the culmination of the perversions of the pink plume on the 1, 4, 7 and 10. It is a total lack of ability to see the Christ in man, it is the epitome of idolatry, it is the killing of the Christ Self in oneself through the destruction of another.

The multitudes, with their mass consciousness, were affinitized to the electronic belt of Barabbas rather than to the Causal Body of the Christ. Because they had not become the Christ, they desired Barabbas. And so they cried aloud. It is written that Pilate knew that the chief priests had delivered Jesus to him because of their envy—of his Light and his Teaching and of his followers—and therefore he said to the crowd, **"Will ye that I release unto you the King of the Jews?... But the chief priests moved the people that he should rather release Barabbas unto them."**

It is the envy of the priests on the 5 o'clock line that precipitates the resentment and the revenge on the 11 o'clock line. And the priests used the mob as the focal point for the precipitation of their envy, which has turned to revenge. **"And Pilate answered and said unto them again, What will ye then that I shall do unto him whom ye call the King of the Jews? And they cried out again, Crucify him! Then Pilate said unto them, Why, what evil hath he done? And they cried out the more exceedingly, Crucify him!"**

And so Pilate, lacking the Christ momentum to reverse the tide of the resentment of people and wishing to content them, **"released Barabbas unto them and delivered Jesus, when he** had scourged him, to be crucified."

The judgment of the carnal mind, the hatred and even the fear and doubt of the Christ are evident in the great thronging and the great extent to which the mob went to put him down. The soldiers clothed him with purple, platted a crown of thorns and put it about his head. They saluted him mockingly, "Hail, King of the Jews!" They smote him on the head with a reed and spit upon him, and bowing their knees worshipped him. All of this is the perversion of the fire element, the fire of the Christ and the pattern of the Christ that is locked within the heart of the earth. They mocked him, **"they took off the purple from him, and put his own clothes on him, and led him out to crucify him."**

On the 2 o'clock line they compelled Simon a Cyrenian to bear his cross as they brought him to Golgotha, the place of the skull, which is the place of the ego at the 3 o'clock line. They gave him wine mingled with myrrh, which he received not. And thus at the third hour where the Christ is glorified and the ego goes down, he was crucified and **"they parted his garments, casting lots upon them, what every man should take."**

The name that the mob gave to the human consciousness of Jesus, which was all that they could see or acknowledge, was "the King of the Jews," and this is the position that they give to the ego in themselves. Jesus was crucified on the cross where Spirit descends to meet the plane of Matter. And in the center of that cross is the place where the ego dies and the Christ is born. This is the center of the clock.

The two thieves, the one on the right and the one on the left, represent the 3 and 9 o'clock lines, which are also crucified with the Christ—these symbolizing the heart chakra. The heart that is impure and wrongly motivated through pride is crucified at the same time as the Christ is being born in the center. And thus the scripture was fulfilled that he was numbered with the transgressors[21]—that is in the sight of the world. This also shows that no matter what his station in life, every man must come to the place where the ego must go down and the Christ is born.

The malefactors were not prepared to become the Christ, they were not prepared for the crucifixion, and therefore they died upon the cross. But it was in the power and in the hand of the Son of God to raise them up, and this he did. The thief who acknowledged him as the Son of God, to him he promised that he would be with him that day in paradise. Thus, by a simple affirmation of the Christ identity and a surrender of the ego, man can attain to the Christ consciousness even at the very last hour. Those who deny the Christ, then, will go down, and to them death is real.

Then came the final temptation given to Jesus. After he was on the cross **"they railed on him, wagging their heads, and saying, Ah, thou that destroyest the temple, and buildest it in three days, save thyself, and come down from the cross."** The final temptation to not go through the initiation of the crucifixion came from the mob, and it came from the chief priests who mocked him and **"said among themselves with the scribes, He saved others; himself he cannot save. Let Christ the King of Israel descend now from the cross, that we may see and believe. And they that were crucified with him reviled him."**[22]

This reviling was carried on by the carnal mind from 3 to 6 o'clock. Thus we see the rebellion, the rationalization, the ignorance, the jealousy of the carnal mind that seeks to preserve itself by tempting Jesus to preserve his own carnal mind and come down and be among them. The challenge to prove that he is the Son of God by forgoing the initiation of the crucifixion is a very great test, and this is the ultimate test of the initiation.

At the sixth hour, where the energies of Spirit that have come forth from the Great Central Sun return in the Mater cycle (the Omega side of the clock), there is darkness over the whole land because it is at that point that the Christ must appear and it is at that point that the Christ in Jesus was completely veiled. This darkness continued in the emotional quadrant until the ninth hour. The planetary momentums of self-pity, self-justification, ingratitude and injustice weighed upon Jesus. His soul is hanging in the balance, and finally at the ninth hour he can bear no more. He says, **"My God, my God, why hast Thou forsaken me?"**[23]

It is the initiation of the 9 o'clock line, where the entire momentum of planetary intrigue gathers, for the Son of God to choose the highest position in the mandala of the Christ without benefit of the guidance or assistance of man or God. And so they brought him **"a sponge full of vinegar, and put it on a reed, and gave him to drink,"** and they wondered whether Elias would come to take him down. But it is at the point of the 9 o'clock line that the ego surrenders, and so **"Jesus cried with a loud voice, and gave up the ghost."** The crystal cord was cut, the threefold flame of the Christ was withdrawn from the plane of Matter (the plane of Mother/ Mater).

At that moment **"the veil of the temple was rent in twain from top to bottom,"** signifying the rending of the veil of illusion that is created by the ego consciousness. When the ego is surrendered and allowed to die, the entire momentum of illusion is broken and God-reality appears. Thus the veil that stands between man and his God is rent in twain from top to bottom, signifying from the 12 to the 6 o'clock line. Throughout the whole clock, all of the illusions of the twelve lines are nullified.

At that moment, the centurion who stood over against him saw that Jesus cried out; and at that moment, when illusion was broken and Reality appeared, when Jesus gave up the ghost of his ego and when his soul left the body, the centurion was able to see, and so he affirmed, **"Truly this man was the Son of God."**

The Antidote for Human Suffering Is the Violet Flame

The antidote for martyrdom and human suffering is the violet flame. When men have not the knowledge of the sacred fire, then the patterns of world maya and world karma are broken through suffering, through the working-out in the physical bodies of the saints of all human hatred and condemnation of the Christ.

The power of the prince of the air, Lucifer, who was given dominion over the mental belt because of mankind's perfidy, is the power that is broken through the crucifixion. For at the place of the cross where Spirit meets Matter, there the energies come forth for redemption in order that the Christ might be born. If the ego is allowed to occupy that position of authority in the being of man, then at the hour of crucifixion, there will come great travail and suffering; but if the Christ occupies the throne of glory in man, then at the hour of crucifixion there is great rejoicing. For the Christ takes upon himself the burdens of the world, the sins of the carnal mind, planetary momentums of effluvia, all of which must be consumed at the meeting ground of the Father-Mother God.

By the action of the violet flame, the entire planetary momentum of martyrdom is consumed and the Christ rises victorious after the three days of transmutation in the astral belt, referred to where it is said that Jesus descended into hell.

These three days symbolize the period, or cycle, required to transmute the perversions of the threefold flame in order that that flame might rise in balanced manifestation and be quickened in the resurrection spiral that the last enemy might be overcome, which is death.

The Initiation of the Crucifixion Must Come to Every Man

The initiation of the crucifixion, then, must come to every man, even John the Baptist, of whom Jesus said that no greater had been born of woman.[24] Even John experienced the crucifixion when he was decapitated by request of the daughter of Herod and his head was brought before the court.

Man, then, must not expect that this cup shall pass from him, but he ought to pray, as Jesus did in that hour of trial, "Nevertheless Father, not my will, but thine, be done."[25] Knowing that the crucifixion will surely come, the devotee must prepare for it by storing within his four lower bodies an intense concentration of the sacred fire through application to the violet flame, to the flame of purity and to the will of God. Thus, when he is required to experience the full weight of the cross, or of his own karma, he will have garnered the spiritual strength to release that karma into the Flame and to stand fast. At that moment, one appointed by the Holy Spirit may come forth as Simon the Cyrenian to assist the initiate in carrying the cross to Golgotha. This is the flame of comfort that does not spare man from the initiation but assists him and upholds him so that he may pass through it, through the fiery trial, and emerge as Shadrach, Meshach, and Abednego, without even the smell of fire upon him.[26]

Though all friends and associates may fail the Christ in that moment, the Holy Spirit will not fail to give him the succor, the strength and the determination to carry on, on behalf of a world that is waiting to be free, that is waiting to rise in the spirals of victory and that is also waiting to be initiated, so that death might be overcome and that Life might be proven to be victorious and eternal here and now.

In order to arrive at the hill of Golgotha, the final test of mastery over the earth element and the physical quadrant, man must accept the assistance of the impersonal personality of the Godhead, which is the Holy Spirit. If someone, anyone, had not carried the cross for Jesus, he never could have received the initiation of the crucifixion. In this final hour of testing, man must acknowledge his dependence upon God and upon the manifestation of God in human form. Without this acknowledgment that a power greater than himself and a power outside of himself is needed, man is not able to put down the weight of his human pride and his human self-sufficiency. Thus in abject humility, the Christ overcomes the world and man is reborn.

At the hour when Jesus walked up the hill, he was bearing the planetary momentums of karma at the etheric, mental and emotional level. In order that he might do that, one was appointed—Simon the Cyrenian—to carry the physical focus of that weight. A parallel example of this moment can be seen in the Old Testament when Aaron and Hur held up the arms of Moses while Moses held back the planetary momentums of opposition.[27]

The crucifixion of Jesus Christ was the crucifixion at the level of the Macrocosm. Therefore there are two initiations of the crucifixion: the one that is of the microcosm at the personal level and one that is at the level of the Macrocosm at the impersonal level. Both rites must be experienced by the soul who has elected to overcome the maya that is anchored in the four quadrants of the clock.

The Crucifixion of the Divine Feminine

It is recorded that there followed after Jesus "a great company of people and of women, which also bewailed and lamented him. But Jesus turning unto them said, Daughters of Jerusalem, weep not for me, but weep for yourselves, and for your children. For, behold, the days are coming, in the which they shall say, Blessed are the barren, and the wombs that never bare, and the paps which never gave suck. Then shall they begin to say to the mountains, Fall on us; and to the hills, Cover us. For if they do these things in a green tree, what shall be done in the dry?"[28]

The green tree is the symbol of the Christ, the man who is redeemed, of the initiate who is preparing himself, in whom there is the flow of the sacred fire, who is alive in Christ. The green tree is ready for the crucifixion, but the dry tree symbolizes the one who is dead to Christ, who has not been reborn. Therefore, when the hour of the crucifixion comes to the dry tree, it is consumed and there is nothing left.

And so Jesus prophesied the day when the Divine Woman would be crucified, when the time would come for the Christ to be redeemed through the Feminine Ray. He foresaw that these daughters of Jerusalem, of the Holy City, would themselves be crucified, and he knew that some among them would not be ready. He also knew that the time would come when the divine office of Woman to bear the Manchild would be repudiated by the mass consciousness, and thus the woman who was barren and did not give forth the Manchild would be blessed among men by men. It is the ultimate degradation and crucifixion of the Divine Woman when she is forbidden to bear the Christ, which is the ultimate fulfillment of her office.

Thus, in this age woman comes forth to fulfill her mission, and because she stands fast in her divine calling she is crucified. When this hour comes, she must not ask to be freed from the crucifixion, she must not run from it, but she must be willing to bear the sins of the world, the planetary momentum of opposition to her divine office. There is no need for martyrdom in the initiation of the crucifixion, for by the power of the Comforter—the Holy Spirit and the sacred fire that is the violet flame—woman may transmute the sins of the world that are directed against her and enter into the joy of the Lord.

Popular movements that espouse the "liberation" of woman from her feminine role typify the final attempt of the carnal mind to deceive woman into running from the crucifixion. We do not say that woman need be oppressed or that she should not fight for the right to express the Christ, to bring forth the Manchild, to fulfill her cosmic mission. But she must be careful that in fighting for her liberation, she does not say "Lord, let this cup pass from me"[29] without repeating the words "Father, not my will but thine be done."[30] Woman must ever seek the freedom to be woman, rather than to usurp the role of man while forsaking her own role.

It ought to be noted that it is written in Luke 23:29: "For, behold, the days are coming, in the which they shall say, Blessed are the barren, and the wombs that never bare, and the paps which never gave suck." Jesus prophesied the day when mankind should consider it a blessing for woman not to bear children. He does not say, behold the days in the which God shall say blessed are the barren. Thus, this is an indication of the perversion of the human consciousness.

Just as Mary in the Magnificat says, "Behold, from henceforth all generations shall call me blessed,"[31] so that typifies the blessing of the Divine Feminine who has fulfilled the role of the Divine Mother, and it is this role that is cursed of men.

Note that in the consciousness of mankind who are unredeemed, the flow of energy is downward because they have not yet entered the path of the ascension. These people are happy in the pleasures of the world, and they are wise in their own generation. The energy they receive from God goes down the drain of their human desires. They have no block in the flow of energy because they are constantly releasing that energy in human desire patterns. Therefore, to the world and in the world they appear happy and content.

Once the individual departs from the world, coming apart in response to the command of the Lord to be a separate people,[32] he must reverse the entire momentum and spiral of his energies, for now they must begin to ascend up the spinal altar to nourish the chakras and prepare him, through the weaving of the wedding garment, for the initiations of the transfiguration, the crucifixion, the resurrection and the ascension. It is the process of the reversal of energies that causes the pain and makes mankind who lack in wisdom to call the Path the via dolorosa.

As long as man identifies with the ego and is ignorant of the process of the reversing of the tide of energy within his being, he will experience pain. But the moment he identifies with the Christ and accepts the challenge hourly and daily to reverse the downward spiral, he is no longer experiencing the pain of the crucifixion, but he enters into the joy of the Lord.

The burden of the cross is lifted when the ego is no more—for all that can feel the burden is the ego. When the Christ displaces the ego in the consciousness of man, it proclaims: "Come unto me all ye who labor and are heavy laden for my burden is light, my yoke is easy."[33] Thus the burden that was borne by the ego becomes a weight of Light in the presence of the Christ.

The End of Banalities

Two thousand years later Jesus dictated a "Watch-with-Me" program[34] that is being given today by his disciples throughout the world. In Part III of this prayer service he gives the conclusion of his Sermon on the Mount, which includes a section entitled "The End of Banalities," a series of fiats that signify the beginning of the end of the inharmonies that have for so long conditioned the race to mediocrity through the substance of their own electronic belts.

We might say that the Sermon on the Mount was a manifestation of the positive (or yang) polarity of the Godhead, the affirmation of the Law by the Father-aspect: Alpha, the Beginning. Upon those who are willing to take their stand for righteousness and Truth, there comes forth the benediction of the Beatitudes as the positive impetus of the Deity.

The denial of evil, on the other hand, the breaking down of human creation that the imprisoned energies of God might be freed, purified and returned to the lake of fire for repolarization,[35] comes under the feminine aspect, or the yin principle, of the Deity—namely, Omega, the Ending. This always occurs at the end of a cycle of ministration or precipitation. Therefore, concluding his two-thousand-year reign in the office of Christ for the earth, Jesus issued forth "The End of Banalities."

Beginning with the **12 o'clock** line, Jesus declares, "**They shall not prevail who scatter seeds of discord and unrest among the brethren!**" These seeds of discord and unrest come through the wedge of 12 o'clock substance as criticism, condemnation and judgment, and as gossip, slander and malpractice. Jesus calls a halt to all such ungodly activities by the universal fiat, "They shall not prevail!"

At the **1 o'clock** line he declares, "**They shall not prevail**

Integrity

who seek to be held in repute by mankind!" For Jesus understands the psychology of the human ego that gains stature by opposing other egos: to be for or against issues or personalities provides the ego with a cause célèbre. By drawing people into the camp of hatred—even a hatred that is based on righteous indignation—the ego can vampirize the energies of other egos as their attentions and emotions are taken up with the issue. This is the strategy of the practitioners of black magic: to mold and manipulate public opinion for and against nations and individuals in order to conquer their very lives by dissipating their daily allotment of energy and destroying what should be the central purpose of their existence—to love one another. Jesus declares, "They shall not prevail!"

At the **2 o'clock** line he states, **"They shall not prevail who seek earthly honor and pay not homage unto divine opportunity!"** All of mankind's efforts to gain recognition in the world of form make up the records—piled layer upon layer and compressed like sedimentary rock—of his involvement with the belief in mortality. It is not by doubting, questioning or fearing his Creator that man attains God-mastery, but by availing himself of divine opportunity—the *op*en *port*al to *unity*—that he experiences the resurrection of his true identity and finds thereby his reason for being and his real mission to the earth.

At the **3 o'clock** line Jesus pronounces the fiat that challenges the lie that seeks through intellectual reasoning to deprive man of the knowledge of the will of God and the God-control of his being: **"They shall not prevail who give not freedom to mankind to accept the progressive revelation of God!"**

Jesus points the finger at the carnal mind, which is ever reasoning against man's divinity, as being the instigator of mankind's rebellion. Therefore, he says of mankind's **4 o'clock** substance: "**They shall not prevail who hearken unto the spirits that are not just and that are not perfected in God!**" Jesus himself, during his forty days in the wilderness, demonstrated the authority of the Son of God over the tempter who defied him to go against the laws of the Universe. He knows from firsthand experience that those who are easily moved by the goadings of specters will not endure the scrutiny of the Lord of Hosts.

Speaking to those whose misdemeanors against the Law fall into the category of the **5 o'clock** line, he says, "**They shall not prevail who abuse their bodies and minds by taking in impure substance knowingly!**" Jesus understands that the abuses of the body temple and the mind are based on man's ignorance of the Law. He knows that man's pitiful sense of incompleteness makes him covet that which he thinks he does not have and then take in impure substance in order to gain it. However, instead of what he hopes to gain by this means, he magnetizes impure thoughts, impure feelings and impure memories.

Challenging the **6 o'clock** substance, Jesus says, "**They shall not prevail who seek by the action of violent drugs to raise their consciousness to a more exalted state!**" Instead of using the currents of the ascension flame and the discipline of purifying the four lower bodies to raise his consciousness to the level of Christhood, he who is wed to the ego seeks the shortcut of violent and unnatural means.

"The kingdom of heaven suffereth violence and the violent take it by force."[36] The storming of heaven by the children of God who think that by taking drugs they will gain something that they do not already possess is proof of their ignorance of the Law. Does not the Law state, "I AM come that all might have Life, and that more abundantly"?[37] Every child of God has the right to the kingdom; therefore, if he will first seek that kingdom and His righteousness, he will find that all of the things that he thinks he is acquiring through the taking of drugs will be added unto him freely as a gift of his Father. It is man's sense of incompleteness that goads him to attempt to secure by fraudulent means the gifts of the kingdom of heaven.

Feelings of ingratitude and thoughtlessness, manifest as emotional density on the **7 o'clock** line, are challenged by Jesus' statement **"They shall not prevail who give not God the glory for each accomplishment!"** How can we fail to be grateful when we recognize God as the doer and as the "open door which no man can shut"?[38] This is the open door through which the stream of Life from the heart of God flows into men to clear away their emotional density. The flushing out of all human effluvia is a prerequisite to the attainment of Christhood, and those who do not clean up their emotional bodies through the power of transmutation will not prevail.

At the **8 o'clock** line Jesus rebukes the sense of duality and the injustice that always results from the attempt of the mortal mind to cater to the human ego. He declares, **"They shall not prevail who carry water upon both shoulders, thinking to serve both God and mammon!"** Jesus is reiterating the fiat that was given to the children of Israel: "Choose you this day whom ye will serve."[39] Injustice, which is the tyranny of uncontrolled emotions, always results from the compromising of principle for personality. "They shall not prevail!"

At the **9 o'clock** line Jesus declares that those who are unable to overcome the defense of the human ego through dishonesty will simply not survive. And so he says, **"They shall not prevail who shall not gird up their minds and hearts and fortify themselves for the victory!"** Victory is the key to God-reality on the 9 o'clock line, and Jesus' own victory at the age of thirty-three was manifest through the overcoming of the intrigue and treachery of the world that sought to place a crown of thorns upon the human Jesus and mockingly proclaim him "king of the Jews."

But he had overcome all need to preserve his identity through the physical self; therefore, he submitted willingly to the crucifixion as a means whereby he might prove the reality of Life over death. Through his final demonstration of alchemy, of victory over the physical body, he won the title of Christ and Saviour of mankind for the two-thousand-year cycle under which he has reigned. Worldly honors gained through one's sense of self can never compare to the rewards that are given by the heavenly Father to those who overcome the world. "They shall not prevail!"

For those enthralled with **10 o'clock** substance, Jesus warns: **"They shall not prevail who senselessly waste the hours God has given them in the continuous seeking of pleasure!"** Here the test of infatuation with the self comes to a head. All self-indulgence must go down before the love of Christ and of God. Self-sacrifice and self-denial are the bywords of the disciple who is overcoming 10 o'clock substance. "They shall not prevail!"

On the **11 o'clock** line Jesus speaks to those who still feel the need for retaliation at the human level. He says, **"They shall not prevail who shall lean upon the arm of flesh and shun the support of the LORD God!"** When people take revenge, they take the Law into their own hands; but when they are calmly seeking the correction of human error by its replacement with the Light of the Christ, they see the battle as the Lord's. They recognize him as the avenger of all human creation, which is overcome and transmuted effortlessly by the power of the sacred fire according to the will of God as that will is invoked by his sons and daughters. "They shall not prevail!"

We hearken to the final commandment of Jesus: **"They**

shall not prevail who shall run with the masses and desire the support of visible numbers in affirming their right action and conduct!"

In order to justify and perpetuate the condemnations and judgments of the carnal mind, men seek to gather the support of the mass consciousness. They tie into the islands of darkness and the blackness of human creation, using that energy to achieve their ends. The judgment of oneself as pursuing right action and conduct is a form of self-righteousness. Therefore, whether the judgment be of self or of others, it is always wrong; for God is the only Judge and Lawgiver.

Jesus knew that in order to accomplish the mission of the Christ, he could not look for support from the masses. This is the cross that all who would become the Christ must carry. The cross symbolizes the victory of the manifestation of God through the four lower bodies of man. With the thirteenth cycle of the giving of the decree, one should rejoice in his Oneness with the Father and in his overcoming of all human attachments—especially one's attachments to the personal self.

The End of Banalities
by Jesus the Christ

Our Father, thy kingdom come!

They shall not prevail who scatter seeds of discord and unrest among the brethren.

They shall not prevail who seek to be held in repute by mankind.

They shall not prevail who seek earthly honor and pay not homage unto divine opportunity.

They shall not prevail who give not freedom to mankind to accept the progressive revelation of God.

They shall not prevail who hearken unto the spirits that are not just and that are not perfected in God.

They shall not prevail who abuse their bodies and minds by taking in impure substance knowingly.

They shall not prevail who seek by the action of violent drugs to raise their consciousness to a more exalted state.

They shall not prevail who give not God the glory for each accomplishment.

They shall not prevail who carry water upon both shoulders, thinking to serve both God and mammon.

They shall not prevail who senselessly waste the hours God hath given them in the continuous seeking of pleasure.

They shall not prevail who shall not gird up their minds and hearts and fortify themselves for the victory.

They shall not prevail who shall lean upon the arm of flesh and shun the support of the LORD God.

They shall not prevail who shall run with the masses and desire the support of visible numbers in affirming their right action and conduct.

SECTION FIVE

The Divine Inheritance

Viewed from the "Summit" of one's Being (i.e., from the heights of the Causal Body), rather than from the marshes of life (from the depths of the electronic belt), all things take on a different expression. Immortality belongs to the highlands and mortality to the lowlands.

Most men and women take life very much for granted, showing little concern for its vast purposes or for the storing up of virtue—treasures in heaven—but showing great concern for their own personal "bit parts," exaggerating their roles, their sufferings, their expectations and the desires of their personal selves—all of which are recorded line upon line in the electronic belt. In a very real sense, God is squeezed out of our lives and forcefields as we let go of the immortal sense and engage in a personal struggle to render unto Caesar that which is Caesar's[1] while forgetting to render equal compensation unto God.

No one can with impunity blame God or another for his

own failures. Each individual has only himself to thank for his failures—and all of the Universe, including the Godhead, to thank for his successes. Hereditary and environmental factors, which seem to play such an important part in molding a lifestream, are actually drawn to the individual by his own past karma. Those who blame parents, neighbors and teachers for their unfulfilled lives must also search the records of Truth concerning the part they played in past incarnations in creating the conditions in which they now find themselves.

The leaves of the Tree of Life and the twelve manner of fruit thereof symbolize the fact that immortal goal-fitting prepares man, regardless of his station or background, to become the manifestation of the Son of Righteousness, whose seed is within himself[2] (whose Christ-power is summoned from the God within) and whose healing wings[3] (whose Light momentum) will lift him out of the socket of mortal delusion into the consciousness of immortality.

The Ritual of Adornment

We call the process of "putting off the old man and putting on the new," spoken of by Saint Paul,[4] the ritual of adornment. This is accomplished as man lovingly, willingly exchanges the limitations of his human consciousness that have accumulated in his electronic belt for the unlimited powers of the Godhead already resident in his Causal Body.

The use of the round the clock decree (see page 166), together with all of the decrees that have been given by the Masters in The Summit Lighthouse decree book,[5] eventually results in the balancing of the threefold flame through man's balanced and masterful use of the four elements. When this time comes, he is nearing his final initiations at the Court of Luxor, which have been described in book 7 of this series, *The*

Path to Immortality.[6]

In preparation for these final tests of the sacred fire, the whirling action of the threefold flame produces in the center of the electronic belt the alchemical heat of the white-fire core of the Central Sun Magnet. This whirling action and the accompanying heat are induced through the individual's invocation of the sacred fire over a period of many years. As the threefold flame rises and expands, the individual's remaining human creation is thrown by centrifugal force to the periphery of the electronic belt, where it is consumed by the violet fire that he has sustained in the center of his tube of light. The vacuum that results from this action of the flame acts as a magnet to draw the qualities of the Causal Body into manifestation in the electronic belt, thereby fulfilling the Law, "As Above, so below."

"As Above, so below," God is omnipresent: by the permeation of the pink plume, his love fills all space. "As above, so below," God is omnipotent: by the action of the blue plume, he is all-powerful because he reigns supreme in the being of man. "As above, so below," God is omniscient: by the wisdom of the yellow plume, he knows all of man because all of man is in a state of awareness of him. When the Law is thus fulfilled, man then stands in the center of his own flaming Christ consciousness. The mighty threefold flame envelops him in a whirling action that touches each line of the electronic belt in an ascending spiral of cosmic faith, hope and charity.

This is the goal of the overcomers of the ages. Those who set their hands to the great plow of life and then turn back are not worthy to be counted among the overcomers. Those who faint before their own human creation or that of the mass consciousness have not truly seen the vision. And those who weary of well-doing cannot be counted among the candidates for the ascension in the Halls of Luxor.

On the threshold of time and eternity, the son of God remembers that his Father is a very present help in time of trouble; and whatever confrontation he may have with the dweller-on-the-threshold—the creation of his own misqualified energies—he knows that the flames of God and the great Hierarchies of the Sun hold the balance of his overcoming. All he need do is to put himself on the side of the scale of Good, of Omnipotence, Omniscience and Omnipresent Reality, and he will win in the battle of life.

Then he, too, shall declare with the risen Christ, "It is finished! Thy perfect creation is within me. Immortally lovely, it cannot be denied the blessedness of Being. Like unto thyself, it abides in the house of Reality. Nevermore to go out into profanity, it knows only the wonders of purity and victory."

The Search for the Tree of Life

Saint Paul's admonishment on the ritual of adornment was beautifully phrased: "Finally, brethren, whatsoever things are true, whatsoever things are honest, whatsoever things are just, whatsoever things are pure, whatsoever things are lovely, whatsoever things are of good report; if there be any virtue, and if there be any praise, think on these things."[7]

It would be well, then, if by the power of directed thought, all individuals would become accustomed to the habit of thinking of themselves not as mortals, wedded to carnality and the life patterns of earth, but as immortal Sons and Daughters of God—deathless, birthless and eternal, whose every act must hold fast to worthy deeds that can endure the acid tests of righteousness and the fire that will surely try every man's work.[8]

The love of the Cosmic Christ, the blessings of the angelic hosts, the communion of saints and the spirit of Life's natural affinity with joy, with righteousness and Truth are the claims of God entered for man in the great Halls of Karmic Justice. The past, with its condemnation of the human, is prologue; but the future, with its affirmation of the divine, beckons.

Thus, the Tree of Life was placed in the midst of the Garden. It cannot be found by a cursory search, but only by a penetration of Life's purposes and by a re-entering of the Garden of the Heart. And this is accomplished through the balancing of one's karmic debts and through the entering into one's novitiate of service. Thus, by dedication to the very principles of Life, the beholder of perfection, who sees in Life the charity of God in action, shall stand before the Tree of Life, put forth his hand, eat and live forever.

Immortality

Immortality and righteousness go hand in hand. How better can immortality manifest here below than as the tangible flame of Life that God has implanted within the heart? The heart that is on fire with His love is the heart that is saturated with right action. The heart that identifies with the thoughts and feelings of God, with the identity of God and with the qualities of His nature is the heart that is determined to manifest His nature here and now at the personal level.

How else can we forge a future that is based on the blueprint of our souls' immortality than through a hope that is cast beyond the veil, beyond mortal reason and feeling, into the domain of the Holy of Holies, the high altar of faith everlasting? For there God's idea of man appears as universal immortality—immortality by creation, immortality by divine right, immortality by worth and immortality by His Law as love in action.

"Who shall separate us from the love of God which is

in Christ Jesus?"⁹ Saint Paul asked. "With what measure ye mete, it shall be measured to you again,"¹⁰ is the decree of God-justice implemented by the Karmic Board. Can we not now, then, call for a dispensation from the LORD's Hosts of that full measure of righteousness that shall enable us to render to our fellow men the service and accord of a living Christ? Shall we not now pass from death unto Life, from the consciousness of darkness unto the consciousness of the dawn? Shall we not now hold fast to that which is good and forsake that which is evil?

Let us come apart, then, from the fate of mortality, shaking its dust from our feet and replacing it by the conscious destiny of an active sense of immortality that is our own, even as we make it so. Let us walk with the Christ not only on the way to Emmaus, where our hearts may burn within us, but also all the way back to a Paradise regained, a consciousness won, a communion reestablished.

"For this corruptible must put on incorruption, and this mortal must put on immortality. So when this corruptible shall have put on incorruption, and this mortal shall have put on immortality, then shall be brought to pass the saying that is written, Death is swallowed up in victory."¹¹

Chapter 3

The One Path above the Many

Enter ye in at the strait gate: for wide is the gate, and broad is the way, that leadeth to destruction, and many there be which go in thereat:

Because strait is the gate, and narrow is the way, which leadeth unto life, and few there be that find it.

GOSPEL OF MATTHEW

The One Path above the Many

SECTION ONE

The Search for Truth

ONE OF THE UNFORTUNATE TACTICS of the sinister force—that is, of the negative powers on the planet—is the continual misdirection of mankind's consciousness into states of criticism, condemnation and judgment of one another. This includes criticizing the doctrines or supposed tenets of various faiths. It is often the case that individuals pass judgment on an individual or a religion when they are not even aware of just what people think or mean by what they print or what they say.

For example, in the name of spiritual progress, the Masters of Wisdom release an idea through one or more spiritual organizations. Other individuals may say, by their misinterpretation of this release, "They think they are the only ones." The result of such criticism is that the intended good cannot flow into their world. Their remark closes the door against Truth, not only for themselves but also for others who come under their sphere of influence.

Nothing can so effectively stop people from receiving their victory as criticizing the faith of others. Nothing constructive is ever achieved by degrading or tearing down any religious faith. (Yet this is not to deny that the standards and conduct of many religious faiths have produced scurrilous effects.)

"Divide and conquer" is a method the negative forces use successfully. Man's propensity to condemn has for thousands of years kept him under the tyranny of negative patterns. In fact, individuals who do the same things they criticize are often the most violent in their condemnation of others.

This criticism comes about because man humanizes the Deity. Making a God in his own image, he justifies all types of mortal thought and feeling that are contrary to what Jesus or any of the great Masters would entertain. We must recognize that all of this is a deterrent intended to keep man from finding the one Path that leads to God-realization.

The Path That Leads to God-Realization

Many religious organizations throughout the world feel that they will successfully perpetuate their own brand of theology, retain their membership and continue to expand by suppressing Truth. There is no question that the failure to practice Christian ethics or divine standards has contributed to setting one religion against another and, by consuming conflict, destroying the noble efforts of both organizations.

A closed mind in religious matters imbues people with the idea that they have the only religious faith by which salvation can be attained. There is something very smug about all this that caters to the human ego. This attitude also closes the door to progress and prevents them from attaining a higher state of being.

No organization or person can be or express something that is not within his capacity. If you dye a white lamb black, beneath it all he is still a white lamb. People and religions, then, are no more than the fullness of their total realization.

Most organizations in reality that have little to give would prefer to seal their members within a prescribed dogma in order to bind them to their particular faith, regardless of the effects upon the person, rather than to loose them and let them have true free will. The leaders of these organizations rule their members by fear. They say other religions are false, their founders are false prophets, their exponents deluded.

It is definitely true that some religious and spiritual organizations are more progressive while others are more reactionary and stultified. But it is also true that there is a thread of continuity that leads through almost every religion that causes the sincere individual to find some element of good there, if he has the good within himself or the potential to acknowledge it.

"The best things in life are free" is a commonly accepted statement. But in reality, the best things of life, because they are the most magnificent, will often prove the most costly in hours of devotion, sacrifice, attention, effort and will.

What, then, is the Reality behind the whole idea of religion?

Religion is basically, whether man admits it or not, mysticism. Religious mysticism is awareness of God. The all-embracing nature of God covers every area of human life.

God is both simple and complex. He is harmony—yet men do not express that harmony, because they themselves have misqualified it by their own thoughts and feelings. This they frequently do not recognize. But a day of reckoning is at hand, and the one Path above the many—which seeks expression in the many—is now coming into manifestation, even as it has always been in the world.

An Open Mind Is Needed

One of the grossest fallacies of human nature is the tendency to honor that which one can accept and to dishonor that which seems unacceptable. This causes people to seek their friends among those who agree with them and to shun those they conceive of as the opposition.

In reality, much can be learned from one's opponents. First of all, there is always the chance that they may be right—and if not, they may have partial realization of some phase of reality exceeding one's own. There is great value, then, in keeping an open mind toward the one Path above the many and extricating oneself from a sense of personal righteousness, i.e., the idea that one has chosen absolute right.

A true religion must possess progressive revelation, else it is already in a state of stagnation—for personal righteousness and the idea that does not see beyond its own nose are limiting. Yet at the same time there is the necessity of becoming tethered to some degree of spiritual Reality, which we will not term dogma but cardinal Truth.

Many religious orders promise that they will impart great wisdom to their followers. They promise them liberty, happiness and future salvation. Those who would speak disparagingly of such religion call it a pie-in-the-sky idea. However, we feel that religion is not only beneficial to man in the future, but also in the here and now.

The seeker seldom realizes whether or not religious orders can deliver the things they promise. Who, in reality, can pierce beyond the veil of the future? Although near-death experiences may shed light on some religious truths, most people have never returned from the dead to verify the truths their religions proclaim.

Oneness with the Father Is Attainable by All

Here is the beauty of the Ascended Masters' presentation of Truth. The Ascended Masters proclaim an essential monotheism, the existence of but one God. But, by the Universal Christ, they reveal the Truth of that one God to be the essential Reality of each individual, which all can realize to the fullest.

Thus, through the Ascended Masters, individuals are made to continually realize that there is a universal level of divine Reality and oneness with the Father that is attainable by all. Reunion with this one supreme God can only be accomplished through the mediatorship of one's own Christ Self and the Universal Christ. For unless the Universal Christ is equated with oneself by acceptance in deed as well as faith, there is no true mediatorship.

When an individual reaches a certain stage in his development, the human monad is no longer identified with the mortal level, but identifies with the level of the Universal Christ and is, in effect, one with the beloved Son, the only begotten of the Father. Thus, in the one Path above the many, all are made to know this Universal Christ and to receive the seamless garment that he wore to wear as their own priceless heritage.

Walking with the Christ before they become the Christ, they enter deeply into his consciousness and merit the gift of his graces. Having attained the status of the Christ, men then walk with God. This walk with God has existed from the foundation of the world.

Incomplete Concepts of Salvation Are Ineffective

In the pure interest of Truth and Truth alone, we honor the Christ, who is the Truth. We declare that the ordinary concepts that most men have regarding salvation are incomplete, and their very incompleteness renders them ineffectual.

For example, conventional interpreters of Christianity have proclaimed that before the birth of the Lord Jesus, salvation and eternal victory were practically impossible for man. They have depicted Jesus not only as the mediator between God and man, but even as the mediator of the time sequence of all history, dating the years before his birth as B.C. and the years after his birth as A.D. They propose that after Jesus' birth, all men are then able to be saved by him. All men who lived before his birth are able somehow through him to attain that which they could not attain prior to his incarnation, "being afar off from God." Just how this is so, they do not explain.

The mystery becomes clearer when we understand that those who lived before him have lived again, and many of them are still living upon this planetary body. We also understand why he said, "Before Abraham was, I AM"[1]—for he knew the timeless Reality of the Universal Christ.

Part of the problem is the theological concepts involving the story of creation and Adam and Eve—that all men had the sentence of death passed upon them with the fall of Adam. Along with this goes the concept of vicarious atonement: that Jesus, by his death on the cross, paid the penalty for this sentence for all of us for all time. However, if this were so, then when the Christ called Jesus spoke the words "It is finished"[2] and gave up the ghost, at that precise instant all of the sin of Adam, called "original sin," would have been wiped out, and from thence onward and forever, men would have had the gift of eternal Life originally held by Adam prior to the Fall.

The real Truth is that the Universal Christ was available from the Beginning and was, therefore, "the Lamb slain from the foundation of the world."[3]

Enoch, the seventh from Adam, proved this. Walking with God through the Christ consciousness, he was able to attain such oneness with that consciousness and with God that he no longer was an ordinary mortal and he never tasted of death. He entered directly into the ascension through his reunion with the Christ, who was the arbiter of all things from the Beginning.[4]

Elijah, ascending into heaven in a chariot of fire, also passed through the ritual of the ascension and achieved his immortal freedom.[5] He subsequently appeared with Moses on the mountaintop to Peter, James and John when Jesus was transfigured before them.[6] A number of others did not taste of death. Some of these have been recorded and some remain unrecorded in the annals of men.

Those who passed from the screen of life and the pages of history to reembody again and again came down through the cycles of time to the time of Jesus and thus entered into the Christian dispensation. Yet in every age—the age of Gautama Buddha, of Mohammed, of Zarathustra, of Confucius and of Lao Tzu—there have been individuals who have contributed much to the well-being of man and to the kingdom of God.

But the significant and all-powerful realization of the one Path above the many is the simple idea of reunion with God and oneness with God, by the grace that is behind the attainment of victory for every man.

SECTION TWO

The Way of the Mystics

THERE HAVE ALWAYS BEEN mystics. And they have always plumbed the depths and scaled the heights of the soul's potential. The Greek word for "soul" is *psyche*. So the mystics are the true psychologists—students of the soul intent on their spiritual quest. Their lives and teachings are a road map that leads scientifically to the summit of being. Thomas Merton wrote: "The spiritual anguish of man has no cure but mysticism."[1]

Mysticism is not exclusive to Christianity. It is the vital, animating element at the heart of every religion. The aspiration of every mystic is one and the same: union with God. He does not postpone it—because he cannot.

The sixteenth-century saint and mystic Teresa of Avila wrote in her autobiography: "I am oblivious of everything in that anxious longing to see God; that desert and solitude seem to the soul better than all the companionship of the world."[2]

Those who long to know and see God are tapping into the

soul's ever-present knowledge of the Higher Self and the higher calling. Although the outer mind may not have a clue, our soul knows at subconscious levels that she is meant to be reunited with her LORD. Lifetime after lifetime this soul-knowledge has impelled us to the feet of our teachers, some true, some false. We have drunk from the communion cups of the world's religions, and we have savored something of the LORD's essence from each one.

Each Age Brings New Revelations of God

God releases new religions in order to give his children a new awareness of himself. We cannot assimilate God all at once. Just as we don't eat the food of a lifetime in a day but portion by portion, so we assimilate God crumb by crumb.

There are specific periods of time, called ages, in which a civilization, a continent or an entire planet is destined to assimilate a certain attribute of God. The opening of these epochs is accompanied by the birth of an Avatar, a God-man, who embodies the Word as it applies to the dispensation he inaugurates.

The length of an age is approximately 2,150 years. It is based on the precession of the equinoxes, the slow rotation of the earth's axis during which the point of the spring equinox moves backwards through the signs of the zodiac. The equinox point takes about 2,150 years to go through 30 degrees of the zodiac, or one astrological sign.

About 4,000 years ago we entered the age of Aries. About 2,000 years ago we entered the age of Pisces. And today we are entering the age of Aquarius. Each 2,150-year period marks a dispensation of Light from the Great Central Sun that gives to earth's evolutions a new awareness of God's Presence.

The dispensation of Aries brought the awareness of God as the Father, the Lawgiver, and as the embodiment of universal Law itself. This age was characterized by God's direct communion with Moses and God's gift to all generations of his name I AM THAT I AM, whereby they, too, could walk and talk with God. Moses showed us that it was the divine right of every son and daughter of God to walk and talk with the Indwelling Presence, the Great I AM. The condition: obey my commandments.

In the Arian age we also note the monotheism of the Egyptian pharaoh Ikhnaton. A century before Moses, he attained mystical union with God through his meditation on the sun—and on the Sun behind the sun. Ikhnaton called God "Aton." The symbol for Aton was the sun with diverging rays ending in hands. This symbolized that man is the hand of God in action—and that as the sun and its rays are one, so there is no separation between Creator and creation. *Ikhnaton* means

Figure 25 Ikhnaton and Nefertiti with the Sun Disk

"he who serves the Aton." The pharaoh believed that he was a son of Aton. He truly knew himself as the Light-emanation of the one God.

The age of Pisces brought the awareness of God as the Son, revealed to us in the Universal Christ personified in the Christ, Jesus. Jesus came to show us how to walk the path of personal Christhood so that we could realize the Son of God within ourselves. The condition: Love me and keep my commandments.

Jeremiah prophesied the full revelation of the Son of God who should appear in the age of Pisces. He saw the son as "The Lord Our Righteousness."[3] In the twentieth century Saint Germain unveiled the Son as the personal, or Inner, Christ. We address this Inner Christ as our Beloved "Holy Christ Self." Knowledge of the Son of God as our True Self, or Higher Self, brings us that much closer to the LORD, I AM THAT I AM.

The dawning age of Aquarius brings us the awareness of God as the Holy Spirit and as the Divine Mother. In this age the Divine Feminine is exalted in male and female as the sacred fire that rises on the altar of our chakras. The condition we must fulfill is self-transcendence through divine love.

Thus, the unfoldment of God's identity within you and your identification with it is progressive through the cosmic cycles. This unfoldment culminates in your direct experience of God followed by your union with God. This is the goal of all of your past incarnations and the goal of your life today.

We do not leave behind the previous ages but we build upon their foundations. Knowledge of the Ascended Masters' teachings is no excuse to set aside the Ten Commandments or the teachings of Jesus Christ or the great truths that come down to us through the Vedas and the Upanishads and all of the teachings of the Avatars of the major world religions.

We have this communion with our I AM Presence because

we have built, stone upon stone, our pyramid. And now we have come to that age and hour when we ourselves must place the spiritual capstone on our personal pyramid.

Through each of the world's major religions God has revealed to your soul another side, or image, of himself. Your soul is the mirror of God. If you allow your soul to mirror the astral plane or discordant images, then there is no room in the mirror for God. If you polish the mirror of the soul and direct that mirror through attention to God, you will always be able to look in the mirror of your soul and see God. That is the first experience of seeing God face to face. You first see God in the mirror of your soul and then directly when he chooses to appear to you.

When God reveals a new image, or attribute, of himself through a world religion, he also reveals in the mirror of your soul a new image, or attribute, of yourself. When you become one with this new image of God and of yourself, you learn a new way of communing with God. A new image is like a new language, a new mode of expression, as though you suddenly discovered love or discovered truth. A whole new world opens to you. You understand more of God and so you can be more of God. Thereby you learn a new way of attaining union with God.

In each age God has also given us one or more new names whereby we may invoke that image and, by reflection, make it our own. Knowledge of the name of God is empowerment. God has empowered his people through many ages. And by that, we have learned to expand the flowers of our chakras. Each time we invoke God by a new name we access a portion of God's Self that was previously beyond our reach.

The name of God is the key to his heart, to his mind, to his spirit, and to that state of consciousness we are destined to mirror and to become.

Eight Pathways to God

Each of the world's major religions facilitates our soul-development on a particular ray and a particular chakra. The seven major world religions and the minor eighth come under the dispensation of the seven rays and the seven chakras and the eighth ray and the eighth-ray chakra:

1. Judaism facilitates your soul-development on the first ray of God's power through the throat chakra.
2. Buddhism facilitates your soul-development on the second ray of God's wisdom through the crown chakra.
3. Christianity facilitates your soul-development on the third ray of God's love through the heart chakra.
4. Hinduism facilitates your soul-development on the fourth ray of God's purity through the base-of-the-spine chakra.
5. Confucianism facilitates your soul-development on the fifth ray of science, healing and truth through the third-eye chakra.
6. Islam facilitates your soul-development on the sixth ray of ministration and service through the solar-plexus chakra.
7. Taoism facilitates your soul-development on the seventh ray of God's freedom through the seat-of-the-soul chakra.
8. Zoroastrianism facilitates your soul-development on the eighth ray through the secret chamber of the heart.

Transforming the Soul

Mysticism is not merely a belief or a philosophy. Mysticism is an experience that transforms the soul. If you aren't transformed, you haven't had the experience. And when your soul is fully transformed, you and God are no longer two but one.

The fifteenth-century mystic Saint Catherine of Genoa experienced the oneness as submersion in the ocean of God's love. She said: "My being is God, not by some simple participation but by a true transformation of my Being.... I am so placed and submerged in His immense love that I seem as though immersed in the sea, and nowhere able to touch, see or feel aught but water.... My Me is God, nor do I recognize any other Me except my God himself."[4]

The mystical path is a spiritual journey into the heart of God's love. But the mystic knows that in order to be completely bonded to God's heart he must transcend the lesser self. Thus the path of the mystic is a path of challenge as well as a path of joy. It is the challenge of working through karma that separates you from God—and then going beyond the pain to the bliss of encountering your Lord face to face.

Origins of Mysticism

The word *mysticism* is thought to be derived from the Greek word meaning to close the eyes or lips. It was first used in connection with the Greek mystery religions. The "mystics" were those who promised to keep secret the rituals of their religion.

Neoplatonic philosophers who later applied the word *mystical* to their doctrines taught their pupils to shut their eyes to the external world and go within, in profound contemplation, to discover mystical truths. Closing their eyes meant they had to go to a plane of consciousness apart from the concrete mind. They had to go beyond the intellectual mind to levels of both the superconscious and the subconscious where the soul has direct awareness of her identity in God beyond the confines of the physical/intellectual self. The Neoplatonists sought to take their pupils to the compartment of being where the soul speaks to God and where God speaks to the soul.

Philo, the Jewish religious thinker and contemporary of

Jesus, used the term *mystical* to refer not to secret rituals but to the hidden meaning of God's word. The early Greek Church Fathers Clement and Origen of Alexandria applied the word *mystical* to the allegorical interpretation of scripture. Origen believed there could be no real understanding of the scriptures without communion with God. For Origen, interpretation of the scriptures was a religious experience. He was the first to use the word *mystical* to describe a way of knowing God.

In later centuries, Christians used the word *mystical* to indicate the hidden and sacred presence of Christ in the scriptures, sacraments and liturgy. The influential writings of the fifth- or sixth-century writer known as Pseudo-Dionysius established the word *mystical* as part of the Christian vocabulary. He didn't just use it to discuss the interpretation of scripture. He also encouraged the exercise of "mystical contemplation"—leaving behind "the senses and the operations of the intellect" in order to gain union with God.[5] Eventually the term *mystical theology* was used in the Church to denote knowledge about God gained through contemplation.

The Path of Mysticism

There are several elements common to the mystical paths of the major world's religions. Among these are (1) the mystics' pursuit of the indwelling Presence of God; (2) their pursuit of direct intercourse with God through prayer and contemplation; and (3) their pursuit of a threefold path of ascent to God.

The mystics believed that the soul is meant to be the dwelling place of God and a partaker of the Divine nature. In Christian mysticism this teaching goes back to the words of Jesus and the apostles.

At the Last Supper Jesus promised his disciples: "If a man

love me, he will keep my words: and my Father will love him, and we will come unto him and make our abode with him."[6]

Paul instructed the Corinthians: "Know ye not that ye are the temple of God, and that the Spirit of God dwelleth in you?"[7] It is a wondrous thing to walk about in a vessel of clay and to realize God inhabits this temple and that we have the power to increase his habitation, to intensify his habitation, or to diminish it to nothing by maintaining a state of anger or selfishness or sensuality. We are the masters of this temple. We decree whether God shall find room in us.

Peter said that through the goodness and glory of Christ we can be "partakers of the divine nature"[8] here and now. Death is not a passport to this experience. Here and now we can partake of the divine nature.

The Divine Spark

The mystics speak of the indwelling Presence of God in two senses. First, they believe that all men are by nature like God and that within every soul there is a spark of the Divine.

The fourteenth-century theologian and mystic Meister Eckhart taught: "There is something in the soul that is so akin to God that it is one with Him.... God's seed is within us."[9] Saint Germain teaches that the indwelling Presence of God is the threefold flame of the Trinity—of Father, Son and Holy Spirit. This is the eternal flame that burns on the altar of our hearts. It is also called the Holy Christ Flame or the Threefold Flame of Liberty—because without it we would have neither free will nor the individuality in God to exercise it.

So long as we tend this flame we have a unique identity in God and are forever tied to his heart. At the moment of a baby's first breath, the Holy Spirit reignites this flame in the physical heart. Child-man now has the potential to become

God-man. In other words, the child-manifestation may, through the threefold flame, put on and become the full God-manifestation.

The goal of not one but many incarnations is to so fan the threefold flame with our devotion to God that it increases to the fullness of the Godhead dwelling in us bodily as it did in Jesus Christ. Jesus is our Lord and Saviour because the fullness of the Godhead dwelt in him bodily. He is our Lord because through him we may have that flame reignited if we have lost it. Through him we may be bonded anew to our Holy Christ Self.

Jesus has saved us for the opportunity to become immortal by taking upon himself our karma in the Piscean age. Jesus was and is the Word Incarnate. Jesus is the supreme mystic who lights the way for all who would follow his Light to the fullness of God's Light in themselves.

The Ascended Master Saint Germain opened the path of mysticism to the world in the twentieth century when he unveiled the Chart of Your Divine Self (see page 105). This Chart is a diagram of your soul's mystical union with God. And it is a sign from the heart of Saint Germain to the mystics of all past ages who reincarnate in this time that the hour of the fulfillment for their reason for being has come.

The unveiling of the I AM THAT I AM as the individual I AM Presence of every child of God is the equivalent of the veil in the temple being rent in twain.* Through meditation on this Chart and a profound adoration of your I AM Presence, you will one day see the Holy of holies of your own God Reality. The rending of that veil in Jesus' time signified that thereafter all who accepted him as the High Priest and Mediator

---

* In the temple at Jerusalem, there was a veil that divided the holy place, into which the priests entered, from the Holy of holies, into which the high priest entered on the Day of Atonement. This veil was rent at the hour of Jesus' crucifixion (Matt. 27:51; Mark 15:38; Luke 23:45).

in their lives would also have access to the Holy Christ Self.

Jesus is the open door. Your Holy Christ Self, the Beloved, is your High Priest who officiates at the altar of your heart. Within the secret chamber of the heart are universes—in this space that is tiny physically. And there that High Priest serves at the altar of your being and delivers to you the communion of God, the Body and the Blood of the Universal Christ.

It is Jesus who reconnects the soul to her Holy Christ Self. Without his intercession as our Lord and Saviour, we could not reestablish this lost tie on our own. We must have him as that Lord and Saviour and that intercessor, for God has so sent him for this very purpose, that we might be saved.

Therefore he comes to restore the threefold flame. And once the flame is restored and the soul has passed her tests, she can be reunited to the Holy Christ Self and to Jesus.

The Indwelling Presence of God

The second way in which the mystics conceive of the indwelling Presence of God is as the indwelling Christ.

The apostle Paul was the first mystic who recorded the concept of the indwelling Christ being "formed" in us. He wrote to the Galatians: "I travail in birth again until Christ be formed in you."[10] Paul proclaimed the Christ within as the inheritance of all Christians. He told the Colossians that God would make known to his saints how great are "the riches of the glory of this mystery: which is Christ in you, the hope of glory."[11]

If you have a Holy Christ Self, then why does Christ need to be formed in you? The Holy Christ Self is above you in higher planes. You can visualize the forming of Christ in you as points of light coming together in concentration, originally dispersed and vapory with no form or shape. As you begin to know who is Christ and what is Christ—his attributes, his works, his words, as he lives daily—there is forming in you your concept of Christ, your image of Christ, the Christ whom you adore and whom you worship, the Christ who is your brother and teacher and friend. Each day that Christ is being formed in you—becoming more concentrated as Light—until the very presence and outline and truly the form of your Holy Christ Self is duplicated here below.

Paul said that Christ lived *in* him; and he discovered that when Christ lived in him, he no longer lived in himself. He said, "I live, yet not I, but Christ liveth in me."[12] And so he was no longer "I, Paul." He was "I, Paul, one with the Christ."

Origen wrote: "Not just in Mary did [Christ's] birth begin ... but in you, too, if you are worthy, is the WORD of God born. If you are so pure in mind, so holy in body and so blameless in deed, you can give birth to Christ himself."[13]

Meister Eckhart taught that the birth of the Son of God within the individual is even more important than the incarnation of the historical Jesus: "It is more worthy of God that He should be born spiritually ... of every good soul than that He should have been born physically of Mary."[14]

The birth of Christ in our consciousness and in our souls comes when we have a companionship with the Christ Presence. It is a certain awakening within us of a larger sphere of selfhood we have yet to fill in. This we accomplish by the intercession of the Holy Spirit. The babe must grow and wax strong in the spirit of the LORD, until he come to the full stature of his Sonship, his Christhood, in God. When that takes place, the soul is fused, or bonded, to Christ—to Jesus Christ and through him to her indwelling Christ.

Mystical Contemplation and Prayer

A second premise of the mystics is that the soul can have direct intercourse with God through mystical contemplation and prayer. I would call this meditation and devotional and invocative prayer. Devotion is where you give your whole heart and soul and love and mind to God. Invocative prayer is when you invoke the whole heart and soul and Mind of God to enter your being.

To the mystics, prayer is not just a prescribed set of devotions and petitions to God. It is an interior prayer wherein we speak with God from the very depths of our soul. It is concentration upon God. It is a profound communion free from distractions within and distractions without.

John Climacus, a seventh-century abbot of a monastery on Mount Sinai, said: "Prayer is by nature a dialogue and a union of man with God. Its effect is to hold the world together."[15] Everyone who maintains this relationship with God is holding the Spirit cosmos and the Matter cosmos together, because in that dialogue and in that union he has come to the point of the center of the Chart, the point of the Son of God.

The mystics taught that true prayer does not take place just at peak moments of the day or week. True prayer is unceasing communion with God even in the midst of daily activities. Teresa of Avila said we should talk with God about even the smallest concerns of our day. Our conversations with him can take place anywhere.

The fifth-century monastic John Cassian wrote: "Through constant meditation on things divine and through spiritual contemplation, the soul is caught up into an ecstasy." Through this practice, said Cassian, the soul can enter into such a close and continuous union with the Lord that "whatever we breathe or think or speak is God."[16]

Teresa of Avila believed that the mystical encounter with God in our day-to-day business is no less valuable than the visions and ecstasies of the saints. "The Lord walks among the pots and pans," she said, "helping you both interiorly and exteriorly."[17]

Unceasing prayer is like being in love. When you are in love, you are always thinking of the beloved. When you are in love with God, you can never take your attention from him. You are consumed by a spiritual passion. Moments apart from him are an agony. Nothing else will comfort you but his love as he rekindles the fiery ecstasy of heart-to-heart communion.

So the psalmist cried out to the living God: "As the hart panteth after the water brooks, so panteth my soul after thee, O God. My soul thirsteth for God, for the living God."[18]

Mother Mary has instructed us on how to fulfill the injunction to "pray without ceasing." She said: "Saint Germain has said that you ought to pray and to pray fervently without ceasing. May each one of you pick his own mantra—not necessarily long, but pick a mantra, beloved—and begin to repeat it without ceasing. [Repeat it in the mind.] Repeat a mantra of Kuan Yin or the Hail Mary, the Om Mani Padme Hum, the Om Namo Narayanaya.

"Understand that it is well to discipline the mind, that through the mind and the heart the soul might travel within over the inner Word that is recited as you serve.... Let it carry thee continually to the secret chamber of the heart, the three-fold flame."[19]

Saint Germain is the great adept who has made the mystical path available to all who will apply themselves by teaching us the path of devotion through the Science of the Spoken Word.

The Threefold Path of Purgation, Illumination and Union

The third element common to the mystical paths of the world's religions is the pursuit of the threefold path of purgation, illumination and union.

Some writers consider these stages a step-by-step path, one stage leading to the other. Others believe the stages can take place simultaneously and that not every mystic experiences every stage. Saint Bonaventure, the thirteenth-century theologian and disciple of Saint Francis, explains that in the purgative stage sin is expelled, in the illuminative stage the soul learns the imitation of Christ, and in the unitive stage the soul is day by day being united with God. He said that in the purgative stage man comes to understand himself. In the illuminative stage, he comes to understand God. In the unitive, he strives to be united with God.[20]

Purgation comes to the soul only after she has experienced her awakening in God. This awakening brings joy to the soul. But when God's Light suddenly enters the world of the mystic, he becomes acutely aware of his faults and weaknesses. More importantly, he sees that his imperfections (or sins, to use a traditional term) are what separate him from God, and he can no longer tolerate the gulf.

Catherine of Genoa described the process by which the soul overcomes her impediments and reunites with God, returning to the "pristine state of her creation," as a kind of purgatory: "As the soul makes her way to her first state, her ardor in transforming herself into God is her purgatory."[21] These words are not an exaggeration. To truly face and conquer the lesser self is arduous. We should not underestimate the challenge. We should know what we are getting into when we want to go all the way back to God in this life.

This is what Paul meant when he said, "I die daily."[22] Paul saw a part of himself dying daily, and some of those parts he was attached to. Some of those parts he didn't necessarily want to see die. But by having Christ be formed in him, something else that was not the Christ had to die.

The Dark Night

During the process of purgation the soul faces testings, trials and temptations that come in many guises. Some mystics have described a certain element of the purgative process as a "dark night." The sixteenth-century mystic Saint John of the Cross said there are two dark nights: the dark night of the senses and the Dark Night of the Spirit.

The dark night of the senses takes place during the purgative stage and as a transition into the illuminative stage. The Dark Night of the Spirit takes place before the ultimate union of the soul in Christ in the spiritual marriage.

Author E. W. Dicken says: "Night is simply the saint's term for 'privation,' eradication of attachment to all that is not God, and it is by this progressively more complete privation that the soul is finally emptied of all that can fill her to the exclusion of God."[23]

Most people do not know the experience of being totally filled with God, and therefore to give up the known for the unknown is not easy. To be totally filled with God does not mean that you need to be a nun or a priest or in a convent or in a cloister. It is also possible to be in the world, yet not of it (though this may be a greater challenge), to be filled with God and to become a radiating point of Light, an extension of the heart of Krishna or Morya or Buddha. Your life will be far greater in joy when there is no room in you for anything but God—because God is everything. God is everything that is

Real. Everything you could ever want he will bring to you.

Mary Baker Eddy said, "Divine Love always has met and always will meet every human need."[24] In other words, when you are filled with God as divine love, God will give you everything that you lawfully need and that you lawfully want.

During the dark night of the senses the mystic disciplines himself to overcome inordinate desires—desires that do not lead to his union with God. Saint John of the Cross advised: "To come to possess all," that is, all of God, if you really want that, "desire the possession of nothing,"[25] and God will give you his All. The mystics recognized that one of the primary laws of spiritual progress is that as the soul becomes increasingly detached from the things of this world, she becomes increasingly attached to God.

John outlined a two-step program to help the disciple get through the dark night of the senses. He said that by these two steps alone the soul could conquer all inordinate desires that separate her from God.

First, the mystic should have a "habitual desire to imitate Christ in everything that he does." He should meditate on Christ's life "so that he may know ... how to behave in all things as Christ would behave." Secondly, "Every pleasure that presents itself to the senses, if it be not purely for the honor and glory of God, must be renounced and completely rejected for the love of Jesus Christ, Who in this life had no other pleasure, neither desired any, than to do the will of his Father."[26]

The path of the imitation of Christ is the path of the Christian mystics. Jesus said: "If any man will come after me, let him deny himself [his lesser self, the carnal mind] and take up his cross daily."[27] Taking up your cross daily means not only the cross of your karma but also your dharma, your duty to be who you really are on the path of personal Christhood in the footsteps of Jesus. Let not your head come to rest on your pillow if you have not dealt with the karma of the day with violet flame, with service, with love.

Saint Philip Neri wrote: "Nothing more glorious can befall a Christian than to suffer for Christ."[28] We can all ask: How can suffering be glorious? Isn't this drive for suffering on the part of the mystics masochistic? Aren't they inflicting this pain upon themselves because they are psychologically sick?

Not when you understand that suffering for Christ means bearing your karma for him so that he doesn't have to bear it for you. If we refuse to bear responsibility for our words, our actions, our deeds, if we are not willing to suffer the consequences of our ungodly words and deeds, this becomes the boulder of pride and rebellion against the laws of God that utterly prevents our soul's reunion with God.

The saints and adepts who willingly underwent what seem to us extreme torments and self-imposed afflictions or severe illnesses were balancing their personal karma (perhaps in the only way they knew how) in order to achieve their soul's realignment with God. Sometimes through their intense physical suffering the saints were balancing planetary karma as well.

Balancing our karma, paying back our debts to God and to every part of life that is God *is* glorious. Because none of us are truly happy—and our souls can never be—until we have undone the wrongs we have done to any part of life. As long as we are enmeshed in a spiral of negative karma with the outer self—our own outer self and someone else's outer self—we cannot know true oneness with the Inner Self—of them or us.

Some suffering may be necessitated by the law of karma. But there is a path of a minimum of suffering. That path is the path of the seventh ray and of the violet flame. Instead of encountering all of the old situations and taking a million years to work through the karma physically, that gift of Saint

Germain has given us this opportunity to accelerate. Sometimes the most suffering you have to bear is to just sit still in one place long enough to get the action of transmutation rolling at peak alchemical pitch.

Saint Germain tells us that the violet flame is the most physical of all flames. Transmutation goes on at all levels when we invoke it. Not only does the violet flame expel toxins lodged in our physical organs but it also transmutes the karmas and traumas of our present and past lives recorded in the four lower bodies.

Saint Germain unveiled the violet flame to the world in the 1930s. It is the gift of his heart to all who would enter the Golden Age of Aquarius. Through the alchemy of the violet flame—the seventh ray aspect of the Holy Spirit—the unredeemed, unperfected soul can become a partaker of the divine nature here and now in this life.

The writings of the mystics tell us that there comes a moment on the purgative path when the intense suffering abates. The flame of love swallows up some aspect of the lesser self, and the soul moves on to a new level. Suffering ceases when the soul has learned her lessons and a certain block of karma has been balanced. This marks the moment when the soul is ready for the illuminative stage.

The Illuminative Stage

"Those who believe that the life of mystics is gloomy and sad," says John Arintero, "do not know what true happiness is.... Indescribable consolations and wonderful illuminations are interwoven amid the many trials."[29]

As mysteries are unlocked, the mystic gains a new perspective on his relationship with God and with his fellow men. He experiences a greater sense of the presence of God. His soul mounts to new heights of joy in communion with the Lord. Radakrishnan, an Indian philosopher, called the second stage on the mystic path "concentration,"[30] for now the mystic's life is focused entirely on God. His sole desire is to be with God and to serve God.

The illuminative stage is often marked by visions, ecstasies, revelations, raptures and other phenomena. However, the Christian mystics often warned, as do the Gurus of the East, that phenomena are not the goal of the mystical path. They said it is dangerous to ask God for such experiences or to expect them because this leaves us open to projections from our own imagination or from the devil.

Author J. Mary Luti writes: "Although Teresa [of Avila] esteemed mystical phenomena, she was also cautious about them,... not only because such experiences could be counterfeited,... but also and especially because she understood the mystical life to involve so much more than peak experiences.... For Teresa, the marks of true Christian intimacy with God were first, last, and always the marks of concrete love: the bearing of the cross [i.e., personal and planetary karma], the service of neighbor. Sensation was not what she was seeking but transformation in God for the sake of God's service."[31]

The Unitive Stage

The illuminative stage, even with its moments of bliss, is merely a foretaste of the splendid and perpetual union with God that comes in the unitive stage. The Christian mystics say that the soul's union with God in this life should be the goal of all Christians. They have referred to this union as the spiritual marriage, the deifying, transforming union, or deification.

To the mystics the soul is feminine in nature and is intended to become the bride of Christ. Thus, some mystics referred to the soul as "she" or "her" rather than "he" or "him." Before the spiritual marriage takes place, some of the mystics passed through a period of a betrothal or engagement. During the mystical engagement, the soul undergoes further tests and purgations in preparations for her marriage, but she also enjoys the delights of God.

Prior to the spiritual marriage mystics also pass through the Dark Night of the Spirit. Saint John of the Cross said that during this period the soul feels that "God has abandoned her, and, in His abhorrence of her, has flung her into darkness." The soul feels "chastised and cast out, and unworthy of Him.... She feels, too, that all creatures have forsaken her, and that she is condemned by them, particularly by her friends."[32]

John described the Dark Night of the Spirit as an "inflow of God into the soul."[33] God is "purging the soul, annihilating her, emptying her or consuming in her (even as fire consumes the moldiness and the rust of metal) all the affections and imperfect habits which she has contracted in her whole life.... God greatly humbles the soul in order that He may afterwards greatly exalt her."[34]

Johannes Tauler, a fourteenth-century mystic, echoed this theme in one of his sermons. He said, "In the measure that a man comes out of himself, in that measure does God enter in with His divine grace."[35]

This is the great mystery that the mystics of all religions have unlocked: In order to be full, you first must be empty.* In order for God to dwell in you completely, you must first empty yourself of all that is not God.

The Ascended Masters teach that the culmination of the Dark Night of the Spirit is the crucifixion. What is crucified in the crucifixion? It is not the outer self. It is the Christ who is

---

* For example, Lao Tzu says, "To be worn out is to be renewed. To have little is to possess. To be empty is to be full" (Tao-Te Ching, ch. 22).

embodied in you. Jesus the Christ was crucified. Had he not been the Christ, they wouldn't have bothered crucifying him.

The crucifixion is the supreme test of your individual Christhood, when your soul is, as it were, cut off from your I AM Presence above. The test is that you must survive in life and in spiritual consciousness on the God-energy, on the Christ-energy, that you have internalized in all of your lifetimes on the Path. You must be able to sustain that God Presence where you are without reinforcement from your I AM Presence.

This is the real explanation of why Jesus suddenly cried out when he hung on the cross, "My God, my God, why hast thou forsaken me?"[36] And this is the meaning of the highest and most difficult initiation that we must pass before we can come to the resurrection. We must have internalized that Word that we are—an individual identity in God, but self-sustaining.

Through the purging that comes with the Dark Night of the Spirit, the soul is at last ready to enter into the bridal chamber. The mystics' description of their love pact with the Beloved has produced some of the most exalted expressions of love ever written. Saint John of the Cross wrote of the personal and intimate contact of the soul with the Divine One:

> All things I then forgot,
>   My cheek on him who for my coming came;
> All ceased, and I was not,
>   Leaving my cares and shame
>   Among the lilies, and forgetting them.[37]

When the soul is "carried away and absorbed in love," said John, it is "as if she had vanished and been dissolved in love,… passing out of self to the Beloved."[38]

The Spiritual Marriage

The mystics have described their spiritual marriage with Christ very graphically. In 1730 Father Bernard Hoyos heard angels singing: "Behold, the Bridegroom is coming, go forth to meet Him." In a vision he saw Jesus, the Blessed Mother and many saints. He heard Jesus say: "I espouse thee, O beloved soul, in an eternal espousal of love.... Now thou art Mine and I am thine.... Thou art Bernard of Jesus and I am Jesus of Bernard.... Thou and I are one."[39]

Commentators on the Christian mystics note that male mystics whom Christ espouses sometimes experience Christ as wisdom or mercy because these are considered to be feminine attributes of God. Jacob Boehme, for instance, spoke of the soul's marriage to the Virgin Sophia (Greek, meaning "Wisdom").[40]

Saint Teresa of Avila recorded that one day in 1572, Jesus gave her his right hand and said, "Behold this nail [print]; it is a sign you will be My bride from today on.... My honor is yours, and yours mine."[41]

A few years later Jesus gave her a ring. "Our Lord told me," she wrote, "that since I was His bride I should make requests of Him, for He had promised that whatever I asked He would grant me. And as a token He gave me a beautiful ring, with a precious stone resembling an amethyst but with a brilliance very different from any here on earth."[42]

He also explained, in the true tradition of a marriage union, that he would share with her all that was his—both the joys and the burdens. "Whatever I have is yours," he said. "So I give you all the trials and sufferings I underwent."[43] Mother Teresa of Calcutta once spoke of the burdens she bore for Jesus, her Bridegroom. "Someone said to Mother Teresa, 'Well, you know, it's easier for you. You're not married or in a relationship.'

"'What do you mean? I am married,' she answered, holding up the ring that signifies a nun's marriage to Jesus, 'and he can be very difficult, too!'"[44]

In the unitive stage some mystics have experienced a close bonding of their heart to the heart of Christ. A mystic by the name of Sister Barbara heard Jesus say to her: "Thou art all Mine, and I am all thine." She later perceived that he had placed a chain around her heart and attached it to his own heart. She said: "From that moment I was so bound to my God and so closely united with Him that I can truly say that between God and myself there was but one will."[45]

The most important sign of the mystical union with God is an active love. The unitive way is, of all stages of the mystical path, the most fruitful. The nineteenth-century French mystic Elisabeth de la Trinité said that in the unitive stage, all the movements of the soul become divine. "Though [the movements of the soul] are God's, they are just as much the soul's," she said, "for our Lord performs them in and with her."[46] Thus the mystic becomes the living instrument of God—the heart, head and hand of God in action.

Teresa of Avila taught that as a result of the spiritual marriage, "the soul is much more occupied than before with everything pertaining to the service of God."[47] All of the energy of the soul who is married to Christ, she said, "goes into finding ways to please him, and into seeing how and where she may show the love she has for him. This is what prayer is for, ... and this is the purpose of the spiritual marriage, which gives rise always to works, works!"[48]

Teresa herself led a very active life, dedicating herself to the reform of the Carmelite Order. She traveled throughout Spain, establishing seventeen monasteries, wrote several books that have become spiritual classics. In Teresa's day and culture, these accomplishments were nothing less than remarkable.

Another very active mystic was Catherine of Siena. Catherine's mystical marriage took place in 1366 when she was 19 years old. As she prayed in the little room of her house where she had lived a secluded life for three years, Jesus promised her "I will espouse you to me in faith" and gave her a gold ring set with four pearls and a diamond.[49] He said that this was her reward for scorning the vanities of the world and desiring only him.

Catherine's life changed immediately and she began a career of unceasing service. She left her cell to care for the poor and sick. She preached, traveled widely and addressed hundreds of letters to the prelates and sovereigns of her day, both advising and rebuking them. Wherever she went she brought a spiritual revival.

The mystical path is truly a practical path. It is practical because we learn how to contact God and find our way back to his heart. It is practical because it deals with the needs of the hour on planet Earth.

Dag Hammarskjold once wrote, "In our era, the road to holiness necessarily passes through the world of action."[50]

"Souls that are on fire," says Thérèse of Lisieux, "can never be at rest."[51]

Becoming God

The spiritual marriage, the mystics tell us, is not simply a conforming of the soul to the ways and will of God but a total transforming of the soul into God. This is precisely how the mystics describe the divine union. And this is the very heart of the teaching that you only whisper: the soul that is transformed into God *is* God. This is the conclusion the mystics inevitably reached—but they were reluctant to tell it, for they feared persecution. The apostle Paul was speaking of purgation and union with Christ when he said, "I am crucified with Christ: nevertheless I live, yet not I, but Christ liveth in me."[52]

John Arintero says that in the unitive stage "the soul, indissolubly united and made one with the incarnate Word, vividly bears His divine image and seems to be Jesus Christ Himself ... living on earth."[53] Saint Francis of Assisi, for example, so dedicated himself to the imitation of Christ that he was called "another Christ." In the act of union, said Tauler, "there is nothing in the soul beside God."[54]

Teresa of Avila said the union of the soul with God is "like rain falling from the heavens into a river or a spring; there is nothing but water there and it is impossible to divide or separate the water belonging to the river from that which fell from the heavens. Or it is ... as if in a room there were two large windows through which the light streamed in: it enters in different places but it all becomes one."[55]

The Spanish mystic Luis de León said that when the soul is united with God she "not only has God dwelling within her, but is indeed God."[56]

Saint Magdalen of Pazzi cried out to the Father: "By means of the union and transformation of Thyself into the soul and of the soul into Thee,... Thou dost deify the soul. O deification! The soul which has the happiness of arriving at the state of being made God—like a sphere irradiating the rays of the sun—is made luminous and resplendent as the sun itself. We are transformed into Thy very image, from clarity to clarity."[57]

These are the words of the Christian mystics and the teachings of the doctors of the Roman Catholic Church. The goal of deification—of becoming one with God or, as some of the mystics say, becoming God—has been a part of the Christian mystical tradition since the time of Jesus Christ.

The Universal Path

The world's major religions have two facets. They have the orthodox system of rules and rituals—an outer religion, a religion of form. As people advance on the Path, they decide this is not enough. They want more. Then there is the inner path of mysticism.

Every one of the world's religions shows the same inner path—the discovery that God is a living fire. Fire is the key in every religion from Zoroastrianism to Taoism to Christianity.

The fire of the Holy Spirit, the flame—whatever way it is seen—is central on the altar of Being. And the goal of the mystic is to unite with the flame, to unite with God, to be transformed, to be purged, to be illumined and to enter into that total oneness.

If religion doesn't give you a path of your soul's reunion with that sacred fire in this life, it is missing the whole heart of the matter. You can engage in rituals for a lifetime but your heart may never have been opened to your Lord. The inner teachings of this mystical path are what we must live and demonstrate so that the world can be freed from religion that has become rote and dead.

The mystical path is a legitimate path. It's not nonsense, it's not hysteria, it's not a manifestation of some kind of a psychological problem. It is legitimate to desire to be one with God. It is your divine birthright. All of the divine love of the universe is surrounding you now, intensifying in your being and telling you that this is the day and the hour when you can transcend yourself.

The mighty angel Justinius, Captain of Seraphic Bands, says, "I ask for you to consider this goal for yourself, the goal of the ascension, and not to postpone it to another lifetime or some undefined future. The ascension is this day. It is every day. And you are ascending moment by moment, erg by erg, as you give back to God the energy that he has given to you—as you give it back in good works, in word and deed, and in the flow of the Holy Spirit that you achieve magnificently by the Science of the Spoken Word in your decrees."[58]

Radiant Spiral Violet Flame

In the name of the beloved mighty victorious Presence of God, I AM in me, my very own beloved Holy Christ Self, beloved Lanello, the entire Spirit of the Great White Brotherhood and the World Mother, elemental life—fire, air, water and earth! I decree:

> Radiant spiral violet flame,
> > Descend, now blaze through me!
> Radiant spiral violet flame,
> > Set free, set free, set free!
>
> Radiant violet flame, O come,
> > Drive and blaze thy Light through me!
> Radiant violet flame, O come,
> > Reveal God's power for all to see!
> Radiant violet flame, O come,
> > Awake the earth and set it free!
>
> Radiance of the violet flame,
> > Explode and boil through me!
> Radiance of the violet flame,
> > Expand for all to see!
> Radiance of the violet flame,
> > Establish mercy's outpost here!
> Radiance of the violet flame,
> > Come, transmute now all fear!

And in full faith I consciously accept this manifest, manifest, manifest! (3x) right here and now with full power, eternally sustained, all-powerfully active, ever-expanding and world enfolding until all are wholly ascended in the Light and free!

Beloved I AM! Beloved I AM! Beloved I AM!

SECTION THREE

The Eightfold Path

WE HAVE REACHED A POINT IN our evolution, both spiritual and material, when we can no longer think of ourselves as Christian or Buddhist or Moslem or Jew. The teachings of the Great White Brotherhood have been given to us, and those teachings and that Light cannot be confined to the narrow lines of doctrine and dogma. They cannot be placed within any sect, because the human spirit can no longer be sectionalized. The teachings of the Mother that come forth from the Great White Brotherhood are for the integration of cosmic law. And this law has been presented by teachers of Truth of all ages.

One of those teachers was Gautama Buddha, who we know today as the Ascended Master Gautama, Lord of the World. This Master has defined Buddhism as "the igniting of the internal being of God."[1] He has also told us: "You can be me and I can be you right where you are."[2] You have the seed of Buddha right inside of you, and because you have it, you have the potential to become a Buddha.

Gautama taught this same message when he walked the earth. He was the embodied Buddha in the sixth century B.C. Sprinkled throughout the Mahayana scriptures is Gautama's teaching that all beings have the essence of Buddhahood. This essence, or seed, has also been called the "Buddha-nature." We read in one Buddhist text: "There exists in each living being the potential for attaining Buddhahood, called the Buddha-essence ..., 'the legacy abiding within.'"[3]

Another text, attributed to Lord Maitreya, speaks of this essence, or seed: "The road to Buddhahood is open to all. At all times have all living beings the germ [seed] of Buddhahood in them."[4]

The Four Noble Truths

In his first sermon following his enlightenment, Gautama outlined Four Noble Truths and the Noble Eightfold Path. This sermon is called "Setting in Motion the Wheel of the Law" or "Turning the Wheel of Truth," and it was delivered at the Deer Park at Isipatana (now Sarnath) near Benares. In it he explained that by avoiding the extremes of self-indulgence and self-mortification one gains knowledge of the Middle Path, or the Middle Way. Gautama preached that the Tathagata* "does not seek salvation in austerities, but neither does he for that reason indulge in worldly pleasures, nor live in abundance. The Tathagata has found the middle path.

"There are two extremes, O bhikkhus, which the man who has given up the world ought not to follow—the habitual practice, on the one hand, of self-indulgence which is un-

---

* *Tathagata:* a title for Gautama Buddha used by his followers and by Gautama when he is speaking of himself. Literally translated as "thus come one" or "thus gone one," the word is variously taken to mean a perfectly enlightened one; one who has come and gone as other Buddhas, teaching the same truths and following the same path; or one who has attained "suchness" *(tathata)* or become one with the Dharmakaya, hence he neither comes from anywhere nor goes anywhere.

worthy, vain and fit only for the worldly-minded—and the habitual practice, on the other hand, of self-mortification, which is painful, useless and unprofitable.

"Neither abstinence from fish or flesh, nor going naked, nor shaving the head, nor wearing matted hair, nor dressing in a rough garment, nor covering oneself with dirt, nor sacrificing to Agni, will cleanse a man who is not free from delusions."[5]

When you are free from your delusions you may or may not choose to engage in those practices. They are helpful but symbolic. And if they are mere covering and we are still full of dead men's bones,[6] then they avail nothing and only convince us we are getting somewhere when we are not.

The Middle Way

I would say that in the East we have a tendency toward greater self-mortification and in the West we have a tendency toward greater self-indulgence. We do need the Middle Way. Gautama taught that this Middle Way leads to six conditions of consciousness. They are insight, wisdom, calmness, higher knowledge, enlightenment and nirvana.

Gautama proceeded to teach his disciples the Four Noble Truths: First, that life is *dukkha,* "suffering." Second, that the cause of this suffering is *tanha,* "desire" or "craving." Third, that suffering will cease when the craving that causes it is forsaken and overcome. This state of liberation through the cessation of suffering leads to *nirvana,* which means literally extinction or blowing out—the blowing-out of the not self. The Fourth Noble Truth is that the way to this liberation is through living the Noble Eightfold Path, or the Middle Way.

The first step on the Eightfold Path is to have right understanding, or right views. The second is right aspiration, right thought, or right resolve. Third is right speech. Fourth is right action, or right conduct. Fifth is right livelihood. Sixth is right effort. Seventh is right mindfulness, and eighth is right concentration, or right absorption.

These eight points of self-mastery are the endowment of your Holy Christ Self. Know this Holy Christ Self as your Real Self, and know your Real Self as possessing all of these attributes. Know that your Real Self has developed them to the full level of Christ-mastery and adeptship and is waiting for you to receive them.

As you put on these attributes in daily striving and attentiveness to the precepts of the Law, you are putting on the robes of righteousness of your True Self. You are putting on your deathless solar body, which Jesus referred to as the wedding garment. You weave this wedding garment by the practice of these eight right attitudes.

Eight Points of the Law

These eight points of the Law fulfill the seven rays of the seven chakras and the eighth ray and chakra, which is the secret chamber of the heart.

The first is right understanding, right viewpoint, right perspective—being centered neither to the left nor the right in relative thinking but being centered in God. This is a quality that is developed through the heart chakra and the third ray, whose color is pink and may intensify to a deep rose. The heart chakra has twelve petals. We remember the prayer of Solomon: "Give me, O LORD, an understanding heart."[7]

Right understanding, or right views, is described as knowledge of the Four Noble Truths; having views free from superstition or delusion; having penetrating insight into reality, or emptiness. Gautama said to his disciples: "What, now,

Brothers, is Right Understanding?

"When ... the disciple understands Evil and understands the Root of Evil; when he understands Good and understands the Root of Good; this is Right Understanding.

"What now ... is Evil? Killing ... is evil. Stealing is evil. Unlawful sexual intercourse is evil. Lying is evil. Slandering is evil. Using harsh language is evil. Vain talk is evil. Covetousness is evil. Cruelty is evil. Wrong views are evil.

"And what, Brothers, is the root of Evil? Greed is the root of Evil; Anger is the root of Evil; Delusion is the root of Evil.

"And what, Brothers, is the root of Good? Freedom from Greed ... freedom from Anger ... freedom from Delusion is the root of Good."[8]

When we think about the conditions of consciousness of greed and anger, we can objectively see them and determine whether they are in us or not. But when it comes to delusion, we are self-deluded by our own desires, by our own pride and ego. We are so much a part of the ego and its pride and its desires that we do not know we are in a state of delusion until increment by increment we catch a higher insight and we observe ourselves mounting an inner spiral staircase, if you will, to a point of enlightenment that, if we are observant, we recognize we did not have yesterday. And if we are wise, we will write down the experience and the insight and anchor into it and take another step.

Freedom from self-delusion is a great necessity on the Path. We need to pursue it with all intensity in our prayer and our thought and our daily consideration of the steps we take and what we do.

The second step of the Eightfold Path is right aspiration, right thought, or right resolve. This is a right attitude that must be had by the soul if the soul is to return to the Christ Self and to the I AM Presence. This point corresponds to the six-petaled seat-of-the-soul chakra, which is the abiding place of the soul. This is the chakra of the seventh ray, the violet ray, which has many shades, from violet-pink to purple.

The soul's aspiration must be centered in God—in having right thought, right contemplation upon the law of God and the right resolve to accomplish her mission in life. This resolution is the use of desire constructively—setting one's desire, setting one's sail and moving in that direction consistently, day after day after day.

The third step of the Eightfold Path is right speech, which relates to the throat chakra. The action of right speech is therefore the right qualification of this ray of power, which is the first ray, the ray of the will of God. The throat chakra has sixteen petals; its color is blue. With right speech we therefore affirm right desire.

Right speech includes abstaining from lying, slandering, harsh or abusive language, vain talk or idle chatter. Right speech is speech that is kindly, open and truthful. Gautama said to his disciples, "What, Brothers, is Right Speech? A man, Brothers, has overcome lying and he abstains from telling falsehood. He speaks the truth, he is devoted to the truth, he adheres to the truth, he is worthy of confidence, is not a deceiver of men.... Thus he brings together those that are at variance; establishes those that are united;... he delights in concord; it is concord that he spreads by his words.

"He has given up harsh language.... He speaks words that are free from rudeness, soothing to the ear, loving, going to the heart, courteous, rejoicing many, elevating many.

"He has overcome vain talk.... He speaks at the right time, speaks in accordance with facts, speaks to the point. He speaks about the Dharma [the law and the teaching] and the Discipline of the Order; his speech is of real value and agrees with its object.

"He bears in mind the injunction which says: 'In meeting one another, Brothers, there are two things that ought to be adhered to: either conversation about the Truth or holy silence.'

"This, Brothers, is Right Speech."⁹

The fourth step is right action, or right conduct. This is the base-of-the-spine chakra. It is the white ray; the chakra has four petals. Action and right conduct are the physical outpicturing of all that we contain in our heart, in our mind, in our soul, in our desires, in our being. The base-of-the-spine chakra is a physical chakra. It is the energy by which life is sustained and life is continued.

The fifth step is right livelihood, and it pertains to the solar-plexus chakra, which has ten petals. It is the sixth ray of purple and gold, the ray of service and ministration. Right livelihood is living honorably by a profession that does not harm any living thing and not choosing an occupation that is not conducive to spiritual progress. It is what we do in life, how we give of ourselves to one another, to society, to our nations. Right livelihood must be based on right desire, and the solar plexus is the chakra of desire. Wrong desire breeds wrong livelihood.

Right effort, the sixth step, is established as right focus through the third-eye chakra, which has ninety-six petals. It is the fifth ray, the emerald ray. By the All-Seeing Eye of God we focus. And as we focus on what our effort will be each day, the direction of our serving and our striving, we must have purity of desire in the inner eye. We must not lust after another, be jealous of another, want what someone else has. Right effort is based upon a direct relationship with God.

Right effort entails right exertion in self-training and self-control. Right effort is following what are called the "four right efforts." We must make an effort to "end existing evil." We must make an effort to "prevent new evil." We must make an effort to "cause new virtue." We must make an effort to "increase existing virtue."

The seventh step is right mindfulness. It is the attribute of the thousand-petaled lotus of the crown chakra. This is the second-ray chakra, and its color is yellow. Right mindfulness is always moving to establish oneself in the Mind of God that was in Christ Jesus,[10] that was in Gautama Buddha and all those who have attained that oneness. It is having an active, watchful mind, an alert mind that tends to details and masters them. Right mindfulness is the captain of one's ship. The crown must be opened, because when one has illumination and then full enlightenment, one can direct the courses of all of the seven rays.

The eighth step is right concentration, or right absorption. This relates to the secret chamber of the heart, an antechamber of the heart chakra. This eight-petaled chakra is the place of the threefold flame. The secret chamber of the heart is the place where you meet the Master, the Guru, the Lord Buddha. Right concentration is upon God and upon the Highest Self and upon the point of Light. It is earnest contemplation on the deep mysteries of Life. It is mental tranquility and the absence of distraction. Right absorption is the absorption of the mind and of the soul in God and in the Teacher. Without right concentration and absorption, we do not attain the full bonding of our souls to the Christ.

In Buddhist teachings, this eighth step involves meditation and proper breathing, as well as the techniques of Hinduism's raja yoga (known as "the royal road to reintegration"). It is a means of finding integration in all of the chakras and in the I AM Presence through direct personal experience of God within by the science of the spoken Word.

Paths of East and West

The teaching on the Eightfold Path is commonly ascribed to Gautama Buddha. In truth, it is the teaching of all of the Gurus who preceded him in the lineage of Sanat Kumara and all who followed him.[11] It is also the teaching of Jesus Christ. Each one of these steps we can also find in Christian teaching.[12]

The paths that have been evolved in East and West are for the selfsame purpose of placing the hand of the soul in the hand of the Christ Self. For only thus can the Way be illumined by right knowledge, right aspiration, right speech, right behavior, right livelihood, right effort, right mindfulness and right absorption.

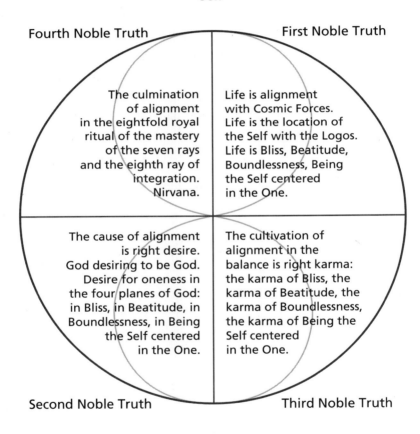

Figure 26 The Four Noble Truths on the Karmic Clock—Spirit

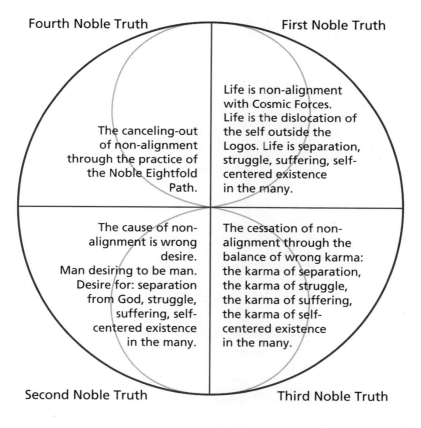

Figure 27 The Four Noble Truths on the Karmic Clock—Matter

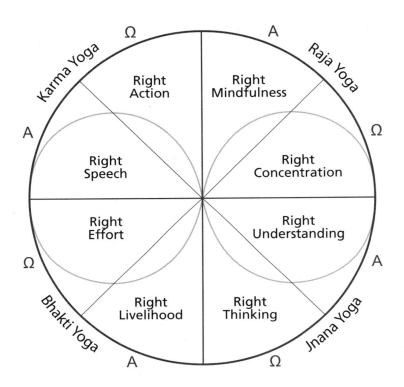

Figure 28 The Middle Way—Eightfold Clock

The eight steps of the Eightfold Path correspond to the seven rays and the eighth ray, as explained in the text. They can also be understood as Alpha and Omega (yang and yin, masculine and feminine) aspects of the four quadrants of being, which correspond to the four paths of yoga outlined in Hinduism. The etheric body corresponds to raja yoga, the mental body to jnana yoga, the emotional body to bhakti yoga, and the physical body to karma yoga. (See book 3 in the Climb the Highest Mountain series, *The Masters and the Spiritual Path,* chapter 1, "The Highest Yoga," for further teaching on these four paths and other forms of yoga.) The Path begins and ends with Right Association with Christ, the point of the 3 o'clock line on this diagram. "Acquaint now thyself with him, and be at peace; thereby good shall come unto thee" (Job 22:21).

SECTION FOUR

The Seeker and the Sought

EVERY LIFESTREAM HAS SOME jeweled expression of divine Reality to reveal to the world when he or she is ready. To make oneself ready, then, is the vital factor in Truth and the business of living. Each individual has a portion of the whole that is his own special lot, for it can rightly be said that no two people are alike. The message of God and the Word of God must go forth to Jew and Gentile, to bond and free, to wise and ignorant, to all in whom the Spirit of Life is active and to those whose hopes in some cases are dead indeed.

The message of hope that is embodied within the power of Truth is the only means of salvation to the planet. Little kernels and crumbs from the LORD's table fall through the channels of the many religions into waiting, hungry hearts. But some men and women are not satisfied with the ordinary, or even with the idea of public acceptance, but choose to make their criteria, "Is it true, and will it produce for me and for my fellow men the fruit of striving?"

These will quickly see that the gift of God to the world is

himself. Only by receiving this priceless gift of his own divine Reality can man become master of himself and thus, hopefully, an Ascended Being, able to aid others and carry on in the method of forward progress into the Infinite.

And what is the Infinite? Is it not also the great circle that contains the little point of Light that is the finite? The lesser is contained by the greater—and more than that, the lesser is a focal point of the greater in the process of revealing itself.

The one Path above the many shows an individual who is steeped in error and molded by darkness how he can be brought to the Light and cut free from human discord. Then he becomes elevated to the stature of candidate for the ascension, and ultimately he becomes an Ascended Being.

The way of the cross was forerunner to the ascension, yet man has stressed the cross and not the crown of the ascension. The divine purpose must be fulfilled, and the one Path above the many must be seen as salvation and liberty now, truth now and progressive revelation.

Man must use the violet transmuting flame and be weaned away from wrong habit patterns of thought and feeling. Christlike concepts and modes of thought must be reestablished in the forcefield of each individual. The reach must exceed the grasp and the Way be made plain.

Seek Until Ye Find

The one Path above the many is that which men do seek in the many. If they find it not, they must continue to seek it until they do find it. They must never lose sight of their search for a standard of faith and purity that is resident within the main religions of the world, so long as seekers do not confine themselves to the "letter that killeth."[1]

If this high standard of living Truth be adhered to in the

spirit, it provides that blessed assurance for every lifestream that God will lead him individually by the power of the Holy Spirit to the one Path above the many.

This one Path is the Path of the spiritual avant-garde. It is the Path of those who are sometimes the lonely ones, until they have passed through the sea of troubles into higher initiations. It is the Path of the seeker who becomes the sought. It is the Path of victory over the long night of error. It is the dawn that breaketh to the eternal day.

Folly and delusions of error melt away in the sunlight of Truth. Truth shows the face of God behind all things and reveals that all things must be shaped in the divine image by a conscious effort of the will.

"Go and do thou likewise,"[2] becomes a fiat to all. "Thou art my beloved Son,"[3] is spoken to all. It becomes the personal charge of God that all learn to accept in the justice of creation.

God Gave the Gift of the Future to Us All

How could it be that the Universal God—whose infinite wisdom framed the world, the star systems, the marvelous tributaries of the nerves and arteries in physical being and the radiant outreach of the mind, who has given his intelligence and the gift of his creative heart to man—would cause that gift to fail?

He will not do so, for God has given the gift of the future unto us all. In our union with that precious gift lies our strength. In our division and our diversity lies the false sense of personal salvation that seeks to laud the efforts of the ego while denying the efforts of God.

Without realizing what he does, man leans on the frail staff of mortal opinion. He seeks out his confessors, the old and familiar, and finds there a pseudo-comfort that will one day pale into insignificance when he learns the Truth. For sooner or later, man must return to the feet of the Masters and perceive that the brotherhood of angels and men is a divine chorus whose anthems, universal in character, will lead all to "the place where the Lord lay."[4]

For where I am, there shall ye be also,[5] holding my hand as you journey, pilgrims all, upon the one Path above the many. Rightly so, for the Lord said unto me, write "It is done," and it was done.

Chapter 4

The Great White Brotherhood

> *The kingdoms of this world are become the kingdoms of our Lord, and of his Christ; and he shall reign for ever and ever.*
> *And the four and twenty elders, which sat before God on their seats, fell upon their faces, and worshipped God,*
> *Saying, We give thee thanks, O Lord God Almighty, which art, and wast, and art to come; because thou hast taken to thee thy great power, and hast reigned.*
>
> REVELATION

The Great White Brotherhood

THE GREAT WHITE BROTHERHOOD is a spiritual order of Hierarchy, an organization of Ascended Masters united for the highest purposes of God in man as set forth by Jesus Christ, Gautama Buddha and other World Teachers. The word *white* refers not to race, but to the white Light of the Christ that surrounds the saints and sages of all ages who have risen from every nation to be counted among the immortals.

The Goddess of Liberty would draw all men into the cooperative spirit of universal liberty under the banner of the Great White Brotherhood. For through such a union will the souls of earth achieve their divinely appointed destiny. She explains:

"The thrust of man's desire for liberty has its origin in the very sun center of the Universe. Man was conceived in the expansive flame of liberty from God's own heart. This Reality, dimmed now by intruding factors, remains the goal of the wise and the sincere.

"The billions who call the planet Earth home are broken fragments of a universal oneness. The liberty of oneness has been lost to the multifaceted sense of separation, and thus, beneath his own fig tree and attached to his own vine,[1] man goes his separate and several ways.

"No specific good would occur in the community of being by forcing the separated segments of the universal into an unwilling alliance. For there, the liberty of oneness would be ignored, and the pull of the senses, like snorting wild steeds, would create its tides of restless energy to pull man away from the balance of true Being.

"Only the pull of the sun center of universal Reality, only the recognition by mankind en masse of the great Laws governing cosmos and the spread of understanding about cosmos can develop within the unfolding identity of the individual a sense of the harmony of universal liberty."[2]

Renewed Opportunity

Trailing clouds of glory, the children of Alpha and Omega come into the world fresh from the octaves of Light, vowing to do His will and to fulfill the noble plan. Descending in a spiral of Light, consciousness involutes, rolling into a ball of fire as it draws within itself the Light-potential for another round of evolution.

The soul, which had full awareness at the end of the previous cycle, in the twinkling of an eye becomes—once again—an embryonic god. Spiraling into the birth canal, she loses the memory of former lives and friendships, of buoyant life at inner levels. The veil of mercy falls, but the positive and negative momentums of past development remain as a sheath of identity.

Secured within the heart is the seed containing the nourishment of solar (soul) destiny. The keys for every right decision are locked within the etheric body. The voice of conscience becomes the steady compass that will guide the frail bark across the high seas of adventure in the world of form.

Through a tunnel of innocence the soul comes, only to find civilization with all its accoutrements waiting like a mammoth beast, eager to devour her purity. The distant memory of exalted spheres makes the soul unwary. How dense the world has become! She is slow to learn its ways.

A Thirst for Brotherhood

Alas, the world to which the soul has come is far from being a reflection of etheric cities and temples of Light where she has sojourned between embodiments. All of a sudden, the soul realizes that she is caught between the synthetic world and the real world, not really a part of either one. Vows easily taken at airy heights become a cross. As the fiery ball evolutes and the soul reaches her farthest point of descent, the dilemma of the ages becomes an unbearable weight.

An idealist in her youth, the soul would turn society inside out and level injustice with a clenched fist and a loud outcry, "It's all wrong!" But those who have become accustomed to the darkness of unreality do not understand her plea.

The soul knows that there are rules to the game of Life, formulas that unlock the secrets of overcoming, laws that govern the release of energy. These keys to Reality provide the links in the chain of Being, and without them neither child nor child-man can make substantial inroads into the existing structures and established traditions that have perpetuated evil as well as good through the centuries.

Entering into the mainstream of life, the soul is often caught in the undercurrents of mass movements and vortices of hatred, prejudice, war and the manipulations of the Luciferians. She cries out for help, and her Elder Brothers and Sisters, who have charted the course before her, heave her the lifeline of the Great White Brotherhood.

The Great White Brotherhood's Reason for Being

The Great White Brotherhood's primary function is to return mankind's consciousness to the liberty of Oneness through the spreading abroad of an understanding of cosmos—the unerring Laws that govern the cycles and destiny of the microcosm (man) and the Macrocosm (his true home of Light).

The purpose of this chapter is to unveil the Brotherhood and to place our readers in direct contact with their Elder Brothers and Sisters, who are fully qualified to lead the way out of the synthetic environment.

The Creator in his wisdom foreknew from the Beginning the consequences of man's misuse of the gift of free will. He foresaw each wrong decision as a negative spiral drawing man downward into shadowed resentment and the darkness of self-delusion—begetting fear, doubt, rebellion and finally total separation from the creative plan and from the freedom of good will.

Having seen how other systems of worlds were penetrated by the darts of that pride that entered into the heart of Peshu Alga,* God knew that it would take only a few rebellious

---

* Peshu Alga was the first individual in this solar system to fall from the high state of the consciousness of Good. The story of his fall and the subsequent fall of the Archangel Lucifer is told in book 8 of this series, *The Path of Christ and Antichrist*.

lifestreams to puncture the balloons of personal happiness for millions of his children. God, therefore, prepared a way whereby eternal Truth might be preserved in every system of worlds, on every planetary body where the children of the sun were sent with wings on their heels to evolve the plan of Life.

Inasmuch as all men came forth from God and were intended to fulfill his plan, the Father, knowing the end from the beginning, conceived of a great Brotherhood of Light, an Eternal Brotherhood wherein those of more advanced attainment on the Path would help their brothers of lesser attainment.

God intended cooperation among his children—a blending of the Light rays, a weaving of the threads of Light that form the universal deathless solar body, the antahkarana, or web of Life, each thread maintaining its identity while at the same time contributing to the universal Oneness.

Mary Baker Eddy glimpsed this cosmo-conception of the brotherhood of man under the Fatherhood of God when she wrote in *Science and Health with Key to the Scriptures:* "God gives the lesser idea of Himself for a link to the greater, and in return, the higher always protects the lower. The rich in spirit help the poor in one grand brotherhood, all having the same Principle, or Father; and blessed is that man who seeth his brother's need and supplieth it, seeking his own in another's good."[3]

Glimpsing the grand fraternity of Light-Beings she remarked, "The universe of Spirit is peopled with spiritual beings, and its government is divine Science.... Advancing spiritual steps in the teeming universe of Mind lead on to spiritual spheres and exalted beings."[4] Observing the service of the builders of form she said, "The eternal Elohim includes the forever universe."[5]

The Formation of the Great White Brotherhood

The idea of the Brotherhood was born in the Mind of God through the universal Christ consciousness who was the Logos, the pure Light of the Great White Way. God the Father could not behold evil nor look upon iniquity,[6] but through the Christ, he was in touch with every situation in the universe. The Christ-intelligence endowed the Father's concept with the tangible Reality of the Great White Brotherhood. Thus was born the seamless garment of the universal Christ consciousness.

The Brotherhood is the hope of every man. It is God's plan for the orderly expression of his love. It is his provision for the raising of the individual through the raising of the whole, as well as for the raising of the whole through the raising of the individual. It is an effective means whereby God reaches out secretly to perform his wonders of deliverance and his miracles of salvation to a world that has departed the path of righteousness.

Although spiritual in origin, the Great White Brotherhood maintains a very real contact with people on the earth today. Higher initiates are quite aware of their contact with the Brotherhood, whereas lesser initiates work and serve without any conscious knowledge of the contact. The Great White Brotherhood functions also on other planets and in other systems of worlds.

Agents of the Brotherhood on Earth

At one time, the Brotherhood adopted a resolution under the aegis of the Karmic Board whereby some of the hidden mysteries and hidden power of past ages (which to the present have been kept from unascended mankind but given in part to certain adepts prior to their ascension) would be released into the hands and use of some among the advanced chelas of the Masters who had demonstrated balance and responsibility over a long period of their lives.

These individuals were given the authority to act as a point of contact with the Brotherhood in the world of form to establish certain talismans upon the planet. These talismans would counteract the negatively qualified compelling forces that have enslaved the minds of the youth, and the aged as well. Absolute humility was necessary in those to whom these powers were given.

Although the Brothers in White made no physical contact with these initiates, each one was given a mystical experience activating internal spiritual powers together with the understanding of how to use these powers. An index of action, together with the plan of cooperation with the invisible Brotherhood, was also released with that dispensation, which was granted by the Karmic Board in order that mighty focuses of Light would be anchored in the world of form enabling mankind to break the power of vicious habit—whether the use of intoxicants and narcotics, the wrong use of knowledge or of tongue, propensities for ego-strutting or the vanity of wasted energy.

The Maha Chohan, representative of the Holy Spirit, explained: "New clarity coming into the mind will enable many among the students to have a greater measure of attunement with their own God Presence, I AM. A sense of personal well-being under God and of universal Brotherhood will permeate the atmosphere of the planet, making many among mankind more vitally aware of the Holy Spirit in its active participation in human affairs as a means of deliverance for the earth from the perils of the past ages and decades—a release from the intensification of mortal delusion and a clarification of the earth's place in the solar scheme."[7]

Cosmic Service

The members of this spiritual fraternity represent the Godhead as rays of Light flooding forth from the sun, each one carrying an aspect of the Creator's consciousness and making it practical to embodied souls. The members are not permitted to divulge their membership—even to other members. They may, however, acknowledge service under the direction of the Masters of the Great White Brotherhood. One of the best-known members of the Great White Brotherhood is the Ascended Master Jesus the Christ, whose Galilean ministry was a magnificent manifestation and fulfillment of centuries of intense preparation and millennia of divine intent.

The higher initiates of the Brotherhood are known as "the Lords of the Flame." It is recorded in the Bible that "our God is a consuming fire."[8] "The angel of the LORD appeared unto Moses in a flame of fire out of the midst of a bush: and he looked, and, behold, the bush burned with fire, and the bush was not consumed."[9] Out of the midst of the bush God said unto him, "I AM THAT I AM."[10] By this we know that God is a flame who has individualized himself in the flaming identity of his many servant sons.

The Mandala of a Root Race

The Masters have said that the universe is a cosmic playpen in which God sits with eyes of wonder, awaiting the moment when humanity will finally recognize who they are; and as they do, they will speak God's name, I AM, and the child will be a man.[11] Thus the lifestreams of the first root race came forth to their playpen earth as gods in embryo—rejoicing, expanding and serving together. They were the first of seven root races assigned to this planet.

A root race is a group of souls, a lifewave, who embody together and have a unique archetypal pattern, divine plan and mission to fulfill. A root race is a design from the heart of God, a solar mandala. Each point of the geometric form, intricate as embroidered lace, is represented by a son and daughter of God—twin flames destined to outpicture a facet of the design through the monadic Whole, the androgynous sphere that was their origin.

Representing the seven rays in perfect balance, as well as the 144 virtues of the Godhead, a root race is a unit of Hierarchy, complete in itself for the purpose it is destined to fulfill. It is endowed with the native affections of brotherhood that come from the illumined consciousness that sees that each monad occupies the central position for twelve other monads.

The cellular structure of brotherhood is like a DNA chain: each link carrying his flame, doing his part, sharing the beauties of God reflected in his energy-pool, thus enhancing the mission of every other monad. Thus brotherhood creates a chain reaction of joy—waves of Light rippling through the interconnecting antahkarana of souls wedded to a common purpose and fulfilling that purpose by the law of geometrics.

Wherever souls are evolving toward Oneness, there is brotherhood in action, an instinctive rapport of heart flames intertwined, braiding energies in a common bond (and a common strength), dancing around the maypole of the white-fire core.

Without brotherhood, the golden chain mail cannot be forged; without brotherhood, sunbeams do not merge. Without brotherhood, there is no contact between the monads, hence an absence of the cosmic flow. Without brotherhood, love is unexpressed, and without brotherhood, the triangle of Father, Son and Holy Spirit disintegrates.

The Representatives of God Come to Earth

The first representatives of Hierarchy on the earth were the seven beloved Archangels, who focused the power of the seven rays and nourished the consciousness of the first root race with the love, wisdom and power of the Universal Christ.

With them came the beloved Manu* of the first root race and his twin flame—fresh from the universal Causal Body—representing the Father-Mother God to the children of the sun. These Manus represented the Ascended Master consciousness to which all members of the root race aspired and which all were destined to attain, for in their sojourns in each of the twelve spheres,† they had studied not only individual mastery but also mastery over the four elements under the Twelve Hierarchies of the Sun.

When all was in readiness and the descent of the first root race was imminent, the Manu and his twin flame superimposed the pattern of the hierarchical design within and around the planetary body. This pattern illustrates the antahkarana, or web of Hierarchy, consisting of the twelve points on the clock, each one connecting with the others, and the point in the center connecting with each of the twelve on the periphery. This mandala, shown in Figure 29, is the matrix for the unfoldment of the thousand-petaled lotus of the crown chakra.

Before they can be appointed by God to the hierarchical office of Manu, twin flames must outpicture within their own forcefield and consciousness the full mastery of this

---

* Manu: Sanskrit for the progenitor and lawgiver of the evolutions of God on earth.
† The journey of the individual I AM Presence through the twelve spheres of the Great Central Sun and the journey of the soul through the twelve spheres of the individual Causal Body are described in *The Masters and the Spiritual Path*, book 3 of the Climb the Highest Mountain series, pp. 231–36, and *The Path to Immortality*, book 7 of the eries, pp. 132–37.

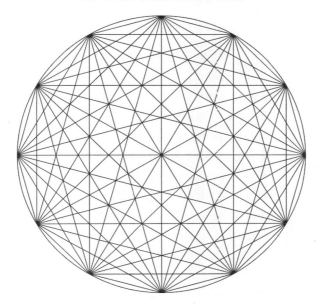

Figure 29 The Mandala of the Manus and Their Twin Flames
Focus of their hierarchical design

hierarchical pattern. They must become the diadem in full expression. The focal point of the consciousness of the representative of the masculine ray is in the center of the pattern, whereas the representative of the feminine ray focuses the consciousness of the Motherhood of God on the periphery.

Within this replica of the diamond-shining Mind of God we see the interaction of the "Alpha-*to*-*Om*ega," the single atom comprising the totality of the Father-Mother God in manifestation, which each set of twin flames is one day destined to become. Each intersection of the lines on the pattern is a focal point for initiation, for a release of cosmic energy and for a position in Hierarchy. All of the services of the Great White Brotherhood come forth from this hierarchical plan.

The Ritual of Descent

The lowering of the design from the consciousness of the Manu to the planet is a magnificent ritual. The Seven Archangels take their positions within the pattern that is held within the consciousness of the Manus. Standing in a circle and facing the center point, they are at that moment actually a part of the thousand-petaled lotus of the Manu himself.

If this is hard to understand, let us think of the question that is often used to relate time and space to infinity: "How many angels can stand on the head of a pin?" Now we ask, "How many Archangels can stand on the head of a Manu?" The answer in both cases is an infinite number, because there is no limitation of time or space in the Ascended Master's consciousness; therefore within the hierarchical pattern there is the opportunity for an infinite expansion of service, initiation and the expansion of the Light through the representatives of Hierarchy.

Let us visualize one, two, twelve, 144 or an infinite number of points on the circumference of the circle between each of the twelve major lines of the clock, which always represent the Twelve Hierarchies of the Sun (Figure 30). If these points were equidistant from one another, they would form the same pattern in groups of twelve, and each pattern would represent a turn of the gear in the wheel of the diamond-shining Mind of God.

As subsequent root races embody upon a planet, each one building upon the momentum of the services of the previous root race, we find that the pattern of Hierarchy becomes increasingly intricate and the Spirit of the Great White Brotherhood becomes more powerful.

During the magnificent ritual of the transfer of the pattern from the mind of the Manu to the planetary orb, the Arch-

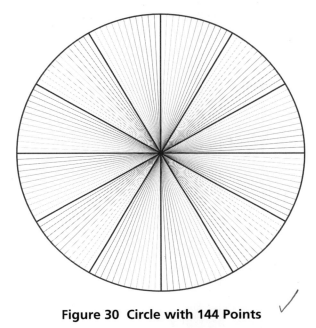

Figure 30 Circle with 144 Points

These 144 points form twelve groups of twelve.

angels form a circle around the focal point of consciousness that is the Manu. The seven intersections that occur on each of the twelve lines coming from the center to the periphery of the mandala indicate the focal points of the seven rays, which are directed through the consciousness of the seven Archangels (Figure 31).

The first to the seventh rays, proceeding in order from the center, show the order of the descent of the root races. The first root race comes forth on the first ray to precipitate the will of God through the seven outer spheres of the Causal Body. The second root race comes forth on the second ray to precipitate the wisdom of God through the same seven spheres. (See the Chart of Your Divine Self, page 105, which depicts the seven rays—spheres within spheres—in the scientific order, proceeding from the center to the periphery, used to magnetize

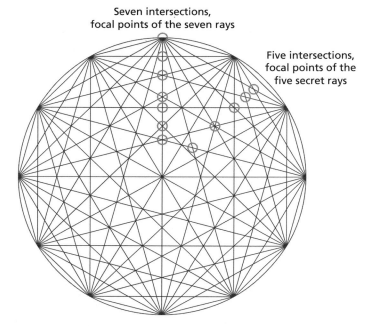

Figure 31 The Seven Rays and the Five Secret Rays

Each of the twelve lines from the center to the periphery has seven points of intersection, which indicate the focal points of the seven rays. Between the twelve lines are series of five intersections, which represent the five secret rays as they interpenetrate the order of the seven spheres and the focal points of the seven rays.

worlds and ideas from the formless to the formed.)

This process of magnetization is called precipitation. Between each of the twelve lines radiating from the center of the mandala, you will note five intersections. These represent the five secret rays as they interpenetrate the order of the seven spheres and the focal points of the seven rays.

The plan is the same for the Ascended Brotherhood as it is for the members of the root race who are to outpicture the plan of brotherhood when they take embodiment: the Manu, therefore, holds the central position—as Above, so below. He is the connecting point between the kingdom of this world and the kingdom of our God, holding the pattern of the City Foursquare, the cosmic cube, on behalf of the evolutions who are to embody.

At the precise cosmic moment, the transfer is made and the Archangels take their positions around the planetary body. It is their responsibility, together with the Manu, to teach the incoming lifestreams how to prepare for and pass the initiations that are required in order that they may take the positions in the Great White Brotherhood in fulfillment of the divine plan for the root race.

The Manifestation of the Hierarchical Design

The plan of God-government for the earth evolves from this pattern, as does the government of the Great White Brotherhood. Thus, an individual who serves at a certain connecting point on earth will no doubt serve in that same capacity after his ascension as he continues to evolve and pass greater and greater cosmic initiations in the infinite and orderly cycles of Hierarchy.

Once it is set, or meshed, with the four lower bodies of the earth, the hierarchical pattern becomes a giant reflector magnet. Polarizing with the Great Central Sun Magnet, it draws to the planetary home the lifewave that composes the root race that is to fulfill this unique, yet universal plan.

Each individual destined to fulfill the plan has implanted within his heart the seed of the hierarchical design, including the pattern of his own individual fulfillment and his own point of relativity within the plan. This is the Law that is written in man's inward parts,[12] the Law of his being and of his destiny.

At a certain point in his development, each lifestream, embracing the pattern of the divine will and pouring forth the fires of divine love from his heart to regenerate the matrix, releases a sufficient momentum—a critical mass of energy, as it were—through the heart chakra that enables the full momentum of the plan to illumine the mind, crowning the soul with the Christ consciousness, the crown of twelve stars that is the key to the unfoldment of the crown chakra. Thus the wisdom of the heart becomes the wisdom of the mind, and the product of that union is wisdom in action—the full cosmic power of the divine plan fulfilled through heart, head and hand.

This pattern of the Great White Brotherhood, emblazoned on every heart, is the key to the mainstream of Life and Light flowing to every soul. It contains not only the keys to precipitation, to self-mastery, to the cycles of time and eternity, to the development of the Causal Body and the overcoming of the negative spiral that forms the electronic belt, but also the secrets of each individual's cosmic destiny, rebirth, regeneration, transfiguration, resurrection and ascension.

All who meditate on this hieroglyph of Light will find the keys to the unfoldment of the seven chakras, each of which has a position within the hieroglyph, each of which becomes superimposed by the hieroglyph when the individual reaches a certain point of self-mastery. And through such meditation, all can draw the power of the Central Sun Magnet in the service of the Great White Brotherhood for the salvation of the planet.

The Crystal Becoming the Mist

It is through this pattern that the mist becomes the crystal and the crystal becomes the mist. The Goddess of Purity has spoken of the action of the flame within the crystal:

"Purity, beloved ones, begins with a single crystal, the

crystal of your consciousness. And from the point of the flame within the center of the crystal begins the expansion of the consciousness of purity. The pure in heart see God through the crystal of their own consciousness, which they have made God's consciousness.

"When you have mastered the many facets of the single crystal, then other crystals will be added unto you with many more facets of opportunity for self-mastery. And so, you see, each crystal denotes another step of initiation to the brothers and sisters serving in my retreat here in Madagascar.

"In our beautiful island in the sea we have consecrated our energies to the crystal diadem of purity that is the consciousness of God, and as the flame passes through the crystal—the mingling of the mist and the crystal, of the formed and the unformed—there is a release of the Cosmic Christ consciousness to the earth.

"Those who truly love will keep the crystal polished so that all of the myriad hues of the diamond-shining Mind of God will be reflected throughout their consciousness.

"Smudges appear easily on the crystal as one moves through the outer world that has been polluted by mankind's consciousness. Carefully one must take from one's pocket the velvet cloth to polish the crystal.

"Keep it clean as though it were the very dearest object of your affection, for at the moment when the Virgins (the holy Ascended Lady Masters) come to infuse you with the momentum of their purity and the Seraphim gather, having come lately from the very throne of God himself to bring to you a drop of purity from his heart—at that moment, precious ones, the crystal must be polished, else it cannot reflect the flame within the drop of purity.

"But if the crystal be polished, then the flame within the drop, taken from the ocean of God's flaming purity, can merge with the flame that is in the center of your crystal. A fiery magnetic attraction impels the purity of God to the center of each flaming crystal.

"But when there is darkness surrounding the crystal—between the flame within and the flame without—then penetration cannot occur. Blessed are the pure in heart, for they shall indeed see the consciousness of God's flaming purity."[13]

The First Three Root Races Ascend

As the members of the first root race completed their individual plan and began to ascend, they assumed the positions in Hierarchy to reinforce the momentums gathered below in the creative scheme above. Retreats and focuses of the Great White Brotherhood were gradually established as members of the first root race arose to fill the positions necessary for an ever-expanding and transcending magnetization of Light upon the planetary body.

In the early days of the first root race, the Royal Teton Retreat was opened as the home of the Manu and the focus of the seven beloved Archangels and their complements, who had also anchored their flames across the planetary body.

The forcefields of the Elohim were likewise intact as the chakras of the earth, which was then transparent crystal, reflecting the seven rays as a replica of the Causal Body. The rays of Alpha and Omega at the North and South Poles held the earth in perfect balance.

The seven root races destined to embody upon this planet come forth in the order of the seven rays. Thus the first root race laid the foundation of the Law, the will of God and the perfect divine plan for all who were to follow thereafter.

After the first root race completed its divine plan and ascended back to the heart of God, the second root race came forth in the same manner as the first, building on the pattern already established. Fulfilling the second ray of divine illumination, the members of this root race added to the pattern what they had been trained to outpicture in the yellow sphere of the Great Causal Body of God. The third root race then came forth, fulfilling the third ray of divine love, and returned to the heart of God. Thus the threefold flame action was complete.

The perfection of these first three Golden Ages is recorded in akasha* upon the planetary body, and the full-gathered momentum of these Sons and Daughters of God, all now Cosmic Beings, can be invoked on behalf of the victory of the four remaining root races who are to fulfill their destiny upon this planet. The magnetic forcefield of all that they attained is still anchored within the etheric body of the earth, waiting to be invoked.

The Interruption of the Cosmic Plan

It was during the time of the fourth root race on the continent Lemuria that the allegorical Fall of man took place. The interruption of the plan is well-known by students of the occult. The tearing of the veils of innocence that had insulated man's world with sheaths of righteousness, Light and fervent devotion took place as man consented to the serpentine lie projected into his thought and feeling processes by the fallen Luciferians.

The first to fall were the high priests, whose subtle sense of superiority over the people yielded to spiritual pride. Once the high priests of Lemuria began to be influenced by the prideful

---

* All that transpires in an individual's world and all events in the physical universe are recorded in an etheric substance and dimension known as *akasha* (Sanskrit, from the root *kas* 'to be visible, appear,' 'to shine brightly,' 'to see clearly'). Akasha is primary substance, the subtlest, ethereal essence, which fills the whole of space; the "etheric" energy vibrating at a certain frequency that absorbs, or records, all of the impressions of life.

rebellion of the Luciferians, wedges of darkness were driven into the consciousness of the people, separating them from their Source. Agitation and inharmony broke down the protection that is always sustained when people express true brotherhood to one another. Fear and doubt widened the gap between man and man, and man and God. Once mankind had shown themselves vulnerable to the illusions of duality, the entire planet lost the protective sheath that always seals the virgin consciousness from intruding Evil.

It was then that Solar councils allowed the remnant of laggard souls to embody through the fourth root race. These came from Maldek, the planet that was destroyed by the dark forces through the same tactics used by the manipulators today to degrade the consciousness of the people. (The remains of the planet Maldek are seen in the asteroid belt between Mars and Jupiter.)

When their home planet was destroyed, the laggards, through the mercy of the Great Law, were given another opportunity. It was hoped that the laggards would be molded and shaped and drawn into perfection by the members of the fourth root race embodied on Lemuria, but instead, the laggards tore down the virtue of the fourth root race.

The degeneration of the fourth root race and their failure to ascend necessitated the coming of the fifth root race during the time when fallen angels, laggards and members of the fourth root race were still embodied. The coming of the fifth and the sixth root races into an imperfect world accounted for their failure to fulfill their plan, as they were also corrupted by the conditions present on the planet when they arrived.

The Great White Brotherhood decided not to allow the seventh root race to come into embodiment until these conditions would be resolved.[14]

The Creation of the Karmic Board

After the coming of the Luciferians and then the laggards, the progression of mankind's misqualification of the energies flowing through the seven chakras (beginning with the crown and moving downward) finally reached its lowest point in the events described allegorically in the Bible as the Fall of Adam and Eve and the misuse of the sacred fire through the base-of-the-spine chakra.*

Eve, the mother of all living, was designed to be the perfect expression of the Motherhood of God; Adam, the Fatherhood. These two, symbolizing those who took embodiment on Lemuria as members of the fourth root race, failed to accept the admonishments of God and were thus driven from the Paradise of God's pure consciousness of holy innocence. God himself yet preserves that consciousness, and the Great White Brotherhood sustains it through their flame focuses maintained in retreats throughout the world.

The Great Karmic Board came into being when man was sent forth from the Garden of Eden to till the ground out of which he was taken[15] (for the laws of alchemy, of divine precipitation, would no longer be operative at the level of duality to which he had descended). The Karmic Board was established and vested with the authority to mete out divine justice and the return of individual and planetary karma as mankind were able to bear it.

---

* There are some who seek to interpret the events described in Genesis literally, and who therefore believe that the earth is no more than several thousand years old. These have had no little struggle with the fact that after Cain slew his brother Abel and became a wanderer upon the earth, he did not choose a wife from among his sisters, but went rather into the "land of Nod" from whence he chose a wife (Gen. 4:16–17). Here we note the record of a society contemporary with that of Adam and Eve. In fact, magnificent Golden Age civilizations existed upon this planet long before our Bible was written. One of the grossest attempts of the sinister force to pervert the Truth has been the dogmatic interpretation of the Bible. The living Word, the essence of Christ Truth, hidden from the foundation of the earth, must be discovered within each one's consciousness.

Man then became a dual being. He is a Spirit, as God is. But he has a soul, born of the flame of the Spirit and possessing a similitude of the Spirit, which he has cast down into the shadowed world of imperfection—the world of good and evil (for the soul has the potential of both good and evil, but the Spirit is immutable).

In order to regain his lost estate, man must now overcome the evil of which he is aware by a goodness other than his own. The righteousness of God, then, that exalteth a nation[16] must also exalt the individual and restore him to the paradise consciousness from whence he came.

The Rescue Mission

After the fall of the fourth root race, when great darkness was spread abroad upon the earth and there was not enough Light to perpetuate the existence of the planet, Sanat Kumara, Hierarch of Venus, came to earth to maintain the focus of Light in Shamballa to restore the evolutions of earth to their lost estate.

Shamballa! jewel of the sea, flame of hope for millions without flame and without hope! Shamballa! the beginning, the middle way and the ending of the Great White Brotherhood upon the planet Earth! With the coming of Sanat Kumara and three of the Holy Kumaras with their legions of Light and volunteers, the cooperative services of Hierarchy under the heading of the Great White Brotherhood began.

Mankind's extremity was God's opportunity. The rescue teams arrived. Their mission was to restore the consciousness of the children of God to primeval single-eyed vision, to raise them from the sense of duality into which they had fallen—the bottomless pit of carnal desire. These lost children, having cut themselves off from all contact with the Christ, required the intercession of Ascended Sons and Daughters of Light. Having lost the torch, they needed others to keep the Flame for them until they were able.

It was the saviour Sanat Kumara whom Daniel the prophet saw as the Ancient of Days. As he and the one hundred and forty-four thousand volunteers came to earth, they said: "We will keep the Flame of Life, the Mother flame and the threefold flame burning in the retreat of Shamballa. We will keep that Flame until the multitudes of the people of earth once again respond to the love of Almighty God."

During the first three Golden Ages, Ascended Masters, angelic hosts and elementals walked and talked with those whose consciousness never departed from the unity of Good. After the Fall, mankind's vision no longer perceived these emissaries of Light; their consciousness no longer penetrated the spheres of purity from which it had fallen.

The Masters retreated from the unholy vibrations of the world, and their focuses of Light became known as "retreats." Henceforth, only those who qualified would be allowed to enter these secret places of the Most High God, each one a focus of the Eden that had been lost—Eden having been the repository of the divine wisdom to which they no longer had access.

The representatives of the Great White Brotherhood who embodied subsequent to the coming of Sanat Kumara held the vision of their assignment by their common bond of Light. Their plan of action was focalized and held intact through the mandala of the hierarchical design.

The quantity of Light that had been sustained in the focuses of the Archangels and the Elohim and at the Royal Teton Retreat had been sufficient for Golden Age civilizations in which every lifestream knew himself as the Christ and drew daily from the heart of the Sun enough energy to fulfill his assigned position in the plan.

But the tremendous burden of world karma—the actual physical weight of misqualified energy superimposed upon the planet by the fallen angels, the laggards and misguided members of the fourth root race—necessitated a much greater release of Light to offset the darkness and hold the balance of Life on behalf of a planet and a wayward generation.

Accordingly, as the energy veil densified and the emissaries of Evil became more highly trained and organized, it became necessary to establish specific branches of service within the Great White Brotherhood for the coordination of the rescue mission. These would make known their findings to all other hierarchical units.

The Brotherhood organized the Cosmic Secret Service to report treacherous activities working against all of their retreats and against their avowed purpose of developing the Christ consciousness in mankind through a concentrated service to each of the seven rays. The legions of Archangel Michael, always active in their devotion to the will of God, now entered into twenty-four-hour service to protect the emerging Christ consciousness of embodied mankind on all of the seven rays and to report threats to planetary safety.

As more Ascended Servants voluntarily enlisted in the liberation of the evolutions of the planet, some joined the focuses of Light already established, while others opened new retreats of their own. Some of these were on the physical plane, while others remained at the etheric level.

Thus the Ancient of Days and all who followed, increasing in number up to the present moment, have taken the vow to keep the Flame and to expand the Light until some among earth's evolutions should be quickened and once again renew their vow to be bearers of the Flame. For Sanat Kumara had made the cosmic decision of seeing to it that the earth should not perish from the solar system.¹⁷

As it gathers more Light through cooperation with unascended mankind, the Great White Brotherhood paves the way for greater dispensations of Light to the earth from the heart of the Solar Logoi.

The Establishment of God-Government

The Great White Brotherhood serves as an integral, albeit invisible, force within every constructive endeavor in which unascended lifestreams are involved, however small or great. Dedicated to the implementation of the will of God, the divine plan of the hierarchical blueprint, the members of the Brotherhood strive diligently to lead each child of God to his place in the solar scheme, the crossroads of his destiny, the place where the lines of force merge in the mandala. For at that place is the release of the Christ Light within the heart of the atom.

At each one of those focal points, identity is born and the potential for an explosion of the Christ consciousness exists. At each intersection, a Messiah is born, and through him, another complete mandala can be formed.

The councils of the Great White Brotherhood consider that their single greatest concern is to establish God-government on earth. For where the governments of the nations reflect Ascended Master Law, the Golden Rule and the precepts of divine brotherhood, there the individual can evolve the Christ flame and become one with his divinity. Where governments are unjust, the image of the mandala cannot be outpictured in society.

In the days of the first three root races, the Manus were the rulers, and those who were appointed to hold office during their reign earned the right to represent the people because they had first represented the Light by passing initiations and proving their self-mastery over cosmic forces. As long as members of the Hierarchy were in positions of rulership, the earth prospered.

However, after the fall of the Luciferians, many of the high priests on Mu in whom the people had placed their confidence became rebellious and used their powers against one another. There followed the war of the priests. The images on Easter Island are a reminder of the decadence to which they fell; the invectives they hurled at one another instantly became crystallized in stone. Astral beasts of prey, mass forms and weird images resulted from the coalescing of their hatred. Divine love, which had once flowed through their chakras, was now perverted and turned to stone.

The Divine Right of Kings

The divine right of kings, a doctrine that persisted to the eighteenth century, came down to us as tradition from the Golden Ages when the Sons of God were invested with the authority of rulership and fulfilled Plato's ideal of the philosopher-king. But as the dynasties became infiltrated with corrupting elements and the stream was no longer pure, the rulers lost contact with the God Source, and they became as other men.

Injustices became so great that the people challenged the divine right of succession. Beginning in the nineteenth century, the Brotherhood endorsed democracy as the means whereby each man should become a king and a priest unto God, developing his Christ potential and being found worthy to rule himself.

With the coming of mass education and the raising of the level of the consciousness of the people, the Masters have been able to pave the way for an age of enlightenment wherein people would not only understand the Law but would behold the character of the Christ in their elected representatives. By this means, they would return to the system of government endorsed in the beginning, and those who by initiation had earned the right to rule would be elected to office under the guidance of the Christ Selves of the electorate.

Side by side with the plan of the Brotherhood to return mankind to a Golden Age, the false hierarchy—the forces of darkness—have moved to thwart the plans of the Brotherhood. Thus, the manipulators staged the French Revolution and through their secret organizations in Europe undermined the plan of Saint Germain for the unification of that continent.[18]

Having failed in his efforts to reestablish liberty in Europe as the Comte de Saint Germain, Saint Germain came to America and inspired the Constitution upon the early patriots. America came to be the cup of Light and freedom to the earth, the virgin wilderness where the World Mother could bring forth the Christ consciousness,[19] building a nation under God that all other nations could emulate.

Just as the Christ showed the way of individual self-mastery, so America was to show the way of national destiny.

Government Is Meant to Facilitate God's Plan

From the very beginning, the infiltrators of the dark forces worked to thwart the plan of God-government for America. One of their first moves was taking the wealth of the nation out of the hands of the people and putting it into the hands of the international bankers. This plot culminated in the Federal Reserve Act of 1913, which places the control of America's money in the hands of a partly private corporation, which in turn can manipulate economic crises according to the schedules of the Luciferians.[20]

The gold standard was ordained by God as the means to keep the balanced radiation of the sun flowing through the hands of the people for the health of their four lower bodies and for the perpetuation of brotherhood. Since gold is precipitated sunlight and a focus of the Christ Light, the removal of gold from circulation is one of the greatest single factors in the degeneration of the consciousness of the people.[21]

Another plot of the manipulators is uniting the nations prematurely—before they have individually attained the Christ consciousness. The giving up of individual sovereignty of the nations to a one-world body that is controlled by neither the Great White Brotherhood nor its appointed representatives can only lead to a Luciferian despotism that will deprive all mankind of the opportunity to return to the Godhead.

This form of tyranny, where the individual is subject to the state instead of the state being subject to the individual, ultimately caused the complete destruction of Maldek and of the planet Mars, where darkness and the passion of war in the evolutions evolving there on the astral plane make that planet a blight on our entire solar system.

The Ascended Masters teach that we cannot unite Good and Evil: "Be ye not unequally yoked together with unbelievers: for what fellowship hath righteousness with unrighteousness? and what communion hath light with darkness? And what concord hath Christ with Belial? or what part hath he that believeth with an infidel?"[22] The Christ does not sit at a conference table with Lucifer, but rebukes him, cuts him off and says, "Get thee behind me, Satan."[23] If this planet is to be preserved for a Golden Age civilization, the nations that are dedicated to the individual ascension of every man, woman and child on earth must not allow their energies to be drained by association with those who are not dedicated to the Christ. Only when all nations are brought to the level of the Christ consciousness can union occur.

Foundations of God-Government

Chananda, the head of the Indian Council of the Great White Brotherhood, explains: "The perfect God-plan for the whole world must be externalized. But this requires enough highly placed people in the governments of the nations of the world who have the vision and legislative know-how to forestall the constant agitation and opposition of the ignorant masses to long-term planning for the evolution of social justice. These clamor loudly to ensure the perpetuation of personal and private advantages for the few over and above the rights of the many.

"Karma, too, plays a part in the affairs of government. But the Lords of Karma have assured the Lord of the World, beloved Gautama, that when the governments of the world are ready and, by reason of the cooperation of their respective leaders, they do accept the divine plan for the earth and its evolutions, a dispensation will then be given that will put the mass karma of the entire earth under a special form of cosmic control.

"Under this system all lifestreams will be able to enter some form of temple training at night in their soul bodies and between embodiments. Thus, after passing from the screen of life from physical embodiment, most of the karma that is now outpicturing for them individually can be balanced at inner levels instead of through toil and suffering, as is presently the case.

"Mass ascensions will likewise be possible, for a utopian form of world government will automatically eliminate many of the present hazards of living. Struggle for place, position, financial advantage, political power and self-seeking will be replaced by that divine justice that affords—as the Constitution of the United States of America really intends—true equality of opportunity for all.

"In this veritable community of the Spirit, where individual dignity is upheld by the Light of its own divinity, the communistic and socialistic doctrines will be stripped of their false veneer and revealed to be—as in reality they are—methods that were evolved humanly as the result of the intellectual rebellion on the part of their founders against their own personal karma.[24]

"The spiritual community of the enlightened will expound the real democracy of the new republic wherein the nobility of life in its God-intended expression is its own acknowledged reward. No one will expect to be given honors or rights he does not deserve. Neither will anyone expect to deny to others their just opportunity to expand their understanding, test their spirituality or pursue life, liberty and true happiness to the fullest....

Blocks to the Brotherhood's Service

"It is to the complete achievement of these goals that the Great White Brotherhood is dedicated. The powers of the Brotherhood have been limited only in appearance or outer expression by mankind's oft-expressed proneness to misuse free will and ignore the advice of the Brotherhood (whether known or unknown).

"The same limitations that operate among men on earth to prevent or hinder man from perceiving and becoming the full manifestation of God as impersonal love in action are also present in mass misqualified thought and feeling as opposition to the universal benign intent of the Great White Brotherhood. Were this not so, the perfect world would long ago have been outpictured in human society.

"One of the principal challenges the Brotherhood itself faces is the training of chelas, or disciples, who will accept the responsibility of serving the eternal purposes while seeking themselves for individual perfection and spiritual victory. This cooperation between heaven and earth increases the Brotherhood's sphere of influence upon earth, bringing into manifestation at the earliest possible date more and more of the world plan of the Brotherhood, which is ever one with the universal will of God, or Good....

Branches of the Great White Brotherhood

"The Great White Brotherhood has many branches—some devoted to spiritual science and some to material science, others to the arts, culture, music, sculpture, architecture and community planning. Jurisprudence, both human and divine, is operative under beloved Portia and the Great Karmic Board; the governments of the world, under beloved El Morya; science and medicine, under beloved Hilarion; and each of the many fields of endeavor, both human and divine, are supervised by a branch of the Great White Brotherhood....

"Seeing clearly the divine plan, the members of the Brotherhood serve to augment and implement every constructive divine idea reflected in government, the social order, man and nature in order to evolve and exemplify the perfect extension of the kingdom of heaven into tangible material form and the manifestation of God-intended happiness everywhere....

Membership and Initiation

"Mundane government seems wholly logical, for on earth it represents the vesting of power in the hands of the few who act for the many in a supposedly just and correct manner. Those who have thought much on the governing aspects of Divinity and who have pondered the truism 'Order is heaven's first law' should have no difficulty in accepting the fact that divine government—which emanates from the Godhead in a wholly impersonal manner—is aided and abetted in its earthly administration by illumined, Ascended and Immortal Beings who, having been cut free from worldly thought and mortal expression, joyously remain connected with the planet Earth and its people in order to serve the causes of divine purpose.

"This august body of the faithful is wholly constructive and may also include spiritually illumined unascended beings dedicated to the will of God, who serve with and under the direction and radiation of those magnificent Ascended and Cosmic Beings who are consecrated to the fulfillment of the divine plan on earth....

"The Great White Brotherhood ... is wholly dedicated to the use of consecrated energies drawn from God through the conscious efforts of the Ascended Masters on behalf of mankind and implemented by the willing cooperation of those unascended beings who, both knowingly and unknowingly, cooperate with the divine intent. In the truest sense, the Great White Brotherhood is a fraternity of the Spirit—recognizing and embracing the Fatherhood of God and the brotherhood of man—which operates with divine authority, divine recognition, foreknowledge and absolute authorization of the Deity....

"The Great White Brotherhood initiates many members, yet none of them can ever admit to or boast of this membership. However, specially trained workers are occasionally authorized to reveal specific information to certain advanced or prospective chelas in order to accomplish a special purpose.

"Membership in the Great White Brotherhood cannot be purchased at any price. Neither can anyone who is unworthy be admitted to its sacred conclaves. By invitation men can rise to this high honor—yet many notable figures of the outer world, unknown to their outer consciousness, are inner initiates of this beloved fraternity.

"Cooperation with the Brotherhood is obtained through membership in the Keepers of the Flame Fraternity, which is chartered and authorized by the Great White Brotherhood in accordance with Ascended Master Light and love.[25] From such faithful cooperating lifestreams as those who remain steadfast in this high calling, the Ascended Masters are able, as the result of proximity and training, to draw initiates and servants of Hierarchy to further the mighty cause (when these show themselves readied and approved unto God). This instruction is designed, then, to help all to keep the flame....

"Initiation into the Brotherhood today is somewhat different than it was in ages past. Long ago the would-be chela was taken to Luxor, Heliopolis, Lhasa or elsewhere and given trials of great endurance involving both physical and spiritual tests. The rigors of these trials almost defy imagination, and many of the would-be chelas fell short of passing the mark. Those who did not are among the Immortals! Today, however, changing times, new methods of communication and transportation, and other factors have altered many old conditions; and new spiritual techniques have been evolved just as material methods have changed.

"Therefore, most of the students living in the present Aquarian age are being given their initiations in the outer world. Karmic events are, so to speak, altered whereby friends, relatives, associates and even the man in the street become the instruments through which their tests come. This makes it necessary for mankind, and especially the would-be disciple, to be extremely vigilant, for one never knows just when a vital and conclusive test may be in the offing.

"However, let me amplify that you must not permit this statement to cause you to become apprehensive. Just be diligent to behave as a Christ, remembering his words, 'Inasmuch as ye have done it unto one of the least of these my brethren, ye have done it unto me!'[26] If you will really follow this, you may well pass any test with flying colors that the Brotherhood sends for your perfection, admonishment and initiation into the highest spiritual brotherhood—the Great White Brotherhood—the fraternity of beloved Jesus, Kuthumi, El Morya, Djwal Kul, beloved Lanto, Kuan Yin, Mother Mary, beloved Serapis Bey, Paul the Venetian and every Ascended and Cosmic Being!

"To this aspire! To this calling be dedicated! There is much, much more to the Great White Brotherhood than either tongue or pen could tell."[27]

Religion

The Goddess of Liberty has told us: "The Masters of Wisdom, in their great outreach in every age and at the beginning of [the twentieth] century, have not neglected to inform mankind about the reality of the Brotherhood. The cloak of religion—which has smothered rather than swaddled mankind's beginnings in Truth—has masked the face of creative expansion, set brother against brother, absorbed mankind's energies in fruitless struggle, and weakened the plan of the Brotherhood for the unity of this age.

"As we inspired the leadership of Abraham, Noah, Moses and other great patriarchs, as we spoke through Zarathustra,

Apollonius of Tyanna and Jesus, as we released holy wisdom to Socrates, Plato and Emerson, so did we come through Madame Helena Petrovna Blavatsky in *Isis Unveiled* and *The Secret Doctrine*. We have also released our instruction through other adherents of Divine Truth, both metaphysical and occult, until the Occult Law was set aside and the pure passion of the flames of liberty and Truth was unleashed in the early 1930s.

"Man, caught in the miasma of his separatist dream, deigning to be fooled, has created a thousand foolish splinters that have taken him from the Truth center of his being. It is not that the germ of Reality and Truth is not active within the many spiritual organizations upon earth; it is simply that individuals do not grasp Truth when they find it, but prefer instead to form their own anthropomorphic God (a god made in their own image) and to embrace concepts that are foreign to Reality."[28]

The Masters sponsor certain activities of an advanced nature in order to bring progressive Truth to mankind. The early Christian church and most of the religions of the world were originally sponsored by the Great White Brotherhood. The Masters of Wisdom knew full well that with the passing of time, crystallization would occur in the tenets of the faith vouchsafed to the early founding fathers. This crystallization would occur through the consciousness of those who inherited the letter without actually receiving the inspiration of the Spirit.

Progressive Revelation Denied

Today there are many religionists throughout the world who are in the bonds of ignorance and the gall of bitterness, opposing the very plans that hold their greatest hope. Ministers and priests cry out against the Truth, supposing that because their traditions are long-enduring, they must be divinely ordained and therefore infallible. They deny progressive revelation, citing as proof the numerous little splinter groups and purveyors of psychicism who mimic and pretend to be true prophets of God.

The Great Divine Director once said: "It is sometimes difficult for individuals to understand just how others can be so gullible about spiritual things as to pin their faith on that which is obviously fraudulent. I do not think that the world is full of frauds, as men might imagine, but rather do I know that it is full of individuals who are often manipulated by forces beyond their ken."[29]

Those who accuse the true prophets of God of being tools of the devil have been tricked by the devil himself. Jesus said, "By their fruits ye shall know them,"[30] and it has been well said that the fruit falls not far from the parent tree.

The release of Truth is not just a series of words, concepts or ideas. It is an actual vibratory action that reaches up to the Godhead and brings the crystal-flowing stream of that action into human affairs. There it is diluted by some, diverted by others, and delighted-in by those whose love for freedom and Truth has raised their own vibrations to the place where they partake of its sparkling effervescence and absorb every bit that comes their way.

Let men seek understanding rather than vengeance. Let them examine the fabric of their own thought, and let them also examine the thoughts of the Ascended Masters. Let them remember that they did not come by their present state of awareness of ideas, ideologies and religious views in the short space of a day or a year.

The "Push-Pull" System of Seeking God

Saint Germain suggests an approach to spirituality that relies on both heavenly and earthly activities: "There are many schools of thought in the world concerning spiritual progress, how to make it and how to keep it. Not recognizing the reason for the existence of these different approaches to spirituality, some chelas become confused.

"They do not realize that outside of those organizations that are directly connected with the Great White Brotherhood, there are few that offer a balanced understanding of all of the many facets of the divine expression. Let me, then, remind those who are sincere to pay special heed to the tenets of the Great White Brotherhood.

"Some schools advocate the development of spiritual consciousness, indicating to their students that this spiritual consciousness will ultimately become so powerful as to cause all negative and baneful influences to drop off from them as overly ripe fruit from a tree.

"Other schools advocate the need for purification, indicating to their chelas that by purifying themselves from the elements of human creation they will naturally find their way back to God. In one sense I would call the former a 'push' system and the latter a 'pull' system.

"Now, let me say that while good exists in both systems, we advocate the use of both rather than one. We believe the 'push-pull' system of seeking God to be the best system of all. Let men recognize the need to purify their worlds of their own human creation, but let them also recognize the need to invoke the assistance of heaven on their behalf. And through attunement with that blessed heaven and the consciousness of the Ascended Masters, let them invoke all beauty unfolding within them here below, as Above."[31]

The Highest Law Is Expressed in Many Ways

A Great Emissary from Venus, speaking at a conference of the Indian Council of the Great White Brotherhood, commented on how the Great White Brotherhood uses many forms of religion to channel the energies of God to his creation:

"Theologians and their followers on Terra often seem incapable of differentiating between a stepped-down release of the Spirit of God and a higher release of that Spirit. Let them understand their own expression, 'God tempers the wind to the shorn lamb.'[32]

"The blessedness of Almighty God, his Spirit and the Spirit of his Sun Radiance, the Christ consciousness, charged with the cosmic illumination of the Divine Mother and her capacity to alter unwanted conditions for mankind, is released from the highest levels of the Godhead and descends into the very heart of the earth to contact the most primitive types, manifesting diversely to each level of awareness in order that everyone might derive the greatest benefits of the Great Law according to his capacity to receive.

"Be not then entangled in the yoke of bondage[33] that differing religious opinion sometimes brings about. Understand, blessed ones of the planet Earth, that many manifestations of the Father-Mother God are necessary in order to reach the various levels of consciousness of embodied humanity. There is no enmity between one manifestation of God and another. There is only the cosmic outreach from the heart of the Spirit of God intended to save that which is lost[34] in the planes of Matter."[35]

The Brotherhood Encourages Practical Spirituality

The Goddess of Liberty offers this advice to those who would put their highest aspirations into practice on earth: "All religion that has had its origin in the spirit of Truth ought (1) to bring to mankind a greater awareness of his divine potential, (2) to serve as a bond of union twixt the Brotherhood of Light and unascended man, and (3) to illumine mankind as to the pitfalls of worldly living.

"These pitfalls are not absent from the spiritual path, not by any means. No immunity has been guaranteed the advancing chela. Indeed, those who consider themselves wise in the teaching are expected to be more alert than those sweet young disciples whose laughing hearts first come to the newness of divine understanding.

"The business of living is a serious business, but it can be indulged with a steadied merriment and a bubbling joy. The mists that have clouded the minds of men must be dispersed. The sun of hope must rise as many hands unite to pluck the harmonic strings of genuine brotherhood.

"The sons of liberty will rally, and the world will know the mounting passion of hearts who love freedom. These love freedom enough to hold high her torch, to look round about them and to pick up the debris that the flame will gladly transmute. No service is too lowly for these, for they follow in the wake of angelic vows, offering eternal service to God.

"Does a humble heart need assistance? They serve. Must a thankless task be done? They do. Shall a seemingly archaic matter require study? They apply their minds. Is organization needed? They organize. Whatever the exigency, they reach up to the abundance of God, magnetize it and offer it in the service of the Light."[36]

False Promises of the False Hierarchy

We wish to point out that dedicated servants of the Great White Brotherhood must beware of organizations that profess to follow the teachings of the Brotherhood, but whose means in obtaining that goal are absolute tyranny. The student must be careful to examine not only the lofty ideals and the aims of such organizations but also their modus operandi.

Is the individual enslaved, controlled in order that the goal of brotherhood be realized? Is he deprived of initiations or tests of self-mastery by compensations, welfare payments or social dividends that he has not earned? Is his initiative to develop his Christ-potential blunted by a superimposed equality that does not take into account the Law that as a man sows, so shall he reap[37]—that each one's talents must first be multiplied before he can receive the dividends of a wise investment of his life's energies?

World Service

Let not men think that the spiritually elect are not needed in the political affairs of the nations, for the God-government of the earth is the first calling of the servant-sons of God. Some spiritual devotees who retreat to the mountains and withdraw from the world show an imbalance of the threefold flame, a lack of true love, a selfishness that is evidenced by their desire to develop their own spirituality at the expense of a total civilization.

It is time for the children of the Light to come forth, to take their place in the so-called mundane affairs of the world. For the Great White Brotherhood teaches that every act done in the name of God is sacred, and inasmuch as we have done it unto the least of these our brethren, we have done it unto the Christ.[38] Public service in his name is one of the greatest callings upon earth at this hour of world crisis.

Like a giant octopus, the Luciferian computer reaches its tentacles to the four corners of the earth to swallow up the children of God in a world machine that is programmed to keep the people ignorant of Reality, of their true Source, of the goal of life that is the ascension, and of the true dignity of the individual—which he has because he is a son of God, because the threefold flame blazes within his heart, because he is destined to be a king and a priest unto God.

John said, "Try the spirits to see whether they be of God."[39] Let us then try the motives of those who would enlist our energies in a supposedly righteous cause. Let us ask the question: Are the means worthy of the ends? And let us never accept the philosophy that the end justifies the means.

Let the children of the sun beware of the philosophies of the manipulators in government, in politics, in social work, in education, in art and in music. For all that tears down the Christ consciousness is unworthy of perpetuation, but all that builds the Golden Age civilization should receive the loyal, prayerful attention of everyone who is homeward bound.

Spiritual Education in the Retreats

During the periods of great darkness upon the planet, which have been present to a greater or lesser degree in every age, the activities of the Great White Brotherhood have been driven underground because of the intense reaction of the darkness in the hearts of the people to the Light of the descending Christ consciousness.

Through a renaissance of art and culture, the release of the music of the spheres through great composers, and an infusion of illumination's flame, the Great White Brotherhood has sought to pave the way for an increasing expression of the Christ Light. But that which has been accomplished on the physical plane and in the outer consciousness has thus far not been enough to secure the blessings of Light for posterity and to hold back the forward movement of the forces of Darkness.

Therefore, in caring for the spiritual needs of mankind, the Brotherhood has found it necessary to utilize many forms of communion and education, including what may be termed "co-education," whereby the soul of man, apart from the mortal form while the body sleeps at night, becomes correctly informed concerning the great Truths of the universe. This education is carried on in the physical and etheric retreats of the Masters, which have been maintained throughout the world for centuries.

The concepts that are taught to these souls are often unacceptable to the domain of mortal reason in the daylight consciousness—simply because teachers, friends, companions and circumstances have already set up a matrix based upon human concepts bereft of the wisdom contained in the record of pure God Truth.

Thus the majority among mankind do not retain the memory of their experiences at inner levels. Nevertheless, an imprint of the events is made upon the mental and emotional bodies. Little by little the memories of the instruction received come to the fore of the outer mind, and the benefits conferred to the soul, which are recorded in the subconscious mind, come to the surface of consciousness.

More advanced initiates are invited to attend the council meetings of the Great White Brotherhood, including the Darjeeling and Indian Councils, the Council of the Royal Teton and committee meetings held by the Masters heading various branches of the Great White Brotherhood's endeavors.

These meetings are not attended in the flesh, but by means

of spiritual projection or the projection of consciousness. (This is never an astral projection or an astral experience.) Some of the more advanced devotees are able to participate in these conclaves of the Brotherhood with the full conscious awareness of the outer mind, even though they attend with only their subtle or finer bodies.

Others who are not allowed to attend these meetings may tune in to them just as we tune in through radio and television to events that are happening at a distance. Those who can attune with the vibratory rate of the Masters' consciousness can in this manner receive the higher Teachings and participate in the council meetings from afar.

The Universities of the Spirit

On January 1, 1986, Gautama Buddha announced that he and the Lords of Karma had granted the petition of the Seven Chohans to open "universities of the Spirit in each of their etheric retreats where they might welcome not dozens or hundreds but thousands and tens of thousands of students who will diligently pursue the path of self-mastery on the seven rays systematically, mastering most especially the first and the seventh rays whereby they might establish the Alpha and the Omega of their identity, whereby they might establish the will of God, the divine blueprint, the inner plan for twin flames and immediately begin an action of personal and world transmutation.

"The plan, therefore, is for students to spend fourteen days in [El Morya's retreat at] Darjeeling and fourteen days with Saint Germain at the Royal Teton Retreat and to alternate these fourteen days as they weave a balance and restore themselves to the commitment of the beginning and the ending of the cycles of life.

"Having successfully passed certain levels, albeit beginning levels, nevertheless strong levels of accomplishment in the use of these rays, they will have a turn also with Lord Lanto and Confucius here at the Royal Teton and Paul the Venetian, who prefers to use in this hour the Temple of the Sun of the Goddess of Liberty, who is the Divine Mother of beloved Paul, and to anchor that action in the Washington Monument, as it has already had anchored there a focus of the threefold flame from the Château de Liberté.[40]

"Beloved ones, this training, then, will be for the rounding out of the threefold flame in the wisdom of the Path and especially in the development of the path of the sacred heart, the expansion of love that they might rid themselves of fear and hardness of heart and records of death surrounding that heart.

"Then, you see, comes the path of ministration and service, which is the logical manifestation of love and a balanced threefold flame. Through ministration and service in the retreat of Nada in Arabia, they will find, then, a place where they can give the same dynamic decrees you give here for all those untoward conditions in the area of the Middle East. And this shall be their assignment at inner levels even as they study the true path of Jesus Christ on that sixth ray as it has never been taught to them before.

"Having come through these retreats, they are now ready to be washed in the purity of the sacred fires of the Ascension Temple [at Luxor, Egypt] for a beginner's course and for the first baptism by water of the Divine Mother. Then they proceed to [the Temple of Truth over the island of] Crete with Paul the Apostle, and there Hilarion shows them the Truth of all ages, and the science of Being is unfolded layer upon layer.

"Thus, having completed a round in all of these retreats—cycling fourteen-day cycles, some repeated in the same retreat, some interchanging—they will come again to second and third levels of training on those seven rays."[41]

Special Training

On occasion, unascended lifestreams are taken in their physical bodies to the retreats of the Brotherhood in order to be trained for special service in the world of form that requires superhuman strength and certain disciplines that can only be imparted to the unascended initiate in the retreats. For example, Jesus was taken into the retreat in Luxor and into the Temple of the Blue Lotus prior to his final three-year ministry.

This rare privilege has also been given to others whose names are still remembered by unascended mankind for their valiant service to Life. Some who have been commissioned to go forth in the name of the Brotherhood, who had not yet transmuted their remaining karma, received the assistance that was given in the Cave of Light to Godfre, Rex, Nada, Bob and Pearl.[42] Through this assistance, their four lower bodies were purified and aligned in order that they might be the immaculate receptacles of the Christ consciousness.

When this dispensation is accorded worthy chelas, their remaining service to Life is magnificently accomplished because their consciousness has become the perfect focal point in the world of form for the release of the entire Spirit of the Great White Brotherhood. Miracles, demonstrations of alchemy and the control of natural forces and elemental life become the mark of those who are so blessed by the opportunity of being "perfected" prior to their final initiation and ascension in the Light.

Protecting the Brotherhood's Focuses

Down through the ages, many of the physical retreats of the Brotherhood have been closed as civilizations crumbled around them and ignorant masses desecrated the shrines. Others were closed before they were destroyed, for the hierarchs of the retreats felt an imminent threat to the physical focus and the ancient relics guarded there. For example, during the ravaging of Tibet by the Chinese Communists,[43] some of the temples of the Brotherhood that were located there were closed and the sacred relics transported to temples of the Brotherhood located in other parts of the world.

In other cases, the temples were sealed within mountains or within the earth itself, preventing any possibility of intrusion by those whose consciousness is unprepared to enter into the Holy of Holies. If it is impossible to save the accoutrements of the retreat and the entrances cannot be sealed, the etheric counterpart of the focus is raised to a point in the atmosphere above the physical structure and the forces of nature are employed through cataclysmic action to destroy the remains.

Inasmuch as the etheric counterpart of the physical is more real than the physical (in one sense the etheric is the cause and the physical is the effect), when the enlightenment of civilization once again reaches a point where it is safe to precipitate in form that which exists as etheric pattern, this will be directed by the Brothers and Sisters of the retreat.

Since all that is on the physical plane has an etheric counterpart, the physical focuses of the Brotherhood already have an etheric counterpart either intermeshing with the focus or located directly above it in the atmosphere. Where both still exist, unascended devotees carry on at the physical level that which the Ascended Masters are carrying on at the etheric level and also in the higher octaves of Light.

The Brotherhood's Retreats Are Strategically Located

The retreats, temples and focuses of the Masters are scientifically located upon the planetary body at certain key points in the design of the mandala. Their positions are calculated for the greatest release of Light to the evolutions evolving here. All of the retreats act as receiving and sending stations for the Light released in all of the other retreats upon the planetary body as well as that sent from near and distant stars and from the flaming Yod in the Great Hub.[44]

The Light emitted from the retreats bounces back and forth between them in magnetic waves. The result of the interaction of these waves of Light is the resonance of a cosmic tone, the sound of the great Amen, the Aum, or the Om, which can be heard with the inner ear. This cosmic keynote bathes the earth, the nature kingdom and mankind in the vibratory action of the sacred Word of creation, which means literally "I AM" or "God is the great Amen." By this we know that every man can become one with the vibration of the lost Word.

From time to time, representatives of the false hierarchy, working through misguided but well-meaning channels in the world of form, have released the information that certain of the Masters' retreats have been moved. Some have even proclaimed that the retreats have been moved to a position above the location of their own organizations, and these releases have caused a great commotion among devotees.

Concerned with the protection of the faithful, beloved El Morya wrote a letter to the students to clarify the position of the Great White Brotherhood on this subject: "Never will we withdraw our support from any sincere, God-loving individual. Neither will we permit anyone to usurp authority with impunity and attempt to present to mankind the false premise that the Ascended Master retreats, which are fixed through love and devotion poured out for milleniums, are to be removed from their etheric locations above the landed areas of the earth, where they have been sustained by the angelic hosts and have served the needs of the entire planet for so long.

"It is a fact that the entire sphere of the etheric mesh in which the etheric retreats are located can (and does at times) rotate independently of the earth at a speed far exceeding the earth's own rotational norm. Thereby there is created a harmonic tone combining the musical keys of the many Ascended Master retreats. These manifest as a wondrous chord of pure love—somewhat in the manner of a child's musical top.

"Therefore, since these retreats were scientifically positioned by the Brotherhood according to cosmic law, it would be in violation of that law and indeed wholly unnecessary to disturb their wonderful etheric pattern in order to convey a blessing to any part of the earth or to any person thereon.

"To do so would be to upset the delicate magnetic field of the entire earth, and this would serve no useful purpose. After all, blessed ones, if the North and South Poles were to be put at the equator, would this not disturb the balance of the earth? Remember that by mighty Light rays we can, and do, reach every part of the earth and expand the Light within men's hearts wherever they are. Inasmuch as the retreats are visited by mankind in their finer bodies, it does not matter where on earth these retreats are located from the standpoint of availability and blessings conferred to all of Life....

"Our retreats remain inviolate—for cosmic purposes. We may from time to time establish new foci or centers that will one day become, by intelligent effort and service, mighty focuses of love. And we have, on rare occasions, moved a flame or reestablished it by mighty Light rays to affect a nation for good."[45]

You Are Welcome to Study at the Brotherhood's Retreats

A number of years ago the false concept was released that only one or several retreats were open each month and that all students of the Masters should therefore go to that specific retreat during that month. This was another attempt of the sinister force to deprive mankind of the full complement of assistance that was and always has been available to unascended mankind.

The fact that all the retreats contribute to the release of Light—and the grids and forcefields that comprise the hierarchical mandala sustaining and balancing the action of the threefold-flame Christ consciousness on the planet—necessarily entails the participation of the students in the action of all the flames of all the retreats that are open.

Before retiring at night, the student should call to his God Presence and his guardian angel to take him in his finer bodies to one of the following retreats, or he may simply ask to be taken to the retreat to which he has been assigned for that particular cycle of his evolution.

In addition to the Universities of the Spirit mentioned earlier, fourteen etheric cities around the earth and also the following retreats are open the year round to qualified and deserving chelas of the Ascended Masters for study and meditation: the retreats of beloved John the Beloved and Eriel, over Arizona; the Cathedral of Nature, in Kashmir; the Cave of Symbols, the Cathedral of the Violet Flame and Tabor's retreat, all in the Rocky Mountains; the Château de Liberté, in southern France; the Rose Temple, over New Bedford, Massachusetts; the Temple of Comfort, in Sri Lanka; the retreat of Hercules and Amazonia, in and over Half Dome, Yosemite Valley, California; the Temple of Peace, over the

Hawaiian Islands; the Temple of Purity, over the Gulf of Archangel, Russia; the retreat of Heros and Amora, over Lake Winnipeg, Canada; the Resurrection Temple, over the Holy Land; the Temple of the Maltese Cross over the House of Rakoczy, in the Carpathian Mountains; Shamballa, over the Gobi Desert; the Temple of Mercy, near Beijing (Peking), China; the Tibetan retreat of Djwal Kul; Maitreya's retreat in the Himalayas; Lanello's retreat, near Bingen on the Rhine River, Germany; the retreat of Orion, the Old Man of the Hills, in the mountains of North America; the Persian retreat, Iran; the Retreat of the Divine Mother and the Western Shamballa, over the Royal Teton Ranch, southwest Montana; Zarathustra's retreat (location not revealed); the retreat of the Master of Paris, in Paris; and the retreat of the Queen of Light, near Messina, Sicily.

In a dictation given May 28, 1987, Jesus Christ spoke of the Archangels as "teachers of Christhood par excellence." He said: "When you have done visiting even the retreats of the Lords of the Seven Rays, may you perchance be invited to a series of studies in the retreats of the Archangels. This, beloved, is my prayer unto the Father, who has responded by saying, 'My Son, let them prove themselves with thy brothers, the Seven Masters of Light, and then they shall truly know the divine interchange with Archangels.' So, beloved, rejoice that not alone Archangel Michael, who has called you in his service, but all of the seven may one day host you in their retreats for the accelerated initiations of Life unto eternity."[46]

On February 27, 1988, Archangel Raphael announced that he and Mother Mary, Archangels of the Fifth Ray, were presenting to the world the opening of the doors of their temple "as the first opening in general of a retreat of the Archangels to those who have passed beyond the levels of the mystery schools of the Lords of the Seven Rays."[47] In the early 1990s it

Figure 32 Retreats of the Ascended Masters That Are Known to Be Open to Unascended Chelas

Retreats of the Chohans

Master	Name of Retreat (if known)	Location
El Morya	Temple of Good Will	Darjeeling, India
Lanto	Royal Teton Retreat	Teton Range, Wyoming
Paul the Venetian	Château de Liberté	Southern France
Serapis Bey	Ascension Temple	Luxor, Egypt
Hilarion	Temple of Truth	Crete
Nada	Rose Temple	New Bedford, Massachusetts
Saint Germain	Cave of Symbols	Rocky Mountains
Saint Germain	Temple of the Maltese Cross	Carpathian Mountains, Romania
Maha Chohan	Temple of Comfort	Sri Lanka

The Chohans of the Rays teach their courses in the Universities of the Spirit at the following retreats:

(1) El Morya, Temple of Good Will
(2) Saint Germain, Royal Teton Retreat
(3) Lanto and Confucius, Royal Teton Retreat
(4) Paul the Venetian, Temple of the Sun
(5) Nada, the Arabian Retreat
(6) Serapis Bey, Ascension Temple
(7) Hilarion, Temple of Truth

Retreats of the Elohim

Master	Name of Retreat (if known)	Location
Hercules and Amazonia		Half Dome, Yosemite Valley, California
Heros and Amora		Lake Winnipeg, Canada
Purity and Astrea	Temple of Purity	Gulf of Archangel, Russia
Peace and Aloha	Temple of Peace	Hawaiian Islands

Retreats of the Archangels

Master	Name of Retreat (if known)	Location
Michael and Faith	Temple of Faith and Protection	Banff, Canada
Jophiel and Christine		near Lanchow, China
Chamuel and Charity	Temple of the Crystal-Pink Flame	St. Louis, USA
Gabriel and Hope		between Sacramento and Mt. Shasta, California
Raphael and Mary		Fátima, Portugal
Uriel and Aurora		Tatra Mountains, south of Cracow, Poland
Zadkiel and Amethyst	Temple of Purification	Cuba

Retreats of the Manus

Master	Name of Retreat (if known)	Location
Himalaya	Retreat of the Blue Lotus	Himalayan Mountains
Vaivasvata Manu		Himalayan Mountains
God and Goddess Meru	Temple of Illumination	Lake Titicaca
Great Divine Director	Cave of Light	India

Other retreats

Master	Name of Retreat (if known)	Location
Cha Ara	Persian Retreat	Iran
Djwal Kul		Tibet
Eriel		Arizona
Goddess of Liberty	Temple of the Sun	Manhattan Island, New York

Master	Name of Retreat (if known)	Location
Jesus and Mary	Resurrection Temple	over the Holy Land
Jesus and Nada	Arabian Retreat	Arabian Peninsula
John the Beloved		Arizona
Kuan Yin	Temple of Mercy	near Beijing, China
Kuthumi	Cathedral of Nature	Srinagar, Kashmir
Lady Master Venus	Retreat of the Divine Mother	over the Royal Teton Ranch, southwest Montana, USA
Lanello		Bingen, on the Rhine River, Germany
Maitreya		Himalayan Mountains
Master of Paris		Paris, France
Orion, the Old Man of the Hills		mountains of North America
Queen of Light		near Messina, Sicily
Sanat Kumara, Gautama Buddha	Shamballa	Gobi Desert
Sanat Kumara, Gautama Buddha	Western Shamballa	over the Royal Teton Ranch, southwest Montana, USA
Tabor		near Colorado Springs, USA
Violet Flame Masters	Cathedral of the Violet Flame	Rocky Mountains
Zarathustra		location unknown
Etheric Cities		seven over the seas, seven over deserts

For detailed descriptions of these and other retreats of the Ascended Masters, see Mark L. Prophet and Elizabeth Clare Prophet, *The Masters and Their Retreats*.

was announced that all of the retreats of the Archangels had been opened to souls of merit.

In 1994, the Great Divine Director announced that his retreat and those of all the Manus had been opened to some among mankind: "The upper tenth of the members of all root races who have incarnated and those who are not of the root races but of the angelic kingdom who have taken incarnation in order to teach those root races—the upper tenth, then, began at summer solstice ... to attend an accelerated course at the etheric retreats of the Manus: at my own retreat and the retreats of the God and Goddess Meru, Lord Himalaya and Vaivasvata Manu."[48]

Calls to beloved Archangel Michael and Mighty Astrea before retiring will ensure the soul's safe passage through the astral belt to the higher octaves of Light and also a safe return. Should the student experience frequent occurrence of disturbing dreams, it is an indication that he is not passing through the lower levels of consciousness like the clean cut of the blade of a knife, and he should redouble his efforts to decree during the day, before retiring at night and during periods when he is awakened by discomforting vibrations during the night.

Impostors of the Ascended Masters

As we have mentioned before, the teachings of the Great White Brotherhood have been imitated by impostors, false hierarchs, black magicians and masquerading entities. The fact remains that every Ascended Master is imitated by one or more dark souls who go forth in his name to release fraudulent material to unascended lifestreams.

These impersonators of the Masters are very clever. They are able to imitate the Masters' vibrations, their etheric patterns and their appearance so well that only an expert is able by the grace of God to determine the synthetic image from the Real Image. Because the language and even the tone of voice of the impostor closely resembles that of the Master whom he imitates, the Great Divine Director has given this practical advice:

"Call upon your own Divine Presence and wait upon the Word of the Lord. Live closely and identify with the precepts of holy Truth that bring to the doorstep of every man the understanding of the full measure of his responsibility to his brother, made in the image of God, to whom he ought to offer the best that is within himself, owing direct allegiance to his great God Being.

"Where there is a dichotomy between the counsels of that great Divine Being and those of another individual or group of individuals, the attention should always flow first to the Divine Presence and then to the Ascended Masters' realm for the resolving of the difficulty. Light always begets Light to nourish and regenerate, whereas darkness may indeed masquerade as intellectual blindness that refuses to accept the Truth of that which it cannot see concretely defined....

"Every doctrine that is rooted in sinister strategies and seeks to cater to the mortal mind of man or to pamper his ego (leading him to believe that he is connected with some 'outer source' that will keep him informed as to what is happening around the cosmic corner) is simply an activity designed to please the little self and to enlarge the boundaries of that self.

"Cosmic magnification, which is the fruit of divine sowing, does not seek to embellish the ego or to make the individual to feel that he is above his fellow men—rather does it seek the identification of the individual with cosmic resources, which enlarge the borders of man's perception by the Light of divine Truth."[49]

The Correct Use of the Ascended Masters' Names

The Great Divine Director also released instruction on the correct use of the Ascended Masters' names: "The Word of God, by which the heaven and earth were framed, was the eternally resonant voice of the Logos, but in the world of form it became drowned by many human voices and many human words. The ringing statement, 'There is no other name under heaven given among men whereby we must be saved,'[50] clearly showed the feeling of the early apostles of the Christian church with reference to the sacredness attached to the Divine Name."[51]

The Master explained that the names of the Ascended Masters are keys to their electronic pattern, to their consciousness and vibration. As each letter in the alphabet keys to a cosmic frequency and release, the combination of letters in an Ascended Master's name comprises his personal keynote.

In the case of well-known Masters, such as Jesus the Christ—whose name has been called upon by devotees for centuries—a great momentum of Light has coalesced around the name, adding the devotion of unascended mankind to the momentum of Light that is released by the name "Jesus." So powerful is this name of the Son of God that it may be used to the present hour to cast out demons and entities.

Disregarding these facts, various channels in embodiment have allowed themselves to be duped by ambitious and calculating minds, who, speaking from the lower astral planes, have sent forth the proclamation that Jesus the Christ is no longer to be called Jesus, but another name. Likewise, these malicious forces have announced that the names of the Great Divine Director, Saint Germain, Cyclopea and Lord Maitreya should be changed.

The names given in each case were those of impostors who had long desired to usurp the office of these magnificent Cosmic Beings.* Dangerous black magicians are they who trick innocent victims into calling upon their names while offering adoration to God in prayer, meditation and decrees. These blackguards then take the energies, the pure energies of the students, and use them to perpetuate the black conspiracy upon the planet.

At other times, inaccurate channels have received the information that not only the names, but also the offices of such magnificent beings as the Lord Maha Chohan and Paul the Venetian have been changed, or that certain Masters such as beloved El Morya have gone on to cosmic service and are therefore no longer available to answer the calls of unascended mankind.

Concerning this subject the Great Divine Director said: "The beloved Master Paul the Venetian remains as the Chohan of the Third Ray of divine love, for his service to Life is far from finished in that office; and the Lord Maha Chohan remains with all of the divine cosmic honor as simply, 'The Maha Chohan,' which means 'The Great Lord.'

"As his consciousness and power soar in the service of the Light and for mankind, the power of his office is not diminished, but transcends itself again and again, illumining and bringing release to many among mankind from the pains of wrong thought and feeling....

"The power of God has for centuries been vested in the names of these Ascended Masters, and to use other names does not increase the power of God or the power of Truth. For if these new names that mankind have tacked on to the

---

* One need only pronounce the name of one of these false hierarchs to key his consciousness into the vibratory rate of the impostor; therefore we will not give their names in this book.

Ascended Masters are called upon, it keys the disciple into the vibratory action of an impostor.

"Thus the disciple, without realizing it, is putting the funnel of his attention into a cesspool and mire of jaded consciousness, while at the same time ignorantly denying the power of the Lords of Light (whom mankind have been taught to call upon from their mothers' knees in some cases, and in others from the date of their illumination). Blessed ones, be not deceived, for the scriptures have clearly stated that there would arise false Christs and false prophets who would show great signs and wonders, insomuch that, if it were possible, they would deceive the very elect."[52]

"The great power of divine love that is in the Ascended Masters' octave remains fixed there. And when the key of the correct name of the Master is used and the attention flows to that Master, it will always return the peace and blessing of that individual Son of God into the world of the seeker.

"When individuals in ignorance call upon other names and their hearts are pure, it does not always mean that they will experience some negative outpouring of which they are consciously aware. But in reality, there is always a diminution of the Light flow into their worlds. In some, there have been awful obsessions created and the infestation of entities into their worlds because they have been thrown off the path of Truth by calling upon others who are, in reality, not Masters of Light but impostors of the black brotherhood, masquerading as angels of Light. 'And no marvel; for Satan himself is transformed into an angel of light.'[53]...

"In Him who has said, 'I AM is my name,'[54] all beings merge into the great Light, but retain the new name they have been given by God, and which is, in reality, the old name which no man knoweth save he who has received it."[55]

In the charts on the Hierarchy that we have released in this volume (see Figure 33, pages 332–33), we have given the correct names of the Elohim, the Archangels and the Chohans.* The Great Divine Director promised that when the time was right for greater clarification on the names of the members of Hierarchy, the students should not be surprised but grateful, waiting for the harvest before removing the tares that the wheat might fully mature.

The Great Divine Director promised the students that the time would come for the revelation of such corrections as were necessary for the maximum release of Light from the Great White Brotherhood to their unascended devotees. Let none, then, be dismayed but all move forward in a greater consciousness of the Truth, which by the action of the two-edged sword cleaves asunder the Real from the unreal.

The Functions of the Brotherhood

Every Ascended Master belongs to the Great White Brotherhood, and those who aspire to union with this Brotherhood must aspire to the Christ consciousness. It is not possible to reveal here all of the myriad functions of the Brotherhood and the methods by which it seeks to assist mankind and protect mankind against himself. It is the agency of God upon earth, and while it has been much maligned and misunderstood, it continues to function and will until every individual upon this earth attains his natural God-intended freedom. Let us however present the sacred goals set forth by the Chief of the Darjeeling Council of the Great White Brotherhood.

At the beginning of the New Year in 1968, beloved El Morya released a fifteen-point program of assistance, which

---

* For biographical information about these Masters and others whose names have been revealed, see Mark L. Prophet and Elizabeth Clare Prophet, *The Masters and Their Retreats*.

the councils of the Brotherhood had determined to release to mankind during that year. These points sum up the purposes of the Brotherhood through the ages, and so we include them in this chapter in order that those who desire to place their hands firmly in the hands of the Brothers in White may understand specifically what they may do to further the divine plan for the earth and invoke the assistance that the heavenly hosts deem most important at this hour of world need.

El Morya writes: "Who can deny the needs of this hour or of humanity? Who should? It is our earnest desire to render the following assistance to mankind individually and collectively as they are able to respond to the ministrations of the Heavenly Hosts:

1. to step up the level of individual service in order to provide for greater clarity of understanding to men of lesser comprehension;
2. to set forth in a most desirable manner the higher teachings of cosmic law for those who are able to grasp them;
3. to create more stable ties with the Hierarchy through our cosmic outposts in the world of men;
4. to introduce new levels of integrity, justice and faith in government and business and in religious, scientific and artistic endeavors;
5. to assist those who have seen or experienced little of the heavenly kingdom by amplifying the power of godly vision among men;
6. to develop the spiritual nature of all peoples in order that they may experience greater joy in carrying out the will of God wherever and whenever they are called upon to serve;
7. to sustain faith in those who yet must walk by it;
8. to meet the spiritual needs of mankind at all levels of consciousness;
9. to promote peace and understanding in order to accelerate

the manifestation of cosmic purpose;

10. to utilize renewed interest in extrasensory perception and matters of the Spirit in order to direct the seeker toward the unfolding of his latent divinity rather than involvement in a search for the phenomenal;
11. to elucidate further to mankind upon the great story of the cosmic Hierarchy;
12. to build mighty pools of reserve energies as reservoirs of spiritual power that can be used by the disciples of the Ascended Masters in their service to mankind and for the blessing of all life directly from the retreats of the Ascended Masters;
13. to secure new dispensations from the Karmic Board that will feed these energy pools and embodied individuals connected with the Hierarchy with sufficient power and cosmic know-how to externalize the plan for the year;
14. to encourage all, even the downtrodden, to keep high their faith in the ultimate outpicturing of the glory of God, right while perceiving the absolute necessity to counteract the ignorant manifestations of mankind involved in their excessive materialism, the use of psychedelic drugs, dissonant music and art forms, and vain pleasure-seeking to their own hurt; and
15. to integrate the whole man in accordance with the original divine plan."[56]

The Summit Lighthouse activity derives its authority from and is sponsored by the Great White Brotherhood. As long as it upholds the tenets of that Brotherhood to the best of its ability, the Brotherhood will, in this age, and we hope in many to come, use the arm of the Summit to uphold the torch of enlightenment unto man.

Figure 33 The Seven Rays and the Seven

Seven Rays of the Flames Magnetized on the Seven Days of the Week	God-Qualities Amplified through Invocation to the Flame	Chakras, or Centers: Chalices of Light Sustaining the Frequencies of the Seven Rays in the Four Lower Bodies
First Ray Will of God (Blue) Magnified on Tuesday	Omnipotence, perfection, protection, faith, desire to do the will of God through the power of the Father	**Throat** (Blue)
Second Ray Wisdom of God (Yellow) Magnified on Sunday	Omniscience, understanding, illumination, desire to know God through the mind of the Son	**Crown** (Yellow)
Third Ray Love of God (Pink) Magnified on Monday	Omnipresence, compassion, charity, desire to be God in action through the love of the Holy Spirit	**Heart** (Pink)
Fourth Ray Purity of God (White) Magnified on Friday	Purity, wholeness, desire to know and be God through purity of body, mind and soul through the consciousness of the Divine Mother	**Base of the Spine** (White)
Fifth Ray Science of God (Green) Magnified on Wednesday	Truth, healing, constancy, desire to precipitate the abundance of God through the immaculate concept of the Holy Virgin	**Third Eye** (Green)
Sixth Ray Peace of God (Purple and Gold) Magnified on Thursday	Ministration of the Christ, desire to be in the service of God and man through the mastery of the Christ	**Solar Plexus** (Purple and Gold)
Seventh Ray Freedom of God (Violet) Magnified on Saturday	Freedom, ritual, transmutation, transcendence, desire to make all things new through the application of the laws of alchemy	**Seat of the Soul** (Violet)

Chakras and the Beings Who Ensoul Them

Chohans, or Lords, Focusing the Christ Consciousness of the Ray; Location of Their Retreats	**Archangels** and Divine Complements Focusing the Solar Consciousness of the Ray; Location of Their Retreats	**Elohim** and Divine Complements Focusing the God Consciousness of the Ray; Location of Their Retreats
El Morya Darjeeling, India	**Michael** **Faith** Banff and Lake Louise, Canada	**Hercules** **Amazonia** Half Dome, Sierra Nevada, California, USA
Lanto Grand Teton, Teton Range, Wyoming, USA	**Jophiel** **Christine** South of the Great Wall near Lanchow, North Central China	**Apollo** **Lumina** Western Lower Saxony, Germany
Paul the Venetian Southern France	**Chamuel** **Charity** St. Louis, Missouri, USA	**Heros** **Amora** Lake Winnipeg, Canada
Serapis Bey Luxor, Egypt	**Gabriel** **Hope** Between Sacramento and Mount Shasta, California, USA	**Purity** **Astrea** Near Gulf of Archangel, southeast arm of White Sea, Russia
Hilarion Crete, Greece	**Raphael** **Mother Mary** Fátima, Portugal	**Cyclopea** **Virginia** Altai Range where China, Siberia and Mongolia meet, near Tabun Bogdo
Nada Saudi Arabia	**Uriel** **Aurora** Tatra Mountains south of Cracow, Poland	**Peace** **Aloha** Hawaiian Islands
Saint Germain Transylvania, Romania Table Mountain, Rocky Mountains, USA	**Zadkiel** **Amethyst** Cuba	**Arcturus** **Victoria** near Luanda, Angola, Africa

Chapter 5

Attainment

*Thou hast been faithful
over a few things, I will make
thee ruler over many things:
enter into the joy of the Lord.*
MATTHEW

# Attainment

THE ASCENDED LADY MASTER Amerissis tells us: "The struggle between Light and shadow is ever one of becoming! O dear hearts, how wondrous is the process of passing through initiation, when the victory of success is perceived blooming upon the stalk of fulfillment. In order to move forward in Light's achievement you must always lay aside the sense of past failure, you must master the method of objectifying the great realities of life and of minimizing the process of habitual response to mass stimuli that pull your precious energies downward."[1]

Dharma

In the matter of attainment, man has often considered the responsibility to be entirely God's. It is a matter of practicing magic. He says, "Abracadabra," and his desires appear or manifest. Whether or not attainment can be this easy is not at all the point. Rather, it is necessary for all people to understand their own personal need to fulfill what has been called in India and Tibet one's *dharma* ("duty")—utilizing one's life for its natural, ordained purposes.

Through the years many have been victims of the purveyors of various occult courses, magic words, special formulas whereby they are expected to manifest tremendous otherworldly power and thus dominate their fellow men and their environment in such a manner that they become the master of all. However, Jesus Christ said, "Let he that is great among you become the servant of all."[2]

The dharma of the Law expects the right attitude to manifest so that the right attainment can manifest. Without the right attainment man becomes but a victim of vanity. All that he does is for the self or for the objects of his affection, with very little indeed done for others—and even this only being accomplished in order that one may have the good feelings of having given.

One should not be attached to feelings—certainly not to bad ones, and therefore, not to good ones either. Let good feelings manifest, but let us exercise discrimination and reject those feelings that are evil.

True attainment is not the acquiring of power over others, but it is the supreme control of the energy that is God within the self.

The True Teachers

God has sent many teachers to show us the way of attainment. There are also those who have come as false teachers, who have told us the lie that it is proud or boastful or ambitious to seek attainment. They have said that the only way to get God is by his grace and all that is necessary for this is the affirmation of the belief in the saviour. This has stopped the path of self-mastery for many who fear to go against what they think to be the truth of scripture.

Yet when we look to the example of Christ himself, we see one who walked the path of attainment. And if we ask ourselves why, we must understand that Jesus, for himself, did not need to walk that path. He had balanced sufficient karma prior to his incarnation to return to the very heart of God. He could have escaped the world and its persecutions. And therefore it was for us. He wasn't putting on a sideshow, it was no vaudeville act. It was a demonstration of supreme law. And this is the meaning of the saviour of the world—he comes to save us by giving us the supreme responsibility for our own salvation.

Those who counsel people today as doctors, as psychiatrists, as social workers or as counselors know that the foundation of helping an individual is to show him how to help himself, and the teacher who takes the responsibility for the learning process of the pupil is no teacher at all. Yet Christ and Buddha were the greatest teachers of all time. They marked a path of attainment by example and by teaching, and they both stressed the works that we must do to arrive at the same place that they had attained, and that we must know the true teaching of the Law.

Measuring Attainment

What is attainment then? Attainment is the putting on of the garment of the Lord.

The Lord's garment is the momentum of his self-mastery. Jesus' supreme manifestation of self-mastery was declared by him only moments before his final victory in the ascension:

"All power is given unto me in heaven and in earth."[3] Jesus did not say these words at the beginning of his mission; he said them after he had passed through every initiation along the way. Jesus was the great scientist of the age. He carved the way of attainment.

The mantle of the consciousness of the Guru is a momentum. It is symbolized in the robe of Christ—the subject of much mystery—which the soldiers would not cut because it was the seamless garment. The robe of Christ, the very mantle of his attainment, is something that can drop upon you—just as the mantle of Elijah fell upon Elisha,[4] just as the succession of the Buddhas in the Far East continues unbroken. The passing of the mantle is the passing of the momentums of attainment.

How do you measure your attainment? Where are you on the path of initiation, if indeed, you are on the path at all? Have you been accepted by a Guru as a chela?

When we speak of Guru, we mean the great Gurus, the Ascended Masters themselves. They are the faultless Gurus. They have the wisdom of the ages. They have the experience of having walked the earth like you and me. They have been through all the trials and tribulations we have experienced before we ever knew what trials and tribulations were. They have walked every step of the way and they know the aspects of the law that need to be applied; they know the science that we need. And this is the concept of Hierarchy.

The Need for Hierarchy

There are many who reject Hierarchy. They say, "All I need is God." They cannot even understand why they would need Christ or Jesus Christ. And many of those who can accept Jesus Christ and God stop there; they cannot acknowledge any need for Mary the Mother or any of the other saints of heaven.

We must learn the lesson of humility. We must understand that just as we would not need to go to the president of a large corporation to buy one of its products, so we don't need to go and trouble God when God has in manifestation his Sons and Daughters, those who are the experts in their fields.

It depends upon our concept of God—God in many aspects. God is very available in the flame within the heart, very available as the still small voice within. Yet these are aspects of God—God personified, God incarnate, God in manifestation. But the God of the Hindus, the God Brahman—the unformed, the uncreated, God the void—I conceive of as energy, and to contact that energy before we have refined the consciousness to enter into it and to assimilate it would be an act of self-destruction, like jumping into an eight-hundred-degree furnace. And so God has created Hierarchy, manifestations of himself throughout a cosmos.

In all of life we see the outpicturing of Hierarchy, in the stars and in the flowers and in nature, even among mankind. We find then that even the Masters that mankind can accept represent a certain way and a certain aspect of Hierarchy.

How do we tell Jesus and Gautama apart? Not so much by their faces, for we aren't really certain of their appearance. We tell them apart by vibration. We tell them by the way and the Truth that they brought. We tell them by the garment of their consciousness. We tell them by attainment.

In fact, each position in Hierarchy—a ladder of cosmic consciousness—has its own frequency and vibration. The one who would hold a position in Hierarchy must equate his vibration with that level on the ladder of attainment, and thereby, being equal to the office, the mantle of that office is given.

You are Hierarchy. The God flame within you has its destiny, its fiery blueprint, its focal point in time and space. Your outer consciousness may not be fully aware of why God has incarnated in you and chosen to place you here and chosen to have you evolve here. The point of attainment is to go within and contact the flame and to bring the flame within to the without, so that it can be in concrete manifestation, so that it can work the works of God as the alchemy of change.

Matter is a frequency, a line in the consciousness of God where we live. It is our home for a time and a space. Matter is a substance that God gives us to prove that level of attainment, and when we have subdued it and taken dominion over the quadrants of Matter as alchemists, we find that we inherit, as Christ did, the all-power of heaven and earth. And that all-power is the release of the soul from the wheel of rebirth and of karma and its cycles. It is the release of the soul in the ritual of the ascension back to the fiery core of God.

God Desiring to Be God

Why pursue this path of attainment? Because God lives in us as Life, and as long as Life is imprisoned within us, bound by our habits, by the enslavement of our souls to our environment, God is crucified within us.

God has a momentum within. We call it God desiring to be God. God desires to come down from that cross. God transfers to us the desire for wholeness because we were created out of the very pattern of the fiery core of that wholeness.

God transfers to each one of us—who live on the periphery, in the sense of separation, in the sense of struggle—the longing for completion. That longing is expressed in many ways among mankind, whether in the pursuit of education or a career, or in seeking one's life partner or a family, or seeking religion or a discipline.

The longing for completion may manifest as the pursuit of a very exacting discipline, an all-consuming life's calling or a sacred labor that we consciously endow with the flame of the spirit. Each day when we get up we are going about our Father's business, to do something to manifest the wholeness that will get God down from that cross.

God is crucified in Matter. The impermanent nature of that which manifests in Matter is the signal of urgency to the soul to pursue the path of initiation. That urgency does not come through a false doctrine and dogma that incites fear or condemnation or guilt or the sense of sin or mortal trepidation about the fires of hell. It comes from the very Spirit of Life itself—life that has an immortal destiny to *be*.

There are only two ways for the Life that is within us as God to attain freedom. God can break the mold at the end of the age or the end of the manvantara, the great cycle of the out-breath. God can draw all of the creation back into that fiery core and dissolve the form, dissolve the mold and take back the flame. That freedom is the total loss of individual identity. This occurs when the God that was encased in form, as the soul, squandered the energy that was God, used it to glorify an ego and a self that was a synthetic self, a not-self, an unreal self, and therefore did not arrive at the point of wholeness, was not worthy to be preserved. That is the path of the downward spiral of self-annihilation. It is the annihilation of God as individuality.

Energy is neither created nor destroyed—it always was, it always is. But these are the cycles of the Creator. First there is the great out-breath, for hundreds of thousands and millions of years. Then there is the great in-breath. And the net gain of that cycle is the increase of God's own self-awareness. Because we conquer in time and space, because we decide to be the fullness of God that we are, we increase God self-awareness. We increase it in manifestation. We increase it in Matter. And the great Sun behind the sun as energy, energy individualized, is likewise increased. Other than this, we can discover no purpose for the creation.

The second way of attaining freedom is through the path of initiation. We contact the God within that is the soul, and we realize that the soul is our potential for wholeness, is our potential to become God. But the soul is not permanent. The Word of the LORD came to the prophet Ezekiel saying, "The soul that sinneth, it shall die."[5] We also learn in the Book of Revelation of the judgment of souls and of some passing through the second death.*

The soul is the portion that went forth from the Spirit of the I AM to gain self-awareness through the correct use of the gift of free will. The soul is given a certain cycle of incarnations for its evolution. And if at the conclusion of these rounds of incarnations the soul has squandered the Light of God, the time comes when the soul must bear witness to the measure of its attainment. If it has not become the wholeness of God, then the form is broken, the identity is canceled out, and that energy returns to the fiery core to be released again in the next age.

But if the soul has followed the path of initiation, has worked for self-mastery in the discipline of energy in service, in love, in interchange with all Life, if the soul has fulfilled the fiery blueprint, then instead of being consumed when she returns to that fiery flame of the I AM THAT I AM, instead of going through self-annihilation, she is fired as a permanent atom in the body of God. Such permanent atoms we know to be the saints and the Ascended Masters of all times. We know they are there. We contact them by the arc of the love of the heart in meditation, and we feel the response.

---

* See Rev. 2:11; 20:6, 11–15; 21:7, 8. For a detailed description of this judgment of souls and the second death, see book 7 of the Climb the Highest Mountain series, *The Path to Immortality*, pp. 224–32.

God allows the sons and daughters who are the overcomers to retain individuality at the same time that they merge with the infinity of the One. This concept is no more mysterious than the concept of nirvana. We haven't been there, and we can only hope to use the very poor approximation of the words of our language to describe it. Individuality in time and space implies a separation, but in the eternity of God it implies wholeness.

The Ascended Masters are the overcomers. They have walked the way of attainment. They are part of the vast Hierarchy known as the Great White Brotherhood. They are the Gurus of the Aquarian age. They are contacting mankind directly and they are contacting us through their dictations and their letters to their chelas.

The Guru-Chela Relationship

Perhaps you would like to be a chela of an Ascended Master, or perhaps you would prefer to be a disciple of Jesus the Christ. In fact, these are one and the same. Jesus, the great Ascended Master of our time, is reverenced by all of the Hierarchies of heaven. And you need not fear that because there are many Gurus that the great Light of the Saviour is eclipsed. It is not eclipsed, it is enhanced. It is also enhanced by your becoming the Christ. As Jesus "thought it not robbery to be equal with God"[6] by declaring himself to be the Son of God, so he also declares it is not robbery for you to make yourself the Son of God.

The promise of Jesus, "He that believeth on me, the works that I do shall he do also; and greater works than these shall he do; because I go unto my Father,"[7] is the illustration in the New Testament of the law of Hierarchy. It is the illustration of the law that John the Baptist declared when he said, "He must increase, but I must decrease."[8] John was talking about the interchange of Spirit and Matter—he, the Guru of Jesus, ascending into Spirit, his presence and image decreasing in the awareness of the people, so that that of his chela could increase, could come into prominence for the demonstration of a new example, a new teaching, a new gospel that would be for the Piscean age.

The Masters want us to increase the Light of the Christ consciousness. The great Master Kuthumi, who was the co-founder with the Master M. of the Theosophical Society, has said to his chelas: "The goal of life is simply the ascension. The ascension is the soul's reunion with God, the individualized I AM Presence in every son and daughter whom God hath made. The ascension is the acceleration of God in man and of man's self-awareness in God. The ascension is the return of the prodigal son to the home of the Father-Mother God. The ascension is the balancing of karma by the law of harmony and the fulfillment of dharma as one's duty to be one's self—one's duty to become one's own real God Self."[9]

That duty is your duty in this life, your duty to be the self that is God within you.

The Need to Go Within

How many of us have been programmed by our civilization, both in East and West, to believe that somehow this was not attainable, or perhaps it was sinful to approach. And then we have been distracted by every aspect of worldly ambition, spiritual ambition, success cults, sex cults, death cults, and a constant bombardment of noise to tear down the delicate balance of the flow of Light in the chakras.

The fallen ones are so frantic with fear that one son of God might get on the path of initiation that they keep us responding to outer stimulus, especially in Western society, where we grow up to respond to externals and we are extroverts by nature. They keep us running here and running there and responding to this and that, and we get all through the day and we haven't made one contact with the inner flame.

And so come the gurus of the East, and they teach meditation. People begin to meditate and we start seeing a movement from externals to internals. It is a step in the right direction. But there is more to the path to attainment than meditation. Meditation is a means to an end: it is not the end itself.

Where are you going in meditation? Are you contacting lower planes of the astral or greater planes of the Christ consciousness? This can only be determined by your state of consciousness in meditation, and if you don't measure your state of consciousness, then how do you really know where you are going?

The fallen ones are extremely concerned lest one son of God contact the fire of the Real Self, because that fire, when contacted, when made manifest as it was in the life of Jesus, is enough to change the entire course of civilization for thousands of years. That same fire that Jesus contacted is available to you. That same fire will have a greater impact on this solar system and this cosmos than the splitting of the atom, than all of science and invention and technology. It will have a greater impact than even the discovery of physical fire itself by the caveman. Such is the power of the release of spiritual fire within you.

But it is necessary to accept the fact that it can be done. This is the age that you've been waiting for, for thousands of embodiments. This point of cycles turning, this moment of the coming of freedom in the Aquarian age, is our time. Our time has come and we are in the right space, we are at the point of contact with the inner divinity.

Energy Is God

Lord Maitreya, whom we revere as the coming Buddha, as the Buddha of the present age, has given us some very important keys to the measuring of attainment:

"The first initiation on the path of attainment is to learn to deal with energy. Inasmuch as energy is God, learning to deal with energy is learning to deal with God—God as Spirit, God as Matter, God in manifestation in man, in woman, in child. God within yourself as the flow of energy from the centers of God-awareness, God as the flow of energy between yourself and other selves—from heart to heart, from soul to soul, from mind to mind. And what of these emotions that flow, God's energy in motion between lifestreams—the one and the many and the masses waiting for the kindling fires of the Spirit? God's energy in motion is the water and the wind and the fire and the earth, for all energy moves as the great fiery sea of God's Being, of Life becoming life.

"Therefore, learn to deal with energy. Learn to give and to receive in harmony. Learn to receive the gruffness and the blunder of the untutored ones and to transmute that overlay by the fires of freedom's ray. Learn to be a buffer for the tender ones charged into your keeping, to absorb the shocks of sacrilege and of the world's ignorance of the flame.

"As you walk the road of life between earth and heaven, be a sifter of the sands of energy—sifting, sifting by the action of the heart; sifting, sifting by the action of the mind. Be a purifier of the strands of darkness, purifying them white on white. Be a refiner of the energies of the world. Carefully, carefully refine that density. Make it light!...

The Purpose of Initiation

"The purpose of initiation is to inaugurate spirals of God-integration within souls who would move toward the center of being that is Life. Life in all of its dazzling splendor, life in its concentrated essence of the sacred fire, is too intense for mortals who have subjected themselves unto the laws of mortality. Those who live by death and death's disintegration are not prepared to live in a life that is God. They think they have life, but theirs is a quasi-existence in a twilight zone of time and space. Whereas they experience that which they call life in a gray band of narrow self-awareness, we who are God-free beings can and shall declare, 'In him we live and move and have our being, for we are also his offspring.'[10]

"I come with the Light of solar initiation to initiate within you the awareness of the abundant Life that flows from the hand of the Mother of the World. I come to break the clay pottery of your materialistic modes, O mankind of earth! I come to shatter the rigor mortis of death and of the death consciousness. I come to dash the hopes of those who have placed their hope in death instead of life. I come to overturn the money changers who have invaded the temple of life, who use the psychology of death to control the masses....

"Were I to place the rod of initiation upon the brow of those who kneel before the altar of the Cosmic Christ prior to their initiation in the cycles of life, I would but lend the momentum of my authority in life as a reinforcement of death as the supreme denial of the Real Self that is God. The Light that flows 'heart, head and hand' from the consciousness of the Cosmic Christ is the Light that makes permanent all that is real and good and beautiful and joyous within you. This is the Light that can endow the soul with everlasting Life, and this is the Light that the LORD God has held back from mortals until they are willing to put on immortality. Thus it is written as the edict of the law that 'this corruptible *must* put on incorruption and this mortal *must* put on immortality.'[11]

"It is an absolute requirement of the law of life that you don the spirals of integration—integration with God, your own Real Self. Day by day, line by line, the challenge of initiation is to integrate the soul, that potential of selfhood, with the Spirit of the living God, the I AM THAT I AM. And the keys to integration are (1) the science of harmony, (2) the science of energy flow, and (3) the science of the spoken Word. Master these three, you who would be chelas of Maitreya, you who would prepare diligently for that expansion of life that is Cosmic Christ-awareness!

"Understand now that when you come to the altar to be initiated, it is a different matter entirely from coming to the altar to pray, to ask for forgiveness in the way of life and death, or to receive the blessings of love, inspiration and Christ-peace. When you come to the altar of the LORD to be initiated, it means that you have striven for perfection in the application of the science of harmony, in the application of the science of energy flow, and in the application of the Science of the Spoken Word. Let us analyze these requirements of the soul's preparation for initiation.

The Law of Harmony

"Harmony begins with the heart. Harmony is the Light of the Mother negating the spirals of disintegration throughout the planes of Mater. Harmony is your own Christ Self dispensing the fires of love, wisdom and power as the communication of the Logos to the night side of life. Harmony is the Light that bursts in winter in the birth of the Manchild. Harmony is the law of a cosmos—the sternness and the fire of the Father who in the Mother becomes the gentle caress of the Holy Spirit.

"Harmony is the energy of God in the white-fire core bursting from the polarity of the Father-Mother God in Spirit unto the fulfillment of creation in Mater. Harmony is the energy of life in perfect alignment on the circumference of being. Harmony is you poised in life. Harmony is you centered in the God flame of the heart. Harmony is the threefold flame burning away the debris of the centuries.

"Your heart is intended to rule your head, your soul, your consciousness, your life and the flow of energy that defines your identity in God. If you are to succeed on the path of initiation, the fires of your heart must be tended, intensified, and expanded....

"Through the exercise of the law of harmony, you make your temple fit, every whit, to be the habitation of the Most High God, who *is* the flame of harmony. The flame of harmony is the flame that contains all of the rays of God as a chord of cosmic fire, as the symphony of the seven rainbow rays spiraling from the white-fire core, moving in the rhythm of the laws of harmony that govern the music of the spheres. When you have the flame of harmony, you contain the indomitable force, the veritable fusion of the Light of Alpha and Omega that courses through your four lower bodies, that flows as the Light of seven spheres and makes of your four lower bodies vehicles for the expression of the Cosmic Christ consciousness.

"The white Light of harmony becomes the crystal of the fiery blueprint of creation. The white Light of harmony may become the resounding chords of the harmonies of the seven rays, each ray having a thousand times a thousand hues, variations and gradations of tone quality and vibration of its own central theme. The flame of harmony is the flame of God resounding in all of the chakras of your being, sacred centers of God-awareness. Through the flame of harmony you can become the symphony of God."[12]

Sometimes we confuse harmony with vegetating. You can sit on a couch all day and do nothing, but that is not harmony. Harmony is rest in motion. Harmony is the movement of cycles turning.

The integration of the outer consciousness with the inner flame is accomplished according to the law of cycles. These cycles include the cycles of your karma and your dharma, the cycles of the flow of Life and the cycles of your meditation and your application of the law.

Cycles of Initiation

Cycles turning are the wheels within wheels spoken of by the prophet Ezekiel.[13] They are the cycles of the flow of energy in your chakras. Until your chakras are cleared you are really not in harmony with life—even if you have attained a relative equilibrium and you are comfortable within yourself.

On the path of initiation, we find that each day the prior level of our awareness is not enough. When we are on the path, the quest of God desiring to be God is like that fire infolding itself that Ezekiel saw. The flame keeps turning; it keeps on demanding more flame to sustain the new level of harmony. Thus the science of harmony begins with striving toward the greatest degree of harmony we can know in our life—holding our peace, watching our tongue, watching the release of the energies of the emotions, watching the level of irritability, keeping our bodies in good health, maintaining the flow of energy through right food and exercise, through yoga. Harmony is something that is a daily refinement.

By and by, you come to the place where your need for this balance that we call harmony is so great that you have to leave the peripheral existence. When you live on the outside of yourself, you are like a cork bobbing on the waves of the mass consciousness—the latest crisis in the stock market, the latest crisis in the world scene or in the Middle East or in China. People go up and down according to the energy sent forth by the media, and therefore they do not have soul harmony. By retreating into the inner core, the inner fire, you find the harmony that you have been seeking.

Then the requirement is to sustain it, to maintain it, to increase it. Because the law of progress is the law of attainment.

Withdraw from All Self-Indulgence

Maitreya also counsels us to withdraw from all self-indulgence—all indulgence of the not-self. We must remove all idolatry of our own self and the selves of others from our consciousness. Idolatry is a result of spiritual blindness, and most people do not know when they are engaging in idolatry. Idolatry, as self-love, is the love of any self before God and before the flame.

Many who consider themselves to be advanced on the Path do not realize that the love of any self must be the love of the God Self within the individual. Many cannot distinguish between divine love and human love, possessive love and non-possessive love, love that is manipulation and love that is freedom. It is a question of refinement. The closer you come to the Real Self within, the less you find yourself in love with your lesser self, pursuing a path of self-preservation, of sensuality, of indulgence.

There are many teachers in our time who teach that you can do anything you want and still be on the spiritual path. None of the real teachers ever told us that—not Jesus, not Gautama, not Milarepa, not Padma Sambhava. The real

Gurus never told us we could take the bag and baggage of our carnality into the consciousness of God. And yet there are many teachers who promise us this attainment. The attainment they promise is a false freedom: it is power over others instead of the God-dominion of the flame within.

In the temptations of Jesus we recognize temptations that come to every one of us. They are the testing of the threefold flame. Can we uphold the Father, the Son and the Spirit as the will of God, the wisdom of God and the love of God? Can we prove that we love that flame more than we love the externals?

"Jesus was led up of the Spirit into the wilderness to be tempted of the devil." This happened to be Satan, a very real being, one who was on the Path of initiation and decided to use all the techniques of self-mastery for self-glory—for the raising-up and the exalting of the carnal mind, the human ego, the not-self, the unreal self.

"And when he [Jesus] had fasted forty days and forty nights he was afterward anhungered. And when the tempter came to him he said, 'If thou be the Son of God command that these stones be made bread.'"

Jesus was able to turn stones to bread—he performed a similar alchemy in the feeding of the multitudes. But he refused to do it when challenged by the adversary. He refused to do it to satisfy the carnal mind. There is a great difference: it is the difference between the black magician and the white magician. It is how we use our alchemy, how we use the laws of God, that makes the difference between Christ and Satan.

Jesus' answer was, "It is written, Man shall not live by bread alone, but by every word that proceedeth out of the mouth of God." It is important that we put ourselves in the place of Jesus. Jesus' victory in this test looks easy with hindsight. But Jesus was in a physical body, he was hungry, he had not eaten for forty days. He could have easily turned the stones to bread. The temptation fit the scene; Satan knew well what he was asking. And therefore we understand the lesson: In the hour of our greatest desperation for a physical or a human need, are we willing to compromise the Law?

On Atlantis the compromise of the Law was spoken: "Let us do evil that good may come." Over the centuries this has become the Machiavellian rationale in church, in state, in politics, in religion. It is the rationalization for the compromise of Truth.

"Then the devil taketh him up into the holy city and setteth him on a pinnacle of the temple and sayeth unto him, 'If thou be the Son of God, cast thyself down. For it is written, He shall give his angels charge concerning thee. And in their hands they shall bear thee up, lest at any time thou dash thy foot against a stone.' Jesus said unto him, 'It is written again, Thou shalt not tempt the Lord thy God.'"

These are tests of power. The madness of the fallen ones is power, ambition, pride and worldly conquest, and they are there to offer us all if we will compromise.

"Again the devil taketh him up into an exceeding high mountain and showeth him all of the kingdoms of the world and the glory of them and sayeth unto him, 'All these things will I give thee if thou will fall down and worship me.' Then sayeth Jesus unto him, 'Get thee hence, Satan, for it is written, Thou shalt worship the Lord thy God and him only shalt thou serve.' Then the devil leaveth him and behold, angels came and ministered unto him."[14]

Satan himself spoke the words, "all power is given unto me, and to whomsoever I will, to him I will give it." The power of this world is in the hands of the fallen ones, and this is their bribery of the children of God.

Satan was tempting Jesus with the very elements of his ministry: the very things that Jesus would go forth to do in the name of the Christ, in the name of God, Satan would have him do in his name.

Assessing Our Motives

Perhaps we don't use these terms today, but everything we do falls to the one side or the other. Are we doing what we're doing so that we can have power and dominion and the pride of the eye and the ambition of attainment before our peers, so that we can get what we want when we want it? Or are we content to wait upon the Lord, to be humble, to sacrifice the lesser self in order to know the glory of the infilling of the temple with the Holy Spirit.

That is how you measure attainment. You ask yourself: Why do I live? Why do I work? Why do I love? Why do I do what I do each day? Do I have the larger purpose of glorifying God, of freeing souls from the bondage of this world? Do I have the greater goal of the ascension in mind, the reunion with the fiery core? Am I living for the great liberation of Gautama Buddha? Am I living to conquer Matter in order to serve my fellow man? Or because I want more money and more things and more of the pleasures of the senses?

When Jesus' time was coming, he made the remark to his disciples, "The prince of this world cometh, and hath nothing in me."[15] There was nothing in Jesus into which Satan could tie—not even a grain of ambition rationalized for the establishment of his church, his Path, for the good of his disciples, for their comfort, for their needs, and so on.

It is so easy to rationalize ambition when it's seemingly for a good purpose. How do we really define these things, when we in the West have been given a path of the subduing of Matter? In fact, it is not the things we do that are really right or wrong: it is the spirit and the motive that is right or wrong.

We are given the science of the Mother to conquer Matter as our gift to mankind. The Masters speak of us as being scientists, physicists, chemists, pushing ahead in the nuclear age—but always we must be sifting the motive. Do we conquer Matter to release the potential of the Christ, or do we conquer Matter so we can have more pleasure and more things? Do we conquer Matter to preserve the flame of freedom for a world in distress, or do we conquer Matter so we can retreat and turn our backs when people around the world cry out for help, for freedom?

Nonattachment

The Bhagavad Gita teaches that we have the right to pursue action only for the sake of the ritual of the action itself—not for the sake of ambition or the results of the action.

Whenever the goal of the action becomes more important than the action itself, we open the door to the compromise of Truth, honor, love; we can accept the philosophy of the end justifying the means—let us do evil that good may come. "I'll cheat a little, because in the end it's for the good of the church, it's for the good of my family, it's for the good of some noble cause. In the end, after I've cheated everybody, I'll give everything I have to some humanitarian endeavor."

How many people have said that? But if you remain unattached, you will never compromise the flame of honor. The flame of honor is the flame of the Holy Spirit, and the flame of the Holy Spirit is our very life. It is the difference between the living dead and those who are quickened to life.

Buddha taught us to be free of desire. Desirelessness means nonattachment. But there is lawful and legitimate desire, and Gautama even taught it himself. It is lawful to desire to be a chela on the Path. It is lawful to desire to attain nirvana, to attain the ascension. You measure your desire by this formula: Is your desire an implementation of God within you desiring to be God? If God desiring to be God within you necessitates that you meditate, that you pray, that you serve, that you balance your karma—and in order to balance your karma you study to have a sacred labor, a profession, a calling—this can be the implementation of God becoming more of himself within you and the means to your mastery of the self on the Path.

To be free of possessions is not quite the object of the Path: the goal is to be free of the desire for possessions and the attachment to possessions. You can have all the possessions in the world if you use them to glorify God and if you are nonattached to them. So the Path of initiation is the fine line that was summed up by Joshua when he said, "Choose you this day whom ye will serve."[16] By that you will measure your attainment.

El Morya confides to us soul lessons on nonattachment drawn from his life and death as Thomas More: "Here in Darjeeling, we are the followers of the path of Christ and the Buddha, which are one. And we follow the byword 'nonattachment to the fruit of action.' This means that we strive for the excellence of divine love in all things and leave the rest to God.

"Therefore, we inform you that it is the ritual of effectively challenging the liar and the lie whereby you will earn your ascension. And when you stand before the Lords of Karma (who are so very real) at the conclusion of this life and you must give answer whether or not you have defended these little ones, the Lords of Karma will not judge you according to whether or not you have accomplished the goal of wiping out planetary Evil—nay, you will be judged by the effectiveness of your effort, by the strength of ritual of your having engaged your energies to counteract the fallen ones.

"Witness my own embodiment as Thomas More. I was well aware of the fact that I would not undo the edicts of the king, nor the separation of the Church of England from the Church of our Lord Jesus Christ. I was well aware that my voice would simply be the testimony of righteousness—not of a righteous man but of a righteous God. For I do not count myself a righteous man but the instrument of the One who is Eternal Righteousness.

"And so, beloved ones, the infamy of the decisions of Henry VIII has continued, multiplied and spawned, as error is wont to do in a corruptible milieu; but the voice of one who chose to be the voice of God remains as the clarion call of a trumpet.

"And the moral of the story is that whereas by and by I entered into the ritual of the ascension at the conclusion of the divine plan for my incarnations on earth, those who valued their lives, their paltry positions, even their flesh, are yet evolving; and I might say that whether or not they indeed are evolving Godward is questionable....

"Blessed hearts, let us not count worthiness as an accrual of good deeds, for if it be so, then unworthiness will become an accrual of wicked deeds. This is a mystery, for at a certain level it is so and at a certain level of life evolving life this becomes the measure and the mark of the judgment of the Lords of Karma; but to be in the center of good deeds, one must be in the center of the awareness that God himself is the doer and the deed. And therefore, one does not make too much, neither of human achievement nor of the little human mistakes, for to do so can cause that insanity that is born of pride and that division in one's members, the schism in consciousness that comes on the heels of failure.

"If one is to acknowledge error or ego as supremely Real, then there is no hope for salvation. For the fulcrum of salvation is not good and bad deeds per se, but it is the forsaking of error and the erroneous consciousness that produced the human ego in the first place and the realization that it is the soul's centering in the will of God, that it is the soul's realignment with that will, that makes all the difference.

"It is not that you are right or wrong but that you are nonattached to your rights and to your wrongs. And with that nonattachment the resolution of your life will be that all that proceeds from you will result in right action, right consciousness, right goals, right mindedness—rightness that is God's Rightness!"[17]

Affirmations for Attainment of the Christ Consciousness

One important technique for attaining mastery is the Science of the Spoken Word. The "Transfiguring Affirmations of Jesus the Christ" are mantras for the attainment of the Christ consciousness.

As you give these affirmations aloud, there is the release of the flow of energy from your heart chakra, from the very heart center that is the seat of the threefold flame of Life. There is also the flow of the throat chakra in the power of the spoken Word setting the blueprint of your self-mastery. There is the flow of the all-seeing eye, the third-eye chakra, which we use to visualize the perfection of God and its precipitation in man. There is the flow of Light through the crown of life, the point of the lotus of the Buddhic consciousness. There is the flow of peace through the solar plexus. There is the flow of the seat-of-the-soul chakra, and finally there is the flow of the Mother in the base-of-the-spine chakra. All of the chakras in your being are points for your realization of levels of God awareness.

How God conceives of himself is how God expresses himself in you, and how God expresses himself in you depends on your releasing of the flow of Light. It's like opening the windows for fresh air—opening the windows of the soul so that the Light of Alpha and Omega can flow. This is why in the East, meditation on the breath—the sacred fire breath, the in-breathing and the out-breathing—is so important.

The flow of the breath through the release of the mantra is also the release of pranic energies into and out of the chakras. The chakras are for the receiving of the life-giving energies of the Mother as prana, as the essence of the Holy Spirit, and they are for the giving forth of spiritual Light, the energies of the creation that come from Alpha. The simultaneous giving and receiving of the energies of the chakras weaves a pattern like basket-weave, the effect of the clockwise and the counterclockwise movement of energy.

As you give these mantras, breathe deeply in the diaphragm and feel your breath as the fire breath: then feel these seven windows of the expression of God with you as being open. You are releasing praise of God through seven centers of God awareness. And instead of the customary conception that we speak through the mouth, speak through all of the chakras having the chord of the seven tones of God's consciousness.

Transfiguring Affirmations
of Jesus the Christ

I AM THAT I AM
I AM the open door which no man can shut
I AM the Light which lighteth every man
    that cometh into the world
I AM the way
I AM the Truth
I AM the life
I AM the resurrection

> I AM the ascension in the Light
> I AM the fulfillment of all my needs and requirements of the hour
> I AM abundant supply poured out upon all life
> I AM perfect sight and hearing
> I AM the manifest perfection of being
> I AM the illimitable Light of God made manifest everywhere
> I AM the Light of the Holy of Holies
> I AM a son of God
> I AM the Light in the holy mountain of God

When you say "I AM," as the name of God, you are really saying "God in me is."

God in me is the I AM. God in me is the affirmation of be-ness and of consciousness and of self-awareness.

God in me is the open door which no man can shut. No man has the power to shut the door of your soul's penetration of God consciousness.

God in me is the Light which lighteth every man that cometh into the world. The same God that is in me is the very fire of creation which lights the life of my brothers and sisters on the path and of all mankind. The acknowledgment of that fire of creation is the great oneness that we can share.

God in me is the way. The way is the path of the Buddha and the Christ.

God in me is the Truth. The Truth can be known—contrary to the lie of the fallen ones that Truth cannot be known.

God in me is the life. Because he is that life I shall live forevermore.

God in me is the resurrection—of my life, my love, my cosmic purpose, my inner blueprint. God in me is the fire of the resurrection to walk in the footsteps of Christ and Buddha.

God in me is the ascension in the Light. God in me is the very fire, the very energy of the creation released in the hour of Jesus' ascension and the hour of the ascension of Gautama, of Mother Mary and countless saints and sages of East and West.

God in me is the fulfillment of all my needs and requirements of the hour. This mantra regulates the cosmic flow in you. In order to have the fulfillment of needs and requirements, there must be the perfect giving and receiving, the perfect flow over the figure-eight pattern. This perfect flow occurs through the chakras, your own centers of God awareness.

God in me is perfect sight and hearing. Sight and hearing are very necessary on this plane, but the sight and hearing that we require above all are spiritual sight—insight to know God, to know Light and darkness, Truth and error, to define, redefine and refine the way of our Christhood—and the hearing of the still, small voice within, the hearing of the Master who calls us, the hearing of the voice of God who spoke to Jesus "This is my beloved son, in whom I am well pleased."[18]

God in me is the manifest perfection of being. We all know that God is perfect, we all know that God is within us. But that he is the manifest perfection of being is the affirmation that brings Light from the plane of Spirit to the plane of Matter whereby we conquer here and now, time and space.

This is the practicality of the avatars of this generation. What does it matter that God is well in heaven? God must be in manifestation here on earth to work the change of the alchemy of the Aquarian age.

God in me is the illimitable Light of God made manifest everywhere. This mantra releases a burst of Light that can illumine a cosmos—because the Light of God cannot be limited. And when we affirm this by the power of God's name, by law it happens.

God in me is the Light of the Holy of Holies. The Holy of Holies is the most sacred innermost core, the fiery core of your being, your very own individualized I AM THAT I AM. This is the flaming flame that will not be quenched. It is the flame that burned though the bush was not consumed. It was the fiery core out of which the LORD God revealed himself to Moses and gave his name as the I AM THAT I AM. You can contact the same Holy of Holies and experience your very own I AM Presence.

God in me is a son of God—the blazing sun of the Christos.

God in me is the Light in the holy mountain of God—the highest point, the very summit of being, of self-awareness, the mountain of God where Moses received the tablets of the law, the mountain of the Buddha, the mount of the transfiguration of the Christ. These are within us, and by initiation we reach that height.

The Science of Mantra

These affirmations of consciousness begin in your etheric body, the plane of the subconscious as well as the superconscious mind, the plane where the blueprint of fire is etched upon your being. When you first begin to give the mantras of Christ and Buddha and the great teachers of all ages, the cycling of that energy begins in this plane, where you perhaps do not see it.

Then it cycles through the mind, the mental plane, and begins to stimulate your mind with creativity and genius and flow. Then it descends into the level of the desire body, into the feelings, and your love of service, manifest as surrender and sacrifice to the Christ in all, becomes deeper and deeper as a feeling as you give the mantras. Finally there is the physical manifestation, when all is balanced in the action of the Trinity of Father and Son and Holy Spirit, as it was in Jesus on the day of the transfiguration.

When the mantras are affecting the physical body, your countenance changes, there is Light in your eyes, Light in your face. Your physical body normalizes, its functions normalize, you take on the appearance and the stature of a disciple of Jesus, a chela of the Buddha, of Maitreya, of Gautama.

Mantras should be given not simply with faith that they work, but with the scientific understanding that they work, beginning from the very depths of being and moving outward. The Ascended Masters have stressed the application of the Law of cosmos as a science, not as a superstition—not as standing before the LORD God and wishing and willing change, but standing before the God of very Gods and knowing that if we apply the Law as Christ and Buddha taught it, that we, too, shall manifest the same perfection in time and space.

We confirm it now by our affirmation. We expect it to manifest according to the law of cycles. Understanding the law of cycles is not to engage in procrastination. It is understanding that all will be fulfilled in us in the fullness of God's time and space, that we are applying the law and that the law works. Therefore we proceed as scientists.

If you do not know that the law works because you have not seen it work, you can take the hypothesis of the mantra and its science that has been proven for thousands of years, in an unbroken chain since the days of Lemuria. You can go into the laboratory that God has given you—your own temple, your own four lower bodies—and you can experiment with the law and that science. But if you are a scientist worthy of the name, you will not give the mantra once and say, "See, it didn't work." This is a science that requires experimentation over months and sometimes years.

The Sanskrit mantras that come down to us from India come from the masters of Mu. Therefore many souls who have walked the earth have scientifically proven the efficacy of the spoken Word. And if thousands have proven this law for themselves, is it not folly to reject their proof?

And when the greatest of all who have ever lived among us have proved this science, would we not be wise to be humble before their attainment and measure our attainment by their demonstration of the Law?

Attainment Is Rooted in the Dharma of God's Law

Attainment comes about because one practices the dharma of God's Law. The fulfillment of one's destiny becomes a practice that radiates through the whole man, as the Law sounding from the center—as though vibrating through rock or other substance—produces its effect all the way through to the periphery.

This attainment will manifest the power of God. But that power cannot actually be invoked by evil people in the same manner as by good people. To attempt to invoke it for evil is a practice of black magic, which cannot help but become self-limiting. White magic is the unfoldment of one's own Reality: it is a blending or congruency with the original pattern envisioned by the Creator himself.

Through the process of eternity, man reaches out of time to actually create himself, and thus a god is born in exactly the fashion ordained by God. The First Cause desired to see many creatures made in His own Image, possessing equal power and harking back to that sublime moment of realization reflected in all and attainable by all. Without this manifestation, man would be a willy-nilly creature of his own desires or habits. His personality would be molded by his lesser desires, his limited concepts, his own thoughts and feelings, and not in the Divine Image.

The Solar Gift of Our Reality

Now attainment is before us; we no longer look entirely to others for our salvation, for our attainment. We look to ourselves, and thus within ourselves to the flame of God, posited there in miniature. This flame must be expanded. It is the solar gift of our Reality (the sole gift of our Reality).

Without it, we literally become nothing. Failing to observe our opportunity, we actually are self-destructing, and thus the soul becomes lost. Reversing the process, man, recognizing that he has the enormous opportunity of the dharma, is able to direct all of the facets of Being—the *citta*, or mind, the body—to obey the powers of the soul, and they are many.

In that full measure of godliness, which Christ dictated as the never-failing light of God, we no longer sense a struggle between the Buddhist and the Christian, between the Muslim and the Jew, between any groups of people. We no longer sense, then, a division in ourselves. We are able to see attainment as possible to us, and once it becomes possible to us through that quality we call grace—the grace of dharma, the grace of the Law, the grace of God—we are able to draw more and more of the divine nature into ourselves by an act of love and faith.

Translated into action, these become the power of God unto salvation. Truly, unless we undertake the direction of our own lives, we cannot expect to achieve attainment.

Every great Master, the entire Great White Brotherhood, all who serve on the various rays, together with the angelic hosts and Cosmic Beings, have one object and one alone, and that is to manifest the will of God. If the will, then, is so sacred to them as their eternal dharma, if the will, then, is so sacred to the universe, it follows that it must be made so sacred to the individual in order for him to practice the ritual of attainment.

Attainment through Grace

It is not unusual to see people who worship with great devotion, but who utterly fail to practice the principles of the Christ, of God, or of the dharma of the Law toward one another. Without this grace they often struggle unnecessarily and repetitiously, the same sequences of events occurring again and again.

They also encounter frustration. And the power of magic that may be invoked from time to time, drawing on the attainment of another or the inherent sounds of universal attainment, can never be made a permanent part of any man until he has actually entered into that personal attainment himself. If he questions his ability to do this, let him seek greater faith from God and realize that he has eternity in which to accomplish all things.

This does not mean that one should not live up to the principles of dharma and the principle of attainment here and now. Salvation is in the here and now. Salvation is today. And the salvation of the individual must be preserved by his living the highest of which he is capable day by day.

Attainment takes many forms of measure. It is always relative, and yet it is transcendent. It is relative because it must be compared to the attainment of yesterday. It is transcendent because it is the attainment of tomorrow and all the tomorrows.

Muse Only upon Your Rate of Progress

Has the individual failed? The universe has not. And as we climb the ladder of realization, we no longer fail God, we no longer think and muse upon our limitation, but upon our rate of progress.

The universe is governed by natural law. Natural law is not subject to the whimsy of man. It works for one as it works for all. Therefore, as an act of faith, we embark upon a journey into the heart of God. We see God as attainment, we see God as ourselves.

Kuthumi says, "The time has come, and it is overripe, when the life-mission of men must be understood; they must recognize that one day they, too, asked to go forth into the realm of form in order to overcome that realm with all of its temptations and achieve the higher purpose of bringing God's kingdom into manifestation. Thus, in the hope of being a faithful servant, they looked forward to the day when God could truly say of such a one, 'Thou hast been faithful over a few things, I will make thee ruler over many things: enter thou into the joy of the Lord!'"[19]

The summit is ever before us; it represents attainment. It is snow-crowned, flooded with the light of the sun. How can the Self be reached in its highest ramifications, and how, step by step, can man climb that ladder?

These things are best known by the God within. For a limited mind cannot discover even its own goals, for they seem to vanish, almost to a point of nihilism. Yet the real goals of man are transcendent.

The Seed of Attainment Is within You Now

While at times beckoning as mirage upon the desert, one knows that the oasis of momentary regeneration is at hand. One knows the permanent promised land lies within the domain of self.

Man is both darkness and Light. He stands created in a sea of his feelings and his thoughts. He dwells both in them and out of them. When he is in them, he is often enclosed around about, encompassed by them. Outside of himself—which in reality he cannot be, but in his mind he still can be, because with God all things are possible—he can stand outside of his limitation, outside of his limited sphere, and behold the great castle of Truth that he must erect.

In imagination he already attains—yet the projected goal must be realistically brought down into the realm of the visible and the practical. Thus he may begin in increments the higher direction of his own way back to the heart of God. That Christ and innumerable Hosts of Light are involved in his direction, on the course transcendent, is unquestioned.

The highest image in which man was created is the Image of God. He is already in that Image. In a higher sense, he has already attained. He is already one with God. His sins are forgiven, for they are no more. He basks in the sunlight of attainment now.

But in this field of duality, as was the intended purpose of duality, he must climb the stairway to the stars, he must seek to dwell upon the mountaintop, he must have a consciousness that examines the love that God has brought to him. This is his attainment. This is his Reality. All else is but illusion.

So a God is born in man.

The Mystical Realization That I AM God

When the microcosm
becomes the Macrocosm,
man knows that he is God,
and the statement of Moses,
"Ye are gods,"* becomes,
"Ye are God's."
All that he is belongs to God, is God
"in eternal, immortal manifestation."

My love is God's Love—
He shall direct its flow.
My mind is God's Mind—
His is the Mind that knows.

My life is God's Life—
His energy here below.
My light is God's Light—
His Light is the Light that glows.

---

* Ps. 82:6; John 10:34.

Mark L. Prophet
Elizabeth Clare Prophet
Twin Flames in the Service of the Masters

*And I will give power unto my two witnesses,
and they shall prophesy a thousand two hundred
and threescore days, clothed in sackcloth.*
— BOOK OF REVELATION

Afterword

The Ascension of Mark Prophet

by Elizabeth Clare Prophet

ONE DAY SOME YEARS AGO, I WAS very much impressed with a statement of Paul. It came out of the Bible to me like letters of living fire: "For this corruptible must put on incorruption, and this mortal must put on immortality."[1] I saw the word "must" and I said, "This is a mandate from heaven. God is impressing this upon me in this hour. I do not know why." And so I asked my secretary to type it on a piece of paper. I taped it onto my mirror, and every day I would read those words.

The weeks and the months passed, and about six months later I went through the experience of observing the transition of my husband, Mark Prophet, the founder of The Summit Lighthouse and our first Messenger. I went through the experience of him being taken from me suddenly, in a moment. And as I tarried with him through the weekend in the hours of his transition, I observed his resurrection, and at the conclusion of three days, in the morning, I saw him ascend.*

I did not see him ascend with my physical eyes, but I saw him with my inner eye. I stood next to him as Elisha stood next to Elijah, and I was able to see him and commune with him and realize that he was taken up in consciousness, in the acceleration into the permanent Being of God. I felt the most magnificent joy and exhilaration, and I was filled with the Light of that experience.

I came home and I gave my witness of that experience to our children and to our staff. And when I returned to my room, I noticed on the mirror the words that were there, which had been burning in my soul those months. As I read them again, "For this corruptible must put on incorruption, and this mortal must put on immortality," I realized that the call of the ascension is not a choice. It is the demand of the very Life that is in us. It is the demand of the fire in our hearts.

And at a certain moment—we know not when it will be—we see our loved ones and fellow disciples on the Path, and suddenly God calls them and takes them by the hand, and we see them going up in that whirling action of the sacred fire.

I had the gentle comfort then in my heart that this truly was the plan of God, as Mark had told me that plan ten years before. I knew that it was the mandate of the cosmos that this soul ascend. I knew it even as I had known when I was just a teenager and I stood on the front steps of a church that it was also true for me. No one had ever given me any teachings on my personal ascension, but as I came out of that church one day, I felt a presence around me. I looked up, and I could see

---

* Mark Prophet suffered a sudden massive stroke early on a Saturday morning. He was taken to the hospital and continued on life support for two more days, never regaining consciousness. He ascended on Monday, February 26, 1973, and is now known as the Ascended Master Lanello.

the light of the sun and even a greater Light. And I exclaimed out loud, "Why, I have to make my ascension in this life." From that moment I knew that I must return to God.

It is a teaching that no one had to teach me and no one has to teach you. You know it in your soul, because God has placed that mandate there—the same mandate that has carried all of the saints who have already returned to the heart of God.

"This corruptible must put on incorruption, and this mortal must put on immortality." May these words also become letters of living fire for you—and perhaps a statement that you place somewhere you will see it each day. When you realize that you must put on immortality, that you must put on incorruption, it becomes the impetus for your daily working of the works of God—steadfast and unmovable.

Elizabeth Clare Prophet

My goal is to take true seekers, in the tradition of the Masters of the Far East, as far as they can go and need to go to meet their true Teachers face to face.

Mark L. Prophet

*Ours must be a message of infinite love,
and we must demonstrate that love to the world.*

Note from the Editor

IT IS WITH GREAT JOY THAT WE release *The Path to Attainment,* the final book in the Climb the Highest Mountain series. Book 1 began with Chapter 1, "Your Synthetic Image," and now Book 9 ends with Chapter 33, "Attainment." Hence, the Climb the Highest Mountain series takes the reader from identification with the limited, human self of the synthetic image to the attainment of the image of the Real Self, our eternal Being.

Much of the material in this book was written by Mark and Elizabeth Prophet in the years 1966 to 1972, when they first worked on the series. I have also included additional material from more recent seminars, lectures and dictations that expand on those original teachings. I feel very fortunate to have been able to attend many of those events in person, and I am grateful to see that those teachings will now reach a much wider audience.

I have been greatly blessed to have been given the assignment to work with the Messengers on Climb the Highest Mountain, the Everlasting Gospel, the scripture for the New Age. I recall sitting in the Messengers' prayer tower at La Tourelle in 1969, working with Mark and Elizabeth and also with Florence Miller, who we know now as the Ascended Lady Master Kristine. We worked on the first volume of this series in a time before personal computers or the Internet, and all of the work had to be done by hand.

The Messengers either wrote the text in longhand or spoke into a tape recorder. Florence and I transcribed, input and proofed the copy, and then it would go back to Mark or Elizabeth for review and further editing. Each time a correction or edit was made, Florence and I had to retype and reproof the entire page. It was laborious work, requiring concentration and attention to detail. But there was also great joy in being present when these sublime teachings were first delivered and assisting in the task of bringing them to the world.

It is now my great joy to see this landmark series completed. It is my fervent prayer that these true Teachings of the great Masters of Light may contact each and every Lightbearer on earth, especially those who are candidates for the ascension.

ANNICE BOOTH
ROYAL TETON RANCH
PARADISE VALLEY, MONTANA

The Thirty-Three Chapters of the Climb the Highest Mountain Series

The Path of the Higher Self	1 Your Synthetic Image
	2 Your Real Image
	3 A Heap of Confusion
	4 What Is Individuality?
	5 What Is Consciousness?
	6 God in Man
	7 God in Nature
The Path of Self-Transformation	8 Karma
	9 Reembodiment
The Masters and the Spiritual Path	10 The Highest Yoga
	11 The Ascension
	12 Ascended and Unascended Masters
	13 Hierarchy
The Path of Brotherhood	14 Brotherhood
The Path of the Universal Christ	15 The Christ
Paths of Light and Darkness	16 The Cult of Hedon
	17 Psychic Thralldom
	18 Armageddon
	19 Thy Will be Done
The Path to Immortality	20 The Law of Cycles
	21 Planes of Consciousness
	22 Immortality
	23 Entities
	24 The Messengers
The Path of Christ or Antichrist	25 Prayer, Decrees and Meditation
	26 Black Magic
	27 Antichrist
	28 The Summit
The Path to Attainment	29 Twin Rays
	30 Integrity
	31 The One Path above the Many
	32 The Great White Brotherhood
	33 Attainment

Notes

Books referenced here are published by Summit University Press unless otherwise noted. Quotes from the Bible are from the King James Version.

Preface

1. Rev. 10:9–10.
2. Elizabeth Clare Prophet, December 29, 1972.
3. Rev. 14:6.

Introduction

1. Rev. 10:9.
2. Ralph Waldo Emerson, *Representative Men: Seven Lectures* (Philadelphia: David McKay, 1893), pp. 286–87.
3. Jer. 31:33–34.
4. 2 Kings 5:1–15.

Chapter 1 · Twin Rays

Opening quotation: Gen. 2:7, 21–23; 5:2.

CHAPTER 1 · SECTION 1 · THE SEARCH FOR WHOLENESS
1. Gen. 2:18.
2. Matt. 19:6; Mark 10:9.
3. Gen. 1:26–28.
4. The original creation of twin flames in the Great Central Sun and their evolution in the planes of Spirit is described in some detail in chapter 4, "Hierarchy," of *The Masters and the Spiritual Path*.
5. The writer of the Book of Genesis described the commingling of Matter and Spirit in the creation and in the ultimate reunion of twin

souls with the simple words: "and they shall become one flesh" (See Gen. 2:7, 21–24).
6. Gen. 3:22, 24; Rev. 2:7; 22:2, 14.
7. For additional teachings by the Ascended Masters on the subject of suicide, see Neroli Duffy and Marilyn C. Barrick, *Wanting to Live: Overcoming the Seduction of Suicide.*
8. Gautama Buddha, May 13, 1976, "The Cosmic Honor Guard of the World Mother," in *Keepers of the Flame Lesson 28*, p. 25.
9. Matt. 19:12.
10. John 2:1–10.
11. 1 Cor. 7:1–9; see also Heb. 13:4.
12. Mother Mary, April 21, 1987, "The Old Order Must Pass Away," *Pearls of Wisdom,* vol. 30, no. 21, May 24, 1987. Magda, the twin flame of Jesus, was embodied as Mary Magdalene. For further teaching on Mary Magdalene and her service with Jesus, see Elizabeth Clare Prophet, *Mary Magdalene and the Divine Feminine.*
13. Mark 10:11–12.
14. Chananda, July 5, 1985, "Twin Flames on the Path of Initiation: How to Join Forces with Your Twin Flame for Freedom," *Pearls of Wisdom,* vol. 28, no. 32, August 11, 1985.
15. Matt. 6:33.
16. Chananda, July 5, 1985, "Twin Flames on the Path of Initiation."
17. Lady Master Venus, March 12, 1978, "Keeping the Flame of Love on Terra," *Pearls of Wisdom,* vol. 21, nos. 34, 35, August 20, 27, 1978.
18. Chananda, July 5, 1985, "Twin Flames on the Path of Initiation."
19. El Morya, July 5, 1985, "The Mission of Twin Flames Today: How to Join Forces with Your Twin Flame for Freedom," *Pearls of Wisdom,* vol. 28, no. 33, August 18, 1985.
20. Matt. 22:4–14.

CHAPTER 1 · SECTION 2 · THE SACRED FIRE
1. Astrea, "Freedom from the Psychic World," in *Keepers of the Flame Lesson 24,* pp. 27–28.
2. Ps. 121:8.
3. Gen. 28:12.
4. Gen. 1:2, 3.
5. John 1:1–3.
6. John 10:30.
7. After his ascension, Saint Germain received a special dispensation from the Lords of Karma whereby he took on a physical body and was known as le Comte de Saint Germain, the "Wonderman of Europe." He was seen around the courts of Europe for at least a hundred years in the eighteenth and nineteenth centuries. For further information about Saint Germain and his accomplishments in this embodiment, see Mark L. Prophet and Elizabeth Clare Prophet, *Saint Germain On Alchemy,* pp. xi–xxxi.
8. Lord Ling, October 13, 1963.
9. Ps. 82:6; John 10:34.

CHAPTER 1 · SECTION 3 · RAISING THE LIGHT

1. Gen. 1:26.
2. Gen. 1:27.
3. It has happened, but it is not common, that twin flames have embodied in the same family as father and daughter, mother and son, brother and sister. However, it is important to beware of the psychological ramifications of dwelling on this concept—whether it be true or not. Engaging in the fantasy that one's mother, for example, might be one's twin flame may have to do with fear of going forth and having a fulfilling, mature relationship with someone of one's own age.

    It is important to mature to the point of being able to provide the polarity to the person that God has ordained for oneself in marriage, if marriage is destined in this life. Entertaining of a fantasy that a family member is one's twin flame may be an avoidance of one's responsibilities and the sometimes fearful place where one may face rejection as well as acceptance from a member of the opposite sex. This problem has also resulted in homosexuality, lesbianism, incest and other inappropriate means by which people seek to meet mental and emotional needs for intimacy. The fantasy itself may be a spiritual violation of the Law. Even if it is not a physical relationship, it may become a spiritual crossing of the barriers in this octave as to the types of relationships that are allowed and ordained.

    In such a situation, role playing can become more important than the issue of twin flames. It is necessary to play the role and not put any other connotations on it, even mentally. There is a sanctity to the offices in hierarchy of father, mother, son, daughter, brother, sister; and one must mature to the place of being capable of delivering love and receiving love in the properly ordained manner.
4. *Sushumnā, idā* and *pingalā:* Sanskrit terms for currents of wisdom, power and love emanating from the white-fire core of the base-of-the-spine chakra and which flow in and around the spinal altar.
5. One example of this misuse still practiced today is the oral stimulation of the genitals. Serapis Bey advises that those who so engage their energies are not able to make their ascension at the close of that embodiment unless or until such time as they cease this practice, erase the record, purify their forcefields and break the momentum by invocation to the violet flame. (The correction can be made within the same embodiment if the disciple is diligent in his application to the sacred fire.) The reason for this is that the juxtaposition of the upper (Spirit) chakras with the lower (Matter) chakras in an inverted position places man in an upside-down relationship to his God Presence at a time when the sacred energies are being released for the purposes of creation. This induces an inverted downward spiral that is the reverse of the ascension current. Once again it becomes clear that concepts of sin and punishment must be replaced by the proper understanding and practice of the precepts of the Law. Whereas knowledge rightly used leads to freedom, ignorance of the Law deprives man of his inheritance.

6. Gen. 18:20–19:28.
7. Goddess of Liberty, October 3, 1965, in *Liberty Proclaims,* p. 21.
8. The Brotherhood does not recommend the use of birth control pills as a means of family planning because they interfere with the normal function of the pituitary gland, which directs the flow of Light from the Presence. In a *Pearl of Wisdom* of January 8, 1967, El Morya said: "I might add, while we are on the subject of the harmful effects of drugs to the spiritual centers, that the birth control pills currently in vogue do interfere with the spiritual activities of the pineal gland, and further, these pills when taken for a prolonged period may induce cancer." The pituitary is the focus in the physical body of the Holy of Holies; therefore, it should never be tampered with. Parents are held karmically responsible for any physical side effects that oral contraceptives might have upon either the mother or future children. Since El Morya's dictation, evidence has been found of links between the use of these contraceptives and an increased risk of breast cancer, cervical cancer, certain liver cancers and cardiovascular disease. See http://www.cancer.gov/cancertopics/factsheet/Risk/oral-contraceptives.

There are methods of birth control (such as barrier methods) that are safe and effective. Abortion, however, should not be considered a means of birth control. Unless there is jeopardy to the life of the mother, it is deemed a violation of the sacred Flame of Life. It is the abortion of the divine plan of a soul whose body temple is being nurtured in the womb. God as a living potential, Christ as a living potential, is in that child from the moment of conception.
9. "Make love, not babies" was taken up as a slogan by the zero population growth movement in the 1960s and 1970s. It was the title of an article in *Newsweek,* June 15, 1970.
10. Unfortunately, this control does not always remain with the woman; for if her consciousness be allied with darkness, the forces of witchcraft and black magic can work through her to vampirize the energies of the man. Wherever illicit relations are practiced, a point of control is established that remains long after the physical relationship has ended, and this point of control can be used decades or embodiments later to hinder the son or daughter of God from moving upward in the Light. Decrees and spiritual work for the clearing of these records will give the student great assistance on the Path.
11. Exod. 20:14.
12. Prov. 14:12.
13. The Ascended Masters warn of the danger of teachings of false gurus of the East who promote sexual and other practices for the raising of the Kundalini. Jesus explains: "May I remind you that this is the path of the *Ascended* Masters and of the ascension. This is not the path of the false gurus of the East who create, out of sensation and a yoga that is not lawful, a sexual activity and attempt to raise that Life-force without the Holy Spirit but only by the stimulation of the chakras, stimulating the energy to rise when the attainment is not there.

"You will discover, beloved hearts, that those who pursue this left-handed path then use that Life-force to endow the dweller-on-the-threshold with permanence. These are the dark ones, and their seeming power is the misuse of the ascension flame to give immortality to the human ego. This, beloved ones, is the means whereby those on the left-handed path, the black magicians themselves, do gain the ability to work their works....

"Beware, then, the magnetism of the aura of those fallen angels who walk by the power of the misuse of the base-of-the-spine chakra, who even claim to take dictations from *me* by this power and these distorted sexual practices.

"Blessed ones of the Light, in the mastery you gain in the divine order which I have taught this day, you will discover that there is no need for Tantric Yoga. For when you raise the Kundalini fire, it is not by the sexual practices but by the lodestone of your mighty I AM Presence, by Christ in your heart who is the magnet for the consummation of that fire in the crown of Life. And this fire is for the deathless solar body, and it *is* the ascension flame" (March 13, 1983, *Pearls of Wisdom*, vol. 26, no. 36, September 4, 1983). El Morya says that under no circumstances does a spiritual seeker need physical sexual union in order to make spiritual progress.

14. Djwal Kul, "The Raising-Up of the Energies of the Mother," in Kuthumi and Djwal Kul, *The Human Aura*, pp. 282–84.
15. Mark L. Prophet and Elizabeth Clare Prophet, *Mary's Message for a New Day*, p. 129.
16. Gen. 1:28.
17. John 5:30; 14:10.
18. Gen. 1:3. A great momentum of Light can be developed by giving the simple yet powerful affirmation that was released by the Brotherhood many years ago, "Light expand (3x) expand, expand. Light I AM (3x) I AM, I AM."
19. Matt. 24:28.
20. Rev. 12:4.
21. "Sleeping Beauty" is a classic fairy tale best known today from Walt Disney's animated film of the same name. In the film, Princess Aurora is placed under a curse by Maleficent, a wicked dark fairy. The princess is awakened from her sleep by the kiss of Prince Philip, her betrothed (archetypal of the twin flame).
22. Rev. 17:1; 19:2.
23. Isa. 54:5.
24. Luke 1:38.
25. Rev. 21:2, 10.
26. Archeia Charity, "The Fire of Love Descending to Implement the Judgment," in Elizabeth Clare Prophet, *Vials of the Seven Last Plagues*, pp. 34–37.

CHAPTER 1 · SECTION 4 · THE ALCHEMICAL MARRIAGE

1. A detailed explanation of the Trial by Fire and the Last Judgment may be found in chapter 3, "Immortality," of *The Path to Immortality*,

book 7 of the Climb the Highest Mountain series.
2. Luke 15:11–32.
3. Mal. 3:10, 11.

Chapter 2 · Integrity

Opening quotation: Rev. 2:7; 22:1–2.

CHAPTER 2 · SECTION 1 · INTEGRATION WITH THE SOURCE

1. Mu, or Lemuria, was the lost continent of the Pacific which, according to the findings of James Churchward, archaeologist and author of *The Lost Continent of Mu,* extended from north of Hawaii three thousand miles south to Easter Island and the Fijis and was made up of three areas of land stretching more than five thousand miles from east to west. Churchward's history of the ancient Motherland is based on records inscribed on sacred tablets he claims to have discovered in India. With the help of the high priest of an Indian temple he deciphered the tablets, and during fifty years of research confirmed their contents in further writings, inscriptions and legends he came upon in Southeast Asia, the Yucatan, Central America, the Pacific Islands, Mexico, North America, ancient Egypt and other civilizations. He estimates that Mu was destroyed approximately 12,000 years ago by the collapse of the gas chambers which upheld the continent.

Atlantis was the island continent that existed where the Atlantic Ocean now is and that sank in cataclysm (the Flood of Noah) approximately 11,600 years ago as calculated by Churchward. The lost continent was vividly depicted by Plato, "seen" and described by Edgar Cayce in his readings, recalled in scenes from Taylor Caldwell's *Romance of Atlantis,* and scientifically explored and authenticated by the late German scientist Otto Muck. In his dialogues, Plato recounts that on "the island of Atlantis there was a great and wonderful empire" that ruled Africa as far as Egypt, Europe as far as Italy, and "parts of the continent" (thought to be a reference to America, specifically Central America, Peru and the Valley of the Mississippi). It has been postulated that Atlantis and the small islands to its east and west formed a continuous bridge of land from America to Europe and Africa.

See *The Lost Continent of Mu* (1931; reprint, New York: Paperback Library Edition, 1968); Otto Muck, *The Secret of Atlantis* (New York: Pocket Books, 1979); Ignatius Donnelly, *Atlantis: The Antediluvian World* (New York: Dover Publications, 1976); Phylos the Thibetan, *A Dweller on Two Planets* (Los Angeles: Borden Publishing Co., 1952).

2. Heb. 11:15.
3. 2 Pet. 2:17.
4. 1 Chron. 16:34, 41; 2 Chron. 5:13; 7:3, 6; 20:21; Ezra 3:11; Pss. 106:1; 107:1; 118:1–4; 136:1–3; 138:8; Jer. 33:11.

5. Matt. 13:12.
6. John 19:23 records that Jesus' coat "was without seam, woven from the top throughout."
7. *The Robe* is an historical novel about Jesus released in 1942. It was number 1 on the *New York Times* Best Seller list for a year. The book tells the story of Marcellus, the centurion who was in charge of the group that is assigned to crucify Jesus. Tormented by his actions, Marcellus is miraculously cured when he touches Jesus' robe. He sets out to find out the truth about the man he had killed, and his life is transformed as he encounters those who met the Master and witnessed his miracles. A film version starring Richard Burton, Jean Simmons and Victor Mature was released by Twentieth Century Fox in 1953. It was the first movie filmed in CinemaScope and won three Academy Awards.
8. The Great Divine Director, March 10, 1968.
9. Gen. 1:27.
10. Luke 12:3.
11. "Though the mills of God grind slowly, yet they grind exceedingly small; though with patience He stands waiting, with exactness grinds He all." From the poem, "Retribution," written originally by Friedrich von Logau and translated from the German by Henry Wadsworth Longfellow. The original is by an unknown Greek poet: "The mills of the Gods grind late, but they grind fine."
12. Matt. 22:21; Mark 12:17; Luke 20:25.
13. James 1:8.
14. The Maha Chohan, June 26, 1994, *Pearls of Wisdom,* vol. 37, no. 28, July 10, 1994.
15. Eph. 6:12.
16. Matt. 7:7–11; 21:22; Luke 11:9–13; John 16:23, 24.
17. Archangel Raphael, June 21, 1986, "The Day of the Coming of the Lord's Angel," *Pearls of Wisdom,* vol. 29, no. 32, June 29, 1986.
18. Cyclopea and Virginia, January 3, 1982, "I Will Stand upon My Watch!" *Pearls of Wisdom,* vol. 25, no. 13, March 28, 1982.
19. Prov. 22:6.
20. Morya was embodied as Sir Thomas More (1478–1535), the "man for all seasons." More's deep devotion to God caused him at one time to consider a religious vocation and to practice extraordinary austerities for over four years to test his own self-discipline. He decided to marry, however, and his wife and four children proved to be his greatest joy and his sole comfort in days to come. Their famed estate at Chelsea housed Thomas' entire family, including eleven grandchildren. Over the years, More's "little Utopia," as he often called it, became a center of learning and culture, likened by Erasmus to "Plato's academie"— a home of good will to which came the most learned men of the day, even the king himself, for counsel and for comfort. At Chelsea, More wrote the famous work entitled *Utopia,* a witty exposé of the superficiality of English life and the flagrant vices of English law.

In 1529, Sir Thomas More was appointed by Henry VIII Lord

Chancellor of England and Keeper of the Great Seal. In spite of many honors and achievements, More sought no man's esteem; he was known for his promptness, efficiency and even-handed justice. He remained sensitive to the needs of the common people by daily walking the back streets of London to inquire into the lives of the poor.

Sir Thomas devoted himself to his duties with utmost zeal until Henry, desirous of but lacking a male heir to the throne, declared his marriage to Catherine of Aragon null and announced his intent to marry Ann Boleyn. Since the divorce was without papal approval and directly opposed to the laws of the Church, More refused to support the king's decision. In 1532, at the height of his career, he resigned his office and retired to Chelsea, where, greatly concerned with the heresies of Luther's revolt, he continued his writings in defense of the Catholic faith. Without friends and without office, More and his family lived in abject poverty. Nevertheless, Henry had been insulted at the chancellor's public disapproval of him. The king, therefore, sought to defame More and thus restore his royal image.

When he refused to take the Oath of Supremacy (which implied the rejection of papal supremacy and made Henry the head of the English church), More was imprisoned in the Tower of London. Fifteen months later, he was convicted of treason on perjured evidence. He was beheaded on Tower Hill July 6, 1535, affirming himself "the king's good servant, but God's first." He was canonized four hundred years later in 1935.

Lawyer, judge, statesman, man of letters, author, poet, farmer, lover of pastoral life, ascetic, husband and father, champion of women's education, humanist and saint, Thomas More was outstanding among the avant-garde of the English Renaissance.

21. Thomas Becket (1118–1170) was Lord Chancellor of England and good friend and advisor of Henry II. When he became archbishop of Canterbury, foreseeing that his duties as archbishop would inevitably conflict with the king's will, he resigned the chancellorship against the king's wishes.

Becket turned his administrative abilities and diplomatic finesse as a distinguished chancellor into ardour and devotion as archbishop. He became as strong a supporter of the papacy as he had once been of the king and freely excommunicated courtiers and nobles for their unlawful use of church property and other breaches. In the face of the king's intent to imprison him, Becket exiled himself to France for six years. He returned to England following a partial reconciliation with the king, only to begin quarreling with him anew.

On December 29, 1170, he was brutally murdered in Canterbury Cathedral when four knights of the court took literally the king's remark that he wished to be rid of "this turbulent priest." Uncompromising to the end, Becket told the knights: "If all the swords in England were pointing at my head, you would never make me betray either God or the Pope." More than five hundred healing miracles were attributed to him only a few years after his death, and he was

canonized three years later.
22. El Morya, October 10, 1973.
23. Mark 8:36.
24. Gen. 3:24.
25. John 8:23.
26. Goddess of Purity, July 29, 1973.

THE CHART OF YOUR DIVINE SELF
1. *The Upanishads: Breath of the Eternal,* trans. Swami Prabhavananda and Frederick Manchester (New York: New American Library, 2002), p. 21.
2. *Ratnagotravibhāga* 1.28, in Edward Conze et al., eds., *Buddhist Texts through the Ages* (1954; reprint, New York: Harper and Row, 1964), p. 181.
3. *The Upanishads,* trans. Juan Mascaró (Baltimore: Penguin Books, 1965), pp. 61, 60.
4. Meister Eckhart, *Sermons and Treatises,* trans. and ed. M. O'C. Walshe (Rockport, Md.: Element Books, 1992), vol. III, p. 107.
5. Matt. 6:6.

CHAPTER 2 · SECTION 2 · THE SCIENCE OF WHOLENESS AND THE TREE OF LIFE
1. Gen. 2:9; 3:22, 24; Rev. 2:7.
2. The mass consciousness may be defined here as the sum of mankind's individual electronic belts, multiplied by the interplay of the forces contained within the belts aided and abetted by the sinister force.
3. Rev. 22:2.
4. "[God] drove out the man; and he placed at the east of the garden of Eden Cherubims, and a flaming sword which turned every way, to keep the way of the tree of life" (Gen. 3:24).
5. *The Random House Dictionary of the English Language,* s.v. "Compensation."
6. Rev. 7:14.
7. Matt. 7:1; Rom. 12:19.
8. Refraining from criticism, condemnation and judgment that is harmful to the well-being of others does not preclude the use of one's Christly faculties of discrimination in determining one's own actions, according to Jesus' admonishment to "judge righteous judgment" (John 7:24). Nor does it preclude trial by jury and the systems of jurisprudence evolved by the Masters to promote order in society.
9. John 21:22.
10. Matt. 6:26–29.
11. "As for man, his days are as grass: as a flower of the field, so he flourisheth. For the wind passeth over it, and it is gone; and the place thereof shall know it no more. But the mercy of the LORD is from everlasting to everlasting upon them that fear him, and his righteousness unto children's children; To such as keep his covenant, and to those that remember his commandments to do them" (Ps.

103:15–18); "For all flesh is as grass, and all the glory of man as the flower of grass. The grass withereth, and the flower thereof falleth away: but the word of the Lord endureth for ever" (1 Pet. 1:24–25).
12. Mark 8:35; Luke 9:24; Matt. 16:25.
13. Jer. 31:33.
14. Portia, September 3, 1972, "Go Forth to Challenge and to Check the Cycles of Injustice," *Pearls of Wisdom,* vol. 19, no. 23, June 6, 1976.
15. 2 Tim. 2:15.
16. Rev. 1:8.
17. We see the plus/minus polarity of the Father-Mother God as not a polarity of good and evil but of the plus/minus factors within the all-good, which is the only reality. Some there are who teach that Good is in polarity with Evil and for everything good there must be something bad, a front side and a back side, something positive and something negative. But this is a worldview of duality, of two-eyed vision. Evil can never be in polarity with Good because Good is the Divine Whole and contains within itself the plus and the minus.
18. Matt. 25:14–30.
19. Matt. 8:11; Luke 13:28.
20. The general term for this effluvia is *animal magnetism:* "ani-mal" (*animus* = "spirit," and *mal* = "evil"). "Animal references the spirit of evil and the form which it takes as a menagerie of lesser images in the electronic belt, and "magnetism" describes the negative or downward spiral—the gravitational pull of this effluvia on the four lower bodies.

There are four general categories of animal magnetism which correspond to the four lower bodies and to the quadrants on the clock. They are: (1) malicious animal magnetism (M.A.M.)—implying malice aforethought, the premeditation or revolving of evil; working through the etheric body on the 12, 1 and 2 o'clock lines. (2) Ignorant animal magnetism (Y.A.M.)—mental density, an inadvertent tool of the sinister force. Accidents and mechanical difficulties can be traced to this form of animal magnetism working through the mental body at the 3, 4 and 5 o'clock lines. (3) Sympathetic animal magnetism (S.A.M.)—sympathies and attractions between personalities. The most dangerous form of animal magnetism because it is usually misunderstood as the milk of human kindness. Family ties and friendships are often falsely based on sympathetic animal magnetism working through the emotional body at the 6, 7 and 8 o'clock lines. (4) Delicious animal magnetism (D.A.M.)—working through the physical body at the 9, 10 and 11 o'clock lines. The indulgences of the physical senses fall into this category and are recorded as the densities of the physical senses and body.
21. Matt. 25:14–30.
22. John 17:22.
23. Luke 2:49.

CHAPTER 2 · SECTION 3 · THE DANCE OF THE HOURS
1. Josh. 25:15; Lord Maitreya, *Keepers of the Flame Lesson 11*, pp. 11–12.
2. The definition of Christhood is the manifestation of God's love, his wisdom and his power. When the individual attains the balance of the threefold flame, he will also be manifesting the perfect God-control of his four lower bodies, for without God-control, the flame will not be balanced.
3. Heb. 13:2.

CHAPTER 2 · SECTION 4 · THE TEACHINGS OF JESUS ON THE TWELVE LINES OF THE CLOCK
1. Gen. 1:28.
2. Ps. 18:35; 2 Sam. 22:36.
3. Matt. 28:18.
4. Luke 15:11–32.
5. Jer. 31:33.
6. Rev. 21:2.
7. The Book of Revelation prophesies the coming forth of the divine manchild, who "will rule all nations with a rod of iron" [12:5; see also 2:27, 19:15]. The term *rod of iron* is a code for the *rod of Aaron*, which turned into a serpent and swallowed up the serpents produced by the magicians at Pharaoh's court [Exod. 7:10–13]. The rod thus symbolizes the raising of the Kundalini energy on the spine. See pp. 37–38.
8. Matt. 7:12.
9. There are three Greek words that are translated as "merciful" in the New Testament: (1) *oiktirmon,* meaning compassionate, (2) *hilaskomai,* meaning propitious, or benevolent, and (3) *eleemon,* meaning beneficent. Tracing the meaning of the "beneficent" to the Latin—*benefactum,* to do well—we find that beneficence is the quality of well-being or being well.
10. Matt. 10:16.
11. Eph. 2:14.
12. John 10:30.
13. Portia, "I Deem Cosmic Justice to Be a Rock!" *Pearls of Wisdom,* vol. 10, no. 8, February 19, 1967.
14. Gal. 6:7.
15. John 3:30.
16. Acts 1:2–12.
17. Exod. 20:3.
18. Deut. 6:4.
19. Matt. 7:2; Mark 4:24.
20. Matt. 7:2.
21. Mark 15:28.
22. Mark 15:31–32.
23. Matt. 27:46; Mark 15:34.
24. Matt. 11:11.
25. Luke 22:42.

26. Dan. 3:27.
27. Exod. 17:12.
28. Luke 23:27–31.
29. Matt. 26:39.
30. Luke 22:42.
31. Luke 1:48.
32. 2 Cor. 6:17.
33. Matt. 11:30.
34. In 1964 the Ascended Master Jesus Christ inaugurated the "Watch With Me" Jesus' Vigil of the Hours—a worldwide service of prayers, affirmations and hymns for the protection of the Christ consciousness in every son and daughter of God. This service commemorates the vigil the Master kept alone in the Garden of Gethsemane when he said: "Could ye not watch with me one hour?" The Lord Jesus has called students of the Ascended Masters to give the Watch individually or in group action once a week, at the same time each week, so that at every hour of the day and night someone somewhere is keeping the vigil.

    In a dictation given October 4, 1987, Jesus promised: "I shall be in your midst, beloved, as you give this prayer service in my name weekly.... All who commit to be my disciple as a Keeper of the Flame shall have my spheres of Light and my Sacred Heart superimposed upon him or her throughout this Watch each week" (*Pearls of Wisdom*, vol. 30, no. 56, November 25, 1987. *"Watch With Me" Jesus' Vigil of the Hours* 44-page booklet and audio recording are available from Summit University Press.
35. Rev. 19:20; 20:10, 14, 15. The lake of fire is a vortex of sacred fire on the God Star, Sirius. This all-consuming sacred fire of God consumes on contact the cause, effect, record and memory of the souls, together with their karma, who have not availed themselves of the continuing opportunity to glorify God in their body and in their spirit. For additional information on this subject, see Mark L. Prophet and Elizabeth Clare Prophet, *The Path to Immortality*, pp. 224–39.
36. Matt. 11:12.
37. John 10:10.
38. Rev. 3:8.
39. Josh. 24:15.

CHAPTER 2 · SECTION 5 · THE DIVINE INHERITANCE

1. Matt. 22:21; Mark 12:17; Luke 20:25.
2. 1 John 3:9.
3. Mal. 4:2.
4. Col. 3:9–10.
5. See *Prayers, Meditations, Dynamic Decrees for the Coming Revolution in Higher Consciousness*. Decrees are a dynamic form of spoken prayer used by students of the Ascended Masters to direct God's Light into individual and world conditions. A decree may be short or long and is usually marked by a formal preamble and a closing or acceptance. It is the authoritative Word of God spoken in man in the

name of the I AM Presence and the living Christ to bring about constructive change on earth through the will of God. The decree is the birthright of the sons and daughters of God, the "Command ye me" of Isaiah 45:11, the original fiat of the Creator: "Let there be light: and there was light" (Gen. 1:3). It is written in the Book of Job, "Thou shalt decree a thing, and it shall be established unto thee: and the light shall shine upon thy ways" (Job 22:28). For more information about decrees and their use, see Mark L. Prophet and Elizabeth Clare Prophet, *The Science of the Spoken Word*.
6. Mark L. Prophet and Elizabeth Clare Prophet, *The Path to Immortality*, pp. 232–47.
7. Phil. 4:8.
8. 1 Cor. 3:13.
9. Rom. 8:39.
10. Matt. 7:2; Mark 4:24; Luke 6:38.
11. 1 Cor. 15:53–54.

Chapter 3 · The One Path above the Many

Opening quotation: Matt. 7:13–14.

CHAPTER 3 · SECTION 1 · THE SEARCH FOR TRUTH
1. John 8:58.
2. John 19:30.
3. Rev. 13:8.
4. Gen. 4:17; 5:22–24; Jude 14.
5. 2 Kings 2:11.
6. Matt. 17:1–13; Mark 9:2–13; Luke 9:28–36.

CHAPTER 3 · SECTION 2 · THE WAY OF THE MYSTICS
Note: Consistent with the teachings of the mystics and our understanding of the soul as the feminine aspect of being in relation to Spirit, we have converted pronouns referring to the soul to the feminine form in some quotes in this section.

1. Encyclopedia Britannica, s.v., "Mysticism."
2. Teresa of Avila, "The Book of Her Life," 20:13, in *The Collected Works of St. Teresa of Avila* (Washington, D.C.: ICS Publications, 1976), vol. 1, p. 133.
3. Jer. 23:6; 33:16.
4. Catherine of Genoa, *Purgation and Purgatory, The Spiritual Dialogue* (New York: Paulist Press, 1979), p. 30; Evelyn Underhill, *The Mystics of the Church* (Cambridge: James Clark, 1975), p. 166; Arthur Clements, *Poetry of Contemplation* (Albany, N.Y.: State University of New York Press, 1990), p. 16.
5. Harvey Egan, *Christian Mysticism: The Future of a Tradition* (New York: Pueblo Publishing, 1984), pp. 2–3.
6. John 14:23.

7. 1 Cor. 3:16.
8. 2 Pet. 1:4.
9. Sidney Spencer, *Mysticism in World Religion* (Gloucester, Mass.: Peter Smith, 1971), p. 245; Meister Eckhart, *Sermons and Treatises*, trans. and ed. M. O'C. Walshe (Rockport, Md.: Element Books, 1992), vol. III, p. 107.
10. Gal. 4:19.
11. Col. 1:27.
12. Gal. 2:20.
13. *Origen, Spirit and Fire: A Thematic Anthology of His Writings*, ed. Hans Urs von Balthasar (Washington, D.C.: Catholic University of America Press, 1984), p. 270.
14. Spencer, *Mysticism in World Religion*, p. 250.
15. John Climacus, *The Ladder of Divine Ascent* (New York: Paulist Press, 1982), p. 274.
16. John Cassian, *Conferences*, x:7, in Spencer, *Mysticism in World Religion*, p. 227.
17. Teresa of Avila, "Foundations," 5:8, in *Collected Works*, vol. 3, p. 120.
18. Ps. 42:1–2.
19. Mother Mary, March 11, 1987.
20. Harvey Egan, *An Anthology of Christian Mysticism* (Collegeville, Minn.: The Liturgical Press, 1991), p. 238.
21. Catherine of Genoa, *Purgation and Purgatory, The Spiritual Dialogue*, p. 81.
22. 1 Cor. 15:31.
23. E. W. Dicken, *The Crucible of Love: A Study of the Mysticism of St. Teresa of Jesus and St. John of the Cross* (New York: Sheed and Ward, 1963), pp. 127, 223, 294, 258.
24. Mary Baker Eddy, *Science and Health with Key to the Scriptures* (Boston: First Church of Christ, Scientist, 1971), p. 494.
25. Saint John of the Cross, "The Ascent of Mt. Carmel," I.13.11, in *The Collected Works of St. John of the Cross*, trans. Kieran Kavanaugh and Otilio Rodriguez (Washington, D.C.: ICS Publications, 1979), p. 103.
26. Saint John of the Cross, "The Ascent of Mt. Carmel," I.13, in F. C. Happold, *Mysticism: A Study and an Anthology* (Middlesex, England: Penguin Books, 1970), p. 359.
27. Luke 9:23.
28. Juan Gonzalez Arintero, *The Mystical Evolution in the Development and Vitality of the Church* (London: Herder Book Co., 1951), vol. 2, p. 126.
29. Ibid., pp. 43, 44.
30. Happold, *Mysticism*, p. 57.
31. J. Mary Luti, *Teresa of Avila's Way* (Collegeville, Minn.: The Liturgical Press, 1991), pp. 10–11.
32. Saint John of the Cross, "The Dark Night of the Soul," II.6, in Arintero, *Mystical Evolution*, vol. 2, p. 195, note.

33. Saint John of the Cross, "Dark Night," II.5.1, in *Collected Works*, p. 335.
34. Saint John of the Cross, "Dark Night," II.6, in *Mystical Evolution*, p. 197.
35. Spencer, *Mysticism in World Religion*, p. 255.
36. Matt. 27:46; Mark 15:34.
37. Evelyn Underhill, *The Essentials of Mysticism, and Other Essays* (New York: AMS Press, 1976), p. 71.
38. Saint John of the Cross, "The Spiritual Canticle," 26.14, in *Collected Works*, p. 514.
39. Arintero, *Mystical Evolution*, vol. 2, p. 171.
40. Jacob Boehme, *The Way to Christ* (New York: McGraw Hill, 1964), p. 20.
41. Teresa of Avila, "Spiritual Testimonies," in *Collected Works*, vol. 1, p. 402.
42. Ibid., p. 404.
43. Ibid., p. 412.
44. Jack Kornfield, in Fred Eppsteiner, ed., *The Path of Compassion: Writing on Socially Engaged Buddhism* (Berkeley: Parallax Press, 1988), p. 27.
45. Arintero, *Mystical Evolution*, vol. 2, p. 171.
46. Spencer, *Mysticism in World Religion*, p. 255.
47. Teresa of Avila, "The Interior Castle," in *Collected Works*, vol. 2, p. 430.
48. Dicken, *The Crucible of Love*, p. 429.
49. Raymond of Capua, *The Life of Catherine of Siena*, trans. Conleth Kearns (Wilmington, Del.: Michael Glazier, 1980), p. 106.
50. Dag Hammarskjöld, *Markings* (New York: Knopf, 1964), p. 122.
51. Thérèse of Lisieux, *Soeur Thérèse of Lisieux, the Little Flower of Jesus* (New York: P. J. Kennedy & Sons, n.d.), p. 176.
52. Gal. 2:20.
53. Arintero, *Mystical Evolution*, vol. 2, p. 38.
54. Johannes Tauler, "Sermon for the Twenty-third Sunday after Trinity," in Margaret Smith, *Studies in Early Mysticism in the Near and Middle East* (1931; reprint, Whitefish, Mont.: Kessinger Publishing, 2003), p. 9.
55. Saint Teresa of Avila, "The Interior Castle," VII.2, in *The Complete Works of St. Teresa of Jesus* (London: Sheed and Ward, 1975), vol. II, p. 335.
56. Spencer, *Mysticism in World Religion*, p. 254.
57. Saint Magdalen of Pazzi, *Oeuvres*, 4:16, in Arintero, *Mystical Evolution*, vol. 2, p. 222, n. 64.
58. Justinius, March 6, 1977, "The Army of the Hosts of the Lord."

CHAPTER 3 · SECTION 3 · THE EIGHTFOLD PATH

1. Gautama Buddha, April 28, 1991, "A Moment in Cosmic Cycles," *Pearls of Wisdom*, vol. 34, no. 24, June 16, 1991.
2. Gautama Buddha, December 31, 1976, "Release of the Thoughtform

for the Year 1977: A Golden Eagle from the God Star Sirius," *Pearls of Wisdom*, vol. 20, no. 23, June 5, 1977.
3. Thupten Wangyal, *The Jewelled Staircase* (Ithaca, N.Y.: Snow Lion Publications, 1986), p. 161.
4. *Ratnagotravibhāga* 1.28, in Edward Conze et al., eds., *Buddhist Texts through the Ages* (1954; reprint, New York: Harper and Row, 1964), p. 181.
5. Paul Carus, *The Gospel of Buddha* (Chicago: Open Court Publishing Company, 1915), p. 49.
6. Matt. 23:27.
7. 1 Kings 3:9.
8. Christmas Humphreys, ed., *The Wisdom of Buddhism* (London: Curzon Press, 1987), pp. 65–66.
9. Ibid., pp. 67–68.
10. Phil. 2:5.
11. Sanat Kumara is the Great Guru of the seed of Christ throughout cosmos. He is the Ancient of Days spoken of in Daniel 7:9, 13, 22. Sanat Kumara (from the Skt., meaning "always a youth") is one of the Seven Holy Kumaras of the planet Venus. Long ago he came to earth in her darkest hour when all Light had gone out in her evolutions, for there was not a single individual on the planet who gave adoration to the God Presence. Sanat Kumara and the band of 144,000 souls of Light who accompanied him volunteered to keep the flame of Life on behalf of earth's people. This they vowed to do until the children of God would respond to the love of God and turn once again to serve their Mighty I AM Presence. Sanat Kumara is known as the Guru of Gurus, the great sponsor of the evolutions of earth. Every true guru who has come to earth has carried his mantle. The Teachings of the Ascended Masters released in these volumes come through the lineage of Sanat Kumara, Gautama Buddha, Lord Maitreya, Jesus Christ, Padma Sambhava, and the Messengers Mark L. Prophet and Elizabeth Clare Prophet.
12. The following are a few passages from the Bible that echo the precepts of the Eightfold Path:
    1. Right knowledge: "The heart of the prudent getteth knowledge; and the ear of the wise seeketh knowledge" (Prov. 18:15). "Wisdom is the principal thing; therefore get wisdom: and with all thy getting get understanding" (Prov. 4:7). "But the manifestation of the Spirit is given to every man to profit withal. For to one is given by the Spirit the word of wisdom; to another the word of knowledge by the same Spirit" (1 Cor. 12:7–8).
    2. Right aspiration, right thought, right resolve: "For though we walk in the flesh, we do not war after the flesh:... casting down imaginations and every high thing that exalteth itself against the knowledge of God, and bringing into captivity every thought to the obedience of Christ" (2 Cor. 10:3, 5). "For he that wavereth is like a wave of the sea driven with the wind and tossed. For let not that man think that he shall receive any thing of the Lord. A double-minded man is unstable in all

his ways" (James 1:6–8).
3. Right speech: "Every idle word that men shall speak, they shall give account thereof in the day of judgment. For by thy words thou shalt be justified, and by thy words thou shalt be condemned" (Matt. 12:36–37). "Let every man be swift to hear, slow to speak, slow to wrath.... If any man among you seem to be religious and bridleth not his tongue, but deceiveth his own heart, this man's religion is vain.... If any man offend not in word, the same is a perfect man and able also to bridle the whole body" (James 1:19, 26; 3:2).
4. Right action: "Woe unto you, scribes and Pharisees, hypocrites! For ye pay tithe of mint and anise and cumin, and have omitted the weightier matters of the law, judgment, mercy, and faith: these ought ye to have done, and not to leave the other undone" (Matt. 23:23).
5. Right livelihood: "No man can serve two masters: for either he will hate the one, and love the other, or else he will hold to the one, and despise the other. Ye cannot serve God and mammon" (Matt. 6:24). (Mammon in scripture is defined as material wealth or possessions, especially when they have a debasing influence.)
6. Right effort: "Then said one unto him, Lord, are there few that be saved? And he said unto them: Strive to enter in at the strait gate: for many, I say unto you, will seek to enter in, and shall not be able" (Luke 13:23–24). "But this one thing I do, forgetting those things which are behind and reaching forth unto those things which are before, I press toward the mark for the prize of the high calling of God in Jesus Christ" (Phil. 3:13–14). "And if a man also strive for masteries, yet is he not crowned, except he strive lawfully" (2 Tim. 2:5).
7. Right mindfulness: "Let this mind be in you, which was also in Christ Jesus" (Phil. 2:5). "That ye put off concerning the former conversation the old man, which is corrupt according to the deceitful lusts; and be renewed in the spirit of your mind" (Eph. 4:22–23). "And thou shalt love the Lord thy God with all thy heart, and with all thy soul, and with all thy mind, and with all thy strength: this is the first commandment" (Mark 12:30).
8. Right concentration: "The light of the body is the eye [the third-eye chakra]. If therefore thine eye be single, thy whole body shall be full of light" (Matt. 6:22).

CHAPTER 3 · SECTION 4 · THE SEEKER AND THE SOUGHT
1. 2 Cor. 3:6.
2. Luke 10:37.
3. Matt. 3:17; 17:5.
4. Matt. 28:6; Mark 16:6.
5. John 14:3.

Chapter 4 · The Great White Brotherhood

Opening quotation: Rev. 11:15–17.

1. Mic. 4:4.
2. The Goddess of Liberty, "Man's Desire for Liberty," *Pearls of Wisdom*, vol. 11, no. 26, June 30, 1968.
3. Eddy, *Science and Health with Key to the Scriptures*, p. 518.
4. Ibid., pp. 264–65, 513.
5. Ibid., p. 515.
6. Hab. 1:13.
7. Maha Chohan, "Hidden Mysteries and Hidden Powers of the Holy Spirit," *Pearls of Wisdom*, vol. 9, no. 28, July 10, 1966.
8. Heb. 12:29.
9. Exod. 3:2.
10. Exod. 3:14.
11. Gautama Buddha, December 31, 1969, "A Magnificent Cause," *Pearls of Wisdom*, vol. 26, no. 15, April 10, 1983.
12. Jer. 31:33.
13. Goddess of Purity, "The Flame in the Center of the Crystal," September 13, 1970.
14. The fourth, fifth and sixth root races (the latter soul group not having entirely descended into physical incarnation) remain in embodiment on earth today. Lord Himalaya and his beloved are the Manus for the fourth root race, Vaivasvata Manu and his consort are the Manus for the fifth root race, and the God and Goddess Meru are the Manus for the sixth root race. The seventh root race is destined to incarnate on the continent of South America in the Aquarian age under their Manus, the Great Divine Director and his divine complement.

    In 1973 the Ascended Lady Master Clara Louise said that some of those who were destined to be parents of seventh-root-race children were at that time living in North and South America. Other parents-to-be were waiting to be born so that they might bring forth those children twenty to thirty years from that time. She said, "When you find yourselves at that age when you can enjoy your grandchildren, you will see by your heightened sensitivity ... that the auras of these precious ones will have a violet hue, and their rosy cheeks and their delicate skin tone will also have a violet cast.... It will take several centuries before the entire seventh root race is in embodiment. They will come in sections according to the rays under which they serve" (Clara Louise Kieninger, *Ich Dien*, p. 156).
15. Gen. 2:7.
16. Prov. 14:34.
17. See Elizabeth Clare Prophet, *The Opening of the Seventh Seal: Sanat Kumara on the Path of the Ruby Ray*, ch. 2.
18. After his ascension in 1684, Saint Germain was given the dispensation by the Lords of Karma to return to earth and manifest in a physical body. The Comte de Saint Germain appeared throughout the 18th-

century courts as the "Wonderman of Europe." His goal: to prevent the French Revolution and establish a United States of Europe. Though the royalty admired his miraculous accomplishments and were always willing to be entertained by him, they were not easily prodded to relinquish their power and move with the winds of republican change. They and their jealous ministers ignored his counsel, and the French Revolution ensued. In a final attempt to unite Europe, Saint Germain backed Napoleon, who misused the Master's power to his own demise. The opportunity to set aside the retribution due an age had thus passed, and Saint Germain was forced to withdraw.

19. "And there appeared a great wonder in heaven; a woman clothed with the sun, and the moon under her feet, and upon her head a crown of twelve stars: and she being with child cried, travailing in birth, and pained to be delivered.... And she brought forth a man child, who was to rule all nations with a rod of iron: and her child was caught up unto God, and to his throne. And the woman fled into the wilderness, where she hath a place prepared of God, that they should feed her there a thousand two hundred and threescore days" (Rev. 12:1, 5–6).

20. At the time the Constitution of the United States was being framed, the nation was in the midst of a terrible inflation caused by the expansion of the Continental, a paper currency that had been issued during the Revolutionary War. This experience taught the framers the importance of a fully gold-backed currency, and they provided for a monetary system based on gold and silver in the Constitution. Article I, Section 10, reads, "No State Shall ... make any Thing but gold and silver Coin a Tender in Payment of Debts."

The framers intended Congress to use gold and silver coin as money even though they did not explicitly state that Article I, Section 10 applied to the federal government. This can be demonstrated by the statements of a number of the framers, by a text analysis of the Constitution and by Supreme Court decisions. The Founding Fathers' intent is also seen in the actions of the First Congress, which in 1792 created a monetary system based on gold and silver (Edwin Vieira, Jr., *Pieces of Eight: The Monetary Powers and Disabilities of the United States Constitution* [Old Greenwich, Conn.: Devin-Adair, 1983], pp. 15–36). During the debate over the wording of Article I, Section 10, Roger Sherman, a delegate to the Constitutional Convention, said he thought this "a favorable crisis for crushing paper money" (*Notes of Debates in the Federal Convention of 1787 Reported by James Madison* [Athens, Ohio: Ohio University Press, 1966], p. 542). Thomas Jefferson and John Adams both wrote about the evils of paper money.

However, contrary to the framers' intent, bankers plotted to control the currency. In his work *The War on Gold,* Antony Sutton explains: "The groundwork for the Federal Reserve System was laid at an unpublicized meeting at the J. P. Morgan Country Club on Jekyll Island, Georgia, in November 1910. Senator Nelson Aldrich, bankers Frank Vanderlip (president of National City Bank and representing

Rockefeller and Kuhn Loeb interests), Henry P. Davison (senior partner of J. P. Morgan), and Charles D. Norton (president of Morgan's First National Bank) met in secret to decide how to foist a central bank system on the United States. Others at the meeting were Paul Moritz Warburg, the German banker, and Benjamin Strong (a Morgan banker who later became first Governor of the Federal Reserve Bank of New York). Out of the Jekyll Island cabal came the basic bill passed by Congress and signed into law by President Woodrow Wilson as the Federal Reserve Act of 1913. Under the earlier sub-Treasury system, bankers had no control over the money supply in the United States and, even less to their liking, none over currency issues" (Antony C. Sutton, *The War on Gold* [Seal Beach, Calif.: '76 Press, 1977], p. 84). The Federal Reserve Act gave the banking community control of the nation's money in violation of Article I, Section 8 of the Constitution, which gives to Congress the power "to coin money" and "regulate the value thereof."

According to Austrian School economist Dr. Murray Rothbard, credit expansion (i.e., easy money) coupled with interventionism beginning in the 1920s interfered with natural business cycles of the free-market system, resulting in the stock market crash of 1929 and the Great Depression. Rothbard cites inflation as the primary cause of the depression. "Government is inherently inflationary because it has, over the centuries, acquired control over the monetary system.... Inflation is a form of taxation, since the government can create new money out of thin air and use it to bid away resources from private individuals, who are barred by heavy penalty from similar 'counterfeiting'" (Murray Rothbard, *America's Great Depression* [Kansas City: Sheed and Ward, 1975], pp. 29, 33).

Today the Federal Reserve System, serving the interests of the banking community, exercises the unilateral right to expand and contract the supply of money and credit and create periods of boom and bust. The ramifications of this state of affairs are almost beyond calculation. Today we could have a financial collapse worse than the Great Depression of the 1930s. And we know that the power elite used the depression to concentrate power in the central government.

Antony Sutton notes in *Wall Street and FDR,* "In modern America the most significant illustration of society as a whole working for the few is the 1913 Federal Reserve Act. The Federal Reserve System is, in effect, a private banking monopoly, not answerable to Congress or the public, but with legal monopoly control over money supply without let or hindrance or even audit by the General Accounting Office. It was irresponsible manipulation of money supply by this Federal Reserve System that brought about the inflation of the 1920s, the 1929 Depression, and so the presumed requirement for a Roosevelt New Deal" (Antony Sutton, *Wall Street and FDR* [New Rochelle: Arlington House Publishers, 1975], p. 75).

21. As explained in the previous note, the intent of the framers of the Constitution of the United States was that the monetary system be

based on gold and silver. The Civil War brought the first deviation from this system, causing steep inflation. In 1879, the U.S. returned to a convertible gold standard and prosperity.

American monetary policy began to change drastically after the passage of the Federal Reserve Act, December 23, 1913, which gave the power to create money to an independent agency, the Federal Reserve Board. The agency issued Federal Reserve notes, which became the only legal tender in America, and progressively reduced the promise to exchange paper dollars for gold. At the time of their original issue in 1914, Federal Reserve notes were 40% gold-backed. During World War II, the gold reserve was reduced to 25%. On March 18, 1968, the gold reserve requirement was entirely eliminated.

President Franklin Roosevelt revalued the price of gold to $35/troy oz. with the passage of the 1934 Gold Reserve Act, which devalued the dollar to 59% of its former value and removed gold from domestic circulation. On April 5, 1938, Roosevelt declared a national emergency and said he was depriving American citizens of the right to own gold and use it as a medium of exchange (Ron Paul and Lewis Lehrman, *The Case for Gold: A Minority Report of the U.S. Gold Commission* [Washington, D.C.: Cato Institute, 1982], p. 129).

On August 15, 1971, President Richard Nixon suspended foreign exchange of U.S. dollars for gold and devalued the dollar by raising the gold price to $38/troy oz. Nixon took the final step on August 15, 1971, when he suspended the convertibility of the dollar for gold internationally. The United States was then fully on the paper standard. In recent years, important steps have been taken towards remonetizing gold. Legislation passed in December 1974 allowed American citizens to own gold. Gold clause contracts, not covered in this legislation, were made legal as of October 28, 1977. And, on December 17, 1985, President Reagan signed the Gold Bullion Coin Act which required the U.S. Treasury to mint and sell gold coins with limited legal tender status. But other steps must be taken before gold circulates as legal tender in the U.S. economy. Essentially, the country is still on the paper standard.

On October 10, 1977, the Ascended Master known as the God of Gold said the formation of the Federal Reserve System "must be challenged and reversed because it is no part of the divine plan of the United States.... The American people must understand the great fraud that has been perpetrated upon them by this printing of money without backing. The grinding out of money by the printing presses will surely cause the collapse of the economies of the nations.... The salvation of the soul of America depends upon the reestablishment of gold" (The God of Gold with the God Tabor, October 10, 1977, "The Flow of Energy in the City Foursquare: Children of God, Demand and Supply the Abundance of the Mother!").

22. 2 Cor. 6:14–15.
23. Mark 8:33; Luke 4:8; Matt. 6:23.
24. For a concise analysis of the doctrines of communism and socialism,

see *The Path of Brotherhood,* book 4 of the Climb the Highest Mountain series, pp. 95–120. An in-depth discussion may be found in lectures by Elizabeth Clare Prophet, October 6, 8 and 9, 1978, "The Economic Philosophy of Jesus Christ," "The Religious Philosophy of Karl Marx" and "The Psychology of Socialism."
25. For more information about the fraternity, write to Keepers of the Flame Fraternity, 63 Summit Way, Gardiner, MT 59030, USA, or call (406) 848-9500.
26. Matt. 25:40.
27. Chananda with the Ascended Master Alexander Gaylord, "The Great White Brotherhood as Inner World Government," *Keepers of the Flame Lesson 5,* pp. 20–27.
28. Goddess of Liberty, "Man's Desire for Liberty," *Pearls of Wisdom,* vol. 11, no. 26, June 30, 1968.
29. Great Divine Director, "The Correct Use of the Ascended Masters' Names II: The Will of God," *Pearls of Wisdom,* vol. 9, no. 41, October 9, 1966.
30. Matt. 7:20.
31. Saint Germain, *Keepers of the Flame Lesson 12,* pp. 11–12.
32. "God tempers the wind to the shorn lamb" ("Dieu mesure le froid à la brebis tondue"). Henri Estienne, *Les Prémices* (1594), quoted in John Bartlett, comp., and Justin Kaplan, ed., *Familiar Quotations: A Collection of Passages, Phrases and Proverbs Traced to Their Sources in Ancient and Modern Literature,* 16th ed. (Boston: Little, Brown and Co., 1992), p. 144.
33. Gal. 5:1.
34. Luke 19:10.
35. An emissary from Venus, quoted by the Maha Chohan, "Hidden Mysteries and Hidden Powers of the Holy Spirit," *Pearls of Wisdom,* vol. 9, no. 28, July 10, 1966.
36. Goddess of Liberty, "Man's Desire for Liberty."
37. Gal. 6:7.
38. Matt. 25:40.
39. 1 John 4:1.
40. In a dictation given in Washington, D.C., September 30, 1962, the ascended master K-17 announced: "There has been held a beautiful and wonderful session at Chananda's retreat in India and a decision was made on the part of beloved Paul the Venetian whereby there was transferred from his retreat in France this day, at the hour of eleven o'clock your time, the full pulsation of the great liberty flame. This flame was permanently placed within the forcefield of the Washington Monument, and the pulsations of the liberty flame are intended to grace the heart of America as a gift from the Brotherhood and from the heart of beloved Paul the Venetian.... It is given as a treasure from the heart of France, from the spiritual government of France to the spiritual government of America.... The liberty flame is a gift of greater magnitude than the former gift of France, the Statue of Liberty, as a tribute to that great being, the Goddess of Liberty. It is

incomparable, for the flame itself shall penetrate the structure of the monument, rising high into the atmosphere above it; and all who visit there shall become, even without knowing it, infused by the pulsations of the liberty flame within the heart of America."

41. Gautama Buddha, January 1, 1986, "The Teaching Is for the Many," *Pearls of Wisdom,* vol. 29, no. 21, May 25, 1986.
42. Godfre, Rex and Nada Rayborn and Bob and Pearl Singleton traveled to the Great Divine Director's retreat in the Himalayas, the Cave of Light, in the early 1930s. Their experiences there are recorded in Godfré Ray King, *The Magic Presence* (Schaumburg, Ill.: Saint Germain Press, 1982), pp. 393–400.
43. In 1950 China invaded and occupied Tibet. The Chinese forces murdered, raped and tortured the people, including Buddhist monks and nuns. They desecrated and destroyed the temples and outlawed the Tibetan Buddhist religion. The Chinese have sought to break the will of the people by eradicating their heritage and traditions. More than a million Tibetans have lost their lives at the hands of the Communists.
44. A *flaming Yod* is a sun center, a focus of perfection, of God consciousness. The very center of Life of the entire Spirit-Matter cosmos is the flaming Yod in the Great Hub, that point in the Macrocosm which received the original fiat "Let there be light!"
45. Letter from El Morya, March 13, 1964. Twelve thousand years ago, prior to the sinking of Atlantis, the Masters transferred the flames from some of the temples of that continent to other locations. Serapis Bey was one such master. In the ascension temple on Atlantis, he trained souls in the mastery of ascension's fires. Before the sinking of Atlantis, he transferred that flame and that focus to Luxor, Egypt. Hilarion, Saint Germain and the Goddess of Liberty transported their flames to other locations.

    More recently, Sanat Kumara announced that the retreat of the Brotherhood that had previously been sustained at Mount Shasta was being transferred. On January 2, 1988, he said: "I make known to you this day, inasmuch as this is a branch of the Great White Brotherhood sponsored by the level of my office with the Seven Holy Kumaras, that in this hour there is the withdrawal of the Brotherhood of Mount Shasta from the retreat physical of Mount Shasta. This entire brotherhood, therefore, does withdraw and does transfer their forcefield and focus both into the Grand Teton and into another area of the Northern Rockies. Blessed hearts, this announcement is a sign unto you and let it be a sign unto every heart and let it be known from within. I give you, therefore, this report that you might accommodate and understand your position as the pillars in the temple of our God.

    "Therefore, deliberations at the Royal Teton Retreat continue, beloved, and we express gratitude for the Light released and the calls given. We, therefore, call to each and every one of you and those who are the creative sons and daughters of God to put your hearts together, to know and to understand how there might be executed a proliferation of the *Word* and of the *Warning* and of the *Message* that has gone forth.

"Let it be so, then, by the release (through the use of such supply as is available to you) of this message that comes from the heart of Saint Germain, that has been shouted from the housetops, delivered by the Messenger and by yourselves wherever you might be received. Let it go forth, then, for the people of the earth must have the warning as they had that warning in the days of Noah, and Noah did preach one hundred years" (*Pearls of Wisdom,* vol. 31, no. 4, January 24, 1988).

46. Jesus, May 28, 1987, "From Temples of Love," *Pearls of Wisdom,* vol. 30, no. 27, July 5, 1987.
47. Archangel Raphael, February 27, 1988, "The Fulfillment of an Ancient Promise," *Pearls of Wisdom,* vol. 31, no. 35, July 3, 1988.
48. The Great Divine Director, June 26, 1994, "I Come to Sound the Alarm: Save Souls Who Will Be Lost without Your Intercession," *Pearls of Wisdom,* vol. 37, no. 29, July 17, 1994.
49. Great Divine Director, "The Correct Use of the Ascended Masters' Names I: The Will of Man," *Pearls of Wisdom,* vol. 9, no. 40, October 2, 1966.
50. Acts 4:12.
51. Great Divine Director, "The Correct Use of the Ascended Masters' Names I."
52. Matt. 24:24.
53. 2 Cor. 11:14.
54. Exod. 3:14.
55. Rev. 2:17; Great Divine Director, "The Correct Use of the Ascended Masters' Names I."
56. El Morya, *Pearls of Wisdom,* vol. 11, no. 1, January 7, 1968.

Chapter 5 · Attainment

Opening quotation: Rev. 3:11–12.

1. Beloved Amerissis, *Pearls of Wisdom,* vol. 6, no. 29, July 19, 1963.
2. Matt. 20:26–27; Mark 10:43–44.
3. Matt. 28:18.
4. 2 Kings 2:8–15.
5. Ezek. 18:4.
6. Phil. 2:6.
7. John 14:12.
8. John 3:30.
9. Kuthumi, "Goal-Setting and Goal-Fitting," *Pearls of Wisdom,* vol. 19, no. 2, January 11, 1976.
10. Acts 17:28.
11. 1 Cor. 15:53.
12. Maitreya, "On Initiation," *Pearls of Wisdom,* vol. 18, nos. 49, 50 and 51, December 7, 14 and 21, 1975.
13. Ezek. 1:16.
14. Matt. 4:1–11.

15. John 14:30.
16. Josh. 24:15.
17. El Morya, in Mark L. Prophet and Elizabeth Clare Prophet, *Lords of the Seven Rays,* pp. 70–73.
18. Matt. 3:17; 17:5; Mark 1:11; Luke 3:22.
19. Matt. 25:21; Kuthumi, "The Mission of the Soul Must Be Understood," *Pearls of Wisdom,* vol. 10, no. 32, August 6, 1967.

Afterword

1. 1 Cor. 15:53.

Publications of Summit University Press that display this crest are the authentic Teachings of the Ascended Masters as given to the world by Mark L. Prophet and Elizabeth Clare Prophet.

Glossary

Terms set in italics are defined elsewhere in the glossary.

Adept. An initiate of the Great White Brotherhood of a high degree of attainment, especially in the control of *Matter,* physical forces, nature spirits and bodily functions; fully the alchemist undergoing advanced initiations of the *sacred fire* on the path of the *ascension.*

Akashic records. The impressions of all that has ever transpired in the physical universe, recorded in the etheric substance and dimension known by the Sanskrit term *akasha*. These records can be read by those with developed soul faculties.

All-Seeing Eye of God. See *Cyclopea.*

Alpha and Omega. The Divine Wholeness of the Father-Mother God affirmed as "the beginning and the ending" by the Lord *Christ* in Revelation (Rev. 1:8, 11; 21:6; 22:13). Ascended *twin flames* of the *Cosmic Christ* consciousness who hold the balance of the masculine-feminine polarity of the Godhead in the *Great Central Sun* of cosmos. Thus through the *Universal Christ* (the *Word* incarnate), the Father is the origin and the Mother is the fulfillment of the cycles of God's consciousness expressed throughout the *Spirit-Matter* creation. See also *Mother.*

Ancient of Days. See *Sanat Kumara.*

Angel. A divine spirit, a herald or messenger sent by God to deliver his *Word* to his children. A ministering spirit sent forth to tend the heirs of *Christ*—to comfort, protect, guide, strengthen, teach, counsel and warn. The fallen angels, also called the dark ones, are those angels who followed Lucifer in the Great Rebellion, whose consciousness therefore "fell" to lower levels of vibration. They were "cast out into the earth" by Archangel Michael (Rev. 12:7–12)—constrained by the karma of their disobedience to God and his Christ to take on and evolve through dense physical bodies. Here they walk about, sowing seeds of unrest and rebellion among men and nations.

Antahkarana. The web of life. The net of *Light* spanning *Spirit* and

Matter, connecting and sensitizing the whole of creation within itself and to the heart of God.

Archangel. The highest rank in the orders of *angels.* Each of the *seven rays* has a presiding Archangel who, with his divine complement, or *Archeia,* embodies the God consciousness of the ray and directs the bands of angels serving in their command on that ray.

Archeia (pl. **Archeiai**). Divine complement and *twin flame* of an *Archangel.*

Ascended Master. One who, through *Christ* and the putting on of that mind which was in Christ Jesus (Phil. 2:5), has mastered time and space and in the process gained the mastery of the self in the *four lower bodies* and the four quadrants of *Matter,* in the *chakras* and the balanced *threefold flame.* An Ascended Master has also transmuted at least 51 percent of his karma, fulfilled his divine plan, and taken the initiations of the ruby ray unto the ritual of the *ascension*—acceleration by the *sacred fire* into the Presence of the I AM THAT I AM (the *I AM Presence*). Ascended Masters inhabit the planes of *Spirit*—the kingdom of God (God's consciousness)—and they may teach unascended souls in an *etheric temple* or in the cities on the *etheric plane* (the kingdom of heaven).

Ascension. The ritual whereby the soul reunites with the *Spirit* of the living God, the *I AM Presence.* The ascension is the culmination of the soul's God-victorious sojourn in time and space. It is the process whereby the soul, having balanced her karma and fulfilled her divine plan, merges first with the Christ consciousness and then with the living Presence of the I AM THAT I AM. Once the ascension has taken place, the soul—the corruptible aspect of being—becomes the incorruptible one, a permanent atom in the Body of God.

Aspirant. One who aspires; specifically, one who aspires to reunion with God through the ritual of the *ascension.* One who aspires to overcome the conditions and limitations of time and space to fulfill the cycles of karma and one's reason for being through the sacred labor.

Astral plane. A frequency of time and space beyond the physical, yet below the mental, corresponding to the *emotional body* of man and the collective unconscious of the race; the repository of mankind's thoughts and feelings, conscious and unconscious. Because the astral plane has been muddied by impure human thought and feeling, the term "astral" is often used in a negative context to refer to that which is impure or psychic.

Astrea. Feminine Elohim of the fourth ray, the ray of purity, who works to cut souls free from the *astral plane* and the projections of the dark forces. See also *Elohim; Seven rays.*

Atman. The spark of the divine within, identical with *Brahman;* the ultimate essence of the universe as well as the essence of the individual.

AUM. See *OM.*

Avatar. The incarnation of the *Word.* The Avatar of an age is the *Christ,* the incarnation of the Son of God. The *Manus* may designate numerous Christed ones—those endued with an extraordinary *Light*—to go forth as world teachers and wayshowers. The Christed ones demonstrate in a given epoch the Law of the *Logos,* stepped down through the Manu(s) and the Avatar(s) until it is made flesh through their own word and work—to be ultimately victorious in its fulfillment in all souls of Light sent forth to conquer time and space in that era.

Bodhisattva. (Sanskrit, "a being of *bodhi* or enlightenment.") A being destined for enlightenment, or one whose energy and power is directed toward enlightenment. A Bodhisattva is destined to become a *Buddha* but has forgone the bliss of *nirvana* with a vow to save all children of God on earth. An Ascended Master or an unascended master may be a Bodhisattva.

Brahman. Ultimate Reality; the Absolute.

Buddha. (From Sanskrit *budh* "awake, know, perceive.") "The enlightened one." Buddha denotes an office in the spiritual *Hierarchy* of worlds that is attained by passing certain initiations of the *sacred fire,* including those of the *seven rays* of the Holy Spirit and of the five secret *rays,* the raising of the Feminine Ray (sacred fire of the Kundalini) and the "mastery of the seven in the seven multiplied by the power of the ten."

Gautama attained the enlightenment of the Buddha twenty-five centuries ago, a path he had pursued through many previous embodiments culminating in his forty-nine-day meditation under the Bo tree. Hence he is called Gautama, the Buddha. He holds the office of *Lord of the World,* sustaining, by his *Causal Body* and *threefold flame*, the divine spark and consciousness in the evolutions of earth approaching the path of personal Christhood. His aura of love/wisdom ensouling the planet issues from his incomparable devotion to the Divine *Mother*. He is the Hierarch of Shamballa, the original *retreat* of *Sanat Kumara* now on the *etheric plane* over the Gobi Desert.

Lord Maitreya, the *Cosmic Christ,* has also passed the initiations of the Buddha. He is the long-awaited Coming Buddha who has come to the fore to teach all who have departed from the way of the Great *Guru,* Sanat Kumara, from whose lineage both he and Gautama descended. In the history of the planet, there have been numerous Buddhas who have served the evolutions of mankind through the steps and stages of the path of the *Bodhisattva.* In the East Jesus is referred to as the Buddha Issa. He is the World Saviour by the love/wisdom of the Godhead.

Caduceus. The Kundalini. See *Sacred fire.*

Causal Body. Seven concentric spheres of *Light* surrounding the *I AM Presence.* The spheres of the Causal Body contain the records of the virtuous acts we have performed to the glory of God and the blessing of man through our many incarnations on earth. See color illustration page 105.

Central Sun. A vortex of energy, physical or spiritual, central to systems of worlds that it thrusts from, or gathers unto, itself by the Central Sun Magnet. Whether in the *microcosm* or the *Macrocosm,* the Central Sun is the principal energy source, vortex, or nexus of energy interchange in atoms, cells, man (the heart center), amidst plant life and the core of the earth. The Great Central Sun is the center of cosmos; the point of integration of the *Spirit-Matter* cosmos; the point of origin of all physical-spiritual creation; the nucleus, or white-fire core, of the *Cosmic Egg.* (The God Star, Sirius, is the focus of the Great Central Sun in our sector of the galaxy.) The Sun behind the sun is the spiritual Cause behind the physical effect we see as our own physical sun and all other stars and star systems, seen or unseen, including the Great Central Sun.

Chakra. (Sanskrit, "wheel, disc, circle.") Center of *Light* anchored in the *etheric body* and governing the flow of energy to the *four lower bodies* of man. There are seven major chakras corresponding to the *seven rays,* five minor chakras corresponding to the five secret rays, and a total of 144 Light centers in the body of man.

Chela. (Hindi *celā* from Sanskrit *ceta* "slave," i.e., "servant.") In India, a disciple of a religious teacher or *guru*. A term used generally to refer to a student of the *Ascended Masters* and their teachings. Specifically, a student of more than ordinary self-discipline and devotion initiated by an *Ascended Master* and serving the cause of the Great White Brotherhood.

Chohan. (Tibetan, "lord" or "master"; a chief.) Each of the seven *rays* has a Chohan who focuses the *Christ* consciousness of the ray. Having ensouled and demonstrated the law of the ray throughout numerous incarnations, and having taken initiations both before and after the *ascension,* the candidate is appointed to the office of Chohan by the Maha Chohan (the "Great Lord"), who is himself the representative of the Holy Spirit on all the rays.

Christ. (From the Greek *Christos* "anointed.") Messiah (Hebrew, Aramaic "anointed"); "Christed one," one fully endued and infilled—anointed—by the *Light* (the Son) of God. The *Word,* the *Logos,* the Second Person of the Trinity. In the Hindu Trinity of Brahma, Vishnu and Shiva, the term "Christ" corresponds to or is the incarnation of Vishnu, the Preserver; Avatāra, God-man, Dispeller of Darkness, *Guru.*

The term "Christ" or "Christed one" also denotes an office in *Hierarchy* held by those who have attained self-mastery on the *seven rays* and the seven *chakras* of the Holy Spirit. Christ-mastery includes the balancing of the *threefold flame*—the divine attributes of power, wisdom and love—for the harmonization of consciousness and the implementation of the mastery of the seven rays in the chakras and in the *four lower bodies* through the Mother flame (the raised Kundalini).

At the hour designated for the *ascension,* the soul thus anointed raises the spiral of the threefold flame from beneath the feet through the entire form for the transmutation of every atom and cell of her being, consciousness and world. The saturation and acceleration of the *four lower bodies* and the soul by this transfiguring Light of the Christ flame take place in part during the initiation of the transfiguration, increasing through the resurrection and gaining full intensity in the ritual of the ascension.

Christ Self. The individualized focus of "the only begotten of the

Father, full of grace and Truth" (John 1:14). The *Universal Christ* individualized as the true identity of the soul; the *Real Self* of every man, woman and child, to which the soul must rise. The Christ Self is the Mediator between a man and his God. He is a man's own personal teacher, master and prophet.

Color rays. See *Seven rays*.

Cosmic Being. (1) An *Ascended Master* who has attained cosmic consciousness and ensouls the *Light*/energy/consciousness of many worlds and systems of worlds across the galaxies to the Sun behind the *Great Central Sun;* or, (2) A Being of God who has never descended below the level of the *Christ,* has never taken physical embodiment, and has never made human karma.

Cosmic Christ. An office in *Hierarchy* currently held by Lord Maitreya under Gautama *Buddha,* the *Lord of the World.* Also used as a synonym for *Universal Christ*.

Cosmic Clock. The science of charting the cycles of the soul's karma and initiations on the twelve lines of the Clock under the *Twelve Hierarchies of the Sun*. Taught by Mother Mary to Mark and Elizabeth Prophet for sons and daughters of God returning to the Law of the One and to their point of origin beyond the worlds of form and lesser causation.

Cosmic Egg. The spiritual-material universe, including a seemingly endless chain of galaxies, star systems, worlds known and unknown, whose center, or white-fire core, is called the *Great Central Sun*. The Cosmic Egg has both a spiritual and a material center. Although we may discover and observe the Cosmic Egg from the standpoint of our physical senses and perspective, all of the dimensions of *Spirit* can also be known and experienced within the Cosmic Egg. For the God who created the Cosmic Egg and holds it in the hollow of his hand is also the God flame expanding hour by hour within his very own sons and daughters. The Cosmic Egg represents the bounds of man's habitation in this cosmic cycle. Yet, as God is everywhere throughout and beyond the Cosmic Egg, so by his Spirit within us we daily awaken to new dimensions of being, soul-satisfied in conformity with his likeness.

Cosmic law. The Law that governs mathematically, yet with the spontaneity of Mercy's flame, all manifestation throughout the cosmos in the planes of *Spirit* and *Matter*.

Crystal cord. The stream of God's *Light,* life and consciousness that nourishes and sustains the soul and her *four lower bodies.* Also called the silver cord (Eccles. 12:6).

Cyclopea. Masculine Elohim of the fifth ray, also known as the All-Seeing Eye of God or as the Great Silent Watcher. See also *Elohim; Seven rays.*

Deathless solar body. See *Seamless garment.*

Decree. A dynamic form of spoken prayer used by students of the *Ascended Masters* to direct God's *Light* into individual and world conditions. The decree may be short or long and is usually marked by a formal preamble and a closing or acceptance. It is the authoritative *Word* of God spoken in man in the name of the *I AM Presence* and the living *Christ* to bring about constructive change on earth through the will of God. The decree is the birthright of the sons and daughters of God, the "Command ye me" of Isaiah 45:11, the original fiat of the Creator: "Let there be light: and there was light" (Gen. 1:3). It is written in the Book of Job, "Thou shalt decree a thing, and it shall be established unto thee: and the light shall shine upon thy ways" (Job 22:28).

Dictation. A message from an *Ascended Master,* an *Archangel* or another advanced spiritual being delivered through the agency of the Holy Spirit by a *Messenger* of the Great White Brotherhood.

Divine Monad. See *I AM Presence.*

Electronic Presence. A duplicate of the *I AM Presence* of an Ascended Master.

Elementals. Beings of earth, air, fire and water; nature spirits who are the servants of God and man. The elementals establish and maintain the physical platform for the soul's evolution. The elementals who serve the fire element are called salamanders; those who serve the air element, sylphs; those who serve the water element, undines; and those who serve the earth element, gnomes.

Elohim. (Hebrew; plural of *Eloah,* "God.") The name of God used in the first verse of the Bible: "In the beginning God created the heaven and the earth." The Seven Mighty Elohim and their feminine counterparts are the builders of form. They are the "seven spirits of God" named in Revelation 4:5 and the "morning stars" that sang together in the beginning, as the Lord revealed them to Job (Job 38:7). In the order of *Hierarchy,* the Elohim and *Cosmic Beings* carry the greatest concentration, the highest vibration of *Light* that we can comprehend in our present state of evolution. Serving directly under the Elohim are the four hierarchs of the elements, who have dominion over the elementals—the gnomes, salamanders, sylphs and undines.

Emotional body. One of the *four lower bodies* of man, corresponding to the water element and the third quadrant of *Matter;* the vehicle of the desires and feelings of God made manifest in the being of man. Also called the astral body, the desire body or the feeling body.

Etheric body. One of the *four lower bodies* of man, corresponding to the fire element and the first quadrant of *Matter;* called the envelope of the soul, holding the blueprint of the divine plan and the image of *Christ*-perfection to be outpictured in the world of form. Also called the memory body.

Etheric octave or etheric plane. The highest plane in the dimension of *Matter;* a plane that is as concrete and real as the physical plane (and even more so) but is experienced through the senses of the soul in a dimension and a consciousness beyond physical awareness. This is the plane on which the *akashic records* of mankind's entire evolution register individually and collectively. It is the world of *Ascended Masters* and their *retreats,* etheric cities of *Light* where souls of a higher order of evolution abide between embodiments. It is the plane of Reality.

The lower *etheric plane,* which overlaps the astral/mental/physical belts, is contaminated by these lower worlds occupied by the false hierarchy and the mass consciousness it controls.

Etheric temple. See *Retreat.*

Fallen angels. See *Angels.*

Father-Mother God. See *Alpha and Omega.*

Four Cosmic Forces. The four beasts seen by Saint John and other seers as the lion, the calf (or ox), the man and the flying eagle (Rev. 4:6–8). They serve directly under the *Elohim* and govern all of the *Matter* cosmos. They are transformers of the Infinite *Light* unto souls evolving in the finite. See also *Elohim.*

Four lower bodies. Four sheaths of four distinct frequencies that surround the soul (the physical, emotional, mental and etheric bodies), providing vehicles for the soul in her journey through time and space. The etheric sheath, highest in vibration, is the gateway to the three Higher Bodies: the *Christ Self,* the *I AM Presence* and the *Causal Body.* See also *Physical body; Emotional body; Mental body; Etheric body.*

Great Central Sun. See *Central Sun.*

Great Hub. See *Central Sun.*

Guru. (Sanskrit.) A personal religious teacher and spiritual guide; one of high attainment. A guru may be unascended or ascended.

Hierarchy. The universal chain of individualized God-free beings fulfilling the attributes and aspects of God's infinite Selfhood. Included in the cosmic hierarchical scheme are *Solar Logoi, Elohim,* Sons and Daughters of God, Ascended and unascended masters with their circles of *chelas, Cosmic Beings,* the *Twelve Hierarchies of the Sun, Archangels* and *angels* of the *sacred fire,* children of the *Light,* nature spirits (called elementals) and *twin flames* of the *Alpha/Omega* polarity sponsoring planetary and galactic systems.

This universal order of the Father's own Self-expression is the means whereby God in the *Great Central Sun* steps down the Presence and power of his universal being/consciousness in order that succeeding evolutions in time and space, from the least unto the greatest, might come to know the wonder of his love. The level of one's spiritual/physical attainment—measured by one's balanced self-awareness "hid with *Christ* in God" and demonstrating his Law, by his love, in the *Spirit/Matter* cosmos —is the criterion establishing one's placement on this ladder of life called Hierarchy.

Higher Mental Body. See *Christ Self.*

Higher Self. The *I AM Presence;* the *Christ Self;* the exalted aspect of selfhood. Used in contrast to the term "lower self," or "little self," which indicates the soul that went forth from and may elect by free will to return to the Divine Whole through the realization of the oneness of the self in God. Higher consciousness.

Holy Christ Self. See *Christ Self.*

Human monad. The entire forcefield of self; the interconnecting spheres of influences—hereditary, environmental, karmic—which make up that self-awareness that identifies itself as human. The reference point of lesser- or non-awareness out of which all mankind must evolve to the realization of the *Real Self* as the *Christ Self.*

I AM Presence. The I AM THAT I AM (Exod. 3:13–15); the individualized Presence of God focused for each individual soul. The God-identity of the individual; the Divine Monad; the individual Source. The origin of the soul focused in the planes of *Spirit* just above the physical form; the personification of the God flame for the individual. See color illustration page 105.

I AM THAT I AM. See *I AM Presence.*

Kali Yuga. (Sanskrit.) Term in Hindu mystic philosophy for the last and worst of the four yugas (world ages), characterized by strife, discord and moral deterioration.

Karmic Board. See *Lords of Karma.*

Keepers of the Flame Fraternity. Founded in 1961 by Saint Germain, an organization of *Ascended Masters* and their *chelas* who vow to keep the Flame of Life on earth and to support the activities of the Great White Brotherhood in the establishment of their community and Mystery School and in the dissemination of their teachings. Keepers of the Flame receive graded lessons in *cosmic law* dictated by the *Ascended Masters* to their Messengers Mark and Elizabeth Prophet.

Lifestream. The stream of life that comes forth from the one Source, from the *I AM Presence* in the planes of *Spirit,* and descends to the planes of *Matter* where it manifests as the *threefold flame* anchored in the heart chakra for the sustainment of the soul in Matter and the nourishment of the *four lower bodies.* Used to denote souls evolving as individual "lifestreams" and hence synonymous with the term "individual." Denotes the ongoing nature of the individual through cycles of individualization.

Light. The energy of God; the potential of the *Christ.* As the personification of *Spirit,* the term "Light" can be used synonymously with the terms "God" and "Christ." As the essence of Spirit, it is synonymous with *"sacred fire."* It is the emanation of the *Great Central Sun* and the individualized *I AM Presence*—and the Source of all Life.

Logos. (Greek, "word, speech, reason.") The divine wisdom manifest in the creation. According to ancient Greek philosophy, the Logos is the controlling principle in the universe. The Book of John identifies the *Word,* or Logos, with Jesus Christ: "And the Word was made flesh, and dwelt among us" (John 1:14). Hence,

Jesus Christ is seen as the embodiment of divine reason, the Word Incarnate.

Lord of the World. *Sanat Kumara* held the office of Lord of the World (referred to as "God of the earth" in Rev. 11:4) for tens of thousands of years. Gautama *Buddha* recently succeeded Sanat Kumara and now holds this office. His is the highest governing office of the spiritual *Hierarchy* for the planet—and yet Lord Gautama is truly the most humble among the *Ascended Masters*. At inner levels, he sustains the *threefold flame,* the divine spark, for those *lifestreams* who have lost the direct contact with their *I AM Presence* and who have made so much negative karma as to be unable to magnetize sufficient *Light* from the Godhead to sustain their soul's physical incarnation on earth. Through a filigree thread of Light connecting his heart with the hearts of all God's children, Lord Gautama nourishes the flickering Flame of Life that ought to burn upon the altar of each heart with a greater magnitude of love, wisdom and power, fed by each one's own *Christ* consciousness.

Lords of Karma. The Ascended Beings who comprise the Karmic Board. Their names and the *rays* they represent on the board are as follows: first ray, the Great Divine Director; second ray, the Goddess of Liberty; third ray, the Ascended Lady Master Nada; fourth ray, the *Elohim Cyclopea;* fifth ray, Pallas Athena, Goddess of Truth; sixth ray, Portia, Goddess of Justice; seventh ray, Kuan Yin, Goddess of Mercy. The Buddha Vairochana also sits on the Karmic Board.

The Lords of Karma dispense justice to this system of worlds, adjudicating karma, mercy and judgment on behalf of every *lifestream*. All souls must pass before the Karmic Board before and after each incarnation on earth, receiving their assignment and karmic allotment for each lifetime beforehand and the review of their performance at its conclusion. Through the Keeper of the Scrolls and the recording *angels,* the Lords of Karma have access to the complete records of every lifestream's incarnations on earth. They determine who shall embody, as well as when and where. They assign souls to families and communities, measuring out the weights of karma that must be balanced as the "jot and tittle" of the Law. The Karmic Board, acting in consonance with the individual *I AM Presence* and *Christ Self,* determines when the soul has earned the right to be free from the wheel of karma and the round of rebirth.

The Lords of Karma meet at the Royal Teton Retreat twice yearly, at winter and summer solstice, to review petitions from unascended mankind and to grant dispensations for their assistance.

Macrocosm. (Greek, "great world.") The larger cosmos; the entire warp and woof of creation, which we call the *Cosmic Egg*. Also used to contrast man as the microcosm ("little world") against the backdrop of the larger world in which he lives. See also *Microcosm*.

Mantra. A mystical formula or invocation; a word or formula, often in Sanskrit, to be recited or sung for the purpose of intensifying the action of the *Spirit* of God in man. A form of prayer consisting of a word or a group of words that is chanted over and over again to magnetize a particular aspect of the Deity or of a being who has actualized that aspect of the Deity. See also *Decree*.

Manu. (Sanskrit.) The progenitor and lawgiver of the evolutions of God on earth. The Manu and his divine complement are *twin flames* assigned by the *Father-Mother God* to sponsor and ensoul the Christic image for a certain evolution or lifewave known as a root race—souls who embody as a group and have a unique archetypal pattern, divine plan and mission to fulfill on earth.

According to esoteric tradition, there are seven primary aggregations of souls—that is, the first to the seventh root races. The first three root races lived in purity and innocence upon earth in three Golden Ages before the Fall of Adam and Eve. Through obedience to *cosmic law* and total identification with the *Real Self,* these three root races won their immortal freedom and ascended from earth.

It was during the time of the fourth root race, on the continent of Lemuria, that the allegorical Fall took place under the influence of the fallen angels known as Serpents (because they used the serpentine spinal energies to beguile the soul, or female principle in mankind, as a means to their end of lowering the masculine potential, thereby emasculating the Sons of God).

The fourth, fifth and sixth root races (the latter soul group not having entirely descended into physical incarnation) remain in embodiment on earth today. Lord Himalaya and his beloved are the Manus for the fourth root race, Vaivasvata Manu and his consort are the Manus for the fifth root race, and the God and Goddess Meru are the Manus for the sixth root race. The seventh root race is destined to incarnate on the continent of South America in the Aquarian age under their Manus, the Great Divine Director and his divine complement.

Manvantara. (Sanskrit, from *manv,* used in compounds for *manu,* + *antara,* "interval, period of time.") In Hinduism, the name used to refer to various cycles, especially the length of the cycle of four yugas (consisting of 4,320,000 solar years) and the length of the reign of one *Manu* (308,448,000 years). The reign of a Manu is one of the fourteen intervals that constitute a *kalpa* (Sanskrit), a period of time covering a cosmic cycle from the origination to the destruction of a world system. In Hindu cosmology, the universe is continually evolving through periodic cycles of creation and dissolution. Creation is said to occur during the out-breath of the God of Creation, Brahma; dissolution occurs during his in-breath.

Mater. (Latin, "mother.") See *Matter; Mother.*

Matter. The feminine (negative) polarity of the Godhead, of which the masculine (positive) polarity is Spirit. Matter acts as a chalice for the kingdom of God and is the abiding place of evolving souls who identify with their Lord, their *Holy Christ Self.* Matter is distinguished from matter (lowercase *m*)—the substance of the earth earthy, of the realms of maya, which blocks rather than radiates divine *Light* and the Spirit of the *I AM THAT I AM.* See also *Mother; Spirit.*

Mental body. One of the *four lower bodies* of man, corresponding to the air element and the second quadrant of *Matter;* the body that is intended to be the vehicle, or vessel, for the Mind of God or the *Christ* Mind. "Let this [Universal] Mind be in you, which was also in Christ Jesus" (Phil. 2:5). Until quickened, this body remains the vehicle for the carnal mind, often called the lower mental body in contrast to the Higher Mental Body, a synonym for the *Christ Self* or *Christ* consciousness.

Microcosm. (Greek, "small world.") (1) The world of the individual, his *four lower bodies,* his aura and the forcefield of his karma; or (2) The planet. See also *Macrocosm.*

Mother. "Divine Mother," "Universal Mother" and "Cosmic Virgin" are alternate terms for the feminine polarity of the Godhead, the manifestation of God as Mother. *Matter* is the feminine polarity of *Spirit,* and the term is used interchangeably with Mater (Latin, "mother"). In this context, the entire material cosmos becomes the womb of creation into which Spirit projects the energies of Life. Matter, then, is the womb of the Cosmic Virgin, who, as the other half of the Divine Whole, also exists in Spirit as the spiritual polarity of God.

Nirvana. The goal of life according to Hindu and Buddhist philosophy: the state of liberation from the wheel of rebirth through the extinction of desire.

OM (AUM). The Word; the sound symbol for ultimate Reality.

Omega. See *Alpha and Omega.*

Path. The strait gate and narrow way that leadeth unto life (Matt. 7:14). The path of initiation whereby the disciple who pursues the *Christ* consciousness overcomes step by step the limitations of selfhood in time and space and attains reunion with Reality through the ritual of the *ascension.*

Pearls of Wisdom. Weekly letters of instruction dictated by the *Ascended Masters* to their Messengers Mark L. Prophet and Elizabeth Clare Prophet for students of the sacred mysteries throughout the world. *Pearls of Wisdom* have been published by *The Summit Lighthouse* continuously since 1958. They contain both fundamental and advanced teachings on *cosmic law* with a practical application of spiritual Truths to personal and planetary problems.

Physical body. The most dense of the *four lower bodies* of man, corresponding to the earth element and the fourth quadrant of *Matter.* The physical body is the vehicle for the soul's sojourn on earth and the focus for the crystallization in form of the energies of the *etheric, mental* and *emotional bodies.*

Rays. Beams of *Light* or other radiant energy. The Light emanations of the Godhead that, when invoked in the name of God or in the name of the *Christ,* burst forth as a flame in the world of the individual. Rays may be projected by the God consciousness of Ascended or unascended beings through the *chakras* and the third eye as a concentration of energy taking on numerous God-qualities, such as love, truth, wisdom, healing, and so on. Through the misuse of God's energy, practitioners of black magic project rays having negative qualities, such as death rays, sleep rays, hypnotic rays, disease rays, psychotronic rays, the evil eye, and so on. See also *Seven rays*.

Real Self. The *Christ Self;* the *I AM Presence;* immortal *Spirit* that is the animating principle of all manifestation.

Reembodiment. The rebirth of a soul in a new human body. The soul continues to return to the physical plane in a new body temple until she balances her karma, attains self-mastery, overcomes the cycles of time and space, and finally reunites with the *I AM Presence* through the ritual of the *ascension*.

Retreat. A focus of the Great White Brotherhood, usually on the *etheric plane* where the *Ascended Masters* preside. Retreats anchor one or more flames of the Godhead as well as the momentum of the Masters' service and attainment for the balance of *Light* in the *four lower bodies* of a planet and its evolutions. Retreats serve many functions for the councils of the *Hierarchy* ministering to the lifewaves of earth. Some retreats are open to unascended mankind, whose souls may journey to these focuses in their *etheric body* between their incarnations on earth and in their finer bodies during sleep or *samadhi*.

Root race. See *Manu*.

Sacred fire. The Kundalini fire that lies as the coiled serpent in the base-of-the-spine chakra and rises through spiritual purity and self-mastery to the crown chakra, quickening the spiritual centers on the way. God, *Light,* life, energy, the *I AM THAT I AM.* "Our God is a consuming fire" (Heb. 12:29). The sacred fire is the precipitation of the Holy Ghost for the baptism of souls, for purification, for alchemy and transmutation, and for the realization of the *ascension,* the sacred ritual whereby the soul returns to the One.

Samadhi. (Sanskrit, literally "putting together": "uniting") In Hinduism, a state of profound concentration or absorption resulting in perfect union with God; the highest state of yoga. In Buddhism, samadhis are numerous modes of concentration believed to ultimately result in higher spiritual powers and the attainment of enlightenment, or nirvana.

Sanat Kumara. (From the Sanskrit, "always a youth.") Great *Guru* of the seed of *Christ* throughout cosmos; Hierarch of Venus; the Ancient of Days spoken of in Daniel 7. Long ago he came to earth in her darkest hour when all *Light* had gone out in her evolutions, for there was not a single individual on the planet who gave adoration to the God Presence. Sanat Kumara and the band of 144,000 souls of Light who accompanied him volunteered to keep the Flame of Life on behalf of earth's people. This they vowed to do until the children of God would respond to the love of God and turn once again to serve their Mighty *I AM Presence*. Sanat Kumara's retreat, Shamballa, was established on an island in the Gobi Sea, now the Gobi Desert. The first to respond to his flame was Gautama *Buddha*, followed by Lord Maitreya and Jesus. See also *Lord of the World*.

Seamless garment. Body of *Light* beginning in the heart of the *I AM Presence* and descending around the *crystal cord* to envelop the individual in the vital currents of the *ascension* as he invokes the holy energies of the Father for the return home to God. Also known as the deathless solar body.

Secret chamber of the heart. The sanctuary of meditation behind the heart chakra, the place to which the souls of Lightbearers withdraw. It is the nucleus of life where the individual stands face to face with the inner *Guru*, the beloved *Holy Christ Self*, and receives the soul testings that precede the alchemical union with that Holy Christ Self—the marriage of the soul to the Lamb.

Seed Atom. The focus of the Divine *Mother* (the Feminine Ray of the Godhead) that anchors the energies of *Spirit* in *Matter* at the base-of-the-spine chakra. See also *Sacred fire*.

Seven rays. The *Light* emanations of the Godhead; the seven *rays* of the white Light that emerge through the prism of the *Christ* consciousness.

Siddhis. Spiritual powers such as levitation, stopping the heartbeat, clairvoyance, clairaudience, materialization and bilocation. The cultivation of siddhis for their own sake is often cautioned against by spiritual teachers.

Solar Logoi. *Cosmic Beings* who transmit the *Light* emanations of the Godhead flowing from *Alpha and Omega* in the *Great Central Sun* to the planetary systems. Also called Solar Lords.

Spirit. The masculine polarity of the Godhead; the coordinate of *Matter*; God as Father, who of necessity includes within the polarity of himself God as *Mother*, and hence is known as the *Father-Mother God*. The plane of the *I AM Presence*, of perfection; the dwelling place of the *Ascended Masters* in the kingdom of God.

Spoken Word. The *Word* of the LORD God released in the original fiats of Creation. The release of the energies of the Word, or the *Logos*, through the throat chakra by the Sons of God in confirmation of that lost Word. It is written, "By thy words thou shalt be justified, and by thy words thou shalt be condemned" (Matt. 12:37). Today disciples use the power of the Word in *decrees*, affirmations, prayers and *mantras* to draw the essence of the *sacred fire* from the *I AM Presence*, the *Christ Self* and *Cosmic Beings* to channel God's *Light* into matrices of transmutation and transformation for constructive change in the planes of *Matter*.

The Summit Lighthouse. An outer organization of the Great White Brotherhood founded by Mark L. Prophet in 1958 in Washington, D.C., under the direction of the *Ascended Master* El Morya, Chief of the Darjeeling Council, for the purpose of publishing and disseminating the Teachings of the Ascended Masters.

Threefold flame. The flame of the *Christ*, the spark of Life that burns within the *secret chamber of the heart* (a secondary chakra behind the heart). The sacred trinity of power, wisdom and love that is the manifestation of the *sacred fire*.

Tube of light. The white *Light* that descends from the heart of the *I AM Presence* in answer to the call of man as a shield of protection for his *four lower bodies* and his soul evolution. See color illustration page 105.

Twelve Hierarchies of the Sun. Twelve mandalas of *Cosmic Beings* ensouling twelve facets of God's consciousness, who hold the pattern of that frequency for the entire cosmos. They are identified by the names of the signs of the zodiac, as they focus their energies through these constellations. Also called the Twelve Solar Hierarchies. See also *Cosmic Clock*.

Twin flame. The soul's masculine or feminine counterpart conceived out of the same white-fire body, the fiery ovoid of the *I AM Presence*.

Unascended master. One who has overcome all limitations of *Matter* yet chooses to remain in time and space to focus the consciousness of God for lesser evolutions. See also *Bodhisattva*.

Universal Christ. The Mediator between the planes of *Spirit* and the planes of *Matter*. Personified as the *Christ Self*, he is the Mediator between the Spirit of God and the soul of man. The Universal Christ sustains the nexus of (the figure-eight flow of) consciousness through which the energies of the Father (Spirit) pass to his children for the crystallization (*Christ*-realization) of the God flame by their soul's strivings in the cosmic womb (matrix) of the *Mother* (Matter).

Violet flame. Seventh-ray aspect of the Holy Spirit. The *sacred fire* that transmutes the cause, effect, record and memory of sin, or negative karma. Also called the flame of transmutation, of freedom and of forgiveness. See also *Decree;* color illustration page 105.

Word. The Word is the *Logos:* it is the power of God and the realization of that power incarnate in and as the Christ. The energies of the Word are released by devotees of the Logos in the ritual of the Science of the *Spoken Word*. It is through the Word that the *Father-Mother God* communicates with mankind. The Christ is the personification of the Word. See also *Christ; Decree.*

World Teacher. Office in *Hierarchy* held by those Ascended Beings whose attainment qualifies them to represent the universal and personal *Christ* to unascended mankind. The office of World Teacher, formerly held by Maitreya, was passed to Jesus and his disciple Saint Francis (Kuthumi) on January 1, 1956, when the mantle of *Lord of the World* was transferred from *Sanat Kumara* to Gautama *Buddha* and the office of *Cosmic Christ* and Planetary Buddha (formerly held by Gautama) was simultaneously filled by Lord Maitreya. Serving under Lord Maitreya, Jesus and Kuthumi are responsible in this cycle for setting forth the teachings leading to individual self-mastery and the *Christ* consciousness. They sponsor all souls seeking union with God, tutoring them in the fundamental laws governing the cause-effect sequences of their own karma and teaching them how to come to grips with the day-to-day challenges of their individual dharma, the duty to fulfill the Christ potential through the sacred labor.

Mark L. Prophet and Elizabeth Clare Prophet are pioneers of modern spirituality and internationally renowned authors. Among their best-selling titles are *The Lost Years of Jesus, The Lost Teachings of Jesus, The Human Aura, Saint Germain On Alchemy, Fallen Angels and the Origins of Evil* and the Pocket Guides to Practical Spirituality series, which includes *How to Work with Angels, Your Seven Energy Centers* and *Soul Mates and Twin Flames*. Their books are now translated into approximately thirty languages and are available worldwide.

FOR MORE INFORMATION

Summit University Press books are available at fine bookstores worldwide and at your favorite online bookseller. For a free catalog of our books and products or to learn more about the spiritual techniques featured in this book, please contact:

Summit University Press
63 Summit Way
Gardiner, MT 59030-9314 USA
Telephone: 1-800-245-5445 or 406-848-9500
Fax: 1-800-221-8307 or 406-848-9555
www.SummitUniversityPress.com
info@SummitUniversityPress.com